ADAM SMITH: CRITICAL ASSESSMENTS

Adam Smith

Critical Assessments

Edited by John Cunningham Wood

Volume II

CROOM HELM
London & Canberra

British Library Cataloguing in Publication Data

Adam Smith
  1. Smith, Adam, *1723-1790*
  I. Wood, John Cunningham
  330.15'3   HB103.S6

  ISBN 0-7099-2748-7

Printed and bound in Great Britain

Contents

SECTION TWO: Smith's *Wealth of Nations*

Commentary

Smith's *An Inquiry into the Nature and Causes of the Wealth of Nations* is considered the first great work in the history of economics. Since its publication in 1776, scholars have often returned to contemplate Smith's thoughts, and the following articles reveal the great richness of Smith's major work. They also make abundantly clear the sheer range and depth of analysis of the *Wealth of Nations* and how Smith touched so many branches of learning.

In 'Adam Smith and his Relation to Recent Economics', L.L. Price indicates what he considers are some of the qualities which have given the *Wealth of Nations* a high and permanent place in economic literature. To Price, the work's greatest claim to fame was the literary workmanship which embodied a scientific treatise. Price stresses that Smith's language was admirably simple and clear, his reasoning direct and forcible and his illustrations abundant and apt. He also discusses how Smith has been regarded as the parent of modern economics and how he employed both an inductive and deductive approach in his writings.

E. Cannan's 'Adam Smith as an Economist' is based on a lecture delivered to commemorate the 150th anniversary of the publication of the *Wealth of Nations*. He argues that very little of Smith's schemes of economics had 'been left standing' by subsequent inquirers and points out that no one now holds Smith's theory of value. Cannan also claims that Smith's account of capital was hopelessly confused and that his theory of distribution was an ill assorted union between his own theory of prices and the ideas of the Physiocrats. However, Cannan contends that Smith accomplished three great things: a new definition of wealth which centred around produce; the substitution of wealth per head for wealth in the aggregate; and fathered 'bourgeois economics', i.e. provided the basis for those economists who looked with favour on working and trading and investing for personal gain. Finally, he notes that Smith's sympathies seem to have been wholly with the industrious wage earner, especially with the poorest.

In 'The Manuscript of an Early Draft of Part of *The Wealth of Nations*', W.R. Scott writes of his delight in discovering a very early draft of what became afterwards the *Wealth of Nations*. Scott relates how he found the manuscript among the papers of Charles Townshend, who was the second husband of the

Countess of Dalkeith, to whose son, Henry the third Duke of Buccleuch, Adam Smith was tutor from 1764 to 1766. Scott notes that the manuscript is definitely intended to be an economic treatise and nothing else and that this is established in the first two draft chapters. He also points out that the treatment of distribution in the manuscript is of immense interest and he outlines the essential features of Smith's analysis. Finally, Scott notes that Smith was a 'positive dandy' in his choice of writing paper and that he used the best government supplied, double folio sheets.

In 'Adam Smith and the Human Stomach', J.S. Davis critically examines three passages in the *Wealth of Nations* which reveal Smith's views on man's demands for food, clothing, housing and 'equipage'. He takes issue with Smith's position that the desire for 'food is limited in every man by the narrow capacity of the human stomach . . .', arguing that the limits to the size of the human stomach have no material bearing on the degree to which wants for food are satisfied or fall short of satiation. Davis also disputes Smith's position that the rich man consumes no more food than his poor neighbour, pointing out that a diet rich in animal protein and in fats is ordinarily several times as expensive as a similar nutritious diet poor in these prized foods. Moreover, he argued that the rich man's consumption entailed much greater waste than the poor man's at the point of consumption.

In 'The Macro and Micro Aspects of *The Wealth of Nations*', J.P. Henderson purports to clarify a number of contradictions attributed to classical value theory and to substantiate the claim that Smith's 'ambiguous and confused' *Wealth of Nations* constituted a valid and coherent attempt to integrate theories of the process of the economic system and the pricing of particular commodities. Henderson argues that those interpretations which show Smith's premarginalist formulations to be confused and irreconcilable, stem from a failure to recognise that this integration was as important a goal of classical economic theory as it is of contemporary economics. He notes, however, that classical theory approached this problem from the standpoint that individual prices were a function, rather than a determinant, of the economic system. He believes that any attempt to interpret the *Wealth of Nations* in the light of orthodox price theory distorted Smith's thinking and Henderson investigates the *Wealth of Nations* in terms of underlying postulates of the classical economists that serve to clarify Smith's basic formulations of value and price. He concludes that the discussion of market price was in the main restricted to Chapter VIII of Book 1 and did not contain anything more than an indication of the direction of Smith's analysis. He points out that in Smith's labour theory of value, value originated in the process of production, and prices tended always to equal cost of production, as the sum of the prices above real value would always equal the sum of the below real value.

In 'The *Wealth of Nations* in Spain and Hispanic America, 1780-1830', R. Smith provides in great detail a survey of the use of Smith's *Wealth of Nations* in Spain and Hispanic America. He discusses the work of José Alonso Ortiz, the translator of the first Spanish version of the *Wealth of Nations*. He concludes that in Spain and Spanish America the main currents of economic thought were enriched by borrowing from streams that flowed across the boundaries of language and intolerance.

In 'Welfare Indices in *The Wealth of Nations*', M. Blaug attempts to dispel the view that Smith tried to formulate a labour theory of value, only to become horribly confused between the purchasing power of a commodity over labour and the amount of labour embodied in its production. Blaug argues that Smith was in fact well aware of the distinction between the measure and cause of value and that he was little concerned with the latter. He notes that the traditional problem of value theory — why relative prices are what they are at any point of time — received only brief treatment. To Blaug, Smith was primarily interested in finding some invariant measure of real income. Blaug examines Smith's labour-standard, Ricardo's views, and concludes that there is nothing wrong with it, per se, only that Smith applied it indiscriminately.

A.L. Macfie's 'Adam Smith's *Moral Sentiments* as Foundation for his *Wealth of Nations*' argues that the influence of utilitarianism on the *Moral Sentiments* was sufficiently minor to prove that this theory had no explicit influence on the *Wealth of Nations*. He also discusses the role of sympathy in the *Moral Sentiments* and seeks to establish that while sympathy is the essential social sentiment for Smith as for Hume, with Smith it was always united with reason and with the operation of the impartial spectator. Generally speaking, Macfie argues that Smith stressed the rational rather than the emotional side of sympathy. Furthermore, Macfie argues that there is *no* evidence for the unlikely view that the theory of economic man in the *Wealth of Nations* is in direct conflict with that of the prudent man in the *Theory of Moral Sentiments*. To Macfie, the *Wealth of Nations* is a special case — the economic case — of the philosophy implicit in the *Theory of Moral Sentiments*. In brief, it worked out that the economic side of that 'self-love' which is given its appropriate place in the developed ethical system of the earlier book.

In 'Some Institutional Aspects of the *Wealth of Nations*', N. Rosenberg attacks the work of such scholars as W.C. Mitchell, who jumped directly from Smith's writings on the conception of man as a rational creature to the policy recommendation of *laissez-faire*, by arguing that it completely short-circuits much of the real substance of Smith's work. In his paper, Rosenberg argues that Smith's unique contribution in the *Wealth of Nations* was that it provided the first systematic guide to the manner in which the price mechanism allocated resources in a free-market economy. At the same time, however, Rosenberg contends that Smith was very much preoccupied with establishing the conditions under which this market mechanism would operate most effectively. He shows that Smith's conception of human behaviour allowed for the free operation of certain impulses and behaviour patterns which were calculated to thwart, rather than to reinforce, the beneficent operation of market forces. Consequently, Smith was very much concerned with providing an exact and detailed specification of an optimal institutional structure. To Rosenberg, generations of economists had ignored this aspect of Smith's analysis by oversimplifying his conception of human behaviour and by invoking a competitive economy. The result, which Rosenberg's paper redresses, has been a neglect of some of the most fruitful and suggestive aspects of Smith's analysis.

In his brief note, 'The First Spanish Edition of the *Wealth of Nations*', R.S. Smith discusses the first Spanish edition of Smith's great work. He outlines the career of Smith's first (and until 1956 only) Spanish translator, José Alonso

Ortiz, a lawyer and professor of canon law and theology at the University of Valladolid.

At the commencement of 'Smith's Travels on the Ship of State', G.J. Stigler states that the *Wealth of Nations* is 'a stupendous palace erected upon the granite of self-interest'. Stigler then offers a list of the instances in the *Wealth of Nations* in which legislation is explained by the interests of several economic groups. Although, Stigler points out, the list is incomplete, he argues that it is sufficient to document the extensive role of self-interest in economic legislation and how Smith singled out the merchants and manufacturers for attack. However, Smith implicitly rejected the use of self-interest as a general explanation of self-interest, a view Stigler sustains on three grounds: (1) for most legislation, no group is identified which could have fostered the law and would benefit from it; (2) puzzles in legislation are posed where none would exist if Smith had considered systematically the role of self-interest in legislation; (3) Smith gave a larger role to emotion, prejudice and ignorance in political life than he ever allowed in ordinary economic affairs.

A.W. Coats' 'Adam Smith's Conception of Self-Interest in Economic and Political Affairs' is both a comment on, and extension of, the paper by G.J. Stigler, 'Smith's Travels on the Ship of State'. Coats argues that like many other historians of economics, Stigler concentrated exclusively on the *Wealth of Nations*, the work in which man's self-interested pursuit of economic gain occupied centre stage. Coats demonstrates that if the *Wealth of Nations* is considered in isolation it conveys a misleading and one-sided impression of Smith's attitude to human nature and conduct, and it had to be supplemented by reference to his other writings, especially the *Theory of Moral Sentiments*. Coats suggsts that self-interest, especially if interpreted 'in perfectly cold-blooded, rational terms', is an inadequate and misleading basis from which to evaluate Smith's account of politics and the legislative process. He demonstrates that Smith's views on self-interest are a good deal more subtle and complex than generally assumed and argues that there is no inherent reason why self-interest should function as effectively in the political arena as in the market-place.

D. White's 'Adam Smith's *Wealth of Nations*' is a review of the R.H. Campbell, A.S. Skinner and W.B. Todd 1976 edition of the *Wealth of Nations* and A.S. Skinner's and T. Wilson's *Essays on Adam Smith*. White finds Campbell's and Skinner's introduction to the *Wealth of Nations* immensely valuable and he agrees that Smith's importance lay in the unique appeal he had to Englishmen of the eighteenth century. White notes that Smith was personally very much a man of the times and he points to Smith's personal collection of books (some three thousand volumes) to give a further indication of the breadth of his learning. He realtes, and agrees with, Skinner's three propositions which were the 'common property' of Smith and the 'enlightened' men of his generation: i.e. (1) the study of human nature is prior in time and importance; (2) the experimental method of Newton is the proper way to study man; (3) human nature was and had been everywhere the same. To these, White adds Smith's belief in a pattern in the affairs of men; a belief in rigid stages of human development. He then briefly considers some of the thirty *Essays on Adam Smith*, which he viewed as a tribute to the wide-ranging genius of Smith.

In 'The *Wealth of Nations* 1776–1976', Sir E. Roll observes that the essential spirit that inspired Smith was the same as that on which the new American republic was to be founded. He considers that in both there was appeal to the 'natural order' or the 'laws of nature'. He notes that the pursuit of happiness as one of the inalienable rights of man is close to the whole approach of Smith's earlier work, the *Theory of Moral Sentiments*. After sketching Smith's biography, Roll discusses Smith's place in economics, arguing that the epoch-making character of the *Wealth of Nations* derived from its bearing on public policy. He outlines Smith's 'brilliant critique' of the state regulations associated with mercantilism, but stresses that it is a mistake to think that the *Wealth of Nations* ushered in an era of unlimited *laissez-faire*.

In his note, 'The Adam Smith Nobody Knows', R.L. Heilbroner points out that although the *Wealth of Nations* is universally admired, it is universally unread. In order to show Smith's many-sided roles, Heilbroner assembles a few less-well-known passages from the *Wealth of Nations*, including quotes on risk, lotteries, imperial preferences, the mixed economy, tariff, labour and capital and mass production.

T.W. Hutchison's 'The Bicentenary of Adam Smith' is a review of the R.H Campbell, A.S. Skinner and W.B. Todd edition of the *Wealth of Nations* and the *Essays on Adam Smith* edited by A.S. Skinner and T. Wilson. While he finds the general introduction to the *Wealth of Nations* informative, Hutchison takes issues with the editors' statement that Smith's 'economic analysis involves a high degree of abstraction', arguing that with the subsequent development of economic analysis, especially since Ricardo, Smith's work involved a markedly low or lower degree of abstraction. Instead of discussing all 32 papers in the *Essays on Adam Smith*. Hutchison concentrates on the essays in Part II which are concerned with the subject-matter of the *Wealtn of Nations*. In so doing, he notes that Smith's treatment of utility and value had vast historical consequences, and his biological, 'moralistic', or objective concept of utility had very dangerous implications.

In his wide-ranging article, 'Adam Smith and the *Wealth of Nations*', Hutchison points out that Smith was in fact, and always considered himself to be, a philosopher in a highly comprehensive sense who penetrated deeply into a social and legal philosophy and the psychology of ethics. To Hutchison, Smith thought of political economy as only one chapter, and not the most important chapter, in a broad study of society and human progress which involved psychology and ethics, law, politics and the development of the arts and sciences. Hutchison argues that Smith was an historical economist not only in the sense that he was empirical, but in that the key theme of progress through natural stages of development ran through his *Wealth of Nations*. He also contends that Smith's treatment of value (1) represented a significant shift of emphasis as compared with his predecessors and (2) involved a serious *under* emphasis or confusion regarding the role of utility and demand. Hutchison discusses how Smith's intellectual horizons in the *Wealth of Nations* ranged in time and place and, with regard to level of development, over every variety of society, economy and human specimen from the primitive savage to his contemporary Scotsmen.

H. Jensen's 'Sources and Contours of Adam Smith's Conceptualized Reality in the *Wealth of Nations*' argues that Smith founded the paradigm of classical political economy which served subsequent nineteenth-century economists as the basis and framework for their own research. He demonstrates that Smith constructed an elaborate paradigm, consisting of a vision of society, a conceptualised reality, a model, a set of theories, an analysis of the model's behaviour and conclusions. Jenson elaborates upon each of the paradigm's components, stressing the inputs Smith used in constructing the component, 'conceptualized society', viz., the egotistical and sympathetic instincts.

In 'The Just Economy: The Moral Basis of The *Wealth of Nations*', L. Billet argues that Smith's famous book was a profoundly political work, which was pervaded by a concern with justice and injustice, with the conflict between private and public interest, and with the problem of liberty and coercion. To Billet, the *Wealth of Nations* was fundamentally concerned with the question, 'what is a just economy?' He feels that this central theme of Smith's treatise has been neither adequately recognised nor emphasised by scholars and commentators on his political economy. He argues that justice is the key to the whole of Smith's work: the link between his philosophy and political economy; the organising concept of the *Wealth of Nations* and the moral basis for the emphasis on natural liberty. Billet discerns three levels of justice in Smith: (1) natural justice which constitutes the basic, normative principles of positive law; (2) systems of general rules in accord with natural justices (e.g. natural liberty) that are the immediate bases of positive law; and (3) the administration of positive law.

The first few pages of H.M. Robertson's 'Euge! Belle! Dear Mr. Smith: The *Wealth of Nations*, 1776–1976' outline how Smith considered the Scots a very miscellaneous collection of real people in a great variety of different circumstances. He also notes how in his discussion of the Scots Smith sometimes denied the universality of 'economic man'. Robertson discusses the alleged inconsistency between the basic premises of the *Wealth of Nations* and those of the *Theory of Moral Sentiments*. He argues that Smith limited the phenomenon of subsistence wages to the stationary state, although he did not regard the stationary state as inevitable and in this context he points out that although Smith's wage theory was diffuse, it was less inconsequent than his critics have alleged. He concludes that Smith painted a frightening vision of a stationary state, in which wages would be at a subsistence level and profits at a minimum.

In 'The Wealth of Nations — The Vision and the Conceptualization', K.R. Ranadive argues that the central theme that inspired the *Wealth of Nations* was the accumulation of capital and that Smith attached such importance to the division of labour because of its dynamic effect in promoting accumulation of capital. He notes that although Smith grasped the prospects of complex relations of trade and industry of a developed economy, the 'early and rude state of society' from which he commenced his analysis was suggested by a primitive community of self-employed peasants, largely self-sufficient and demanding only a rudimentary system of exchange. Ranadive stresses that the fundamental doctrines of the *Wealth of Nations*, especially in regard to economic nature and natural liberty, led to Smith being labelled the 'apostle of individualism'.

However, he contends that the *Wealth of Nations* cannot be understood without a knowledge of Smith's *Theory of Moral Sentiments* which reflects the common ethical background of the eighteenth century as well as Smith's own individual contributions within that common framework. In his section on Smith's concept of man, Ranadive believes that Smith argued, like Aristotle and Hume, that man was by nature *social* and he regarded the dominant human end as the interests or welfare of society. Although he notes that Smith also created the 'economic' man as an abstraction which typified social behaviour in the market place, he argues that such a creature was a very different one than that invented by subsequent economists. He also argues that some of the inconsistencies *within* Smith's two major works could be traced to the combination of deductive and inductive methods.

In 'A Centenarian on a Bicentenarian: Léon Walras's *Eléments* on Adam Smith's *Wealth of Nations*', W. Jaffé points out that Walras's *Eléments* mentions the *Wealth of Nations* only twice: to criticise Smith's alleged definition of economic science and to denounce as a sophism Smith's labour theory of value. Jaffé finds this surprising because Smith had a theory of general equilibrium similar to, but less rigorous than, Walras's. He also points to other similarities between the authors: their analysis was inspired by Cartesian methodology; Newtonian celestial mechanics was their model for social science; they were both exposed to the natural law philosophy of Gratuis and Pufendorf in their youth. Despite these similiarities, Jaffé argues that Walrus stubbornly refused to open his eyes to Smith. He explains this in terms of Walras's fanatical anglophobia, an anglophobia which in the nineteenth century made no distinction between the Scots and the English.

In 'The Wealth of Nations', R.H. Coase describes Smith's *Wealth of Nations* as a masterpiece which contained interrelated themes, careful observations on economic life and powerful ideas. He notes that the work also contained some obscurities and inconsistencies which might have been removed had Smith not been so solitary but had consulted more with others. To Coase, Smith's main point was not that benevolence or love is not the basis of economic life in a modern society, but that it cannot be. In brief, society had to rely on the market, with its motive force, self-interest. Coase argues that although Smith's analytical system may seem primitive to us, he reached results which would be accepted today. He notes how Smith used the concept of natural price (the long-run supply price) and considered the effectual demand to be the amount demanded at that price. Coase concludes that Smith's main contributions to economics were the division of labour, the working of the market and the role of government in the economic system.

54

Adam Smith and his Relations to Recent Economics[1]

L.L. Price

Source: *Economic Journal*, Vol. 3 (10), June 1893, pp. 239-54.

It is with a feeling of some hesitancy that I submit to the Economic Section of the British Association these fragmentary and inadequate remarks. To say anything new on Adam Smith is not easy; but to say anything of importance or profit, which has not been said before, is well-nigh impossible. I have indeed heard that rumours have been whispered of late in economic circles that he may be more than suspected of the charge so commonly advanced against writers who seem to have made some new contribution to the development of human knowledge, or to have given some fresh exhibition of the fertility of the human imagination, and that, like so many before and after him, he is guilty of plagiarism. It is certainly true that the references to other authors in the *Wealth of Nations* are comparatively few and far between, that the years, during which the work was in process of composition, were sufficiently numerous to afford time for accumulating a mass of material in common-place books and the like, which may have been included among the papers destroyed, as we know, before Adam Smith's death, that his notorious excellence of memory would have assisted conscious or unconscious appropriation, and that the comparative absence of systematic continuous development through the separate books of his treatise might be held to point to the reproduction of the views of others rather than the formation and statement of his own independent opinions. It is certain that there were economists before him, and he himself is emphatic in his recognition of the merits of his French predecessors; and it is no less certain that he was influenced by the particular circumstances of his time, and that he breathed in the atmosphere of thought by which he was surrounded to an extent which recent historical inquiry and criticism have enabled us to apprehend more fully. But I have neither the wish nor the knowledge to enter on the interesting discussion which these considerations suggest. The determination of the line, where plagiarism ends and originality begins, calls for a fine power of discrimination, and the limits of borrowing without acknowledgment constitute a most delicate and difficult question of literary etiquette. If the ideas, which you are accused of plagiarising, form part of the common stock of the discussions of the day, you may perhaps be allowed to use them without an express recognition of their original ownership. If, in passing them through your mind, you have given them the stamp of your own individuality, it becomes doubtful how far you may claim that they are, in part at least, your own, and how far you are bound to exhibit the precise process by which they have arrived at their present shape. With these nice questions I do not propose to deal, but to attempt the more modest and agreeable task of trying to indicate some of the qualities which have given the *Wealth of Nations* so high and, as I venture to think, so permanent a place in economic literature. For, explain it as we please, it would be difficult to deny that Adam Smith's great treatise has taken, and retained, a position which is unique. It has become a 'classic.' It has, unlike the mass of economic writing, established itself in the affections of the layman as well as the expert; and, unlike the mass of economic writing also, it has exchanged the fading laurels of ephemeral renown for a crown of abiding glory.

First among its titles to enduring fame I should place the fact that it is a piece of literary workmanship as well as a scientific treatise. I have seen it stated somewhere that Political Economy in its scientific character has suffered from the literary treatment, which it has often received at the hands of practised writers, who wield the effective instrument of a facile pen. This has, so we are told, led to the sacrifice of accuracy of reasoning to finish of expression, and has permitted sciolists to enter the domains of science. That there is some truth in this argument no one, who knows anything of the history of Economics, would be prepared to deny; and it might perhaps be urged that Adam Smith himself offended against the conditions of scientific exactitude no less than the graces of literary style by his diffuseness and repetition. But it remains true that the *Wealth of Nations* has a charm in its composition which reveals the literary artist, and that the happiness of many of its phrases has aided the recollection of what would otherwise have been speedily forgotten. Literary form is, no doubt, a means to an end, which must not be exalted to an end in Economics more than in any other science; but, despite of all the objections which have been raised, and of drawbacks which it is easy to indicate, there can be no doubt that the layman will concern himself more closely and frequently with it than with most other sciences, and that he will be attracted by grace, and deterred by awkwardness, of composition. If he cannot, and it is surely doubtful whether such a result, if attainable, is really to be desired – if he cannot be prevented from straying into the preserves of the scientist, it is preferable that he should seek the companionship of the best writers rather than the worst, and it is therefore a matter for congratulation that in Adam Smith he will find a stimulus to thought added to a gratification of taste.

But the attraction of the *Wealth of Nations* as a literary performance is largely due to the presence of another characteristic, which is held by some critics, and not unreasonably, to militate against scientific exactitude. The exposition of the theory of Economics, we are told, must be carefully distinguished from its application to practice. The theoretical expositor must sternly preserve himself from the dangerous and deteriorating influence of motive or purpose of a practical nature. He must pursue truth and truth alone, turning neither to the right hand nor to the left. Here, again, it would be difficult to deny the force of these arguments, or to ignore the serious mischief which has resulted from the intrusion of partiality or prejudice into the region of scientific inquiry. There can be no doubt that the distinction between the theory of

Economics and the art of political or social or philanthropic practice, which has, by dint of constant repetition and urgent insistence, been forced home on the mind of the student, has helped to clarify his views and to save him from hasty unwarranted conclusions. There can be no less doubt that, if the 'man in the street' could be brought to recognise this distinction, the process would be wholesome for himself and for the science which he so often misappropriates to his own ends. But in his case it is almost hopeless to expect to achieve success, and the student, with all his watchfulness, will find the subtle influences of motive and purpose continually trying to reassert their sway and, not infrequently, triumphing over resistance. To look for any other result is to listen to 'counsels of perfection' rather than the plain lessons of common experience. And, whatever may be urged on this point, it is at least certain that in Adam Smith's time the distinction between the scientific study of the causes, which govern the production and distribution of wealth, and the art of increasing the 'wealth of nations' had not passed beyond its rudimentary stage, if it had even emerged from obscurity at all. And it is no less certain that the persuasive fascination of his writing is largely due to the presence and prominence from beginning to end of his book of one dominant motive and one ruling purpose. It has been said that every page of his treatise is 'illumined' by the 'passion' for freedom, and the most cursory reading of the *Wealth of Nations* could scarcely fail to disclose this ardent feeling as the most diligent and protracted study would serve but to strengthen the original impression. It is the possession of the whole man by such a passion which renders writers cogent arguers and their readers willing listeners; and, though the passion may, if it is not curbed and bridled, sometimes run away with the judgment, it may also lend a wonderful force to accurate reasoning, and carry conviction to minds unwilling otherwise to listen to wholesome and important truths. As a literary instrument it is unsurpassed; as a weapon of science it is by no means to be lightly esteemed or carelessly dismissed.

This instrument Adam Smith possessed in admirable perfection, and this weapon he wielded with marvellous effect. But it has been said that his passion for freedom was largely a product of the times and an outcome of French speculation in the period before the Revolution; and it has been urged that it led him into an excessive euology of the 'obvious and simple system of natural liberty,' which was soon to receive a terrible corrective in the misery and suffering apparently due, to a large extent, to unfettered competition in the early days of the factory system. It has been maintained that, while the removal of the old barriers, which impeded the course of trade, and the shackles, which cramped the movements of industry, was then needed, and was powerfully aided by the strenuous energy and perseverance of Adam Smith, the requirements of later times are different, the extension rather than the limitation of the functions of government, and the enlargement rather than the contraction of the sphere within which the State should regulate or supersede the action of individuals, constitute the pressing need of our day and the most urgent question alike of practical politics and of political theory, and therefore the teaching of Adam Smith is obsolete and the *Wealth of Nations* has no message for us. But, on the other hand, it has been pointed out that Adam Smith himself was too shrewd an observer of human nature, and too keen a judge of the exigencies of practical affairs, to believe in uncontrolled individualism or, as it has been happily called, 'administrative nihilism;' and he recognised that there was a sphere for State action, and departments of life where its absence would be fraught with social injury and danger of the gravest kind. The question is often stated as if the choice lay between no interference on the part of the State and complete arrangement and control; but it is really a question of degree, and in this lies its difficulty. Adam Smith, no doubt, inclined to the less rather than the more; we perhaps have latterly been disposed to go some way in the opposite direction. But he would be a bold man who would deny that the crying need of the days of the *Wealth of Nations* was the limitation of State meddling, and the removal of multitudinous restrictions and narrow exclusive regulations. Nor would it argue less ignorance of human nature, or less unintelligent acquaintance with the movement of affairs, to dispute the pertinence to all time of much that Adam Smith urges in defence of liberty. Attacks upon freedom are the melancholy feature of more than one condition of society and of more than a single epoch in the world's history. The argument in favour of liberty may be pressed too far, and Adam Smith may have fallen into this error; but it is rarely inopportune, and it is seldom, if ever, superfluous. Liberty is assailed in so many and such subtle forms that the claims of its champions have a perennial application; and, when the advocacy of freedom means, as in Adam Smith's case, the pleading of the cause of the weak oppressed by the strong, and the vindication of the rights of the defenceless, it is premature, as it is ungracious, to say that he has no message for our time. His passion for liberty, which illuminates all his pages, sheds its lustre over the problems of this and every age; and it gives a permanent value as well as imparts a persuasive charm to the *Wealth of Nations.*

Adam Smith's merits do not appeal to the lover of the interesting alone. In fact the number of minds, which have agreed, while differing on other subjects, to unite in praising the *Wealth of Nations,* is not the least remarkable or conspicuous testimony to its unique character. We have already observed that it appeals, and appeals successfully, to the layman as well as the expert; and statesmen and men of affairs, from Pitt downwards, have derived instruction, and obtained guidance, from its pages no less than academic economists. The causes of this wide popularity are not far to seek. The language of Adam Smith is admirably simple and clear, his reasoning direct and forcible to a degree unsurpassed, and perhaps unapproached, by other writers on a subject which it is only too easy to make repellent and difficult, and his illustrations are at once abundant and apt. The strong motive, by which his argument is informed, gives an air of unmistakable reality to his writing, and he always seems to be in the closest touch with actual present fact. These are the very qualities to appeal to the plain practical man; but the remarkable characteristic of Adam Smith is that he appeals with equal strength to the trained economist. The position of the *Wealth of Nations* in strictly economic literature is as unique as is the fact that it occupies a recognised place among the classic productions of men of letters of all times. The comparative simplicity of economic theory in Adam Smith's day, as contrasted with the more elaborate and complex development of latter periods of thought, might have been expected to render the *Wealth of Nations* attractive to the outsider, deterred by the terms and formulae of more specialised, but exact, knowledge and inquiry; but for this very reason the professed economist might have been supposed to be likely to regard the book as interesting rather as evidence of what Economics had been in a comparatively unadvanced stage, and as an example of the early form which doctrines, developed since, had then assumed. But he might not improbably have thought that its antiquarian interest was its strongest point, and that later reasoning had superseded it as an engine for inquiry and speculation. Such a conclusion would, no doubt, be natural; and chapters in Adam Smith might be cited in its support. The importance which, in spite of his criticism of the system of the Physiocrats, he assigned to agriculture, in which, he said, 'nature laboured along with man,' and the order in which he ranged the employments of capital in the same chapter,² very suggestive as it is in the light it throws on his mental environment, but containing also not a little which would now be stated differently, if it were not regarded as obsolete, are examples of this. But the surprising fact remains how little is really unimportant now, and how much is supplied in germ in the *Wealth of Nations*, which later investigation has done no more than develop into the maturer plant. Few, if any, writers on a subject, which has to deal with the changing phenomena of human society, could stand so well the test of a hundred years of study and criticism, or, after the lapse of so long a time, appear so fresh and apposite.

To this point I propose to return later; what I wish now to emphasise is the way in which by writers of almost every school, in England at least, Adam Smith has been regarded as the parent of modern Economics. It is true that recent research has called attention to the important contributions of authors before this time, who had been over-shadowed by his fame and greatness; and the *Wealth of Nations* was no more the end than it was the beginning of economic study. But throughout the subsequent history of Economics, at any rate in this country, there has been one writer and one treatise to which all others have in turn traced the origin of most of their ideas; and that writer has borne the name of Adam Smith, and that treatise the title of the *Wealth of Nations.* Even in the generation which immediately followed its issue, it seemed as if in the persons of Malthus and Ricardo Political Economy would break up into two opposite schools of thought pursuing two different methods of inquiry. Certain it is that many of the fundamental issues raised in later controversy were started at that time; and the *Letters of Ricardo to Malthus* may from this point of view be read even now with interest, although they refer in many instances to passing practical questions of the day. And yet Malthus and Ricardo, in spite of their fundamental differences, owned Adam Smith to be their common teacher, although, like able pupils, they were not afraid to criticise, and improve on, their master.

The same feature has repeated itself through the course of subsequent discussion. In Germany, no doubt, Smithianismus has become a term of reproach, and the ghost, conjured up under this name, has been assailed with all the weapons which painstaking research, and wide erudition, and enthusiastic zeal for a new creed, could command; and the attack, perhaps we may add, has after all been eluded owing to the unsubstantial and imaginary character of the object of assault. But, if we turn to the representative of the German historical school, who in recent times has led the onslaught in England, we find that, while he criticises Adam Smith with perfect freedom, and shows how he was influenced by the facts and thought peculiar to his time, he places him on quite a different level from Ricardo, and claims the *Wealth of Nations* as a brilliant illustration of the advantages of the inductive as opposed to the deductive method of inquiry. In one of the most interesting of his essays,[3] Cliffe Leslie observes that the followers of the orthodox school now reply to their opponents by a cry 'of greatness of Adam Smith.' 'And,' he adds, 'it is well that the cry is now for him instead of Ricardo.' But, he proceeds later, 'it reminds one of the contest between the spirits of darkness and light for the body of Moses to find the followers of Ricardo claiming Adam Smith for their prophet.' '"Whom ye ignorantly worship, him declare I unto you," the true disciple of Adam Smith may say to those who raise altars to his name, but to whom he is virtually an unknown being.' And he goes on to argue that the method employed by Adam Smith was inductive, and to illustrate this point in particular by the 'famous tenth chapter of his first book.' 'The notion of evolving from his own consciousness the circumstances and motives that diversify the employments of a nation, and the remuneration obtained in them, would be preposterous, even if Adam Smith himself had not expressly stated at the beginning of the chapter that he had gathered them from observation.' Cliffe Leslie's opinion is entitled to great respect, for the influence which his writings have exercised on the conception of method, and the development of theory, has been considerable; but it is curious to turn from his assertions to the conclusions drawn by other writers.

For what does the author of the most recent English treatise on economic theory say? Professor Marshall is even more emphatic than Cliffe Leslie in his praise of the *Wealth of Nations*. 'The next great step in advance, the greatest step that economics has ever taken, was the work,' he declares,[4] 'not of a school, but of an individual.' 'Wherever' Adam Smith 'differs from his predecessors, he is more nearly right than they; while there is scarcely any economic truth now known of which he did not get some glimpse.' And what are the grounds on which Professor Marshall bases this ungrudging eulogy? 'His chief work,' he observes, 'was to combine and develop the speculations of his French and English contemporaries and predecessors as to value. His highest claim to have made an epoch in thought is that he was the first to make a careful and scientific inquiry into the manner in which value measures human motive, on the one side measuring the desire of purchasers to obtain wealth, and on the other the efforts and sacrifices undergone by its producers.' The work, however, thus described is largely deductive as well as inductive, and at any rate it places Adam Smith in the direct line of descent to Ricardo and the so-called abstract school. It is opposed to Cliffle Leslie's verdict, as it is more comprehensive; and Professor Marshall proceeds to remark that the *Wealth of Nations*, 'though not well arranged, is a model of method; for' Adam Smith 'saw clearly that while economic science must be based on a study of facts, the facts are so complex, that they generally can teach nothing directly; they must be interpreted by careful reasoning and analysis. And, as Hume said, the *Wealth of Nations* "is so much illustrated with curious facts that it must take the public attention." This is exactly what Adam Smith did; he seldom attempted to prove anything by detailed induction or history. The data of his proofs were chiefly facts that were within every one's knowledge, facts physical, mental, and moral. But he illustrated his proofs by curious and instructive facts; he thus gave them life and force, and made his readers feel that they were dealing with problems of the real world, and not with abstractions.'

Discussions on method are perhaps never very profitable, and Economics has had more than its full share of such discussions. I do not propose to enter now on the treatment of the questions, interesting though they may be, whether Adam Smith reasoned in the main inductively or deductively, and whether he more generally constructed his theory from observation of collected fact or used his facts to verify and illustrate his theory. It is hard to draw a rigid line between deduction and induction, and to say where the province of the one ends and that of the other begins. It is now generally allowed that Economics may and, if it is to advance, must avail itself of all the aids to inquiry and speculation which the wit of man has discovered. It must use in turn, as the circumstances favour, induction, deduction, observation, experiment, hypothesis, and verification. Later investigation has, no doubt, emphasised the importance of facts, but it has not lessened the advantage of employing the instrument of method in all its varieties and patterns to handle facts. And so it seems probable that Adam Smith, like other writers, sometimes used what would probably be called an inductive, and sometimes what would be broadly distinguished as a deductive method, that sometimes he constructed his theory from his facts, and sometimes he employed his facts to verify and illustrate his theory. That it should be, as it still is, a disputed question whether the one or the other form of reasoning predominated in his treatise is a testimony to the catholicity of his work; that he should be labelled now deductive, and now inductive, may not unreasonably be held to point to the conclusion that he was not exclusively either, but embraced elements of both. And, whatever may be said as to the method he employed, it is certainly remarkable that he should be highly esteemed alike by what we may perhaps without offence call historical dissenters and orthodox believers, and that the germs of the 'theory of measurable motives,' as well as illustrations of the systematic knowledge slowly built on the observation of a mass of facts, should be discovered in the *Wealth of Nations*. In this respect it is surely unique in economic literature.

Nor does the theorist find in its pages merely the rudiments of the central theory of Economics, but, if he examines the different departments of the science, he is astonished to discover how close Adam Smith is to the latest results of economic inquiry. There is, it is true, no formal or regular division in the *Wealth of Nations* into separate departments dealing with production, distribution, exchange and consumption; and the arrangement of the treatise is lacking in system. But the early treatment given to exchange as arising naturally from division of labour, and facilitated by the use of money, the tool of exchange, the prominence assigned to value as the dominant fact in exchange, the distinction drawn between natural and market value, and then the manner in which, after substituting the consideration of price for that of value, and noticing demand, the natural price is resolved into the elements of which it usually consists, and the wages of labour, the profits of stock, and their differences from occupation to occupation, whether due to artificial or natural causes, and the rent of land, are successively considered, are in accordance with the general tenour of recent investigation; and the first two books of the *Wealth of Nations* may be said to contain a theory of production, exchange and distribution, which presents in essence the fuller development of later criticism and speculation.

If we take, for instance, the laws governing the earnings of the different classes of participators in the distribution of wealth, it is truly surprising to find how successfully Adam Smith seems to have avoided many of the errors of subsequent thinkers, as they now appear, and to have seized hold of the essential elements of the truth. It appears tolerably certain that he did not fall into the characteristic fallacies of the wage-fund theory, although he speaks of the 'funds' from which wages might be paid, and he seems to have grasped the notion of a lower limit to wages in the standard of comfort of the labourer, and an upper limit in the wealth of a nation, between which the market forces might operate. On the subject of profits he writes with a domestic system of industry before his eyes, where there was little scope for the work of management, as compared with the huge industrial and commercial undertakings of the present day. And so he uses the term profits to denote the interest of capital, varying, as he says, entirely according to the amount of the stock employed; and he will not allow the element of wages of management to come into prominence. In the case of the 'apothecary' and the 'village grocer' he expressly brings under the category of wages, and excludes from the class of profits, what we should now term earnings of management. The American economist General Walker has, on the other hand, employed the term profits to denote these wages of management exclusively, and separated the interest of capital from it, and, in doing so, he has marked the change which has taken place in the organisation of industry. But the common English use of the term embraces both elements, and Adam Smith is in accord with the most recent tendency of economic speculation to consider under one and the same general head the wages of management and the wages of labour, and to regard as similar the general laws governing the earnings of all descriptions of labour – whether that of direction or that of obeying direction. On the matter of rent there are reasons for doubting whether he fully grasped, or consistently held, the theory known as the Ricardian theory, but he went some way towards doing so, and his statement that the rent of land 'not only varies with its fertility, whatever be its produce, but with its situation, whatever be its fertility' has the merit of stating concisely, and yet explicitly, what Ricardo mentioned but allowed many of his readers to forget.

So far for Adam Smith's treatment of distribution; and, before we pass to the later books of his treatise, it may be asked whether the advantages and dangers of paper money have ever since been more pithily expressed than in his remark that 'the gold and silver money which circulates in any country may very properly be compared to a highway, which, while it circulates and carries to market all the grass and corn of the country, produces itself not a single pile of either. The judicious operations of banking, by providing, if I may be allowed so violent a metaphor, a sort of waggon-way through the air, enable the country to convert, as it were, a great part of its highways into good pastures and cornfields, and thereby to increase very considerably the annual produce of its land and labour. The commerce and industry of the country, however, it must be acknowledged, though they may be somewhat augmented, cannot be altogether so secure, when they are thus, as it were, suspended upon the Dædalian wings of paper money, as when they travel about upon the solid ground of gold and silver.' The temptation to quote from the *Wealth of Nations* is very powerful, and may easily become irresistible; but I have not time to make, and you would scarcely have patience to listen to, more on the present occasion. The quotation, which I have just made, seems to me to afford so perfect an example of the qualities, which have contributed to give Adam Smith's treatise its high position, that I could not forbear to cite it. We see in it that power of direct and lucid statement, that facility of expressing in a sentence a profound and far-reaching truth, that felicity of apt illustration, which render the book at once so pleasant and so valuable. Adam Smith is sometimes diffuse, but he can also be remarkably terse, and he has the rare merit of luminous exposition and of relieving the tedium of dry reasoning by interesting and appropriate illustration. His wide acquaintance with fact, and his strong sense of its importance, combine with his extensive knowledge of the learning, with which the educated minds of his age were furnished, to enable him to employ within the compass of a paragraph a homely metaphor, which he may call 'violent' but his readers deem as suitable as it well can be, and also a parallel, just as apt but as classical as the metaphor is drawn from the common knowledge of the average man.

But we are returning to the consideration of the literary side of the *Wealth of Nations*; and, with a repetition of the opinion that it is only too possible to underrate the value, even for scientific ends, of literary excellence, and a mere passing allusion to the admitted belief of economists of different schools that Adam Smith's treatment of the division of labour, of the origin and use of money, of the rules and maxims of taxation, has perhaps been added to and improved, but has not been superseded, by later inquiry, we must press on to the consideration of that part of the book which has been most generally associated with the name of its author, and has achieved the most remarkable success in the domain of practical affairs.

Adam Smith's examination of the Mercantile System has been critically reviewed by writers of great ability and learning. Historians have shown that the Mercantilist views were more reasonable than the reader of the fourth book of the *Wealth of Nations* might suppose, and that they were actually in keeping with the practical exigencies of the times in which they were advanced. Able Protectionists have opposed to Adam Smith's undoubted cosmopolitanism a National System, and no fair-minded student can read List, for example, without recognising his persuasiveness and the force of some of the arguments he uses in reply to Adam Smith. Economic theorists, who believe in Free Trade, or at any rate in Free Trade for England, have brought into the light possibilities of which Adam Smith did not take full account: and the encouragement of 'infant industries' by Protection, to be withdrawn when they are able to stand by themselves and have attained maturity, has been allowed an economic justification by writers of the rank of Mill, who shocked some of his admirers by his candid admission. But those writers have been careful in most cases to add that the selection of the 'infants' to be specially nurtured requires an extraordinarily impartial and prudent government, and the removal of the protection, when it is no longer needed, calls for a remarkably strong and discreet administration. The economic basis of the argument is sound, but the political foundation is weak and shifting. Again, the difference between a country whose commodities obey a law of increasing returns, and one whose commodities are governed by a law of diminishing returns, as exchanging parties, has by recent writers been applied to the theoretical question of Free Trade and Protection, and some economic defence discovered for opinions and acts of a seemingly heretical character. Nor can it be denied that the tariff policy of so many European States of the great American Republic, and of our own colonies, although in the first case the eminent desirability of raising a large revenue for military purposes by the easy, imperceptible, and indirect means of taxation of imported commodities, in the second the immense area – perhaps the largest of its kind – of the United States, throughout which complete freedom of trade prevails, and the comparative unimportance of the question, and in the third the revenue considerations, which render direct taxation so difficult and expensive in a comparatively new country, might be advanced in explanation – it cannot be denied that this tariff policy has shaken the hopes raised by the more liberal movement of tariffs some little while ago.

But, with all these adverse influences, it is still surprising to find how fresh and forcible is the reasoning of Adam Smith's fourth book, and with how sure an instinct he seized on the most important and enduring arguments. There are two main grounds on which he may be said explicitly to base his contentions, and a third is implicitly contained in his language. The first of these arguments is the justice and advantage of freedom. Every individual, he maintains, in his own place and station can judge of the proper employment of his capital better than a lawgiver on government can do for him. It would be difficult to deny the force of this argument, though the further conclusion which he draws, that the consideration of a man's own interests will lead him to promote the interests of the community, might now be received with some qualification. But the general drift of the argument in favour of individual freedom in the employment of capital is admittedly very powerful. Connected with this is the argument, implied rather than stated, that there is a division of labour between nations as between individuals; that similar advantages result from its institution in encouraging production and developing capacities; and that, as domestic division of labour implies, and follows on, freedom of exchange, so the necessary condition of territorial or international division of labour is Free Trade.

But after all neither of these two arguments, though they are forcibly urged and aptly illustrated, seems to be that to which he is inclined to give the greatest prominence. It is the erroneous conception of money in the Mercantilist doctrine to which he devotes most continual attention, and it is on the correct idea of its function and place in industry and commerce that he lays repeated insistence. No doubt this emphasis was naturally suggested by the arguments of the advocates of the Mercantile System, to whom he was specially replying, but it seems also, in a higher degree than the other arguments which he advances, to give an enduring application to his reasoning. The conception that trade is an exchange of goods for goods in international as well as domestic transactions is a touchstone to which protectionist arguments may be brought with, as an almost invariable rule, serious, if not fatal, consequences to their validity. The fact that a nation pays for its imports by its exports is one which it is hard, if not impossible, to contest, if it is once apprehended; but there are few protectionist reasonings which can successfully confront it. That the process might be circuitous and indirect Adam Smith freely admitted; and the circuit has extended, and the accomplishment of its passage taken a longer time, since he wrote. The 'invisible exports,' as they have been called, of the capital and labour engaged in our shipping industry in carrying goods from one country to another, and the interest due on our investments abroad, have grown in volume since the publication of the *Wealth of Nations*. That gold and silver might form part of those imports and exports Adam Smith unhesitatingly allowed; but that they formed a small and insignificant part he stoutly maintained, and that the transit of bullion was avoided as far as possible he strenuously affirmed. Nor, in the case of countries like Great Britain, which did not themselves produce the precious metals to any large extent, could they be procured in the first instance except by the exchange of goods. These arguments have not lost their validity of pertinence, and any one acquainted with the difficult theory and complex practice of the foreign exchanges will remember that they turn on the anxiety to avoid the transit of bullion, while the growth of credit and its use in international trade have diminished the proportion of that trade effected by the passage of money to an extraordinary extent. And yet it is scarcely possible to read a protectionist pamphlet, however able and well-informed, without finding the old mistakes about money making their reappearance in some cunning disguise. It is as true now as it was when Adam Smith wrote it that 'even they who are convinced' of the 'absurdity' 'that wealth consists in money, or in gold and silver,' 'are very apt to forget their own principles, and, in the course of their reasonings, to take it for granted as a certain and undeniable truth.' Nor is it less true that 'writers upon commerce set out with observing that the wealth of a country consists, not in its gold and silver only, but in its lands, houses, and consumable goods of all different kinds. In the course of their reasonings, however, the lands, houses, and consumable goods, seem to slip out of their memory; and the strain of their argument frequently supposes that all wealth consists in gold and silver, and that to multiply those metals is the great object of national industry and commerce.'

Adam Smith never anticipated the 'complete restoration' of freedom of trade in Great Britain; and, had he lived to see this result accomplished, his disappointment as a mistaken prophet might have mingled with his satisfaction as a convincing reasoner. Few triumphs of a higher kind have ever been achieved by a speculative philosopher in the region of practical affairs; for, while it was the stern logic of fact, enforced by the famine in Ireland, which brought about the repeal of the Corn Laws, some of the most persuasive arguments used by Cobden on the platform reflected the spirit, if they did not reproduce the language, of the *Wealth of Nations*; and certainly Cobden himself and the succession of reforming finance ministers from Pitt, who showed that, had he enjoyed the opportunity, he would have anticipated the liberalising measures of later times, to Mr. Gladstone, who put the crowning touches on a purified tariff, would have been proud to own that they were pupils of the Glasgow professor. It might, indeed, have been well, had it been possible, if the common people had learnt their lesson also from the book and not from the facts. Facts may be forgotten when they have passed away, but 'litera scripta manet,' and it almost seems as if before long the battle may have to be fought over again.

May I add one word in conclusion, and that is simply to express the pleasure of being permitted as an Oxonian to do honour to the memory of Adam Smith in this famous and beautiful city, where he first lectured and established a reputation, where he formed that intimate friendship with David Hume which endured throughout life, and where he spent the greater part of his closing years and, dying in the ripeness of age and honour, was laid in his last resting-place? If Oxford treated Adam Smith ill as a student in her unregenerate days, she, in common with the World, accords him a high place on the roll of the World's worthies, and she is proud to number him among the most distinguished of her own sons. But it is to Scotland that Adam Smith owed most, and it is to Scotland also that students of Economics are in duty bound to express their gratitude for having given birth to the bearer of the greatest and most honoured name in the annals of this branch of learning.

Notes

1. Read before Section F of the British Association at Edinburgh, August 12, 1892.
2. Book II, Chapter V.
3. *Political Economy and Sociology.*
4. *Principles of Economics,* Vol. I., Book I., Chapter IV., Section 3.

55

Adam Smith as an Economist[1]

E. Cannan

Source: *Economica*, Vol. 6, June 1926, pp. 123-34.

I have no responsibility for this choice of subject. I would not have chosen it myself, because I was acutely conscious of the difficulty of saying, one hundred and fifty years after the publication of the *Wealth of Nations*, anything which is both new and true about it. I do not profess to have solved the difficulty now. I hope what I shall say is true; but as for newness, I can only be like the candidates for Ph.D. degrees, who when their supervisor says, "I can't see that you are discovering any new facts," plead "But don't you think I might be held to have 'exercised independent critical power'?" (Ph.D. Regulations, section 5[b]).

Very little of Adam Smith's scheme of economics has been left standing by subsequent inquirers. No one now holds his theory of value, his account of capital is seen to be hopelessly confused, and his theory of distribution is explained as an ill-assorted union between his own theory of prices and the physiocrats' fanciful Economic Table. His classification of incomes is found to involve a misguided attempt to alter the ordinary useful and well-recognised meaning of words, and a mixing up of classification according to source with classification according to method or manner of receipt. His opinions about taxation and its incidence are extremely crude, and his history is based on insufficient information and disfigured by bias.

But three great things he did accomplish.

The first was the definite substitution of income – "produce" as he called it – for the older idea of a capital aggregation of "treasure" or something akin to "treasure." He was quite aware of what he was doing here. The Introduction and Plan which he prefixed to the *Wealth of Nations* begins with two paragraphs in which the continuous attainment of a large quantity of the necessaries and conveniences of life is treated as the end of economic endeavour, and it ends with a sentence in which the "real wealth" of a nation is taken to be "the annual produce of the land and labour of the society."

Of course this idea was not new in the sense of springing from Adam Smith's head like Athene from that of Zeus. The seed for it had been sown by the calculations of the English political arithmeticians in the end of the seventeenth century, and its germination had been assisted by the physiocrats' discussion of what they called "the annual reproduction" and its "distribution." But Smith must be given the credit of getting in the harvest.

Right down to his time the reigning school of economic thought was open to the reproach which he levels against it when he says that it represented the great object of the industry and commerce of a nation to be the multiplication of gold and silver within it. It is no use to pretend that this was confined to the small fry of less reputable writers. With the possible exception of Sir William Petty, Cantillon was the acutest economist of the period before Adam Smith, and in some directions anticipated doctrine which did not come into fashion till a century and a half after his own time; but what does he say? At the beginning of his *Essai* he says "*la richesse en elle-même n'est autre chose que la nourriture. les commodités et les agréments de la vie,*" and he heads chapter xvi of Part I "*plus il y a de travail dans un Etat, et plus l'Etat est censé riche naturellement.*" This raises great hopes, but they are rudely shattered by what follows. Calculating that only 25 per cent. of the population can be regarded as available for any labour other than that required for the production of the absolute necessaries of life, Cantillon says that if some of these persons are employed in beautifying the people's apparel and refining their food, their country "will be considered rich according to the amount of this labour, though it adds nothing to the quantity of things necessary for the subsistence and maintenance of men." But, he thinks, if the same persons are employed in getting metals out of the earth and fashioning them into tools and plate, the country will not only appear richer but "will really be so."

"It will be so especially," he proceeds, "if these persons are employed in drawing from the bosom of the earth gold and silver, metals which are not only durable, but so to speak permanent, which cannot be consumed even by fire, which are generally received as the measure of value, and which can at all times be exchanged for everything necessary for life: and if these persons work so as to bring gold and silver into the country in exchange for manufactures and wares which they have made there and which are exported to foreign countries, their labour will be equally useful and will really benefit the country.

"For the point which really seems to determine the comparative grandeur of states is the body of reserve which they have over and above the annual consumption, like stores of cloth, linen, corn, etc., to serve for lean years in case of need or in case of war. And inasmuch as gold and silver can always buy all these things even from the enemies of the State, the true body of reserve for a State is gold and silver, of which the greater or less actual quantity necessarily determines the comparative grandeur of Kingdoms and States." (*Essai*, pp. 117 *ff.*)

Sir James Steuart brought out his book – the first in English with the title of *Political Economy* – in 1767, and its 1,300 quarto pages quite fail to make clear what he thought constituted the wealth of society. Even the great Turgot, though he is sound enough about money and bullion, does not adopt the idea of produce or income being the wealth of society, but says the riches of a country are to be found by multiplying the annual value of land by the number of years' purchase and adding the value of moveable goods. (*Réflexions*, xci.)

The statesmen or politicians were, as usual, worse than the economists. Necker, in 1776, the year which we are now commemorating, included in the riches of the State "neither the land which supports the people nor the advances in tools, in animals, in buildings, in things necessary for sowing and cultivation;" because "all this is absolutely a part of the population since it is impossible to separate man from his subsistence."

"So," he continued, "the only riches which form a power distinct from the population are the surplus of goods of all kinds which are gradually amassed in a society, and which, being susceptible of exchange against the services of foreigners, can increase the public power.

"These goods consist to-day chiefly in treasures (*matrières précieuses*) such as gold and silver; because these metals have become the common measure of exchanges, and the sure means of acquiring everywhere all the productions of the land and the labour of men." (*Sur la législation et le commerce des grains*, chap iv.)

To change all this, to recognise that not a hoard of gold and silver, nor even a store of all kinds of valuable and useful things, is the end of economic endeavour, but instead, a large continuous produce or supply of consumable necessaries and conveniences – that, in short, as Smith himself put it (vol. ii, p. 159), "Consumption is the sole end and purpose of all production," was a great service. It marks the transition from the state of mind of the savage who can only think of what he has in hand, to the state of the civilised man who looks before, and considers himself well off when he is assured of having adequate supplies of food and other necessaries and conveniences in the future.

The second great change which Adam Smith made in general theory was to substitute wealth per head for wealth in the aggregate, whatever that may be. He does this in the second sentence of the *Wealth of Nations* in his stride, so to speak, apparently without noticing that anything important was happening: "The nation," he says, "will be better or worse supplied with all the necessaries and conveniences for which it has occasion" according as the produce "bears a greater or smaller proportion to the number of those who are to consume it." That is, he will consider the nation wealthy or not wealthy according as its average worker is wealthy or not wealthy, and not according as the sum of all its members' wealth is great or small.

By this he threw over the old idea of an entity called the state or the nation existing outside the individuals who constitute its subjects or members, and flourishing or languishing irrespective of their prosperity. To us that may seem a small thing. We are accustomed to think of Switzerland or of Denmark as a rich nation compared with Russia. But it was a great break with tradition in 1776, so great that Smith himself often fails to live up to it, and drops back into speaking of China as rich, while at the same moment insisting on the extreme poverty of the Chinese. Cantillon had had a glimmering of it in 1730, when he wondered whether it might not be better to have a smaller well-to-do population than a larger poor one, but he dismissed consideration of the matter as outside his subject.

It was a change in accordance with the humaner spirit of the age. The "nation" was henceforth to be the whole people and not merely the King or the ruling classes, who, being themselves above the reach of want, could afford to pursue national glory and power and despise the sordid considerations which invade the homes of the people. No longer were the people to be regarded as mere pawns to be used as required in the queer game of accumulating a hoard of treasure of which the only conceivable use was to be sent abroad again in time of war. They were to be a body of persons whose individual necessaries and conveniences of life were to be the objects to be pursued. "Political Economy," Smith says himself in the Introduction to Book IV, had to teach the Statesman how to get revenue for the State, but also, and firstly, to "provide a plentiful revenue or subsistence for the people, or more properly to enable them to provide such a revenue or subsistence for themselves."

There are difficulties, of course, about accepting the average wealth as conclusive. Those which concern the validity of the average (whatever average is taken) as a measure of general individual wealth we may dismiss as matters of detail, but it is otherwise with the difficulty which confronts us when we are asked whether indefinite diminution of numbers, provided it is accompanied by increasing wealth, is good from an economic point of view. Smith himself evaded this difficulty by his firm belief that prosperity and population move together, but we know that they often do not. Yet at any rate Smith's view was better than the one which it displaced. Within certain limits, at any rate, we may be satisfied to prefer the high average to the high aggregate.

The substitution of the average for the aggregate involved that approval of high wages which marks off the economists from the more ill-disposed employers whom the socialists persist in supposing them to represent. Nowadays even, there are some persons who will tell you that low wages are a great "advantage" to Japan and Germany. In Smith's day they were probably more predominant. With them he reasons gently but persuasively: "What improves the circumstances of the greater part can never be regarded as an inconveniency to the whole. No society can surely be flourishing and happy of which the far greater part of the members are poor and miserable" (vol. i, p. 80). Wage-earners are the most numerous income-receiving class, so that an increase of wealth per head is not likely to take place without an increase of wages.

Smith's sympathies, indeed, seem to have been wholly with the industrious wage-earner, and especially with the poorest. In the *Lectures* we find him telling his Glasgow students:

"The division of opulence is not according to the work. The opulence of the merchant is greater than that of all his clerks, though he works less; and they again have six times more than an equal number of artisans . . . The artisan who works within doors has far more than the poor labourer who trudges up and down without intermission. Thus he who as it were bears the burden of society has the fewest advantages" (p. 163).

The employers of his time and their spokesmen were always complaining that high wages ruined their workmen by making them drunken and disinclined to work more than half the week. In his lectures Smith speaks as if he accepted the fact so far at least as the "commercial parts of England" and especially Birmingham were concerned, summing up the result in a Ruskinian phrase, "So it may very justly be said that the people who clothe the whole world are in rags themselves" (p. 257). He does not, however, suggest reduction of wages as a remedy, but elementary education and a consequent abolition of early employment of children. In the *Wealth of Nations* he pooh-poohs the whole theory of high wages ruining workmen. Industry, he thinks, is improved by encouragement:

"A plentiful subsistence increases the bodily strength of the labourer, and the comfortable hope of bettering his condition, and of ending his days perhaps in ease and plenty, animates him to exert that strength to the utmost. Where wages are high, accordingly, we shall always find the workmen more active, diligent, and expeditious than where they are low; in England, for example, than in Scotland" (vol. i, p. 83). It is said, he observes, that "in cheap years workmen are generally more idle and in dear ones more industrious than ordinary," but this, he believes, is merely the result of masters being able to make better bargains with their men in dear years, which they then naturally commend as more favourable to industry.

"Some workmen, indeed," he admits, "when they can earn in four days what will maintain them through the week, will be idle the other three. This, however, is by no means the case with the greater part." The majority, he thinks, are more likely to overwork themselves when paid liberally by the place; "excessive application during four days of the week is frequently the real cause of the idleness of the other three, so much and so loudly complained of" (vol. i, pp. 83, 84). "If masters would always listen to the dictates of reason and humanity they would have frequently occasion rather to moderate than to animate the application of many of their workmen."

Smith thus started the line of thought which was continued by what are called the classical economists. A recent writer has actually said that those economists "defended subsistence wages." Of all the libels upon them invented by socialist and semi-socialist writers this is about the worst. They may have been, they certainly frequently were, wrong about the causes of high wages, but they were always in favour of them. Malthus devoted years to his propaganda for raising wages by reducing the supply of labour. Ricardo certainly reckoned himself among those "friends of humanity," who, he says, should wish the labourer to have expensive tastes so as to keep the supply of labour down and wages up. McCulloch, who is so often a very present source of comfort to the enemies of the classical economists, is never tired of insisting on the advantage of high wages, as a glance at the heading of Wages in the index to his *Principles* will show.

Thirdly, Adam Smith may fairly claim to be the father, not of economics generally – that would be absurd – but of what in modern times has been called, with opprobrious intention, "bourgeois economics," that is the economics of those economists who look with favour on working and trading and investing for personal gain. We are apt to forget that the idea that a wage-earner, a trader, or an investor may be, and indeed generally is, a very respectable person is very modern. From Homer we learn that the people whom Odysseus visited on his travels thought it all the same whether he was a trader or a piratical murderous marauder. Primitive people are said to have regarded exchange as a kind of robbery rather than as a mutual giving. Greek philosophers thought wage-earners incapable of virtue, and money-lenders have been objects of antipathy throughout the ages. In Smith's own time Dr. Johnson and Postlethwayt very seriously considered whether a trader could be a gentleman.

Smith came forward as the admirer and champion of the man who wants to get on. Probably, like many another Scotch boy, he had learnt that gospel on his mother's knee. He did not get it from his master, Hutcheson, for he complained that Hutcheson did not sufficiently explain "from whence arises our approbation of the inferior virtues of prudence, circumspection, temperance, constancy, firmness." Regard, he said, for "our own private happiness and interest" is often a laudable principle of action. "The habits of economy, industry, discretion, attention and application of thought are generally supposed to be cultivated from self-interested motives, and at the same time are apprehended to be very praiseworthy qualities which deserve the esteem and approbation of everybody . . . Carelessness and want of economy are universally disapproved of, not, however, as proceeding from a want of benevolence, but from a want of the proper attention to the objects of self-interest" (*Moral Sentiments*, pp. 464-6). Far from making people inclined to cheat, he held, commerce made them honest and desirous of fulfilling their contracts. He told his Glasgow students, according to the report of one of them:

"Whenever commerce is introduced into any country, probity and punctuality always accompany it. These virtues in a rude and barbarous country are almost unknown. Of all the nations in Europe, the Dutch, the most commercial, are the most faithful to their word. The English are more so than the Scotch, but much inferior to the Dutch, and in the remote parts of this country they are far less so than in the commercial parts of it. This is not at all to be imputed to national character, as some pretend; there is no natural reason why an Englishman or a Scotchman should not be as punctual in performing agreements as a Dutchman. It is far more reducible to self-interest, that general principle which regulates the actions of every man, and which leads men to act in a certain manner from views of advantage, and is as deeply implanted in an Englishman as a Dutchman. A dealer is afraid of losing his character, and is scrupulous in observing every engagement. When a person makes perhaps twenty contracts in a day, he cannot gain so much by endeavouring to impose on his neighbours as the very appearance of a cheat would make him lose. When people seldom deal with one another we find that they are somewhat disposed to cheat, because they can gain more by a smart trick than they can lose by the injury which it does their character.

"They whom we call politicians are not the most remarkable people in the world for probity and punctuality. Ambassadors from different nations are still less so . . . The reason of this is that nations treat with one another not above twice or thrice in a century, and they may gain more by one piece of fraud than lose by having a bad character . . . But if states were obliged to treat once or twice a day, as merchants do, it would be necessary to be more precise . . . a prudent dealer, who is sensible of his real interest, would rather choose to lose what he has a right to, than give any ground for suspicion" (*Lectures*, pp. 253-5).

In the *Wealth of Nations* Smith says, like a true bourgeois: "Bankruptcy is perhaps the greatest and most humiliating calamity which can befall an innocent man." Throughout the book he treats prodigality with bourgeois contempt; it is a kind of mental aberration: sane men save:

"With regard to profusion, the principle which prompts to expense is the passion for present enjoyment; which though sometimes violent and very difficult to be restrained, is in general only momentary and occasional. But the principle which prompts to save is the desire of bettering our condition, a desire which, though generally calm and dispassionate, comes with us from the womb and never leaves us till we go into the grave. In the whole interval which separates those two moments, there is scarce perhaps a single instant in which any man is so completely satisfied with his situation as to be without any wish of alteration or improvement of any kind. An augmentation of fortune is the means by which the greater part of men propose and wish to better their condition. It is the means the most vulgar and the most obvious; and the most likely way of augmenting their fortune is to save and accumulate some part of what they acquire, either regularly and annually or upon some extraordinary occasions" (vol. i, pp. 323-4).

All this approval of the man who wants to get on in life, succeed in business, or whatever you like to call it, would have been a very poor gospel if such success were only purchased at the cost of depressing other people. But in Adam Smith's view it was not. On the contrary, he held that commerce and investment having been introduced, each man by trying to help himself, in fact, not only helped himself, but all others.

So, in his opinion, when "the butcher, the brewer, and the baker" provide us with our dinner, not because they love us, but because they wish to benefit themselves, they need not be ashamed of the fact. Let them go on doing their best to serve their own interest, and they will serve us and society generally better than "if they affect to trade for the public good," and better than if the State tries to regulate their prices.

He pictured the vast multitude of persons in various parts of the world co-operating in the production of the modest coat of the labourer; he showed how their specialising in their respective occupations increased their product; he described this division of labour as the greatest cause of the superior opulence of civilised mankind over their primitive ancestors and their uncivilised contemporaries. And he pointed out that the co-operation was not due to any effort of collective wisdom, but to men's natural propensity to serve their own interest by "truck, barter, and exchange of one thing for another." He described the increase of capital as another great cause of prosperity, and said very truly that it was not the result of Government foresight, for Governments were generally prodigal and profuse, but of the frugality and good conduct of individuals desirous of bettering their own condition.

It is easy to object to the confidence in "Nature" which he displays, in accordance with the fashion of the time, when he assumes that the coincidence between self-interest and the general good establishes itself "naturally," in the absence, that is, of all human institutions except a few which were regarded as being themselves natural. In our day, with the law of property just put into an Act of several hundred pages in length, and the relations between husband and wife, and between parents and children in a state of flux, we are not likely to believe in an orderly and harmonious state of "natural liberty" in which society does not presume to "interfere" with individual action. We see that self-interest, which might lead many of us to snatch jewellery from shop windows in the Strand, is made to flow in quite unnatural directions by the existence of those very artificial institutions, the Metropolitan Police and the Bow Street Police Court and Dartmoor Prison. Throughout history society has been fashioning and modifying its institutions so as to make it the interest of its members to do the right thing.

It is just the incompleteness of those institutions which have been the great obstacle to the acceptance of Smith's view in the realm of international trade. International trade is still looked on with quite primitive suspicion: each country imagines that it must be very careful not to allow its subjects to buy and sell across the national boundary as freely as they do inside it. There is no confidence that the fact that they find it profitable indicates that the country as a whole will benefit by it.

Adam Smith could see no sense in a country's refusing to let its inhabitants buy from abroad what they could buy cheaper than at home. No prudent head of a household, he said, has anything made at home when he can buy it at less expense outside, and what is prudence on the part of the householder can scarcely be folly on the part of a nation. Why, then, this persistence of fear of cheap imported goods, rising almost to panic when the price falls to zero, as when a defeated enemy consents to pay reparations and it is realised that the reparations will be paid not in paper money or gold but in goods?

The simplest explanation that may be proposed is that nations, trying to think collectively, are stupider than ordinary house-holders thinking individually, so that they do by mere stupidity what the householder will not do. But there is probably more in it than that, and I am inclined to think that the true explanation is to be looked for in the very fact which Smith ignored, namely, that such harmony as is found between the pursuit of self-interest and the general good is dependent on the existence of suitable human institutions.

As between country and country "natural liberty" in the completest sense still very largely prevails. Any sovereign state may declare war upon another except in so far as it is hindered by some very recent arrangements, the strength of which has yet to be tested. Hence a prudent nation has some excuse for considering whether the immediate advantage to itself of a particular branch of foreign trade may not be outweighed by the greater strength which that trade may cause the other country to possess in some future conflict of arms. The nation, in fact, in contemplating its foreign trade, is always asking, "What if there is war?"

The existence of protection in British overseas dominions and even in the Irish Free State may be brought up against this suggestion that want of institutions giving security against foreign attack is the chief root of the general refusal to regard international trade as favourably as internal domestic trade. The Dominions, it may be said, protect themselves against the metropolitan country and each other as well as against foreign countries, and it cannot be that they suppose that there is danger to be apprehended from either. But it is doubtful if there is much strength in the objection. Tradition has enormous force in these matters. The Dominion which feels itself a separate entity is likely to behave from mere force of imitation in the way which the nations which have complete independence and sovereignty ordinarily do.

Adam Smith himself never really faced the difficulty. He was too much in the thrall of old ways of thinking which have come down from the ancient very partial civilisation when the barbarians were regarded as just as much outside society as the wolves and other wild beasts. His followers have scarcely improved on him to this day, and still get themselves into inextricable difficulties by at one moment treating "the nation" as if it were synonymous with human society, and at another recognising that it is only a section which may be doing its level best to harry, kill, and erase the memory of some other section or sections.

But though Smith was wrong in supposing that the desire for individual gain would pull the industrial chariot safely along in the absence of harness, and though this error vitiated his doctrine and accounts for its ill-success in the international sphere, so far as internal trade and specialisation of persons and places to particular occupations were concerned, he was on firm ground, because the institutions which are required for making self-interest take the beneficent road were actually there – not, of course, in a perfect form – they never will be that but sufficiently developed to justify his view. When he describes the co-operation necessary for making the labourer's rough coat and contrasts the situation of the humblest member of a civilised and thriving nation very favourably with that of many an African king, the absolute master of the lives and liberties of ten thousand naked savages, he was in fact taking things as they were in his time. That he failed to see that self-interest had been put in the shafts and harnessed by law and order, products of collective wisdom, detracts little from the value of his exposition that it was a very good horse.

By that exposition he elevated the conception of gainful occupation and investment from a system of beggar-my-neighbour to one of mutual service. The new conception has steadily gained ground in the more advanced countries of the world. It is true that there is a numerous sect which tries to convince the wage-earners that they are working not for the public and not for the consumers of the things or the services which they produce, but for the capitalist employer who gets what is left after wages and other expenses have been met; but their sour propaganda loses force as the old theory of the iron law of wages drops into oblivion in face of obvious facts, and the nature and necessity of interest becomes more clear.

So we do not now think of work being done as by a slave for a master, and of business being engaged in as by a gambler to win gain at the expense of other players. We work for our wages and our salaries, and even for those residues which are called profits: we save and invest for our interest and our dividends: knowing full well that the more successful we are, the better not only for ourselves but for the consumers of our products.

I hope that no teacher in the School will ever give any countenance to the pernicious belief that steady and honest service in satisfying the demand of the people for the necessaries and conveniences of life is something to be ashamed of because it is profitable. The modern workman and the modern trader can practice virtue as well as a Greek philosopher, a mediaeval begging friar, or a twentieth century social reformer.

Note

1.   The first of a series of seven lectures delivered by various lecturers at the London School of Economics in Lent Term, 1926, to commemorate the completion of a hundred and fifty years since the publication of the *Wealth of Nations*.

56

The Manuscript of an Early Draft of Part of *The Wealth of Nations*[1]

W.R. Scott

Source: *Economic Journal*, Vol. 45 (179), September 1935, pp. 427-38.

It gives me very great pleasure to announce to the Society a discovery of the greatest possible interest to students of Economics. It is the finding of a very early draft of what became afterwards *The Wealth of Nations*. The general character of it may be best explained by certain circumstances connected with the manuscript. As a part of a plan to obtain more information about Adam Smith, I obtained permission from the Duke of Buccleuch to examine any manuscripts at Dalkeith House which were likely to be useful. Amongst these were the papers of Charles Townshend, who was the second husband of the Countess of Dalkeith, to whose son, Henry the third Duke of Buccleuch, Adam Smith was tutor from 1764 to 1766. These papers have been kept together in a separate collection. The relative failure of my original objective was compensated for many times by the finding of a fairly thick folded folio manuscript which had very close affinities both with the *Glasgow Lectures* and *The Wealth of Nations*. It is written on stout handmade paper, consisting of twelve double folio sheets, making forty-eight pages in all. Each double folio sheet is marked with a number – N 1, N 2 up to N 12 – in Adam Smith's writing. As was the case with his other works,[2] it is in the hand of an amanuensis, similar to that of one of the Glasgow College scribes, as can be seen by a comparison of the script with that of some of the University records of the period. There are a number of corrections and additions made by Adam Smith in his own hand. At the foot of each page there is a catchword; and, since there is one of these on p. 48, it is evident that there had been originally more, perhaps considerably more, of the manuscript. The existing portion consists of 12,113 words.

The form of the manuscript is connected with the engagement of Adam Smith as travelling tutor to the Duke of Buccleuch. It will be remembered that Rae records how Hume wrote to Adam Smith on April 12, 1759, that Charles Townshend had said to Oswald that "he would put the Duke of Buccleuch under the care of the author of *The Theory of Moral Sentiments*," at the same time warning Smith of the instability of many of Townshend's projects, as to which Rae has several amusing anecdotes to relate.[3]

It seems that Adam Smith always had a hankering after a tutorship. It was to this end that he gave much of his energy after he returned from Oxford, and it was one of the objects he had before him in arranging for his lectures in Edinburgh from 1748 to 1751. A new fact sheds some light on this fixed purpose. It turns out that Adam Smith had a relative, probably a cousin, William Smith, who was a tutor and curator according to Scots law, or, in other words, a trustee, for Adam Smith's half-brother Hugh. This William Smith had been governor to Lord Charles Hay, afterwards Earl of Errol; and, on the termination of his engagement, was nominated as a Regent of Marischal University,[4] Aberdeen. No doubt in Adam Smith's youth this was impressed on him as an example to follow and the early impression remained, even though the main purpose, namely, the procuring of promotion, had disappeared in his own case. Accordingly, it is easy to understand that Adam Smith was careful to keep himself before Townshend. The latter had visited Smith in Glasgow and Smith had been to Dalkeith, but still the appointment was not made. It is likely that, in order to maintain himself in Townshend's mind, Adam Smith had this manuscript prepared; or, alternatively, it may have arisen from something that was said at one of the meetings of the two. In view of the fact that he himself stated in July 1764 that he had begun to write a book at Toulouse,[5] the possibility that this was a draft sent to Townshend from France is not to be wholly excluded. However, for the present, since the finding of the manuscript is so recent and there has not been time to examine several problems connected with it, I do not wish to commit myself as to date, though there seem to be strong reasons against it having been sent from France. In any case the relation with Townshend determined the form of this draft.

It will be remembered that the *Glasgow Lectures* consist as to more than one-half of a treatment of Jurisprudence. It is the remainder, named "Police," which constituted the economic portion of these lectures. In the manuscript there is a new and most significant departure. It is definitely intended to be an economic treatise and nothing else. The first words on p. 1 are sufficiently arresting. They are "Chapter 2, The Nature and Causes of Public Opulence." Here the keynote of the later book is struck with no uncertain touch. The subject-matter is Division of Labour. Evidently at this time Adam Smith had in view a general introductory chapter, corresponding to the Introduction of *The Wealth of Nations*, and the beginning of the manuscript consists of material corresponding to Chapters 1 and 2 of the completed book. The unwritten first chapter of the manuscript would have, no doubt, repeated Sections 1 and 2 of "Police" in the *Glasgow Lectures*, namely, "the natural wants of mankind" and "the arts subservient to these." Then comes the existing Chapter 2, which takes in §§ 3-6, *i.e.* "Opulence arising from Division of Labour," which multiplies the product, what occasions it, and that it must be proportioned to the extent of the market.

After this point the remaining chapters are in skeleton form. Though thus less full than the *Lectures*, they are of the greatest interest as showing how close and integrated the argument is – an impression which is in fact lost in *The Wealth of Nations*, through the additional matter subsequently inserted. Chapter 3 is entitled "Of the Rule of Exchanging or of the Circumstances which regulate the Price of Commodities;" Chapter 4, "Of Money, its Nature, Origin and History considered, first as the measure of value, and secondly as the instrument of Commerce;" Chapter 5, "Concerning the Slow Progress of Opulence." The manuscript ends in the middle of the criticism of the prohibition of the exportation of corn at the point where Cicero quotes "Old Cato."[6]

Professor Cannan has a note at the end of the second chapter of *The Wealth of Nations* that "the concluding paragraph was probably taken bodily from the manuscript of the author's lectures." Now that we have these, or a revision of them, it is possible to say that not only this paragraph but the rest, after the beginning of Chapter 1, is taken practically word for word from this manuscript. What I mean to imply by "practically" is, subject to the alterations which one makes in the revision of something written previously. These revisions are fewer than one would expect. They consist (1) of matters of style; (2) of change of adjectives, involving a change of meaning, sometimes reducing the emphasis of the *Lectures*, occasionally adding to it; (3) additions to the *Lectures* by the insertion of a sentence or two, and – what comes rather as a surprise – a much greater reduction, for purposes of condensation, usually by cutting out a quite considerable part of a paragraph. The portion of the manuscript consisting of Chapter 2 (corresponding to Chapters 1 and 2 of *The Wealth of Nations*) comprises twelve long paragraphs, amounting to over 7,800 words. A great part of Chapters 1 and 2 of *The Wealth of Nations* is made up of repetitions of the manuscript which amount to close on 3,500 words, in the sense of being quoted textually subject to verbal alterations. Some of these are of interest. The relation of the invention of window glass to "the making of these northern parts of the world habitable" has an addition, the cancellations of which may be a loss to *The Wealth of Nations*, namely, "without which these northern parts of the world would scarce have been habitable, at least by that effeminate and delicate race of mortals who dwell in them at present." The African king, "the absolute master of the lives and liberties of ten thousand naked savages," appears in the manuscript as "an Indian prince, the chief of a savage nation in North America," which presents a complete picture. At a later stage, during the fighting in the American colonies, the "naked savages" (or some of them) became "noble allies," and it was necessary or politic to substitute "the African king," who is, artistically, less satisfying.

Besides a number of cuts in the manuscript for purposes of condensations the reason the word for word transfer to *The Wealth of Nations* is not higher, coming very close to the whole of these two chapters, is that I have excluded the opening of the first chapter of the manuscript, though, all through, it is very near to *The Wealth of Nations* in its phraseology. That is the part relating to pin-making and amounting to about two pages in Cannan's edition. This is involved in the considerations of another interesting question, namely, how far the reporter of the *Lectures* has given a correct and adequate summary of what he had heard. We have now the opportunity to check this report with the original or something very close to it. In view of the fact that the portion, which is given in full in the manuscript, is barely one-eleventh of the economic part of the *Lectures*, this is obviously a matter of considerable importance. Subject to one important reservation, the reporter was quite exceptionally competent. He had the rare faculty of understanding Adam Smith's argument, restating it in a much briefer form, while retaining the main line of thought, and at the same time incorporating in his summary a number of the more picturesque and striking phrases. The condensation is greater than one would have expected. He reduces by as much as 70 per cent. More precisely he represents Adam Smith by 29.9 per cent. of the number of words in the manuscript. The reduction is by no means equally distributed. The short paragraph on the three advantages of the Division of Labour is nearly as full as the manuscript – the report containing as much as 70 per cent. of the number of words in the latter.

It is to be expected than an average contraction of 70 per cent. would result in the omission of nearly all Adam Smith's finer points and most of his qualifications. A closer inspection reveals the fact that the average is by no means representative. The condensation is very unequal. It is easy to understand that the copious illustration of the manuscript is capable of much abbreviation, and Adam Smith himself applied the pruning knife when moving these passages to *The Wealth of Nations*. But there is more in the situation than this. Comparing the *Lectures* and the manuscript, it is most remarkable to find that, when questions relating to Distribution are touched on, they are abbreviated almost to the point of disappearance, sometimes they find no place in the summary. Omitting incidental references, topics connected with Distribution amount to over one-third of Chapter 2 of the manuscript – that is, 1,891 words out of 5,441 – the reporter represents these by only 322 words, or 17 per cent. against a general average of 30 per cent. Since he is accurate elsewhere, this suggests the problem whether the lectures he heard contained much less on this subject than is to be found in the manuscript. This is a question which I hope to discuss in the edition of the manuscript which I am preparing.

This brings us back to the paragraphs on pin-making, and at the same time affords a better idea of the plan Adam Smith had in mind than is to be found in the *Lectures*. He begins with the advantages of the common day labourer, thus his proem in the *Lectures* and the manuscript becomes the peroration in *The Wealth of Nations*. Arising out of this he finds himself faced with the problem how this can be so when the poor provide both for themselves and for the enormous luxury of their superiors. From their produce comes the landlord's rent, the interest of the monied man; and "the indolent and frivolous retainers of a Court" are supported by the labour of those who pay taxes. Reviewing the various claims on the produce of a great society, the poor labourer seems to bear on his shoulders the whole fabric of the building – how then, he asks, "shall we account for the superior affluence and abundance commonly possessed even by this lowest and most despised member of civilised society, compared with what the most respected and active savage can attain to"? The answer is, of course, the principle of Division of Labour. What is of much interest is that the analysis of pin-making is treated, not only from the Productive, but also from the Distributive point of view. As specialisation increases profits emerge, and, at each stage, the wage of the worker increases. As the illustration is developed further it is significant to observe that Adam Smith has the conception of real wages, imagining the pin-maker paying so many pins for the wire he uses and for the loan of the tools.[7] On this basis he finds it a mark of an opulent, commercial society that "labour becomes dear and work cheap." This is worked out with an amount of elaboration and detail that is very scantily represented in the *Lectures*. In particular, he has a distinct conception of National Wealth, which looks somewhat disguised as "National Opulence," and is treated in the stimulating manner "as that of the whole people diffused universally through all the members of the society." In the remainder of Chapter 2 of the manuscript there are occasional references to distributive problems, as, for instance, when *The Wealth of Nations* has "that universal opulence which extends itself to the lowest ranks of the people," the manuscript reads after "opulence" "notwith-standing the inequality of property."

The same subject is continued in Chapter 3 of the manuscript, which, unfortunately, is represented only by a summary. The first section deals with wages under three heads: (1) "what is sufficient to maintain the labourer, (2) to indemnify him for his education in that particular business, (3) to compensate him for the risk he may run, either of not living long enough to receive this indemnification, or of not succeeding in the trade let him live ever so long." This is reproduced in the *Lectures*.[8] Then there follow discussions on the price of country labour, that of handicraft work, of the ingenious arts and of the liberal professions. In the fourth section of this chapter, "national or public opulence" is said to consist in the cheapness of commodities in proportion to wages, and therefore "whatever tends to raise their price above what is precisely necessary to encourage the labourer tends to diminish national or public opulence." Chapter 5 is an early form of Adam Smith's attack on the Mercantile System. The first head begins with the great importance of Agriculture, which is of interest from the references to the stock of farmers, but the summary does not show how the resulting distributive questions are developed.

This treatment of Distribution in the manuscript is of immense interest. Professor Cannan in his Introduction to the *Lectures* says "there is no trace whatever in them of the scheme of Distribution which *The Wealth of Nations* sets forth," and again, "the dissertations on the division of labour, money, prices and the cause of the differences of wages in different employments, evidently existed very nearly in their present form before Adam Smith went to France, and the scheme of distribution, on the other hand, was wholly absent. It is plain that Adam Smith acquired the idea of the necessity of a scheme of distribution from the Physiocrats, and that he tacked his own scheme (very different from theirs) on his already existing theory of prices."[9] If "trace" in the first sentence be taken in the sense in which it is used in chemical analysis, I cordially agree with Professor Cannan, with the necessary limitation that the quotation applies to the *Glasgow Lectures*.

The finding of this manuscript may involve some reconsideration of the reference in the last sentence to the influence of the Physiocrats. There has not been time to pronounce on the rather involved questions which emerge; but, since these can only be investigated gradually, an incomplete and tentative statement of what a preliminary view suggests may be pardoned, all the more since I am proposing to include an edition of this manuscript in a book on parts of Adam Smith's life which is unlikely to be issued earlier than the year after next.

The manuscript has considerably more concerning Distribution than the *Lectures* suggest. It is remarkable as containing passages including just those points which Professor Cannan signalises as being wanting in the *Lectures* and which he considered Adam Smith learned from the Physiocrats, namely, stock or capital, productive and unproductive expenses and the conception of a National Dividend.[10] In the second paragraph of the manuscript a vivid and even highly coloured picture is painted of the labourer and the peasant on the one hand, and on the other the slothful landlord supporting his vanity by the rent he receives, "the monied man indulging himself in every sort of ignoble sensuality at the expense of the merchant and the tradesman to whom he lends out his stock at interest," and, finally, "all the indolent and frivolous retainers of a Court." As has been seen, Adam Smith had already the conception of something closely corresponding to a real National Dividend, which he describes as dividend amongst various classes of persons. He imagines a great society, illustrated by one of 100,000 persons, and again simplified by the favourite example of pin-making as carried on by undifferentiated labour and by labour in various degrees of specialisation. The resulting Distribution is worked out both in money and in kind. In each example the master of the work receives so much for materials, for tools and for his own profits. To this skeleton exposition Adam Smith adds in his own hand, "I do not mean that the profits are divided in fact precisely in the above manner, but that they may be divided in such manner."

It seems, then, that in this manuscript we have a document which, in this as in other respects, is different from the report of the lectures. It may be, the person who took the notes omitted these particular passages, but he is found to be exceptionally reliable elsewhere. There are characteristics which indicate that this manuscript was dictated by Adam Smith and not copied from an existing set of his lectures. The summary of the later chapters would require to be prepared for this special occasion. There are some erasures in the manuscript where it has been overwritten either by the amanuensis or by Adam Smith himself. These are of the type which would be unlikely in a copy from a document, but to be expected in something dictated. For instance, there is a case of "overrunning," where a new paragraph should have been begun; two lines are erased and the new paragraph started in the proper place. There are a few instances of words likely to be misheard or mis-spelt in dictation, but which should have been written correctly from a copy, *e.g.* coarse, earned and plough.

Since at the time of writing it is less than three weeks from the finding of this document, I wish to speak with all reserve as to its date. Without committing myself in any way, there are some matters of much interest which enter into the problem of fixing a date, and the omission of which would render this preliminary account very incomplete. The extreme limits are from about April 1759, when Hume wrote on the 12th that Charles Townshend, after reading *The Theory of Moral Sentiments*, wished Adam Smith to take the Duke of Buccleuch to France,[11] and 4th September, 1767, when Townshend died. Thus it is possible that it could have been written after Adam Smith had been in close contact with the Physiocrats at Paris. At first sight this possibility seems to become highly probable when it is noticed that, when in Chapter 5 he comes to summarise different types of cultivation of land, he has a heading "Of the Cultivation by the ancient Métayers or Tenants by Steel bow," adding in the margin (by the hand of the amanuensis), "the first of these expressions is French, the second Scotch . . . I know no English word for it at present." It might be natural to infer that such a passage was written after he had seen, or heard of *Métayage* in France. But it so happens that there were several books in the Glasgow University Library from which he could have obtained full particulars, amongst them the first seven volumes of the *Encyclopédie* which he had ordered for the Library before 1760, the sixth volume of which contains the article by Quesnay on "Fermiers" in which the Métayer is described.[12] Judging by the corresponding passage in *The Wealth of Nations*, Adam Smith did not wholly agree with Quesnay on the nature and results of this kind of tenure.

At the other extreme in favour of an early date is one interpretation of a sentence which occurs at the beginning of the summary of Chapter 4, where Adam Smith, speaking of the nature of money, writes, "I have very little to say that is new or particular; except a general history of the coins of France, England and Scotland." Does this refer to material which he had collected but which was not yet written up? And the summary of the third and succeeding chapters might be adduced to support that view. Against this it has to be remembered that after 1759 or 1760 there was some kind of manuscript of the *Lectures*, and therefore he may have meant "when the book I am writing, based on the material I have, comes to be printed it will be found there is nothing very new on this head."

Another fragment of evidence is somewhat curious. Adam Smith once said he was a beau in his books – it might be added that he was a positive dandy in his writing-paper. It was not only that he used the best, but he had a special quality supplied in double folio sheets to the Government offices. He used this freely. Judging by his letters, when he was at the Custom House in Edinburgh, he divided the double folio into halves, then doubled one into four pages, making his letter-paper quarto size. In the muniments of Glasgow University there are a number of specimens with his writing on them – some used as outer covers for documents. There were several issues of this paper either successively or simultaneously for the use of different offices. On the left-hand half-sheet there was a watermark consisting of a double circle, containing a laurel wreath encircling G R, crowned. This mark is 1¾ in. in diameter. On the other half-sheet the watermark was larger and varied according to the issue. One type had the ribbon of the garter, with the motto, enclosing the Royal Arms. This one was about 3½ in. high. Another was a fine flight of fancy and capable of various interpretations. There was an elliptical picket fence upon which Britannia seems to sit, but probably she is really on a throne; she holds a trident (on the end of which is what appears to be the cap of Liberty), which protects a lion rampant, crowned. The motto is "pro Patria." The fighting forces could think of the sea-grit isle, the Foreign Office of the balance of power, and the Customs of the duties they administered. Nowadays, if this mark were used, the fence would need to be increased to a wall and Britannia would either be lost or her seat would have to be raised. This measures about 3½ in. by 4 in. A third, 4 in. high by 3 in. wide, consists of the garter ribbon crowned, containing the motto "Pro Patria eiusque Libertate," and within is a crowned lion, regardant, grasping a trident. Now all the sheets of the manuscript bear the last watermark, *i.e.* the small G R to the left, and the crowned lion, regardant, within the crowned ribbon. It follows that this manuscript must have been written when paper of this type was available. Adam Smith had it before the earliest possible date. Therefore the manuscript could have been written any time between 1759 and the end of 1763. The entourage of the Duke of Buccleuch travelled with a considerable amount of impedimenta. Accordingly, if Adam Smith attached special importance to his supply of manuscript paper, there is no reason why he should not have brought some with him. We know, too, that he wrote to Hume from Toulouse on July 5, 1764, that he "had begun to write a book in order to pass away the time."[13] There are three letters, extant, written from Toulouse, but they are on a totally different paper, thinner, and without watermark. Then we come to the Paris visit, represented by the letter to Hume, dated July 6, 1766, and relating to the quarrel between Hume and Rousseau. This is on paper of the type Adam Smith favoured, but the watermark does not appear to be British. It has a ducal crown with what seems to be either a flag or a double four on a mound with the inscription VAN DER LE . . . From November 1766 till May 1767 Adam Smith was in London. A complicated set of circumstances, not yet described, would have enabled him to get plenty of official paper. Curiously enough those circumstances would have prevented or made it unnecessary for him to write this particular manuscript. There is only one letter in this short period. It is now in America and, except by chance, is too small to show a watermark. In any case, as it happens, the official paper to which he could have had access was of a different watermark from that used for this manuscript.[14]

Without risking a premature and ill-founded opinion, it would be unwise to carry the matter further at present. The apology for venturing to offer incomplete evidence to the Society is that this course gives the earliest opportunity for others to consider the interesting problems which this manuscript presents.

Notes

1.   An Address delivered before the Annual Meeting of the Royal Economic Society, May 23, 1935.

2.   The statement of McCuloch that the manuscript of *The Theory of Moral Sentiments* was in Adam Smith's own writing and the reason he gives for it is one of those ridiculous sayings – the result of excessive acuteness – which only a person usually intelligent succeeds in perpetrating. Allowing for the character of booksellers' catalogues, it is likely that the cutting from a Caxton Head Catalogue, sent to Dr. Bonar by Mr. Henry Higgs (*Library of Adam Smith*, 1932, p. 204), describing a manuscript "Meditations on Seneca's Epistles," may be of the same character as the document now described, namely, in the hand of an amanuensis, with possible additions by Adam Smith himself.

3.   *Life of Adam Smith*, pp. 141-48.

4.   At this time Marischal and King's were separate Universities.

5.   Rae, *Life of Adam Smith*, p. 179.

6.   It is perhaps of interest to mention that in the *Lectures*, p. 229, the passage is referred to; in *The Wealth of Nations*, I. p. 151, it is translated. Here it is given in the original and the reference is correct, being Bk. II of *De Officiis*, not Bk. III as in *The Wealth of Nations*.

7.   The manuscript reads, "the case here is the same as if he gave five hundred pins to his master for affording him the wire, the tools and the employment." The implication of the last three words is not clear.

8.   P. 176.

9.   Pp. xxviii, xxxi.

10.   *Lectures*, pp. xxviii, xxix.

11.   Rae, *Life of Adam Smith*, p. 144.

12.   Adam Smith wrote a letter to the *Edinburgh Review* in 1755 commending the *Encyclopédie*, the first volume of which had appeared in 1751 (Bonar *Library of Adam Smith*,

1932, pp. 3, 4). This account may have been taken from D'Alembert's "Discourse Préliminaire," from an analysis in a review, from a copy at the Advocates' Library, Edinburgh, or he may have purchased some of the volumes for himself. In any case, the reference above shows that he was interested in the actual book and had access to it before he set out for France. It is curious that though there were French books on various economic subjects in the Glasgow University Library during Adam Smith's time, the *Catalogue* of 1791 does not contain the name of any Physiocrat.

In relation to the parallels between R. Cantillon and the *Glasgow Lectures*, it may have been that, at this time, Adam Smith had not acquired the copy of the *Essai* which is recorded as being in his Library. If this were so, the University Library Catalogue of 1791 records:

M. Postlethwaite, *Plan of the Universal Dictionary of Trade and Commerce*, Lond. 1749. This at the period 1751-63 was in the possession of Smith's colleague, Simson, the mathematician, and it came to the Library after his death. Since both men lived near each other in the College and were friends, Adam Smith could easily have borrowed it from Simson.

M. Postlethwaite, *The Universal Dictionary of Trade and Commerce*, Lond. 1757.

J. Savary, *Le Parfait Négociant*, 2 vols., 4°, Amst. 1726.

The two last were recommended by Adam Smith.

13. Rae, *Life of Adam Smith*, p. 179.

14. While the watermark on the right-hand half-sheet is the same, or similar to that on the manuscript, that of the other half-sheet is quite different. It is also G R but without the laurel wreath, crown and circle and the letters are of a different size and shape.

57

Adam Smith and the Human Stomach

J.S. Davis

Source: *Quarterly Journal of Economics*, Vol. 68, May 1954, pp. 275-86.

How many people can the world support? What sets the limits to the amount of food consumed, by individuals and by whole peoples? Is capacity to produce food the prime determinant of population growth? These are perennial questions on which new light can be thrown by a critical examination of passages in a famous old classic.

I

Adam Smith's discussion of man's wants for food, clothing, housing, and "equipage" is mostly compressed into the following three paragraphs:[1]

"After food, cloathing and lodging are the two great wants of mankind." . . .

"Countries are populous, not in proportion to the number of people whom their produce can cloath and lodge, but in proportion to that of those whom it can feed. When food is provided, it is easy to find the necessary cloathing and lodging. But though these are at hand, it may often be difficult to find food. In some parts even of the British dominions what is called A House, may be built by one day's labour of one man. The simplest species of cloathing, the skins of animals, require somewhat more labour to dress and prepare them for use. They do not, however, require a great deal. Among savage and barbarous nations, a hundredth or little more than a hundredth part of the labour of the whole year, will be sufficient to provide them with such cloathing and lodging as satisfy the greater part of the people. All the other ninety-nine parts are frequently no more than enough to provide them with food.

"But when by the improvement and cultivation of land the labour of one family can provide food for two, the labour of half the society becomes sufficient to provide food for the whole. The other half, therefore, or at least the greater part of them, can be employed in providing other things, or in satisfying the other wants and fancies of mankind. Cloathing and lodging, household furniture, and what is called Equipage, are the principal objects of the greater part of those wants and fancies. The rich man consumes no more food than his poor neighbour. In quality it may be very different, and to select and prepare it may require more labour and art; but in quality it is very nearly the same. But compare the spacious palace and great wardrobe of the one, with the hovel and the few rags of the other, and you will be sensible that the difference between their cloathing, lodging, and houshold furniture, is almost as great in quantity as it is in quality. The desire of food is limited in every man by the narrow capacity of the human stomach; but the desire of the conveniencies and ornaments of building, dress, equipage, and houshold furniture, seems to have no limit or certain boundary. Those, therefore, who have the command of more food than they themselves can consume, are always willing to exchange the surplus, or, what is the same thing, the price of it, for gratifications of this other kind. What is over and above satisfying the limited desire, is given for the amusement of those desires which cannot be satisfied, but seem to be altogether endless. The poor, in order to obtain food, exert themselves to gratify those fancies of the rich, and to obtain it more certainly, they vie with one another in the cheapness and perfection of their work. The number of workmen increases with the increasing quantity of food, or with the growing improvement and cultivation of the lands; and as the nature of their business admits of the utmost subdivisions of labour, the quantity of materials which they can work up, increases in a much greater proportion than their numbers. Hence arises a demand for every sort of material which human invention can employ, either usefully or ornamentally, in building, dress, equipage, or houshold furniture; for the fossils and minerals contained in the bowels of the earth, the precious metals, and the precious stones."

These passages contain a few errors of fact or of implication that have surprisingly persisted for 175 years.

Smith's oft-quoted dictum is this: "The desire of food is limited in every man by the narrow capacity of the human stomach . . ." The continued acceptance of this idea may be indicated by the following recent statement: "Our wants and desires for foodstuffs are satiable, and may become fulfilled eventually, for there is a limit to the size of our stomachs."[2] Let us start with this quotation and come back to Adam Smith.

II

The inherent satiability of wants for particular foodstuffs, and for many other specific goods, can be accepted as a fact. Moreover, an individual's wants for some specific foods are actually satiated, in ordinary times, in the sense that he recurrently eats all he wants of these without stint. Indeed, for a few things, such as water, salt, and pepper, this may commonly be true of the great mass of mankind. But under exceptional circumstances, one or more of these becomes so scarce that even their food use must be curtailed. More or less extreme deprivation may then be felt in the cases of water and salt, because certain minimums of these are absolute essentials for life, health, and activity. The use of pepper, on the other hand, can ordinarily be curtailed without serious deprivation, or acceptable substitutes may be made available as during World War II.

The limited extent to which wants for most specific foods are actually satiated, day by day and year by year, is not generally realized. A considerable fraction of the world's population, in ordinary times, finds its wants for a few staple foods recurrently satiated. But even this is not true for probably a much larger fraction of the world's people, including huge populations in Asia, Africa, and the poorer countries of Europe, as well as smaller fractions even in countries that are economically most advanced. The wants for fats, meats, and other animal products are satiated for only a small fraction of the population, even in the more advanced countries in prosperous periods. During a great war and its aftermath, as compared with ordinary times of peace, all these wants are satisfied for smaller fractions of the world's population.

An individual's wants for food as a whole, in contrast with those for specific foods, are also satiable. The experience of many individuals attests this, and physiological and psychological experiments would easily prove it. But it may safely be asserted that such wants are actually satiated for only a tiny fraction of the world's population at any time, and for a still smaller fraction of the world's population over the life span of the individuals concerned. Even the primary want for food – to satisfy hunger – is probably not continuously satisfied for the majority of mankind. Most of those whose hunger is recurrently satisfied find it impossible to satisfy regularly all the secondary wants for abundance, variety, palatability, and refinements of food. Moreover, despite notable progress in technology and nutritional knowledge, amid the teeming expansion of population in the ill-fed countries, there seems no ground whatever for expecting that such desires will ever be "fulfilled." The more restricted goal of the Food and Agriculture Organization – freedom from want for the nutritional essentials of an optimum diet – is conceivably attainable if it were accorded top priority; but it is doubtful whether in fact it will ever be attained by most of the world's people, especially if optimum is liberally defined and accords considerable weight to preferences for what are relatively expensive foods.

III

The limits to the size of the human stomach, however, have no material bearing on the degree to which wants for food are satiated or fall short of satiation. The stomach is not a simple container of fixed size.[3] It is an elastic and distensible sac, and capable of permanent enlargement. Normally full, the average capacity of an adult human stomach is about one liter or quart, but its size varies greatly among individuals. (Empty, the sac may have a volume only about one-fifth as large as when normally full.) Most individuals have had the experience of filling their stomachs beyond this level, on special occasions such as Christmas dinners, even to the point of considerable discomfort. How much larger the distended capacity is, apparently is not known. In primitive societies, and in the cases of some individuals in modern societies, occasional or habitual gorging may enlarge the stomach far above the average.

The stomach, however, serves only in part as a reservoir to keep the bowels from being overwhelmed by too sudden a flow of food. It is also part of the digestive system, a processing apparatus in which the stomach plays some part along with other organs, while the small intestine plays the largest role.

One does not measure the capacity of a flour mill by the number of bushels of wheat that its bins will hold at one filling, but by the amounts of wheat that it will mill or of flour that it will produce if it runs continuously for twenty-four hours a day. The annual capacity of a flour mill is usually computed as a multiple of its daily capacity, leaving enough idle days for necessary maintenance operations that can be performed only when it is shut down, and for occasional necessary overhauling. In some degree, moreover, the effective capacity of a flour mill varies somewhat with the wheat available and the types of flour that it produces. It is somewhat greater for fine, clean wheat that is well adapted to its equipment, and for turning out standard types and grades of flour, than it is for wheat that is difficult to mill and for flours of peculiar types.

The digestive system's processing capacity per twenty-four hour day, under normal conditions, is several times one filling of the stomach. Indeed, at a single meal one may eat and drink more than one filling. Experiments might reveal the maximum processing capacity in a twenty-four hour period, but this maximum would undoubtedly vary over a considerable range with different types of food, rates of feeding, kinds of work, etc. So far as the writer knows, such experiments have not been made. This is probably chiefly because the human digestive apparatus, unlike a flour mill, does not turn out products for use outside, and apparently no one has been interested in ascertaining its processing capacity in this sense.[4]

Actually, the digestive system is seldom used to its maximum capacity. Its function is to process what the body needs for operations, maintenance, growth, and energy, without any great excess. These requirements vary a good deal, particularly with the different kinds of foods eaten and the varying amounts of energy required. Consequently, while the stomach may be filled once, twice, or three times a day, it rarely operates continuously at the peak which it occasionally reaches; and the peak operating capacity that it reaches is typically well below the maximum that it could reach if the function of the digestive system were to turn out products for use outside the body. For the most part, neither the size of the stomach nor the processing capacity of the digestive system sets effective limits to the quantity of food eaten.

The limited processing capacity of the digestive system is of some dietary significance, in special cases, primarily in influencing choices of types of food. Heavy manual workers such as lumbermen, especially in cooler climates, typically expend a great number of calories in their work and therefore require an exceptionally high-calorie diet for maximum working efficiency. To get these calories mainly from the bulkier carbohydrate foods, such as bread and potatoes, would put an excessive load not only on the stomach but on the whole digestive system. Hence liberal amounts of fats, which are several times as rich in calories per unit of bulk, are a normal part of a lumberman's diet, whereas much smaller quantities of fat, however agreeable its consumption may be, are nutritionally ample in the diets of sedentary workers.

IV

When all this is said, however, the largest correction of the erroneous notion remains to be made. The various combinations of foods with which hunger may be satisfied, or with which optimum nutritional needs can be met, or with which tastes may be gratified as well, vary enormously in economic cost. At a given time and place, for example, one can meet nutritional needs at a minimum cost of 25 cents a day, or one can spend $20 or more by using the most expensive combination. In practice, few people choose either extreme. But the range is still wide between the costs of the more economical and of the more luxurious diets, roughly equal in nutritional value, that are customary in different families in the same community. Only part of the differences in cost is due to overeating, or to inefficient shopping, which are fairly common among both rich and poor under ordinary conditions. It is principally due to the fact that the richer choose to gratify more kinds of wants in their eating, including the wants for rare or unusual foods, while the poorer necessarily eat more largely to satisfy simple hunger, to keep alive and in health and strength.

"The rich man consumes no more food than his poor neighbour. In quality it may be very different, and to select and prepare it may require more labour and art; but in quantity it is very nearly the same." So Adam Smith wrote, and others continue to echo him. This view, however, is open to serious misinterpretation.

In what terms shall the quantity be measured? It may be true that the poor ingest as much as the rich, in terms of weight, or even more if potatoes and bread bulk large in the poor man's diet and light in the rich man's; but pounds are a wholly inappropriate unit of measure in this connection.[5] Reductions of intake to a dry-weight basis, or a dry-weight digestible basis, would not improve the comparison significantly. It may also be true that the poor, in a relatively well-fed country, eat as many calories per day as the rich – or indeed even more, especially if they expend more energy and use more food to maintain body heat; but calories, important though they are, are an inadequate measure of economic significance. Food provides calories among other things, but calories are not food. The economic facts must not be ignored in considering the quantity eaten.

A diet rich in animal protein and in fats is ordinarily several times as expensive as a comparably nutritious diet poor in these prized foods; far more resources must be used in their production than in the production of cheaper diets, even prior to selection and preparation in the home or restaurant. The same is true of different grades and qualities of the same food, as the trade and consumers have come to appraise quality. Typically, moreover, the rich man's consumption entails much more waste than the poor man's, at the point of consumption. In terms of economic resources, from the standpoint of either the individual or the nation, an expensive diet is several times as large as a cheap one, apart from the "labour and art" required to select, prepare, and serve it.

The United States, nowadays the richest nation in the world, consumes much more food per capita than India, one of the poorest. This is certainly true in terms of calories, inclusive of wastes at the consumer level and perhaps even more if real wastes in channels of distribution are included. In good times the Indian people may consume two-thirds as many calories per capita as Americans, and in periods of special food shortage the proportion may fall below half. The contrast in terms of calories would remain, but would be reduced, if one were to make the consumption for age-adjusted populations in adult-male equivalents. It would be further reduced, but by no means eliminated, if due account were taken of the smaller requirements of Indians as smaller heat requirements, and lesser energy requirements of Indians as compared with Americans. But the American diet, rich in animal products and in variety, much of it highly processed and embellished with services, requires several times the amount of labor and other economic resources per capita that a diet of the Indian type would require here. In India, the American type of diet would require several times the economic resources that the prevailing Indian diet requires. In terms of economic resources, the rich country's diet is a much higher multiple of the poor country's diet than is suggested by the relative number of pounds or calories consumed per capita, unadjusted or adjusted.[6]

V

Adam Smith began his brief discussion with the statement: "After food, cloathing and lodging are the two great wants of mankind." This statement has an important measure of truth, for most people, as one can see if he observes instances when the consumption level is drastically cut. The satisfaction of most other consumer wants is sacrificed, in considerable degree, before these three, and heavy curtailment in consumption of lodging and clothing would be endured if necessary to insure a sufficiency of food. If insufficiency in all is inescapable, the cuts will usually be relatively lightest in food.

Yet the quoted statement easily conveys an erroneous impression. Man does not give adequacy of food full priority over clothing and housing. A low minimum of these two is more urgently desired, at least by most people in the more advanced countries, than even a sufficiency of simple food. What most people seek, however divergently, blindly, or unwisely, is a balanced combination in consumption, at any level. The proportion of the components changes as the aggregate level rises from low to high, or falls from a high to a low level. In economic terms, however, the food component rises with the rise of the aggregate level, though not so fast after a certain low point is reached. Beyond this point, the "income elasticity" of food as a whole is below unity, but it is not zero or negative. Negative income elasticity characterizes only certain non-preferred foods in the presence of preferred alternatives – for example, millets, sorghums, corn, manoic (variously called cassava, yuca, and tapioca), and sweet potatoes in most countries where these are eaten liberally, even rye nowadays, and margarine. In other words, the admittedly high priority for food is true only for a limited economic quantity, in many cases far below one's customary consumption. Beyond this, wants for clothing, housing, and many other goods effectively compete with wants for additional food. Sir Jack Drummond reported some years ago that tenants of much improved housing in Great Britain after World War I, whose larger rent payments for better quarters left less to spend for food than before they moved, showed appreciable effects of undue skimping on food.

In advanced nations, moreover, wants for other consumer goods effectually compete with wants for food. Since the democratization of the automobile in the United States, many individuals and families have come to sacrifice housing comforts, and even sufficiency of food, in order to have and use an automobile. Whether or not one accepts Veblen's distinction between clothing and dress[7] – clothing that provides essential protection and dress that primarily satisfies the urge to appear well to others – one can say that expenditures on the combination of clothing and dress are often accorded priorities over sufficiency of food and other appreciated comforts of housing.

VI

Adam Smith further said: "Countries are populous, not in proportion to the number of people whom their produce can cloathe and lodge, but in the proportion to that of those whom it can feed." In the light of the foregoing discussion, we are now prepared to examine this statement.

How many people a country can feed depends in the first place on how they are fed. The people of India are notoriously ill-fed, and have been for generations, if one judges by available measures either of nutrition or of preference, and even if one ignores acute famines which have become rare only since about 1900. Yet India is one of the countries of relatively rapid population growth, at least since 1921. Poor as the diet of the Indian people has been, and extremely low as their customary level of living has been, the country has fed, after a fashion, a population that has risen from 306 million in 1921 to about 438 million in 1951 (India and Pakistan).[8] In this half-century, rates of infant mortality have tended downward and over-all death rates as well, though both continue high in comparison with such rates in most western countries of the Northern Hemisphere. Even the experts do not fully understand how this has been possible, and the evidence is conflicting as to how far the level of living of the people has changed for better or worse.

In India, if anywhere, one might expect the Malthusian positive checks to population increase to operate effectively. They do operate, of course, but not vigorously enough to prevent a striking excess of births over deaths. If population growth there should continue more rapid than food production, with no significant change in net imports, one might predict (without forecasting the date) that a stage would be reached at which the effectiveness of the Malthusian checks would increase and the population stop growing. But we have no basis for confidently asserting that this will occur. In other words, no one can estimate with assurance how many more people India can feed, at some level of diet, or how much the prevailing diet might deteriorate below current low levels without forcing deaths into balance with births.

In China, the size of the population, and changes in it, are among the many unknowns; but there is an approach to a consensus that the population has not grown significantly for several decades. Perhaps in that "land of famine" the Malthusian positive checks actually operate to keep the population broadly constant. But certainly many factors beyond China's ability to produce food contribute to this stability in the midst of grave instability. If civil order could once be achieved, transportation facilities developed, and known techniques of production applied, China could unquestionably feed many millions more at the current average level of diet, or conceivably a lower one if it were differently distributed through the year and over the people as a whole.[9]

By contrast, if Americans were willing to subsist on diets like those of the Indian or Chinese peoples, the United States could unquestionably feed several times the present population, and several times the changing peak of population that demographers have until recently projected for this country. Indeed, if we chose to maintain our present diet, and to eliminate or radically reduce wastes of food and to cut down on consumption of other goods, this country could now feed many millions more as well as the present population is fed. The significant limits on the growth of our population are in no way set by the amount of food that we can produce, but by the character of our whole standard of living, which involves much more than food. The way in which food is consumed, and the level of the diet that we insist upon, make important differences.

The cases of Great Britain, Belgium, and Japan require emphasis on another factor, international trade, which is of lesser importance in the cases of India, China, and the United States. None of the first three countries comes close to feeding its people from the food that it produces. Each conceivably could if its people were willing to be satisfied with diets less poor than those of the Indian and Chinese peoples, and with moderate reductions in other consumption goods. Instead, the British, Belgians, and Japanesse can and do specialize in various kinds of exports and colonial products and services, and thereby supplement their domestic food production by imports of foodstuffs and feedstuffs. With most countries, international trade is a factor, but with these it is a highly important means of maintaining diets far above those that they could maintain without trade.

VII

These considerations are pertinent when one faces the larger question: How many people can the world support? Those who give pessimistic answers point to the rising rate of population growth and the limited amount of potentially arable land, and cite some accepted ratio of arable land requirement per thousand inhabitants. The optimists, on the other hand, point to the substantial improvement of diets that has occurred in many countries since 1800 despite greatly enlarged populations, and to the current flow of scientific and technological improvements at an increasing pace. Where does the truth lie?

No definitive answer can be given. No one can safely forecast the rate of population growth, the rate and significance of applications of technology, or the extent to which migration barriers will in the future be raised or lowered. Both history and analysis, however, make it clear that there is no fixed ratio of arable land to 1,000 persons; that yields as well as areas are subject to important changes; that the manner of utilizing agricultural output – especially as between food and animal feed – makes great differences in the number of people that a given output will support; and that dietary adjustments of major degree are feasible under pressure to contract or with opportunities to expand.

The standards of living that peoples insist upon, which affect the rate of population growth, per capita productivity, and the composition of the consumption level, will surely continue to be powerful factors influencing the growth of the world's population. Other factors will contribute in fixing the effective limit on the total, as of any given time, but no one factor will fix that limit for any period. There is yet no sign of an upper limit for all time.

The keynote of Sir William Crooke's famous address of 1898 was: "England and all civilised nations stand in deadly peril of not having enough to eat." Despite the distressing food shortage of postwar years, recent emphasis on the wide extent of undernutrition, and alarmist books that keep coming out, Crookes' statement now appears more extremist than it did fifty-five years ago.[10] Yet the time is far distant when everyone, everywhere, will have "enough to eat," even in the sense of regular satisfaction of recurring hunger; and optimum nutrition for all the world's billions seems a millennial goal.

Notes

1. Adam Smith, *Wealth of Nations*, Bk. I, Chap. XI, Part II (Cannan ed., I, 162, 164-65).
2. Committee on Public Debt. Policy, *Our National Debt and Our Savings* (National Debt Series, No. 5, New York, Jan. 1948), p. 4. Many other citations over the past two decades could be given, with names such as A.G.B. Fisher, E.F. Heckscher, J.P. Cavin, and Hazel Stiebeling.
3. In this discussion I have had the benefit of comments from Professor John Field, Jr., a physiologist.
4. In this context it is proper to ignore the waste products, which nowadays typically involve more or less expense in disposal, but which in some countries (e.g., Japan, China) are secondary by-products used for fertilizer.
5. The author of "The Fabulous Market for Food" (*Fortune*, Oct. 1953, p. 138) quoted Adam Smith's dictum to explain the very limited year-to-year variability in the calculated per capita poundage of food consumed in the United States over a period of years. Better explanations surely must be sought.
6. Worthy of mention in this connection, though not precisely relevant, is the Bureau of Labor Statistics mimeographed paper, "A Method of Measuring Comparable Living Costs in Communities with Differing Characteristics" (Oct. 1953).
7. Thorstein Veblen, "The Economic Theory of Woman's Dress," *Popular Science Monthly*, XLVI (Dec. 1894), 198-205; reprinted in Leon Ardzrooni (ed.), *Essays in Our Changing Order by Thorstein Veblen* (New York: Viking, 1934), pp. 65-77.
8. *UN Demographic Yearbook, 1952*. Including Kashmir, Jammu, and the Kabul areas of Assam.
9. The impact of local or regional famines or food shortages is typically mitigated mainly by migrations to places where food is less short. Professor T.H. Shen has mapped the historic routes that the migrants take. Cf. R.L. Harrison, "International Movement of Foodstuffs," *Foreign Agriculture*, XII (March 1948), 43.
10. Cf. "The Specter of Dearth of Food: History's Answer to Sir William Crookes," in J.S. Davis, *On Agricultural Policy, 1926-1938* (Food Research Institute, 1939), pp. 3-23; and M.K. Bennett, *The World's Food* (New York: Harper, 1954), passim.

58

The Macro and Micro Aspects of the *Wealth of Nations*

J.P. Henderson

Source: *Southern Economic Journal*, vol. 21 (1), July 1954, pp. 25-35.

This article purports to clarify certain contradictions attributed to classical value theory,[1] and to substantiate a claim that Adam Smith's "ambiguous and confused" *Wealth of Nations* constitutes a valid and coherent attempt to integrate theories of the process of the economic system and the pricing of particular commodities. Current interpretations in which Smith's premarginalist formulations appear confused and irreconcilable[2] seem to stem from a failure to recognize that this integration was as important a goal of classical economy theory as it is of contemporary economics, but that classical theory approached the problem from the standpoint that individual prices were a funtion, rather than a determinant, of the economic system.

Basically the constructs which draw the lines of demarcation between classical economics and post-Ricardian utility analysis are those which touch upon this relationship between the macrocosm and the microcosm. Classical theory, formulated in the age of mechanical law which received its fullest expression in the works of Newton,[3] concerned itself with problems of general equilibrium and looked upon partial analysis as subsidiary to the generic. Micro analysis was the study of the particular and, essentially, an inquiry which took its position within the macroscopic movement of the system as a whole. Post-Ricardian utility analysis, on the other hand, has taken the microcosm as its starting point, with the individual household and firm at the center of gravity. Claiming that the classical formulation of the relationship between the economic system and the actions of individuals was incorrectly stated, the leaders of the utility school shifted the emphasis to the microcosm as the activating force in the economic system.[4] The generic system of the classicists was pushed to the background and made subordinate to the interaction of microscopic forces.

Present-day theory has, for the most part, accepted this reversal of the major emphasis which classical economics developed. Under the influence of marginal analysis, the basic postulates of the classical school, which were concerned with the economic system as a whole, were cast aside until the advent of the "new economics" of J.M. Keynes. Except for this "modern lapse into mediocrity," economics has come to view classical theory from the bench mark of the utility school in which value is synonymous with price and the economic process is activated by the individual firm and consumer. Böhm-Bawerk, Marshall, and Wicksell each claimed that a new theory of the functioning of the macrocosm, which would allow for historical development and the dynamics of the economic system, would be developed from the basic postulates vis-a-vis the individual consumer and producer.[5] But such a theory, based upon the assumptions of utility analysis, has never seen the light of day. All three authors failed to go beyond micro analysis, and orthodox contemporary thought has not yet made the transition they anticipated.

Therefore, any attempt to interpret the *Wealth of Nations* in the light of orthodox price theory distorts the thinking, not only of Adam Smith but of Ricardo and Marx whose works also reflect the change in outlook upon economic and political phenomena which accompanied the rise and development of capitalism. This article represents an investigation of the *Wealth of Nations* in terms of certain underlying postulates of the classical economists that serve to clarify Smith's basic formulations of value and price.[6]

The first of these is the homogeneity of money, which was assumed by classical economics in the determination of any essential relationships in the system. More recently, this has been referred to as the absence of "money illusion,"[7] and the importance of money is stressed only as a medium of exchange. The assumption views money, as such, as a convenient technique of exchange, either for calculation or as an exchange intermediary, and as having passive influence on the essential productive relationships in the system. Any change in the quantity of money would affect all prices equally, leaving relative prices unaffected; the prices of all things would simply be raised or lowered proportionally, leaving the ratios the same as before.[8] This assumption, with respect to money, formed the basis for most of Smith's attack upon the Mercantilists and their theories of value, and for Ricardo's essays upon the monetary question.[9]

Second is the distinction made between productive and unproductive effort. Classical theory postulated that a consuming class which had no active function to perform in the production of material commodities, was not an active factor in economic society. The existence of such a class, consequently, meant a drain upon the "wealth" of nations and did not aid the productive process. This process, for all classical theorists, was the direct result of labor and the incentive to accumulate capital. That emphasis upon the productive process was the basis for the rent theories of both Smith and Ricardo, and provided the raw material for the political attacks upon speenhamland and the corn laws, and the protection of land rents. "Productive" implied the actual creation of commodities with emphasis upon that labor which contributed to the production of tangible goods. These were the domain of analysis.[10]

Thirdly, the famous law of markets, which has been given the name of J.B. Say, stated that demand, in the aggregate, was a dependent variable. Thus, when looking at the whole system rather than at particular sectors, supply was the determinant of production and price and demand referred only to the distribution of the total product between alternative producers and consumers.

These were the major assumptions in the background of the *Wealth of Nations* and as such they constituted value judgments which were implicit in

the analysis. The first assumption reveals the classical concept o
factors are significant in the determination of wealth. The s
foundation for the labor, or productive, theory of value and, tog
third assumption, forms the basis for the analysis of the economic system as a
evolving process. In the process of production was to be found the activating
force in history, with capital accumulation as the central theme. Value was the
creation of tangible goods, and labor was the source of that value. Viewing the
labor theory of value as Smith's theory of the process of production, Book II
becomes significant as a history of capitalistic production, and Smith's theory
of individual price appears, not as a contradiction, but as the micro aspect of his
analysis.

Smith's Theory of the Economic Process

While it is easy enough to claim that mankind should not be interested in the
purely material world, it is something again to claim that, historically, men and
women have not been seekers after commodities of a tangible and substantial
nature. The spirit may seek the finer things in life, but the body has
pragmatically gone about its everyday task of acquiring and producing those
material objects upon which it is dependent. For the proper understanding of the
18th century, nothing is so important as the recognition that the age of the early
industrial revolution looked upon the production of goods and more goods as
the *sine qua non* of activity. The long draught of commodities which had
characterized the decline of feudalism had given way to the growing abundance
that accompanied industrialization. All classes, regardless of their institutional
source of income, looked upon increased production as the ultimate purpose of
economic activity. Emphasis upon productivity rapidly replaced the restrictive
philosophy of Mercantilism as the fluidity of society required production for all,
and not the few.

Smith's *Wealth of Nations*, stressing the productivity of society which would
be brought about by the division of labor and competition, was the touchstone of
the age. Statements like "The annual labour of every nation is the fund which
originally supplies it with all the necessaries and conveniences of life which it
annually consumes, and which consist always either in the immediate product
of that labour, or in what is purchased with that produce from other nations,"[11]
reflect the dominant attitude which prevailed in 18th century England. As
Professor Bladen has suggested, the *Wealth of Nations* can be viewed as "a
plea for consumer's sovereignity."[12] The output of commodities was dependent
upon (1) the state of technology, and (2) the ratio of productive to unproductive
in the allocation of the labor force.[13] The higher the proportion of labor used in
productive activity, *ceteris paribus*, the greater the flow of goods in real terms.
The state of technology, in turn, depended upon the state of the arts and the
advancement of the division of labor which directly increased the productivity
of the nation. These were the notions and the method juxtaposed to the
mercantilist philosophy which depended upon scarcity for value. The latter was
true for the few, the former would increase the welfare of all.

The increased productivity which an advanced and improved division of labor manifests necessitated the development of institutions and mores to facilitate exchange as each individual produced a greater number of specific commodities than could be personally consumed. The surpluses were exchanged in the market and, in this sense, exchange became a system of distribution. The quantity of goods in the distribution process, however, was determined at the time of production, if the latter term is understood in its classical meaning as a process by which commodities are increased by the exertion of human energy. The ratio of the exchange of the surpluses had to do with the conditions surrounding their production, and it was the analysis of these conditions which took the substantial position in theory.

The famous dictum of two kinds of value, value in use which is peculiar to the individual consumer, and exchange value which the market gives to commodities, was the starting point of the analysis. This distinction had its roots in a philosophical concept which has only incidentally been recognized by students of classical economics. Adam Smith was first and foremost a philosopher, and secondly a political economist. He brought to his economic analysis a general philosophical background which certainly influenced his formulation of problems and their solutions. As successor to Francis Hutcheson's position, he represented the "materialist" aspects of 18th century philosophy. That is, he dealt with the objective aspects of economic phenomena which were *common* to the society. While he was a friend of Hume and was familiar with the subjective notions of reality expressed by 18th century skepticism, his economics remained objective in the philosophical meaning of the term.[14]

As a part of the Lockian extension of the Newtonian *Weltanschauung* into the area of political and religious thinking, the 18th century came to recognize a distinction between the "real," material forces of the world (its primary qualities) and those perceived by man through his senses (the secondary qualities).[15] The latter, in as much as they were peculiar to each indivual, were specific and nongeneric. They were special to the individual in question. On the other hand, there was the real and objective world which was independent of the sense perceptions of individuals. Part of this material world was the economic system which existed as an entity, unaffected by the individuals who made up society. In the system there was homogeneity of data, whole individual datum were heterogeneous and particular. Within the system the analysis of market phenomena dealt with value in exchange, while value in use pertained to the individual consumer. For classical economics, therefore, the real world of analysis was homogeneous and devoid of the distortions of sense perception. The essential distinction between classical theory and the utility approach of the 19th century is that the latter looked microscopically at the economic process and, consequently, value in use became the only significant basis of analysis.

The influence of Immanuel Kant on the subject of the nature of matter must be considered in any attempt to understand the utility school. The Kantian concept that matter is what the mind perceives it to be exerted great influence upon all German-Austrian thinking. Its logical conclusion, that all phenomena are purely personal, makes macroscopic analysis irrelevant since personal perceptions are not additive. This trend of thought is apparent in Austrian economics and is the position taken by those who claim that, "to form social aggregates is an operation with a very limited meaning."[16] However, both the history of science and the present state of science indicate that the systematic organization of facts and their conceptual relationships has only been fostered by the elimination of the purely subjective elements in analysis by reductions to nonqualitative formulations.[17] The labor theory of value, with its emphasis upon exchange value and the rejection of utility as the foundation of analysis, appears to be in keeping with this tradition.

Within this framework, Smith turned to investigation of production and exchange.

System of Exchange

To investigate exchange in the system, Smith set up three problems: (1) The determination of the real measure and source of exchange value, (2) the analysis of the component parts of real exchange value, and (3) the understanding of the circumstances which caused some goods to exchange at other than their real value.[18]

Smith sought to define an underlying and absolute value determined by the material forces at work in the economy.[19] He assumed that, through particular circumstances of the market, some commodities might exchange at other than their real prices, but that, independent of market price, there existed an absolute value derived in the process of production.[20] Such a value, materially determined and therefore measurable, would remain unfettered by the use value which individuals might attribute to commodities.[21]

This notion of absolute value was similar to those of just price which were at the base of ecclesiastical value theory. Smith had expressed his general notions of justice toward others in *The Theory of Moral Sentiments*, dealing with contemporary philosophical inquiry into the relationship of the individual to the system. Locke had postulated the right of each individual to formulate his own morals – religious, political, and economic. Granted that premise, the crucial question was whether the macrocosm could be advanced by the egocentric action of individuals. The solution worked out by Shaftesbury was that individuals had a "sympathy" for the rights of others which acted as a restraint upon their selfish interests. His was an aristocratic and esoteric sympathy, residing with the benevolent despot, and was inconsistent with such notions as the brotherhood of man. Hutcheson democratized the notion and deduced, in *The System of Moral Philosophy*, a universal sympathy which held competition between individuals in check and guaranteed the greatest good to the greatest number.

Aware of this problem and of the disadvantage through exchange possible in a system of competition between ego-motivated individuals, Smith looked upon value in exchange as *originally* synonymous with that involved in production. Labor was, accordingly, the source of this value, and gross national product, in real terms, was the material result of productive labor.[22] Use value he viewed as independent of the conditions of production because it depended upon the ideas and perceptions individuals had about commodities and the estimated satisfaction to be derived from them. In the general philosophical framework of Smith's day, as presented by Hume and before him Locke, ideas and perceptions were the effects of matter reacting upon the mind. They were personal, and were meaningful only relative to particular persons. Therefore, notions of utility were non-addictive, dependent variables from which no common or abstract value could be hypothesized. The independent, objective forces were the economic laws of causation in the philisophical tradition of Shaftesbury, Hutcheson, Locke, and Hume, who had all attributed the source of wealth of labor in production.[23]

The real value of commodities, which could be increased through human effort,[24] was a function of the toil and effort of producing them as, "all of the wealth of the world was originally purchased by labor."[25] But while the creation of all wealth was attributed to labor, it was not assumed that labor received all it produced. It was true in a primitive economy, before the accumulation of stock and the appropriation of land, that "the whole produce of labor belongs" to those who produce it,[26] but this did not remain true in stages in which private ownership of the means of production was characteristic, because the laborer "must share it [produce] with the owner of the stock which employs him . . . [and] give up to the landlord a portion of what his labour either collects or produces."[27] Consequently, "the whole of what is annually either collected or produced by the labour of every society . . . is in this manner originally distributed among some of its inhabitants."[28]

This left profit and rent as deductions from the produce of labor arising, like value, in the process of production and in the particular institutions which characterized the latter under conditions of private ownership. These institutions were considered strictly in terms of the differential between those who owned the means of production, capital and land, and those who worked to produce. "Many workmen could not subsist a week, few could subsist a month, and scarce any a year without employment," and it seldom happens "that a person who tills the ground has wherewithal to maintain himself til he reaps the harvest. His maintenance is generally advanced to him from the stock of a master, the farmer who employs him, and who would have no interest to employ him, unless he was to share in the produce of his labour, or unless his stock was to be replaced to him with a profit."[29]

Thus, in Smith's general equilibrium or macro analysis, profits and rents, in the aggregate, were explained as deductions from the produce of labor, not as arising in the process of distribution as suggested by later economists. The distinction can be seen by comparing Smith's discussion with that of any member of the utility school. Schumpeter, for example, explains entrepreneurial revenue in terms of innovation.[30] Speaking microscopically, it is certainly possible to hypothesize profit as the return, above costs, to the individual entrepreneur. But in the aggregate, if innovation is to yield income over and above the wages involved in its production, there must be a group of workers who are in need of working for less than the value they produce. The difference, profit, was by far the most important variable in all of the classical thinking. It provided the motive behind capital accumulation that was considered to be the major kinetic force in the system of capitalist production.[31]

This classical formulation in which profit was assumed to originate in the differences between the economic status of the laboring and the nonlaboring classes did not exclude the possibility that individual profit could arise in exchange. Such cases, however, were special because, in the competition between markets, individuals and resources would be mobile and prices flexible. The advantages and disadvantages which some would experience in the short run would be eliminated through the forces of the market and commodities would tend, in the long run, to their real exchange values.[32]

It might be suggested here that for the terms long run and short run, with their time connotations, it is useful to substitute macro and micro to point up the difference between profit in the aggregate, and profit on the individual level. Viewing the classical concept of the origin of profit in its rightful place in the general equilibrium analysis, the notion of no profit in the long run is nonsense. For Smith, profit did not arise as the result of exchange, but existed in the sense of the difference between output produced by labor and the total wage bill. Though this was implicit in the analysis, aggregate profits were always explained in this way and, in the aggregate, the economy was always considered to be in equilibrium in terms of gains and losses through distribution. Prices in the aggregate always equaled the cost of production and, therefore, profit could only *originate* in the process of production. This the classical system attempted to make explicit.

But Smith's system of analysis, unlike Ricardo's, made assumptions with respect to both the macrocosm and the microcosm, recognizing the importance of setting the two problems in some relationship of functional consanguinity. On the micro level, the part played by demand was that it might determine market price for particular commodities with the cost of production in a very minor role. Use value becomes significant in that the market price of "every particular commodity is regulated by the proportion between the quantity which is brought to market and the demand of those who are willing to pay [at least] the natural price."[33] Competition among demanders might tend to make particular market prices different from the real price "according as the acquisition of the commodity happens to be of more or less importance to them."[34]

But what role can demand play in such a system as the classical political economy? According to Say's law, that total demand is a function of total supply, the amount of purchasing power which individuals have at their disposal, in either net or gross terms, is limited and set by the level of production. In this way the amount of "value" in the system is determinate and can not be increased through individual exchange unless the materialistic notions of value are rejected, as they are by Lionel Robbins. Within the system of Smith, however, and we should use his postulates and assumptions if we are to understand his analysis, the individual demand is always functioning within the framework of the system and the consumer equations, as such, are dependent and not independent variables. The degree of freedom which consumers can exercise lies in their ability to reallocate the ratios at which particular goods exchange. But no value is added by this process; value has arisen in the process of production and the total amount of it is unaffected by the *ex post* decisions of consumers. In this way it is correct to say that the utility school does not have a theory of production and concerns itself exclusively with the redistribution of goods because it always assumes that the production process is *ex post* to the *ex ante* decisions of consumers. In the classical formulation, the relationship is reversed and consumer demand functions within the framework of the production process wherein individuals assign different "use values" to particular goods, but no exchange value is thus created.

The same is true of the classical theory of profits. The aggregate amount of profits is the difference between the output of labor and the total wage bill. There may be a redistribution of this profit fund, but this will not affect its size. The latter is a function of the production coefficients which accompany the labor-capital contract.

The theory of individual prices, and therefore individual profits, takes its direction from, and exists within, the framework of the general accumulation of capital which, in the classical system, is the dynamic factor in the economic system. In this "growth" analysis,[35] individual prices and profits are subsidiary to the general equilibrium problem, and should only be understood in such a relationship. But Smith, has been suggested, did have a discussion of these strictly microscopic phenomena. His theory of price, in its modern terminology, is that price reflects the influence of market conditions upon the transfer of particular commodities. Leaving aside the effects of what Marx called the "organic composition of capital," these influences are grouped under five categories: Accidents,[36] natural causes,[37] police regulation,[38] ignorance,[39] and, most important, monopoly.[40] The latter receives by far the longest discussion, as the inequality and distortion of some prices from their natural or real price, "is upon every occasion the highest which can be squeezed out of the buyer." But price could not affect the aggregate amount of exchange value unless monopoly implications caused such a distortion of distribution that funds were misused and the amount of investment in future periods retarded. Then the monopoly problem becomes a "growth" problem, since the size of future annual flows becomes influenced by the distribution of goods in previous periods. In this framework monopoly is assigned a quite different role than that usually associated with the theory of price, and it was just this designation which concerned Smith and the rest of the classical school.[41]

To return to the central theme, the supply and demand analysis, in which demand is an active influence upon price, can be looked upon as remaining within the boundaries of Say's law, wherein aggregate demand is dependent upon the cost of production. The law appears valid in an *ex post* analysis. It is only when period analysis is introduced that its usefulness comes into question. Marshall, among others, modified the early attempts of the utility school to dispose completely of cost of production analysis by pointing out the necessity for long-run considerations.[42] But the contradiction between the cost of production theory and the demand analysis of the utility school is not just one of market period as against long run, as Marshall claimed. In classical theory the dichotomy is always present, but is explained in terms of microscopic movements within the dynamics of the aggregate system. When the relationship between pricing and the economic process is so viewed, there is no contradiction. It is only in the light of utility assumptions that contradictions appear.

Conclusion

In conclusion we can say that the discussion of market price is in the main restricted to Chapter VIII of Book I and does not contain anything more than an indication of the direction of Smith's analysis. Later *micro-oriented* economists were certainly correct in claiming that Smith's discussion was not as elaborate as it might have been. But this was the nature of classical economics. As Professor Lange has said, "The range of validity of partial equilibrium theory is . . . very limited . . . we need, therefore, to study the repercussions of the changes in the price of one factor upon the prices of other factors and upon the prices of products. This leads us from partial equilibrium to general equilibrium."[43] This was what the classical school attempted to do, and it was in the macrocosmic formulation of their system that the labor theory of value was the key to the understanding of the movement in the base of the system.[44] The partial analysis was concerned with the superstructure wherein the distribution of the output of labor was allocated among the different members of society in accordance with sociological and institutional parameters.

According to Smith's labor theory of value, wherein value originated in the process of production, prices tended always to equal cost of production, as the sum of the prices above real value would always equal the sum of those below real value. This was true in the aggregate and in the long run – which we should consider synonymous terms. Smith's discussion of the causes for the distortion of the market price from the real price are indications of partial analysis which the *Wealth of Nations* contained. But they do not necessitate the scrapping of the labor theory of value, as the microcosmic movements of individual prices below or above real price were always assumed to be governed by the process of capital accumulation.

Notes

1.   "It is not easy to give a summary account of Adam Smith's ambiguous and confused theory of value. Subsequent economists have found two or three different strands of thought which Smith did not separate sufficiently clearly. He developed the labor theory inherited from Petty and Cantillon, but he also added to it certain elements of the supply and demand analysis of Locke. And in his struggles with the difficulties of the concept of capital and its place in the economic process, he *contradicted his own labor theory of value and bequeathed to later generations what became a mechanical cost of production theory.* According to their predilections economists have stressed one or the other of these different principles. But not even adherents of the same school can agree on their interpretations of Smith's theory . . . It is true that Adam Smith's theory is inconsistent." Eric Roll, *A History of Economic Thought* (New York: Prentice-Hall, 1942), pp. 164-165. (Italics added.)

2.   "Smith, *having discarded labour,* finds a new determinant of value in cost of production, and if socialists rallied to his first hypothesis the great majority of of economists right up to Jevons have clung to his second. As for Smith himself, *he never had the courage to choose between them.* They remain juxtaposed in the *Wealth of Nations* because *he never made up his mind which to adopt.* As a result his work is full of contradictions which it would be futile to try to reconcile." Gide and Rist, *A History of Economic Doctrines* (New York: D.C. Heath and Co.), p. 78. (Italics added.)

3.   Elie Halevy, *The Growth of Philosophic Radicalism* (New York: Augustus Kelley, 1946), p. 6; J.H. Randall, *The Making of the Modern Mind* (New York: Houghton Mifflin Co., 1940), Book III; F.S.C. Northrop, *The Meeting of East and West* (New York: Macmillan Co.,

1946), Chap. III.

4. See, for example, T.W. Hutchison, *A Review of Economic Doctrines, 1870-1929* (Oxford: Clarendon Press, 1953).

5. For the Marshallian formulation of this problem see Allan Gruchy, *Modern Economic Thought* (New York: Prentice Hall, 1947), pp. 37-39.

6. As Keynes suggests in a footnote, *General Theory*, p. 3, the word "classical" was applied, by Marx, to Ricardo and his predecessors. Marx also considered himself to be a member of the classical school. This meaning of the term, rather than Lord Keynes' "solecism," is used in this article. Excluded are the writings of Malthus and the Physiocrats which reflect the opinions of the agricultural classes and consequently formulate the significant queries in a quite different framework.

7. J.M. Keynes, in the *General Theory*, breaks the continuity of economic thought vis-a-vis money, and introduces, in some detail, the concept of "money illusion" which had been suggested by R.A. Fisher. Keynes' assumption (Chap. 19) is a throwback to the Mercantilist theory of money. See W.W. Leontief, "The Fundamental Assumption of Mr. Keynes' Monetary Theory of Unemployment," *Quarterly Journal of Economics*, November 1936, pp. 192-197.

8. M. Dobb, *Political Economy and Capitalism* (New York, 1947), p. 39.

9. See *Wealth of Nations* (Modern Library Edition) discussion of real and nominal prices, Book I, Chap. V; D. Ricardo, *Collected Works*, ed. by Sraffa and Dobb (New York: Cambridge University Press, 1951), Vol. III, and Vol. I, p. 22.

10. Ricardo, *Collected Works*, Vol. I, pp. 11-12; *Wealth of Nations*, Book II, *passim*.

11. *Wealth of Nations*, p. lvii.

12. V.W. Bladen, "Adam Smith on Value," *Essays in Honor of E.J. Urwick*, ed. by H.A. Innis (Toronto: University of Toronto Press, 1938), p. 40.

13. *Wealth of Nations*, p. lvii.

14. Northrop, *op. cit.*, p. 128. For the distinction between materialistic and subjective economics, see L. Robbins, *An Essay on the Nature and Significance of Economic Science* (London: Macmillan Co., 1946), pp. 4-23.

15. Northrup, *op. cit.*, p. 122 ff; also A. Smith, "Of External Senses," *The Collected Works of Adam Smith, Ll.D.* (ed. by Dugald Stewart), Vol. V., pp. 331-399.

16. L. Robbins, *op. cit.*, pp. 56-57.

17. For a discussion of the problem of subjectivism in science, see Marvin Farber, "Experience and Subjectivism." *Philosophy for the Future*, ed. by Sellars *et al.* (New York: Macmillan Co., 1949), pp. 591-632.

18. *Wealth of Nations*, pp. 28-29.

19. This is suggested by a rather obscure paper published posthumously under the title, "History of Astronomy and Its Influence upon the Development of Other Sciences," *Collected Works of Adam Smith*, Vol. V. This paper deals with the successes of Newtonian physics and attributes these to Newton's ability to systematize the body of knowledge. Smith suggests that attempts should be made to extend this procedure into other areas of thinking and to get away from the purely personal and nonmaterial forces at work. As for the significance and importance which Smith attributed to this paper, see J. Rae, *The Life of Adam Smith* (London, 1892). See also Ricardo, *Collected Works*, Vol. IV. "Absolute Value and Exchangeable Value," pp. 358-412.

20. *Wealth of Nations*, p. 52.

21. W.R. Scott, *Francis Hutcheson* (Cambridge, 1900), pp. 235-237.

22. The estimation of gross national product in real terms was the index problem which Smith attempted to work out in his long discussion as to whether corn or money was a better measure of the real value of goods. The whole classical school tended to ignore the contribution of services as unproductive labor. (Book II, *Wealth of Nations*.) Smith's use of labor, rather than utility, as the measure of real value, somewhat anticipated the problem which Keynes discusses as one of the "Perplexities which most impeded my progress in my writing," the *General Theory* (Chapter 4). It is not a coincidence that both Keynes and the Classical school used labor as the measure of value, for both were concerned with the macrocosm rather than the microcosm.

23. J. Bonar, *Philosophy and Political Economy in Some of Their Historical Relations* (London, 1893), p. 117; Scott, *op. cit.*, p. 233 and *passim*. With the development of the utility school, value was considered to originate in the process of consumption, rather than production, and labor lost the significant role it had played in the classical analysis. It is suggested that this was essentially due to the orientation of utility analysis to the microcosm rather than the macrocosm.

24. The classicists recognized of course that some commodities were outside the boundaries of increase through human effort and derived their value mainly by being scarce. Scott, *op. cit.*, p. 238.

25. *Wealth of Nations*, pp. 30-31.

26. *Ibid.*, pp. 47, 64.

27. *Ibid.*, p. 49.

28. *Ibid.*, p. 52.

29. *Ibid.*, pp. 65-66.

30. *The Theory of Economic Development* (Cambridge: Harvard University Press, 1949), Chapter IV.

31. See L. Robbins, "On a Certain Ambiguity in the Conception of Stationary Equilibrium," *Economic Journal*, 1930, pp. 194-214.

32. Dobb, *op. cit.*, pp. 38-39. Ricardo considered this to be such a minor aspect of the analysis that he ignores the short run problem altogether and concerns himself with profits in the macrocosm. *Collected Works*, Vol. IV, "Essay on Profits," pp. 9-41. See also G. Stigler, "The Ricardian Theory of Value and Distribution," *Journal of Political Economy*, June 1952, p. 200.

33. *Wealth of Nations*, p. 56.

34. *Ibid.*, p. 57.

35. For a discussion of the growth theory of classical economics, see R.F. Harrod, *Towards a Dynamic Economics* (London: Macmillan, 1948), pp. 15-18; B.S. Kierstead, *The Theory of Economic Change* (Toronto: Macmillan Co., 1948), Chap. IV; W.J. Baumol, *Economic Dynamics* (New York: Macmillan Co., 1951), Chap. II.

36. *Wealth of Nations*, p. 60.

37. *Ibid.*, pp. 58, 6-61.

38. *Ibid.*, pp. 59 and 62.

39. *Ibid.*, p. 60.

40. *Ibid.*, p. 61 and Book IV, Chaps. 1-8.

41. It is interesting to note that Schumpeter also saw this as the major repercussion of monopoly. See *Capitalism, Socialism and Democracy* (New York: Harper & Brothers, 1947), Part II; also E. Domar, "Investment, Losses and Monopolies," *Income, Employment and Public Policy*, Essays in honor of Hansen (New York: W.W. Norton, 1949), pp. 33-53.

42. J. Viner, "The Utility Concept of Value and Its Critics," *Journal of Political Economy*, 1925, pp. 369-387, 638-659.

43. *Price Flexibility and Employment* (Bloomington, Ill.: Principia Press, 1944), pp. 3-4.

44. For a discussion of the adequacy of Smith's analysis as an introduction to general equilibrium theory, see Bladen, *op. cit.*, pp. 41-43.

The *Wealth of Nations* in Spain and Hispanic America, 1780–1830

R.S. Smith

Source: *Journal of Political Economy*, Vol. 65 (2), April 1957, pp. 104-25.

I

Eighteenth-century Spain, as Jean Sarrailh has so ably demonstrated,[1] was not wholly the benighted land that foreigners, and even more often Spaniards themselves, were wont to disparage. Enlightened statesmen, economists, scientists, professors, and even a few clergymen made up an elite who eagerly embraced new ideas and earnestly strove to apply rational methods to the solution of grave national problems. To men like Feijóo, Campomanes, and Jovellanos – to mention the most illustrious of a goodly host – reforms in agriculture, industry, education, and public administration seemed to offer the hope of rescuing Spain from its material and spiritual backwardness.

Mercantilist thought reached its zenith in 1724 with the publication of Gerónimo de Uztáriz's *Théorica y práctica de comercio y de marina*.[2] During the rest of the century few writers on economic questions failed to acknowledge the authority of Uztáriz, but the ideas of foreign economists made up a significant part of the migration of thought which nourished the Spanish Enlightenment. For those unable to read foreign languages, Spanish translations of Addison, Belloni, Biefeld, Condillac, Condorcet, Davenant, Filangieri, Galiani, Genovesi, Herbert, Hume, Necker, Quesnay, Smith, Turgot, and probably others were available before 1800.[3]

Despite the number and variety of foreign economic works chosen for translation, often the Spanish version appeared many years after the publication of the original. Thus Quesnay's *Maximes générals* did not have a Spanish translator until 1794, thirty-six years after the first French edition. By this time many Spaniards were familiar with Smith's criticism of physiocratic ideas and, of course, with his attack on the mercantile system. I have found no statistics of sales or library circulation to show how widely known in Spain was the *Wealth of Nations*; but the perusal of Spanish economic writings makes it possible to identify those who read Smith, quoted him, or developed ideas directly or indirectly inspired by the English classic. While the prompt translation of Say's *Traité*[4] undoubtedly served to widen the sphere of Smith's influence, the assertion that in Spain and Italy "Smith became popular in large part through the influence of Say and other French writers"[5] minimizes the accomplishments of eighteenth-century economists in both countries. Spaniards read the *Wealth of Nations*, in English or in French translations, prior to the publication of the Spanish version of Condorcet's synopsis in 1792 and Ortiz' translation in 1794. Even in the Spanish colonies the *Wealth of Nations* "was not long in becoming known . . . to the enlightened youth, who longed for the independence of these territories."[6]

Colmeiro, usually a reliable guide, appears to have erred in crediting Danvila y Villarrasa with use of Smith in the preparation of a text published in 1779.[7] Danvila cites Cantillon, Condillac, and "David Hum" (*sic*); but the date of publication, the failure to mention Smith, and the superficiality of Danvila's seven "lessons" in economics persuade me that he was unfamiliar with the *Wealth of Nations*.[8] In the 1780's Vicente Alcalá Galiano, secretary of the Segovian Economic Society, lectured widely on economic questions; and, in discussing taxation, he reflected "much foreign influence, especially of Adam Smith."[9] In the schools sponsored by the Economic Society of Saragossa, Lorenzo Normante y Carcavilla taught courses in "civil economics and commerce," expounding principally the ideas of the French economist Jean François Melon. Although his defense of luxury and usury, his attack on sacerdotal celibacy, and other "audacious doctrines" provoked "no small scandal" in Spain, I lack direct evidence that Normante knew Smith's work.[10]

Valentin de Foronda, a member of the Basque Economic Society and a fellow of the Philosophical Society of Philadelphia, where he resided as Spanish consul-general, defended extremely liberal views on economic questions. Addressing an imaginary prince, he recommended the reading of the *Wealth of Nations* for a clear explanation of physiocracy. Although he referred to Quesnay as the "ingenious author of this system," Foronda condemned "the economists" for applying the "humiliating designation of sterile or unproductive class" to artisans, manufacturers, and merchants. He called himself "a copyist, a translator, a plagiarist"; he mentioned Smith several times; but he left largely unfulfilled his promise to disclose the "warehouses" from which he stocked his mind.[11]

Foronda denounced guild privileges, government subsidies to industry, and price-fixing; but it is his uncompromising defense of free trade that sets him apart from his Spanish contemporaries, most of whom espoused liberalism guardedly. Foronda challenged those who, accepting the principle of free trade, insisted on making an exception of trade in grain. This was as absurd as to argue that the earth, unlike the other planets, does not revolve around the sun. Tariffs and embargoes on grain imports raised prices to consumers; restrictions on exports discouraged growers and increased the threat of scarcity. Ruling out the possibility of monopoly, because grain dealers were numerous and scattered, Foronda maintained that competition would naturally set prices which would protect the public and reward the producers.

In breadth of vision, catholicity of interests, and respect for the scientific method, Gaspar Melchor Jovellanos had few peers among eighteenth-century economists and statesmen. Though Jovellanos' liberalism was not the product of a single influence, Smith impressed him profoundly. His unpublished papers include a thirteen-page "Extract from the Work of Mr. Smith" and a translation of parts of the *Wealth of Nations*.[12] Jovellanos' diary reveals that on May 23, 1796, his secretary, Acevedo Villarroel, "began to read Smith" to him; but for Jovellanos this was a third reading. He first read the "anonymous French translation" (perhaps the 1778-79 edition); then the original English; and in 1796 the "Roucher translation, made for Condorcet's notes."[13] Almost daily from May to November, he recorded "reading Smith," or simply "Smith," frequently noting that Villarroel was reading with him. In June he exclaimed, "What a remarkable picture he analyzes"; and in July he was moved to comment, "How well he proves the advantages of free trade with the colonies." He finished the final volume on November 9 and, apparently forgetting the previous entry, declared that he had now read the book four times.[14]

Long before he became familiar with Smith, Jovellanos had doubted the wisdom of restrictive commercial policies. In 1774, while sitting as a judge in Seville, he was called upon to write an opinion concerning the embargo of olive-oil exports when the domestic price rose to a specified level. He took the position that no one could say what price would sufficiently encourage the producer without hurting the consumer. "We should like," he said, speaking for the court, "to restore completely the liberty which is the soul of commerce, which gives to exchangeable things that appraisal corresponding to their abundance or scarcity, and which fixes the natural justness of prices." Never a complete non-interventionist, Jovellanos foresaw circumstances under which exports might be curtailed in the public interest.[15] In 1784, writing a report for the Royal Board for Money and Commerce, he vigorously defended navigation acts.[16] England, he asserted, owed the "astonishing increase of its merchant marine . . . in great part" to the acts of 1652 (i.e., 1651) and 1660. Jovellanos, possibly referring to the *Wealth of Nations*, observed that the first law was directed against the Dutch; but he did not cite Smith's dictum that "national animosity at that particular time aimed at the very same object which the most deliberate wisdom would have recommended" (Book IV, chap. 2).

One of Jovellanos' most forceful essays (1785) was an attack upon guild privileges. In addition to abridging the individual's free choice of occupation, guilds restricted output, thwarted the introduction of new crafts, and impeded the technical progress which specialization and the division of labor made possible. Prophetically, he observed:

> The greatness of nations will no longer rest, as in other times, on the splendor of its triumphs, in the martial spirit of its sons . . . Commerce, industry, and the wealth which springs from both, are, and probably will be for a long time to come, the only foundations of the preponderance of a nation; and it is necessary to make these the objects of our attentions or condemn ourselves to an eternal and shameful dependency, while our neighbors speed their prosperity upon our neglect.[17]

Jovellanos wrote boldly and extensively on other questions of economic policy, but his fame as an economist rests largely on his treatise on agrarian reform.[18] Sponsored by the Economic Society of Madrid, this celebrated report attacked the century-old privileges of the grazers' guild, which had impeded the inclosure of arable land, denounced (as had Count Campomanes thirty years earlier)[19] the perpetuation of large entailed estates, and advocated the expropriation of the inalienable real property of numerous religious foundations. Jovellanos cited Smith, as well as other foreign authors, in support of his analysis of the benefits of small-scale peasant proprietorship, improved farming practices, and free access to markets for agricultural products. Within two years of its publication, the report was denounced as "anticlerical"; and its illustrious author, who had advised the crown to strip the Inquisition of its power to censor books, was driven from his post as minister of justice.[20] Posthumously, Jovellanos' *Informe* was added to the Roman index of prohibited books.[21]

II

Carlos Martinez de Irujo helped to make Smith better known in Spain by publishing, in 1792, a partial translation of Condorcet's analysis of the *Wealth of Nations*.[22] The Inquisition had just placed the French translation of Smith's work on the Index of Prohibited Books;[23] but Martinez' *Compendio* was printed at the Royal Press, by government order, without benefit of inquisitorial review. The translator, a one-time official in the State Department, apparently had the support of the prime minister, Manuel de Godoy, whose relatively liberal ideas often thwarted the Inquisition.[24]

Martinez may not have been certain that his work would escape an unfavorable scrutiny. Hoping, perhaps, to confuse those who had condemned Smith, the translator of the *Compendio* always refers to the English economist as "the Author." The *Wealth of Nations*, he said, was "the best work on political economy which has been written until now." It was to be regretted, however, that the author made some "improper applications" of his theories. Such "levity" ought not to be an excuse for depriving Spaniards of the "treasures" found in the book. The *Compendio* effaced the blemishes of the original work but preserved "those principles which can be looked upon as the axes of political economy."

In his Preface, Martinez advised the reader that Smith's work was "authoritative, abstract and profound" but "almost useless for those who read it without [an understanding of] principles." Dealing with the "first elements of a science until now little known in Spain," the author employed a "special nomenclature, which it is necessary to understand." Indeed, a "knowledge of economics" was required "to comprehend the important results which the *Compendio* affords." The translator was inspired by love for his country; and, if Spain should apply Smith's "solid principles" to the furtherance of national prosperity, he would feel well rewarded.

The *Compendio* closely follows Condorcet's book-by-book analysis of the *Wealth of Nations*.[25] Martinez frequently paraphrased Condorcet's text, instead of making a literal translation; and he suppressed entire paragraphs. The most serious expurgation occurs in connection with Smith's article, "Of the Expense of the Institutions for the Instruction of People of All Ages" (Book V, chap. 1, Part III, Art. III). Condorcet's condensation reduced the article (twenty-six pages in the Cannan edition) by more than a half, but the Spanish translator retained only two paragraphs.[26] If Martinez had followed Condorcet, he would have reproduced a fair share of Smith's discussion of religious tolerance, sectarian differences, and clerical sinecures.

Using the "original English," Martinez added his own summary of Smith's digression on the Bank of Amsterdam. In a solitary footnote he took issue with the Smithian dictum that the individual is more competent than the state to select the most advantageous employment of capital. This may be so, Martinez observed, in an enlightened country; elsewhere "capitalists need the government, so to speak, to lead them by the hand so that they may put their funds in circulation and employ them gainfully."

The translator of the first Spanish version of the *Wealth of Nations* was José Alonso Ortiz, a lawyer attached to the royal councils and chancery in Valladolid and a professor of canon law and sacred theology. Godoy mentions Ortiz' translation as one of the works on political economy which he helped to get published,[27] and the evidence suggests that this is true.

On February 15, 1793, Ortiz appeared before the Inquisition, explaining that "some time ago" he translated the English text of the *Wealth of Nations*, "purging it of various impious proposals . . . and eliminating entirely an article . . . in which the author favors tolerance on points of religion, so that it stands cleansed of anything that could lead to error or relaxation in moral and religious matters."[28] The next day the Supreme Council of the Inquisition sent Ortiz' translation, together with a copy of the proscribed French translation, to its examiners (*calificadores*). Ortiz, meanwhile, asked the royal Council of Castile for permission to publish the work, pleading that the Inquisition had not banned the English *Wealth of Nations*, from which he made his translation, and asserting that he had deleted the passages which led to the prohibition of the French edition. He thought the Council should grant his request, since it had allowed Condorcet's *Compendio* to be published. The Council submitted Ortiz' work to the Royal Academy of History for censure.

On April 30 Ortiz declared that the three censors appointed by the Academy of History had approved his translation. He requested the Inquisition to concur in this decision or advise him what had to be changed. Not satisfied with the opinion of two censors that Ortiz' work avoided the errors of the French text, on May 29 the Inquisition named a new panel of examiners, including the friar who had condemned the French translation. In July, however, the latter had to be replaced by another clergyman. On September 27 the reviewers reported that they found one passage "a little dangerous." Smith said that the revenue derived from stock by one who lends it to another is called "interest or the use of money." Ortiz had paraphrased this as "interest or lawful usury." To meet the censors' criticism, he reworded the passage to read "usury or revenue from money"; and, further on, he changed Smith's phrase "interest of money" to "interest on money or usury understood in this sense." These minor textual changes, together with the expurgation discussed below, satisfied the Inquisition. The manuscript was returned to Ortiz on October 22, and the work was published, with government permission, in 1794.[29]

The 1794 edition was republished in 1933-34.[30] The editor, José M. Tallada, referred to his work as a "revision and adaptation to modern Spanish" of Ortiz' translation; in fact, he made little more than unimportant orthographical and grammatical changes. Neglecting to consult the English text, Tallada perpetuated the errors, omissions, and distortions committed by Ortiz in 1794.

Finally, in 1956, Amando Lázaro Ros gave the Spanish-speaking world the first faithful and unabridged translation of the *Wealth of Nations*.[31] Ignoring completely the work of Ortiz, Ros translated directly from the Cannan edition, omitting Cannan's notes. In a brief prologue Ros observes that, even after two centuries, Spaniards and Spanish-Americans should find interesting what Smith had to say about the results of the discovery of America. Equally notable, Ros observes, is Smith's condemnation of the seizure of Gibraltar, which lost to England its "natural ally," Spain. Finally, the "clarity and historical insight" with which Smith analyzed the problems of the British Empire, when the American colonies were revolting, "today produces astonishment."

III

Ortiz dedicated his translation to Manuel de Godoy, who encouraged him because of his (Godoy's) desire to spread "throughout the nation the deepest understanding of civil economy." Spain, Ortiz correctly observed, had not been without able economists; but, generally, they failed to treat economics in a "scientific method" or to make it a "true science." Smith succeeded, to a greater extent than any of his predecessors, in constructing a "general system" and in "expounding economic ideas in an abstract manner." He discovered the "universal principle of wealth, which is the productive labor of man." The reader, Ortiz warned, would find Smith's ideas "profound" and "highly metaphysical," requiring "repeated reading to penetrate the spirit of his assertions."

Ortiz erroneously identified his work as a translation of the eighth (and latest) English edition – the edition published in London two years after the appearance of the Spanish version.[32] He was drafting the translation in 1792 and could not have used the seventh edition (1793). He may have had the sixth edition (1791) before him, but I think it more likely that he had the fifth edition (1789) and mistook "5th" for "8th." For the purposes of the following discussion I have compared Ortiz' translation with the well-known Cannan edition.

In the Preface, Ortiz announced the suppression of "some details, but very few, either because absolutely irrelevant to our country or hardly in keeping with the holy religion which we profess." The "essence of the work," he insisted, was "in no way adulterated" by the expurgation. He failed to reveal that he omitted all of Article III, Part III, chapter 1, Book V – the section which Martínez de Irujo reduced to two paragraphs. Furthermore, in Ortiz' translation the heading "Article III" was transposed to another place in the chapter, as though nothing had been deleted.

Smith's discussion of tithes and taxes (Book V, chap. 2, Part II, Art. I) also suffered serious expurgation in translation. "In the dominions of the king of Prussia," Smith related, "the revenue of the church is taxed much higher than that of lay proprietors." This sentence Ortiz retained, but he dropped the following sentences: "The revenue of the church is, the greater part of it, a burden upon the rent of land. It seldom happens that any part of it is applied towards the improvement of land; or is so employed as to contribute in any respect towards increasing the revenue of the great body of the people." Smith continued: "His Prussian majesty had probably, upon that account, thought it reasonable, that it should contribute a good deal more towards relieving the exigencies of the state. In some countries the lands of the church are exempted from all taxes. In others they are taxed more lightly than other lands." Ortiz revised these sentences, as follows: "His Prussian majesty concluded that these revenues [taxes on church property] should contribute more than any others to the exigencies of the state; but there are some countries in which the lands of the church are entirely exempted from every tax or lay contribution and others in which they are not entirely tax-free but are much less burdened than lay property."

In the same article Ortiz suppressed an entire paragraph, beginning with the sentence: "The tythe, as it is frequently a very unequal tax upon the rent, so it is always a great discouragement both to the improvements of the landlord and to the cultivation of the farmer." In a footnote the translator endeavored to explain the difference between inequality and justice in taxation. The tithe, as Smith observed, was "very unequal," but Ortiz regarded it as just. Furthermore, as "all the canonical authors" had pointed out, tithes had never been uniformly exacted at the rate of one-tenth of the produce or rent but were subject to downward adjustment in many cases.[33]

In Book V, chapter 1, Part III, Article II, Smith said: "The more they [the inferior ranks of people] are instructed, the less liable they are to the delusions of enthusiasm and superstition, which, among the ignorant nations, frequently occasion the most dreadful disorders." Smith concluded the paragraph with the observation that "in free countries, where the safety of government depends very much upon the favorable judgment which the people may form of its conduct, it must surely be of the highest importance that they should not be disposed to judge rashly or capriciously concerning it." In Ortiz' words, this sentence becomes: "All these advantages, and many others infallibly follow from the principles of good education." Such discrepancies are surely too great to excuse on the grounds of linguistic difficulty.

Elsewhere, Ortiz saw fit to add a sentence, apparently for the purpose of softening the bluntness of Smith's criticism. In the conclusion to chapter 11 of Book I, Smith noted that merchants and manufacturers generally had a better understanding of their own pecuniary interests than country gentlemen had of theirs. Consequently, landowners were often prevailed upon to accept policies beneficial to the mercantile classes "from a very simple but honest conviction" that the measures were in the interest of the public. Ortiz mutilated these sentences in such a way as to conceal the thought that the interests of merchants and landlords might conflict. Then, after reproducing faithfully the sentence in which Smith denounced "an order of men . . . who have generally an interest to deceive and even oppress the public," Ortiz manufactured the following conclusion: "We are speaking thus with respect to the tendency of the class in general, not with reference to those individuals who, loving the nation and mindful of the common welfare, administer their affairs to their own point and without injury to the public interest."

Understandably, Ortiz found it superfluous to reproduce verbatim the long discussion of the English malt tax (Book V, chap. 2, Part II, Art. IV); and he gave due notice that he had condensed the text and suppressed the statistics. Similarly, he paraphrased a large part of Book IV, chapter 8 ("Conclusion of the Mercantile System"), in which Smith explained in detail the rise and development of bounties and embargoes. It may not be true, as Ortiz insisted, that the illustrative material from English history would be "without the slightest use" to the Spanish student of economics; in any case, it is not a serious matter. By the same token, one need not be too critical of his manipulation of the tables at the end of Book I, chapter 11. Of the three columns of wheat prices for 1202-1601, Ortiz retained only the "average price of each year in money of the present time"; but he added his own dubious estimates of equivalent prices in Castilian vellon reals. He also computed a Spanish price series to match Smith's wheat prices at Windsor, 1595-1764; and he published a series of wheat and barley prices for Burgos, 1675-1792, purporting to show yearly averages of high and low prices in the Castilian market. Finally, he devoted two pages to reporting legal maximum prices for wheat and barley in Spain from 1350 to 1699.

Unlike the original, Ortiz' *Investigación* is heavily interlarded with footnotes, in which the translator compares Spanish conditions with Smith's description of England, raises questions concerning the author's historical accuracy, especially in connection with Spain, or challenges the correctness of Smith's views on economic policy. No fawning adulator of the Glasgow professor, Ortiz gives the lie to Spanish writers who have ridiculed their countrymen for blind acceptance of economic liberalism.[34]

Most offensive to Ortiz were Smith's strictures on the motives for founding colonies (Book IV, chap. 7). Parts of the text, he declared, might well have been omitted in translation, but he finally decided that it would be better to refute the charges than to suppress them. In discussing the Spanish conquests in America, Smith fell into the error of most foreigners, who wilfully overlooked the "just causes which motivated the Spanish establishments in the New World." The "incontestable facts of history" proved that Spain settled "deserted land and islands, or lands whose natives were neither familiar with a civilized state nor lived in a society, wherefore no one doubts that under the law of nations their occupation was just." While admitting that the discovery of gold mines was sometimes the deciding factor in the settlement of a particular region, Ortiz declared: "It is not absolutely certain that it happened this way generally, as the author [Smith] supposes, and as all those foreign writers suppose who lose no opportunity to besmirch our nation with the stigma of greed, solely because there may have been in Spain, as in all nations, some greedy individuals, whose vice our government always punished severely." To spread the "true religion,' to gain markets for its industry, "at that time more flourishing in Spain than in other European countries," to bring savages the benefits of a civilized community – these were some of the fundamental reasons for Spain's overseas ventures, and they were not essentially different from the aims of other colonizing powers.

With respect to Spanish imports of American gold and silver, Ortiz knew of no way to improve upon the estimates which Smith derived from the works of Megens and Raynal (Book I, chap. 11). Indeed, he considered it unimportant as well as impractical to attempt the sort of statistical verification of imports of treasure which Profesor Hamilton brought to fruition nearly a century and a half later.[35]

What Smith had to say about paper money, Ortiz asserted, provided "as much as can be desired for complete instruction in the matter"; and he urged that the entire chapter (Book II, chap. 2) "be meditated with much reflection." Spain's first experiment with paper money consisted of an issue of interest-bearing treasury certificates (*vales reals*) in 1780. After circulating at a discount for many months, the *vales* rose to parity with silver in 1785. Ortiz believed that the public's unfamiliarity with this type of money had contributed significantly to its depreciation. Eventually, the "good opinion with which the public was accepting this paper money" facilitated new issues. The government, Ortiz said, realized that the paper money stimulated the circulation of immobilized funds and kept within the country the interest payments which in the case of a foreign loan would have gone abroad. In any case, Spain in the 1780's "exiled the hoary misconception that only gold and silver can be useful instruments of commerce and the sole means of increasing national wealth."

Following Smith's "Disgression concerning banks of deposit, particularly concerning that of Amsterdam" (Book IV, chap. 3), Ortiz inserted a forty-page appendix on the Bank of San Carlos (later styled the Bank of Spain).[36] He thought the bank had been "scarcely scrupulous" in making loans against its own shares as collateral, and he expressed a mild criticism of the bank's role as a contractor for provisioning the armed forces. On the other hand, he noted with satisfaction that the bank had settled foreign balances by remitting specie, confident that "the country from which that precious metal is withdrawn need not remain less wealthy as, falsely, common prejudice is accustomed to imagine." Two years after the appearance of his translation of the *Wealth of Nations*, Ortiz published a substantial treatise on paper money and public credit.[37] Believing that "the subject in itself is not susceptible of much that is new," Ortiz disclaimed having made any contribution except that of making available to Spaniards the ideas of French and English economists. Besides Smith, the greatest authorities on paper money were Mortimer, Hume, Genovesi, and Dutot. All their teachings, Ortiz concluded, proved that "the only support and the true foundation on which rests the soundness and stability" of paper money "is the public credit."

In expounding the "interest of money" (Book I, chap. 9), Smith, Ortiz noted, had in mind "compensatory or mercantile interest" not "lucrative usury, generally known by the generic term usury, prohibited as illicit by all laws, which is to give something more than the principal at risk by reason of mere accommodation [*mutuo*]." It is doubtful that this clarified the matter for the readers of footnotes or that they were enlightened by the note (Book II, chap. 4) in which Ortiz made another attempt "to obviate the errors of the uninformed reader on the point of interest on money." The gist of his argument is that interest is permitted, up to the maximum legal rate, in ordinary mercantile and commercial transactions; but, when a loan is made "with no other reason than the benefit it bestows in ministering to the need of the borrower," the taking of interest is unlawful.

Ortiz devoted several notes to the exceptions which he presumed Smith had overlooked in propounding the principles of free trade (Book IV). He agreed that a "natural tendency" would be obstructed by protecting any industry in a country which, because of a high level of industrialization, had little to fear from foreign competition. But a generally backward economy, of which Spain seemed to be the prime example, could never advance without tariffs. Domestic manufacturers had to have the "privilege of an exclusive market, at least for a certain time and until national industry may place itself in a position to complete for the foreign." Free trade, in Ortiz' mind, was "advantageous when it does not serve as a positive obstacle to the improvement of the domestic industry in a backward country." It was necessary, Smith to the contrary notwithstanding, to limit Spanish exports of gold and silver; otherwise excessive quantities of the precious metals would be exchanged for foreign wares, "with recognizable harm to our factories, because these are not yet in a state to compete with the foreign factories."

With respect to the grain trade, Ortiz thought Spanish policy had been "much more lenient and prudent than that of England." A new departure from age-old Spanish legislation was the corn law of 1765, recommended by Count Campomanes, who had been greatly influenced by the Physiocrats. The act abolished legal price ceilings and removed most of the restrictions on the domestic grain trade. Exports of wheat were permitted as long as prices remained below 35 reals per fanega in Asturias, Galicia, Andalucia, Murcia, and Valencia, below 32 reals in the Cantabrian provinces, or below 22 reals in the border towns. Imported wheat had to be warehoused within six leagues of the port of entry, but it could be withdrawn for sale in interior markets when domestic prices were above the prices specified in the regulations governing exports. The corn laws of 1789 and 1790 restored many of the pre-1765 restrictions on the grain trade, but (Ortiz insisted) Spain had "adopted the maxim of free trade, if not in an absolute manner, at least in a way most compatible with the circumstances of the country." The "circumstances" included the machinations of greedy and unprincipled grain dealers who persistently conspired to raise prices.

Commending Smith's attack on privileged trading companies, Ortiz pointed out that Spanish policy had been "more prudent" than that of England, because Spain "never granted such companies sovereign power nor the right to have and maintain garrisons and fortifications." Furthermore, Spain had granted exclusive rights to trade only for a limited number of years. Ortiz noted the privileges possessed by the powerful Five Greater Guilds of Madrid but failed to make a vigorous attack, as others had done, on the Guilds' virtual monopoly of several branches of trade, industry, and government procurement.

Ortiz generally agreed with Smith on the harmful effects of craft guilds (Book I, chap. 10). A case could be made for guild regulations limited to the improvement of the workers' manual skills and to technical innovations in production. Inherently, however, guild objectives exhibited a "prejudicial tendency; and it will be a very rare case, if one is found, that keeps them within legal and just limits, according to the intentions of the government." In one matter Spain was ahead of England, Ortiz found, because it had never interfered with the migration of workers within the country. There were laws to control vagrancy and mendicancy but nothing comparable to English laws "to remove a man who has committed no misdemeanour from the parish where he chooses to reside," in "evident violation of natural liberty and justice."

Ortiz disagreed with Smith's explanation of the low pay for military service as compared with the wages of common laborers (Book I, chap. 10). It was not the prospect of honors and metals that caused young men to enlist but genuine hatred of the country's enemies, eagerness to defend its religion, and patriotism. Similarly, Smith's comparison of the worker's wages with the emoluments of curates was considered inapplicable to Spain, where some bishoprics were well endowed and others had meager means for supporting the parish priests. On the other hand, the constant concern of both church and state lest the number of Spanish clergy increase inordinately lent support to Smith's observation that the "hope of much more moderate benefices will draw a sufficient number of learned, decent, and respectable men into holy orders."[38]

The article, "Of the Expense of the Institutions for the Education of Youth" (Book V, chap. 1, Part III, Art. II), evoked thirteen long notes in Ortiz' translation. In one place Smith observed that, when the university professor was salaried and not dependent upon student fees, his interest was "set as directly opposite to his duty as it was possible to set it." Ortiz found this view "quite judicious, well-founded, and in keeping with experience." He saw no way to make the buying and selling of education competitive: "stimulus and advancement in the arts and sciences and costly education in these subjects are two entirely incompatible things." But Smith's charge that the professor tended "to consent that his neighbor may neglect his duty, provided he himself is allowed to neglect his own," struck Ortiz as "false" and "impudent." Similarly, he doubted that students had to choose a college or university "independent of the merit or reputation of the teachers"; he felt that "emulation" was strong enough to make the education afforded scholarship students as good as that provided those who paid full fees.[39] The translator vigorously objected to Smith's insistence that the "discipline of colleges and universities is in general contrived, not for the benefit of the students, but for the interest, or more properly speaking, for the ease of the masters." On the other hand, Ortiz regretfully corroborated Smith's reference to "some Spanish universities . . . in which the study of the Greek language has never yet made any part of that course" (theology). Only three universities, Ortiz said, had chairs of Greek and Hebrew.

Elsewhere, Smith made the caustic comment: "Were there no public institutions for education, a gentlemen, after going through, with application and abilities, the most complete course of education which the circumstances of the times were supposed to afford, could not come into the world completely ignorant of every thing which is the common subject of conversation among gentlemen and men of the world." Baffled, apparently, by the abstruseness of the sentence, Ortiz rewrote it, as follows: "If these public institutions did not exist, men perhaps would receive a more useful and beneficial education." In any event, he regarded the statement as "puerile," equivalent to saying: "If there had been no masters who taught science, there would not have been masters who taught erroneous things; so, in order that there be no one who teaches errors, all the masters who teach science must be removed from the world." I doubt whether either Smith or Ortiz furnishes much help on means to rid educational systems of pedantry, sophistry, error, and nonsense.

Ortiz' footnotes on the second chapter of Book V are devoted to describing the Spanish tax system and to commenting on Smith's criticisms of fiscal policy. He agreed with Smith that it was improper to tax "revenue arising from stock," and he deplored inheritance taxes, which in certain parts of Spain and Portugal deprived close relatives of the major portion of even paltry estates. Wages were taxed in Spain, but Ortiz considered the Spanish practice "never . . . so burdensome as in other parts of Europe." On the other hand, sales taxes, both general and selective, had reached intolerable levels. For more than a century, as Ortiz pointed out, Spanish economists had deplored their depressing effect upon trade and the unfair burden on the poor. As a general rule, Ortiz asserted, "the principal defects which customarily underly taxes . . . are the inequality in their imposition and arbitrariness in their collection, which originate either in the very nature of the tax, concerning which our author [Smith] reasons skilfully, or in the extrinsic or accidental circumstances which by reason of the difficulty of reducing them to an exact calculation are, as it were, another [defective] characteristic." If called upon to improve the tax system, Ortiz would have favored the introduction of a single property tax (*contribución única*), a reform proposed by the Treasury in the first half of the eighteenth century.

Commenting on public debts (Book V, chap. 3), Ortiz spoke of the sinking fund as a necessary guaranty of the repayment of a loan as well as a bulwark of credit which would facilitate new borrowing in an emergency. He also considered it praiseworthy that the nation's paper money had been protected by a redemption fund for its eventual retirement from circulation. Although he had misgivings about the accuracy of the available data, he thought the Spanish national debt was smaller in relation to national wealth than the public debts of England and France. This consideration seemed to Ortiz to be more to the point than Smith's reminder that part of Spain's public debt, contracted in the sixteenth century, had never been retired.

For the serious student of the *Wealth of Nations* the usefulness of Ortiz' translation was greatly enhanced by a sixty-page synopsis ("Indice General") of the five books.

After Ortiz, the most influential critic of the work of Smith was the Catalan jurist Ramón Lázaro de Dou y de Bassols. In a work on public law, composed during the closing years of the eighteenth century, he acknowledged the "profundity" of the *Wealth of Nations* as well as the superiority of Englishmen in "economic speculation," but he refused to accept Smith's views on commercial policy. Dou criticized his compatriots who, "in the spirit of novelty and scepticism," were "opposed to tariffs and taxes on the import and export of produce and manufactures, defending themselves with the authority of Smith, whom they represent as the Achilles of their opinion." England had never adopted free trade; and Dou believed that "the further a nation is from equaling or surpassing other nations in industries, the further it must be from adopting Smith's system."[40] Without examining the logic of the case for free trade, Dou eagerly espoused a vigorous program for the industrialization of Catalonia behind tariff walls.

After serving as president of the Cortes of Cádiz in 1810, Dou became chancellor of the University of Cervera.[41] Here he published, in 1817, a commentary on the *Wealth of Nations*, based on excerpts from the second edition of Ortiz' translation.[42] Calling Smith the "Neuton [*sic*] of political economy," Dou declared that the Scotsman's genius consisted in having discovered, as from a high watchtower, that Europeans, dazzled by the brilliance of the mercantile system, were straying very far from the paths they ought to follow." On the other hand, Dou thought, Smith had erred in not presenting "with as much extension and force as it seems they should be presented some important exceptions in the matter of the mercantile system." Dou set out to show how the wisdom of Smith would profit the reader, but he felt free to refute him at will, especially on points which "do not seem to me consistent with his own system."

Dou said he had heard many complain that they could not fathom some of Smith's ideas; and Dou admitted his "embarrassment" because he had had to read parts of the *Wealth of Nations* several times before understanding the "sublimity" of the doctrines. Furthermore, he thought that poor organization and Smith's failure to elaborate points which would be obscure to all except the most erudite helped to explain the "scarce fruit" which the *Wealth of Nations* had borne in Spain.

Criticizing Smith, Dou repeated much of his earlier defense of protectionism. Duties on imports, which incidentally constituted a good source of revenue, were essential for an industrially backward country: "Whatever may be said against tariffs . . . seems to me an illusion or economic madness." Uztariz proved to be a better guide to commercial policy than Smith. Furthermore, Dou thought Smith had "confessed" the "utility, or to put it better, the necessity of the mercantile system."

Dou also reached a conclusion "somewhat contrary to the disdain which some, with the title or the pretext of being disciples of Smith, have for the precious metals." The poverty of Spain and Portugal, in the midst of a plethora of gold and silver, had been exaggerated: what these two countries lacked was the necessary intelligence to use their money as a means of expanding agriculture and industry. Gold must be counted as a part of the wealth of nations, since its production demanded "an astonishing quantity of labor . . . permanent labor which does not perish with time or with fire."

Usury, Dou cautioned, was "a delicate matter . . . on which, because of the sole circumstance of religion, we should depart from Smith"; but Dou supposed that Smith's views, applying to purely mercantile transactions, supported his own position. Unfortunately, Ortiz had given Dou a garbled translation of the third chapter of Book V. Smith said: "To trade, was disgraceful to a gentlemen; and to lend money at interest, which at that time was considered usury, and prohibited by law, would have been still more so." Ortiz' version reads: "To trade (he is speaking of olden times) was not well thought of for a gentleman: to lend money at interest, without taking into account the circumstances which can make this contract lawful, was then commonly regarded as usury, and consequently prohibited, as it now is, [and] which in reality is usury." In other words, Dou supposed that Smith recognized "lawful usury" as interest on loans qualifying under the Thomist doctrine of *lucrum cessans* and *damnum emergens*. He challenged the idea that the Catholic position was inimical to national prosperity. "Economics in all its parts and in a thousand ways, blended perfectly with religion, governs and must govern affairs so as to destroy usury."

Dou regarded the labor theory of value an "enlightening principle." So clearly had Smith shown that the quantity of labor determined the value of goods that it was "unnecessary to look for other sources of wealth than labor." But Dou objected that land and capital were not independent sources of value; they created wealth only "in proportion to the labor they contain." Dou disagreed with Smith and the "majority" of economists who regarded large entailed estates as inimical to agricultural progress and contrary to natural rights. He also doubted the wisdom of Jovellanos' views that the "interest of cultivators will never be more active than when they are proprietors."[43] Finding strong sanction for entail and primogeniture in civil, natural, and divine law, Dou proposed to remove the obstacles to better farming by the use of emphyteusis. In two pamphlets published in 1829 and 1831, apparently Dou's last work, he found support in the *Wealth of Nations* for his scheme to generalize the practice of long-term hereditary leases for small holdings.[44]

IV

Toward the end of the eighteenth century Ramón Campos, a physics professor and the author of works on logic, attempted to make the ideas of Smith better known through a text on "economics reduced to exact, clear and simple princiles." Smith, he declared, "made himself immortal by the brilliance with which he presented the substance of Stewart's [*sic*] work." It was Campos' ambition to publicize the findings of both economists, so that the science, "so mysterious until now, may through my work become widely known, being universally accepted among the number of exact sciences." In eight chapters Campos covered concisely, but accurately, the Smithian theories of prices, wages, profit, capital, and taxation; and he devoted an appendix to public debts. It is not clear for whom the miniature volume was intended or how widely it was read.[45]

In the Preface to the 1821 edition of Say's *Tratado* the translator, Juan Sánchez Rivera, exclaimed: "How much honor befalls our nation and how much happiness we should promise ourselves, and even more our children, from a great number of laws and dispositions of the Spanish legislature of 1820, all founded on the brilliant ideas of Say, Smith, Ricardo, Steward [*sic*], Filangieri, Beccaria, and other celebrated writers, who have dedicated their talents to enlightening this essential part of human knowledge"! Foremost among the liberal deputies in the Cortes of 1820 was the economist, Alvaro Flórez Estrada. A member of the commerce committee, Flórez Estrada supported legislation to reduce tariffs and remove other restrictions on trade. "As far as I am concerned," he declared, "would to God that I could persuade Congress to abolish all tariffs from this day forward!" To prohibit imports was "contrary to all the principles of political economy." Equally bad were the exclusive privileges of the Philippines Company, and those who thought the example of the English East India Company proved the advantages of trading monopolies were mistaken: "There is no informed Englishman who has touched on that Company who does not consider it inimical to public happiness."[46] José Canga Argüelles, one of Flórez Estrada's colleagues in the Cortes of 1820, cited Smith in defense of the proposition that lower tariffs increase the revenue from customs duties.[47]

Both Canga Argüelles and Flórez Estrada were exiled to England upon the restoration of Fernando VIII's absolute rule in 1823. A former finance minister (1811), Canga Argüelles published in London a number of works on public finance, including a five-volume *Diccionario de hacienda*. A potpourri of economic, historical, and statistical information, the *Diccionario* cites Smith several times. It was the *Wealth of Nations* which explained the fallacy of the favorable-balance-of-trade argument, showed the beneficial effects of circulating capital in domestic trade, and revealed the "prodigious increase" in production made possible by the division of labor. Canga Argüelles quoted Smith – but not accurately – in an article which denounced the granting of exclusive privileges to foreign traders.[48]

Flórez Estrada's *Curso de economia politica*, first published in 1828, has been described as the "first sytematic treatise on economics written by a Spaniard." Although relying primarily on the *Wealth of Nations* and other English works, Flórez Estrada advanced the original doctrine that private ownership of land is the cause of the "laborer's failure to obtain the entire fruit of his labor," anticipating Mill and Henry George.[49] Neglecting Say, he asserted that no Spaniard had ever written a "complete treatise on political economy" or translated into Spanish a work which unfolded the "great discoveries" in the science during the preceding thirty years. Flórez Estrada's *Curso* attempted to inquire methodically into the means of increasing national wealth. He considered Smith the "true founder of the modern system of political economy" and held that the *Wealth of Nations* "ought to be placed among the works which have brought the most good to the human race." But Smith's masterpiece had its faults: it lacked clarity; it was not well organized; and its digressions, if not useless, were often unnecessary. Smith was mistaken, Flórez Estrada believed, in regarding agriculture as the most productive type of economic activity, and he erred in calling labor unproductive unless expended on an exchangeable commodity. But Smith's "capital error" was his insistence on the stable value of wheat and the natural adjustment of wages to the price level.[50]

In the *Elementos de economia politica*, first published in 1829, the Marqués de Valle Santoro endeavored to synthesize the theories of Smith and Say, eliminating the "discussion and digression" found in the economists' works, "so that beginners may form forthwith a clear idea of the status of the science without being distracted by other purposes." Smith was often mistaken, but "no one can take away from him the glory of having been the founder of Political Economy." Unfortunately, the "error of Smit [*sic*] in believing and writing that the creators of immaterial goods were not producers of wealth did much harm during the past revolutions because, dividing men into useful or productive and sterile or unproductive classes, it was easy to inflame one against the others, considering them as just so many leeches who lived at the expense of their sweat and robbed them of their sustenance." Finally, the "celebrated Adam Smith" thoroughly discredited the tenets of mercantilism. What he failed to recognize was the dependence of commercial policy on a country's stage of economic development; only the most advanced nations could afford to adopt free trade.[51]

V

Liberal economics seeped into the Spanish colonies through several channels. The Ordinance of 1778, which introduced the policy of *comercio libre*, has sometimes been identified as a free-trade measure.[52] It was, of course, nothing of the sort; it merely opened to trade a number of Spanish and American ports which for two and a half centuries had been denied the right to engage in overseas commerce. Possibly, as González Alberdi suggests,[53] the *Wealth of Nations* encouraged some colonists to press for even greater freedom in their economic affairs – freedoms which proved inconsistent with Spain's concept of colonial dependence. Few, it would seem, were persuaded to accept all the principles in defense of which Smith and Say wrote so cogently.

In Buenos Aires, in the early years of the nineteenth century, Juan Hipólito Vieytes founded a weekly newspaper to disseminate useful information on agriculture, industry, and trade.[54] The pages of the *Semanario* constitute, according to Weinberg, the "most intensive and systematic exposition of political economy which had been achieved up to that time in the Rio de la Plata."[55] Actually, although Vieytes called Smith the "sublime economist," he gave his readers little more than extracts of some Smithian ideas found in Samuel Crumpe's essay on the means of providing employment for people.[56]

The ablest and most prolific writer on economic questions in Argentina was Manuel Belgrano. Educated in Spain, Belgrano learned of Smith through Martínez' *Compendio*; but, as Gondra points out, no Smithian influence marks the addresses on agriculture, industry, and commerce which Belgrano delivered before the Consulado of Buenos Aires in 1796-1802.[57] He showed his predilection for the Physiocrats in a book published in 1796.[58] In the first number of the *Correo de comercio*, founded by Belgrano in 1810, he discussed Smith and published a résumé of the first chapter of Book IV of the *Wealth of Nations*. In subsequent issues Belgrano attacked monopoly, championed laissez faire, and echoed many of the views of liberal economists. "Self-interest," he declared, "is the only motive force in the heart of man and, well managed, it can furnish infinite advantages." Elsewhere, he assured his readers that he would "never tire of repeating to you that competition is the judge which is able to regulate the true price of things." In an essay on commerce (1810) he enumerated "nine principles which the English, that is to say, the wisest people in matters of trade, propound in their books in order to judge the utility or the disadvantage of commercial undertakings." Unfortunately for Belgrano's reputation as a student of English economics most of the "principles" may be traced not to Smith but to seventeenth-century mercantilists.[59]

The *Wealth of Nations* was one of several European works which influenced Chilean economic thought in the early years of the nineteenth century. Manuel de Salas, Juan Egaña, and Camilo Henríquez, the founders of the Instituto Nacional (1813), recommended the works of Genovesi, Say, and Smith for the Institute's course in political economy.[60] Salas, the energetic syndic of the Santiago Consulado, wrote voluminously on questions of agricultural and commercial policy. He cited Hume; but, if he knew Smith's work, he never found it worth mentioning. For Salas, the ideas of the Spanish reformers Campillo and Ward seemed adaptable to Chilean conditions.[61] Egaña owned copies of Say's *Tratado*; but the only writing in which he may have expressed an opinion of Say (and Smith) has not survived.[62] Although Henríquez, the founder of two periodicals, *La Aurora* (1812) and the *Mercurio de Chile* (1822) learned English for the sake of reading the works of English economists, his writings make no direct reference to Smith.[63]

An anonymous "Economist," writing to the editors of the Santiago *El Telégrafo* (May 25, 1819), quoted Say and Smith in defense of the right to export coin and specie freely. "The silver and gold . . . produced in Chile," he asserted, "should be regarded in the same light as copper, wheat, wool, or any other product." Export duties on precious metals should be so moderate that it would not be worth the risk of confiscation to engage in contraband trade. Adam Smith, he said, "explains this doctrine very well."[64]

José Joaquín Mora, a Spaniard who had lived several years in London, came to Chile in the 1820's. After establishing the Liceo de Chile, which included political economy in its curriculum, Mora launched *El Mercurio chileno* to popularize his political and economic beliefs. In the issue of May 1, 1828, he explained Smith's canons of taxation, supplementing them by four "precepts no less just" which he took from Say. In an article on banks and money he attacked the "principal dogma" of the mercantilists that "true wealth consists only in the abundance of precious metals." He extolled agriculture and noted that "Adam Smith, whose opinions can be contradicted or modified, but who is rarely mistaken in matters of fact, calculates the value of the land rent as the fourth part at least of the product of the labor employed in its cultivation." This represented a better return than was possible from the use of labor in manufacturing. Furthermore, as Smith pointed out, "the merchant and the manufacturer . . . are citizens of no country" and, hence, less desirable than agriculturists. In later articles Mora's paper referred to Smith as the "father of political economy" and asserted that the Scotch economist had demonstrated that the only way to eradicate smuggling was to lower tariffs. Smith, Mora wrote, first explained the advantages of the division of labor; but Say "expresses the same idea in a still more convincing manner." Quoting the "most respectable of the authorities in political economy who can be cited," Mora called attention to Smith's observation that complaints of the dearth of money are universal; like wine, money necessarily appears scarce to those who lack the wherewithal to buy it.[65]

Debates over economic measures in the early legislatures of Chile frequently elicited references to Smith, usually as one of several European economists whose views threw light on the matters under consideration.[66] There was, apparently, no continuing influence of this early acceptance of the doctrines of Smith and other classical economists. Chile, however, experienced a rebirth of academic and official interest in economic liberalism in the 1850's, when the government employed the French economist Jean Courcelle-Seneuil to serve as a professor of economics and an advisor on economic policy.[67]

The *Wealth of Nations* is included in a list of "recognized works of political economy" recommended for the library of the Consulado of Veracruz (1802), but it is not clear that the merchant guild ever acquired the books.[68] In the Mexican Congress of 1823 Manuel Ortiz de la Torre presented an unusually vigorous and enlightened discourse on commercial policy. Quoting the Spanish edition of the *Wealth of Nations*, as well as the works of a dozen other European economists, he argued that a new nation could best maintain its independence by trading with all countries on equal terms. After analyzing the harmful effects of a prohibitive tariff, Ortiz concluded that the level of important duties should be adjusted to accomplish two objectives: (1) produce needed revenue, taking into account the yield of other taxes, and (2) equalize the prices of imported and domestic goods. But protective duties should be reduced gradually over a period of years, during which the protected industries would either acquire sufficient skill to compete with foreign producers or give way to domestic industries which could survive without protection.[69] Ortiz had no influence on legislation and, apparently, little influence on the writings of other Mexican economists.[70]

In Guatemala the Economic Society inaugurated a course in political economy in 1812 and selected the outstanding intellectual, José Cecilio del Valle, to teach the subject. In a preliminary statement on the curriculum, Valle said that he accepted Smith's principles but considered the *Wealth of Nations* too difficult for an elementary course. Smith was the "man from whose mind the science [of economics] sprang already formed"; but much of his thought was too abstract for the beginner. Say, he felt, was "capable of greater perfection in style and thinking" than Smith.[71] In 1814 Father Francisco Garcia Pelaez prepared a syllabus of "Notes on Civil Economy Taken from Adam Smith" for the first course in political economy offered in the Guatemalan University of San Carlos. The surviving records indicate that after one or two meetings Father Garcia abandoned the course for lack of students.[72]

Francisco de Arango y Parreño, an official of the Havana city council, drew upon the "opinion of the profound and wise Smith" in preparing essays on agricultural improvement (1792 and 1808). Arango thought that Smith "had given the mortal blow to the mercantilist system," though other exceptions than navigation acts, which Smith had praised, should be admitted to the rule of laissez faire.[73] In 1818 the Economic Society of Havana founded a chair of political economy in the Seminario de San Carlos. Justo Velez, the first professor, used his own translation of Say's *Traité* as a text but lectured on both Smith and Say.[74]

VI

In Spain and Spanish America the main currents of economic thought were enriched by borrowing from streams that flowed, not always uninterrupted, across the boundaries of language and intolerance. If, perchance, the present essay has identified the principal channels through which the ideas of Adam Smith moved, many rivulets remain for others to explore. A search of unpublished lectures and university curriculums, for instance, might reveal a wider diffusion of the *Wealth of Nations* than may be surmised from the published works of Foronda, Ortiz, Jovellanos, Dou, and Flórez Estrada. It is improbable, though, that Spain ever experienced an academic interest in Smith comparable to the movement which made the Scotsman so well known in German universities.[75] Works on political and legal questions, especially in the period which brought forth the first Latin-American constitutions, may yield further evidence of familiarity with, if not respect for, the tenets of classical economics.[76] Not only Smith but Say, Ricardo, Malthus, and other liberal economists had their translators and followers among Spanish-speaking people. If their number was not legion, nor their influence far-reaching, explanations may be sought in the pages of social and political history, in the New World as in the Old.

Notes

1.   *L'Espagne éclairée de la seconde moitié du xviii⁰ siècle* (Paris, 1954).

2.   Earl J. Hamilton, "The Mercantilism of Gerónimo de Uztáriz," in *Economics, Sociology and the Modern World* (Cambridge, Mass., 1935), pp. 111-29. The English translation of Uztáriz (*Theory and Practice of Commerce and Maritime Affairs*, trans. John Kippax [London, 1751]) was, apparently, the only work of a Spanish economist found in Adam Smith's library (James Bonar, *A Catalogue of the Library of Adam Smith* [London, 1894], p. 116). Smith cited Uztáriz in the *Wealth of Nations*, Book V, chap. 2, Part II, Art. IV.

3.   Joseph Addison, *Reflexiones sobre las ventajas que resultan del comercio al estado*, trans. Cristóbal Cladera (Madrid, 1785); Girolamo Belloni, *Disertación sobre la naturaleza y utilidades del comercio*, trans. José Labrada (Santiago, 1788); Jakob Friedrich Bielfeld, *Instituciones políticas: Obra en que se trata de los reynos de Portugal y España*, trans. Valentín de Foronda (Bordeaux, 1781), and *Instituciones políticas: Obra en que se trata de la sociedad civil, de las leyes, de la policía, de la real hacienda, del comercio y fuerzas de un estado*, trans. Domingo de la torre y Mollinedo (6 vols.: Madrid, 1761-1801); Étienne Bonot de Condillac, "Tratado sobre el comercio y el govierno, considerados con relación recíproca," in *Memorias instructivas y curiosas sobre agricultura, comercio, industria, economía, chymica, botánica, historia natural*, &. (12 vols.; Madrid, 1778-91), III, 219-386, and IV, 3-116; Charles Davenant, "Del uso de la aritmética política en el comercio y rentas," in Nicolás Arriquivar, *Recreación política* (2 vols.; Vitoria, 1779), I, 1-24; Cayetano Filangieri, *Reflexiones sobre la libertad del comercio de frutos* (Madrid, 1784) and *Ciencia de la legislación* (5 vols.; Madrid, 1787-89); Fernando Galiani, *Diálogos sobre el comercio de trigo* (Madrid, 1775); Antonio Genovesi, *Lecciones de comercio o bien de economía civil*, trans. Victorián de Villalva (3 vols.; Madrid, 1785-86); Claude Jacques Herbert, *Ensayo sobre la policía general de los granos, sobre sus precios y sobre los efectos de la agricultura*, trans. Tomás Anzano (Madrid, 1795); David Hume, *Discursos políticos* (Madrid, 1789); Jacques Necker, *Memoria reservada sobre el establecimiento de rentas provinciales*, trans. Domingo de la Torre y Mollinedo (Madrid, 1786), and "Sobre la legislación y comercio de granos," in *Memorias instructivas y curiosas . . .*, VIII, 3-237; François Quesnay, *Máximas générales del gobierno económico de un reino agricultor* (Madrid, 1794); A.R.J. Turgot, "Reflexiones sobre la formación y distribución de las riquezas," in *Memorias instructivas y curiosas . . .*, XII, 3-100. The translations of Condorcet and Smith are noted below.

4.   Juan Bautista Say, *Tratado de economia política o exposición simple del modo como se formen, distribuyen y consumen las riquezas* (3 vols.; Madrid, 1804). There were at least seven other editions of the *Tratado* (1807, 1814, 1816, 1817, 1821, 1836, 1838), three editions of the *Cartilla de economía política* (1816, 1818, 1822), two editions of the *Catecismo de economía política* (1822, 1823), two editions of *Cartas a Mr. Malthus* (1820, 1827), and an *Epítome de los principios fundamentales de economía política* (1816).

5.   Melchior Palyi, "The Introduction of Adam Smith on the Continent," in *Adam Smith, 1776-1926* (Chicago, 1928), p. 191.

6.   Paulino González Alberdi, *Los Economistas Adam Smith y David Ricardo* (Buenos Aires, 1947), pp. 42-43.

7.   Manuel Colmeiro, *Biblioteca de los economistas españoles de los siglos xvi, xvii y xviii*

(Madrid, 1880), p. 78.

8. Bernando Joaquin Danvila y Villarrasa, *Lecciones de economia civil* (Madrid, 1779). The book, written for use in the Royal Seminary for Nobles, was reprinted (Saragossa, 1800), with the author's last name changed to Villagrasa.

9. Jaime Carrera Pujal, *Historia de la economia española*, IV (Barcelona, 1945), 343. Carrera Pujal takes Alcalá Galiano to task for his "great attachment to direct taxes, when the idiosyncracy of the country required preferably indirect taxes, since the former were more easily mocked by false declarations than were the latter by fraud." In his early addresses, published in the *Actas y memorias de la Real Sociedad Económica de los Amigos del País de la Provincia de Segovia*, Vol. I (Segovia, 1785), Alcalá Galiano showed no Smithian influence. I have not located the fourth volume of the *Actas*, containing the piece to which Carrera Pujal refers.

10. Sarrailh (*op. cit.*, pp. 274-77, 591-92) details the controversy between Normante and his clerical opponents. The "scandal" is referred to in Marcelino Menendez y Pelayo, *Historia de los heterodoxos españoles*, Vol. VI (Madrid, 1930 ed.), 272-73, and in Clemente Herranz y Lain, *Estudio crítico sobre los economistas aragoneses* (Saragossa, 1885), pp. 58-60. Apparently, influential friends at court saved Normante from official censure. One of his attackers, Father Gerónimo José de Cabra, declared that Normante's errors included the assertion that the study of the causes of human happiness represented "the most sublime use of one's reason and intelligence"; the belief that "free trade in grain is useful in Spain"; the condemnation of "some laws and observances of ecclesiastical bodies and establishments" which checked the increase of population; the argument that "sales taxes are inimical to the development of industry"; the view that sumptuary laws are "contrary to the true spirit of economics"; and the insistence that restrictions on interest-bearing mercantile loans keep money out of circulation (*Pruebas del espiritu del Sr. Melon y de las proposiciones de economia civil y comercio* 2 parts: Madrid, 1787).

11. *Cartas sobre los asuntos más exquisitos de la economia politica y sobre las leyes criminales* (2 vols.; Madrid, 1789-94). The letters were first published in the *Espiritu de los mejores diarios literarios que se publican en Europa* (Madrid), from November 10, 1788, to November 23, 1789. An earlier work, *Miscelánea o colección de varios discursos* (Madrid, 1787), contains speeches on agriculture, banking, and trade delivered before the Basque Economic Society.

12. Julio Somoza de Montsoriu, *Inventario de un jovellanista* (Madrid, 1901), pp. 81, 125.

13. *Obras de D. Gaspar Melchor Jovellanos: Diarios (Memorias intimas), 1790-1801* (Madrid, 1915), p. 304. On May 10, 1795, Jovellanos saw the "entire translations of Smith" at the home of Vicente Salamanca but failed to say whether it was the Spanish translation published in 1794. In November, 1795, he loaned the *Wealth of Nations* to his friend, José Pedrayes, a mathematician; the following May he referred to the "original English, which I gave to Pedrayes" (*ibid.*, pp. 222, 277, 304).

14. *Ibid.*, pp. 304-323. But "things repeated sevenfold will be pleasing" (*septis repetita placebunt*), Jovellanos concluded.

15. "Informe del Real Acuerdo de Sevilla al Consejo Real de Castilla sobre la extracción de aceite a reinos extrangeros," in *Biblioteca de autores españoles* (Madrid, 1859), L, 1-6.

16. "Informe de la Junta de Comercio y Moneda sobre formento de la marina mercante," *ibid.*, pp. 20-28.

17. "Informe dado a la Junta General de Comercio y Moneda sobre el libre ejercicio de las artes," *ibid.*, pp. 33-45.

18. *Informe de la Sociedad Económica de esta Corte al Real y Supremo Consejo de Castilla en el expediente de ley agraria* (Madrid, 1795).

19. Conde de Campomanes, *Tradado de la regalia de amortización* (Madrid, 1765).

20. Edith F. Helman, "Some Consequences of the Publication of the *Informe de ley agraria* by Jovellanos," *Estudios hispánicos: Homenaje a Archer M. Huntington* (Wellesley, Mass., 1952), pp. 253-73.

21. The *Index librorum prohibitorum Sanctissimi Domini nostri Pii IX. Pont. Max. iussu editus* (Rome, 1877) continued the ban of the *Informe*, first decreed in 1825.

22. *Compendio de la obra inglesa intitulada Riqueza de las naciones, hecho por el marqués de Condorcet* (Madrid, 1792). There were two other editions: Madrid, 1803, and Palma, 1814.

23. León Carbonero y Sol, *Indice de los libros prohibidos por el Santo Oficio de la Inquisición Española* (Madrid, 1873), p. 607. In a letter dated Munich, December 4, 1792, Sir

John Macpherson wrote Edward Gibbon that the Spanish govenment had "permitted an extract of the Wealth of Nations to be published, though the original is condemned by the Inquisition." Macpherson, referring to sentences of the Inquisition "pasted upon the church doors," says that Smith's work was banned because of the "lowness of its style and the looseness of the morals which it inculcates" (*The Miscellaneous Works of Edward Gibbon Esq.* [London, 1814], II, 479). Fernando de los Rios believed that the proscription, far from hampering "its spread inside and outside of the universities," was "an incentive to its diffusion" (*Encyclopaedia of the Social Sciences* [New York, 1930], I, 296).

24. "Royal censors of the press," declared the "Prince of the Peace," "were ordered gradually to slacken the reins, and to allow great latitude to literature; always providing, that religion and the principles of monarchy were respected. The same indulgence was extended to foreign books and journals, so that they did not openly preach atheism or anarchy, and were calculated to promote the progress of science or of art" (J.B. D'Esmenard [ed.], *Memoirs of Don Manuel de Godoy, Prince of the Peace* [2 vols.; London, 1836], II, 176).

25. "Recherches sur la nature et les causes de la richesse de nations," in *Bibliothèque de l'homme public*, III (Paris, 1790), 108-216, and IV (1790), 3-115. The article is not signed, but Condorcet, one of the founders of the *Bibliothèque*, was undoubtedly the author. Doctor Robinet (*Condorcet, sa vie, son œuvre, 1743-1794* [Paris, n.d.], pp. 98-99) claims that Condorcet also wrote a volume of "notes on political economy" for the Roucher translation of the *Wealth of Nations* (*Recherches sur la nature et les causes de la richesse des nations, traduites de l'anglais de M. Smith, sur la quatrième edition, par M. Roucher, et suivies d'un volume de notes par M. le marquis de Condorcet* [4 vols.; Paris, 1790-91]). There were several editions of the Roucher translation, but I have seen none which contains Condorcet's notes. A French review of the first edition was printed in translation in the *Espiritu de os mejores diarios literarios*, X (1790), 282-85.

26. As follows: "The establishments concerned with the instruction of people of all ages are principally those which have for their object religious instruction. Those who give this instruction are maintained, as are teachers of any other kind, either by the voluntary contributions of their hearers or by funds to which they are entitled under the laws of the land; and they ordinarily manifest more zeal and industry when they live solely on the liberality and charity of their hearers.

"There is probably not a single Protestant church in which the zeal and industry of the clergy is as active and fervent as in the Roman Church. The clergy of its parishes obtain the greatest part of their support from alms and voluntary oblations of the people; and the parochial clergy, like those teachers whose compensation in part depends on a fixed fund and in part upon the contributions of their students, consequently depend for their well-being on their reputations and good conduct."

27. *Memoirs of Don Manuel de Godoy*, II, 169.

28. Archivo Histórico Nacional, Madrid, *Papeles de Inquisición*, No. 1327. Excerpts from this document were kindly furnished me by Don Miguel Bordonau y Mas.

29. *Investigación de la naturaleza y causas de la riqueza de las naciones* (4 vols.; Valladolid, 1794). Ortiz, apparently, was responsible for the second "greatly corrected and improved" edition (4 vols.; Valladolid, 1805-6). Published in a smaller format (but with 15 per cent more pages), the second edition represents a comparatively minor revision of style and terminology. The most notable omission is the flowery dedication to Manuel de Godoy, who was no longer influential at court. Ortiz also dropped his own apprndix (Book IV, chap. 3) on the Bank of Spain.

30. *Investigación e la naturaleza y causes de la riqueza de las naciones* (2 vols.; Barcelona, 1933-34). There were several printings, some in three volumes.

31. *Investigación de la naturaleza y causas de la riqueza de las naciones* (Madrid, 1956).

32. C.J. Bullock, *The Vanderblue Memorial Collection of Smithiana* (Boston, 1939), p. 4.

33. The further mutilation of the text in this section includes the suppression of such phrases as: "As through the greater part of Europe, the church"; "The parson of a parish"; and "The tythe in the greater part of those parishes."

34. Menéndez y Palayo was particularly harsh on eighteenth-century economists who found something of value in the work of Smith and the Physiocrats. Smith's so-called science of wealth, "developed in an incredulous and sensual century, came forth contaminated with a utilitarian and basely practical spirit, as though it aspired to be an independent science and not a branch and end of morality. In the Latin nations, furthermore, it was from the very beginning a powerful aid to revolution and a formidable battering ram against the property of the Church" (*Historia de los heterdoxos españoles*, VI, 22.)

35. Earl J. Hamilton, *American Treasure and the Price Revolution in Spain, 1501-1650* (Cambridge, Mass., 1934), pp. 11-45.

36. Earl J. Hamilton, "The Foundation of the Bank of Spain," *Journal of Political Economy*, LIII (1945), 97-114.

37. *Ensayo económico sobre el sistema de la moneda papel, y sobre el crédito público* (Madrid, 1796).

38. Ortiz practically rewrote Smith's paragraph on this point, cutting out altogether the phrases, "In England, and in all Roman Catholic countries" and "The example of the churches of Scotland, of Geneva, and of several other protestant countries."

39. In the first edition Ortiz deleted without comment the paragraph in which Smith discussed the bad effects of assigning tutors to students, instead of allowing them to choose their tutors. The passage was restored in the second edition.

40. *Instituciones del derecho público general de España* (9 vols.; Madrid, 1800-1803), V, 247.

41. Now Cerbère, France, but no longer a university town.

42. *La Riqueza de las naciones, nuevamente explicada con la doctrina de su mismo investigador* (2 vols.; Cervera, 1817). Dou refers to the 1805-6 edition of Ortiz's work as though it were the first translation of Smith.

43. *Informe*, p. 74.

44. *Conciliación económica y legal de pareceres opuestos en cuanto a laudemios y derechos enfitéuticos* (Cervera, 1829); *Pronta y fácil egecución del proyecto sobre laudemios, fundada principalmente en una autoridad del Dr. Adam Smith* (Cervera, 1831).

45. *La Economia reducida a principios exactos, claros y sencillos* (Madrid, 1797). Four years before the publication of Say's *Tratado*, Johann Herrenschwand's *Principios de economia politica*, translated by the probably pseudonymous Juan Smith (Madrid, 1800), gave Spaniards another smattering of Smithian economics.

46. *Diario de las sesiones de Cortes: Legislatura de 1820* (3 vols.; Madrid, 1870-73), Vols. II (1664) and III (1705, 1737-38, and 1877). The tariff acts of 1820 occasioned Jeremy Bentham's *Observations on the Restrictive and Prohibitory Commercial System: Especially with a Reference to the Decree of the Spanish Cortes of July 1820* (London, 1821).

47. *Diario de las sesiones de cortes*, I, 110.

48. *Diccionario de hacienda para el uso de los encargados de la suprema dirección de ella* (5 vols.; London, 1826-27), I, 263; II, 146, 374; V, 97-98, 109. There was another edition of the *Diccionario*: Madrid, 1833-34 and 1840 (*Suplemento*). Earlier, Canga Argüelles published the *Elementos de la ciencia de hacienda* (London, 1826; Madrid, 1833).

49. G. Bernacer, "Alvaro Flórez Estrada," *Encyclopaedia of the Social Sciences* (New York, 1931), VI, 285.

50. The second edition of the *Curso* was published in Paris (2 vols., 1831), as was the French translation (*Cours éclectique d'économie politique* [1833]). There were Spanish editions, published in Spain in 1833, 1835, 1840, 1848, and 1852. Blanqui considered Flórez' work "one of the most notable treatises which have been published since that of J.B. Say . . . methodical like Say, social like Sismondi, algebraic like Ricardo, experimental like Adam Smith, it differs in many respects from all these great masters and shares in its good qualities without falling into all their defects" (Adolphe Blanqui, *Histoire de l'économie politique en Europe* [Paris, 1837], pp. 299-300).

51. Marqués de Valle Santoro, *Elementos de economia politica con aplicación particular a España* (Madrid, 1829). There was a second edition (Madrid, 1833). Valle Santoro also wrote a *Memoria sobre la balanza del comercio y examen del estado actual de la riqueza en España* (Madrid, 1830).

52. *Reglamento y aranceles reales para el comercio libre de España a Indias de 12 de octubre de 1778* (Madrid, n.d.).

53. See above, n. 6.

54. *Semanario de agricultura, industria y comercio: Reimpresión facsimile publicada por la Junta de Historia y Numismática* (5 vols.; Buenos Aires, 1928-37). The original paper commenced publication on September 1, 1802, and suspended on February 11, 1807.

55. Félix Weinberg, "Estudio preliminar," in *Antecedentes económicos de la Revolución de Mayo* (Buenos Aires, 1956), pp. 18-19.

56. Twelve issues of the *Semanario* (February-July, 1805), about forty pages in all, were

devoted to extracting Crumpe's *An Essay on the Best Means of Providing Employment for the People* (London, 1793). This essay, awarded a prize by the Royal Irish Academy, appeared in a second edition (London, 1795) and was translated into French and German.

57.   Luis Roque Gondra, *Las ideas económicas de Manuel Belgrano* (Buenos Aires, 1923), pp. 71-74.

58.   The *Principios de la ciencia económico-política, traducidos del francés por D. Manuel Belgrano* (Buenos Aires, 1796) is based on and in part taken directly from the writings of Dupont de Nemours and Karl Friedrich of Baden.

59.   Thus: "The importation of foreign goods of pure luxury in exchange for money, when money is not a product of the [importing] country . . . is a real loss to the state" (Manuel Belgrano, *Escritos económicos* [Buenos Aires, 1954], p. 201). See also L.R. Gondra, "Argentina," in *El pensamiento económico latinoamericano* (Mexico, 1953), pp. 9-19.

60.   Domingo Amunátegui Solar, *Los Primeros años del Instituto Nacional* (Santiago, 1889), pp. 160-61.

61.   Miguel Cruchaga, *Estudio sobre la organización económica y la hacienda pública de Chile* (Madrid, 1929 ed.), I, 155.

62.   "Tratado de economia política: encargado a mi hijo don Joaquin." Another son, Mariano Egaña, was Chilean minister to Great Britain in the 1820's. While in Europe he collected a library of over four thousand volumes, one of the largest private collections in Latin America. Letters to his father indicate that he bought Smith's *Theory of Moral Sentiments* as well as the works of Malthus, Lauderdale, Hume, and Steuart (*Cartas de don Mariano Egaña a su padre, 1824-29* [Santiago, 1948], pp. 207-8).

63.   Miguel Luis Amunátegui, *Camilo Henríquez* (Santiago, 1889), I, 59; II, 238.

64.   Another Santiago paper, *La Clave* (November 2 and 12, 1827), published an article on tariffs copied from the Buenos Aires *La Crónica*, in which José Mora quoted the *Wealth of Nations* to show how duties tended to foster monopoly.

65.   *El Mercurio chileno*, No. 2 (May, 1828), pp. 53-55; No. 4 (July, 1828), pp. 149-52; No. 5 (August, 1828), pp. 203-7; No. 6 (September, 1828), pp. 245-60.

66.   *Sesiones de los cuerpos legislativos de la República de Chile, 1811-1845* (Santiago, 1889, VI, 134-6; VII, 196-98.

67.   I owe practically all this material on Chile to the kindness of Robert M. Will, who put at my disposal many of the notes he made in preparation of a doctoral dissertation (Duke University, 1957) on the development of Chilean economic thought.

68.   I.A. Leonard and R.S. Smith, "A Proposed Library for the Merchant Guild of Veracruz," *Hispanic American Historical Review*, XXIV (1944), 84-102.

69.   *Discurso de un diputado sobre la introduccion de efectos extrangeros* (Mexico City, 1823), reproduced in *El Trimestre económico* (Mexico City, 1945), XII, 283-315. Ortiz, a deputy from Baja California and a signer of the constitution of 1824, also wrote a *Discurso sobre los medios de formentar la población riqueza e ilustración de los Estados-Unidos Mexicanos* (Mexico, *ca.* 1825).

70.   Jesús Silva Herzog (*El Pensamiento económico en México* [Mexico City, 1947], pp. 34-39) discusses Tadeo Ortiz, who wrote a tract on economic liberalism in 1832; but Ortiz de la Torre escaped his attention.

71.   José del Valle y Jorge del Valle Matheu, *Obras de José Cecilio del Valle* (Guatemala, 1829), II, 25, 55, 269-70.

72.   Archivo General del Gobierno, Guatemala, Al. 3, leg. 1905, exp. 12,609: "Fundación de la primera cátedra de economia política." I owe this note to the kindness of Professor John Tate Lanning.

73.   *De la factoria a la colonia: Cuadernos de cultura* (2d ser., No. 5 [La Habana, 1936]). See also H.E. Friedlaender, *Historia económica de Cuba* (La Habana, 1944), pp. 139-41.

74.   Gerardo Portela, "Cuba," in *El Pensamiento económico latinoamericano*, pp. 125-27.

75.   Carl William Hasek, *The Introduction of Adam Smith's Doctrines into Germany* (New York, 1925), pp. 60-94.

76.   Antonio Nariño, one of the heroes of Colombian independence, mentioned the "famous Smith" and the *Wealth of Nations* in a speech to the electoral college in June, 1813 (Thomas Blossom, "Antonio Nariño, Precursor of Colombian Independence" [Ph.D. thesis, Duke University, 1956], p. 193).

60

Welfare Indices in *The Wealth of Nations*

M. Blaug

Source: *Southern Economic Journal*, Vol. 26 (2), October 1959, pp. 150-3.

I

Adam Smith, an old legend has it, tried to formulate a labor theory of value but got horribly confused between the purchasing power of a commodity over labor and the amount of labor embodied in its production. The origins of this legend are to be found in Ricardo's *Principles* but the authorized version is by Marx.[1] As a result, generations of critics have dealt unkindly with Smith as a theorist who identified such totally different things as the labor-price and the labor-cost of a product.

An unprejudiced reading of *The Wealth of Nations* destroys the legend. Adam Smith was well aware of the distinction between the measure and cause of value. He was little concerned with the latter. The traditional problem of value theory – why are relative prices what they are at any moment of time? – received only summary treatment. Rather he was interested in finding some invariant measure of real income. To be sure, the order of topics in *The Wealth of Nations* invited misunderstanding of his purpose. Book I, chapter 4, "The Origin and Use of Money," closes with a promise to analyze the determination of "relative or exchangeable value of goods." But the next chapter, "The Real and Nominal Prices of Commodities," attempts instead to define an inter-temporal standard to evaluate changes in money prices. The determination of relative prices is not discussed until chapters 6 and 7 where Smith rejects the notion that capital can be reduced to labor expended in the past, ending up with a simple money-cost of production theory. But this conclusion does not affect the labor-yardstick advanced in chapter 5. All this would have stood out much better if chapter 5 had followed, not preceded, chapter 6 and 7.

Most of the difficulties created by the Marxian interpretation of Adam Smith have been cleared up by modern commentators. Smith's discussion of "the measuring rod of labour" is now properly regarded as a stab at subjective welfare economies, involving an effort to surmount the index-numbers problem. Few critics, however, have gone beyond generalities in discussing Smith's standard of welfare. Myint's stimulating analysis is a notable exception.[2] But Myint's analysis is not always free from ambiguity. Other readers may have been left wondering, as I was, exactly why Ricardo or anyone else should have objected to Smith's yardstick. It is to this question that the following note is devoted.

II

Smith employs a labor-standard in two distinct senses: as an index of the rate of capital accumulation and as an index of the magnitude of subjective income. The spearhead of his argument is to show that in a developing economy the two indices come to the same thing. And so they should not upon Smith's assumptions.

The first idea is, relatively speaking, plain sailing. The notion is that capital accumulation involves a definite trend in the money value of the national product expressed in wage units (the going money wage rate of unskilled labor). In Book II, chapter 3 of *The Wealth of Nations* "productive labour" is defined as activity producing storable items of wealth, particularly wage-goods, which can put "more labour in motion" in the next cycle of production. That is to say, measuring all value in current wage units, productive labor produces physical output whose value exceeds the value of labor embodied in it.[3] This is, of course, nothing but a cumbrous way of stating that such labor normally produces a value-surplus above its cost of maintenance and replacement.[4] Now, if "net revenue" is always promptly reinvested and if the supply of labor is perfectly elastic, an upward trend in the number of wage units commanded by total output is guaranteed (p. 54).[5] Capital and labor are combined in fixed proportions (p. 421). Hence, the volume of employment will increase *pari passu* with the increase of capital. With real wages constant, the growth of output must result in a positive trend of the labor-index.

A growing labor force, Smith was wont to say, is a "decisive mark" of increasing real income (p. 70). But, on the other hand, so is a "liberal reward of labour" (p. 73). The latter, however, creates a dilemma: when real wages are rising, a positive rate of investment does not necessarily imply an increase in the purchasing power of total output over wage units. Indeed, if real wages rise as fast as the average productivity of labor, the labor-standard will show no change through time. We return to this difficulty in a moment.

Consider now the second proposition, the index of subjective income. In the chapter on "Real and Nominal Prices" Smith takes a leaf from the pages of Locke's *Second Treatise on Civil Government*, by posing the question of how to measure real income in the context of a "rude and original state of society." For all practical purposes, this is a single-factor world in which the personal labor embodied in products coincides with the labor these products can purchase. A man is "rich or poor" according to the value of his own labor services or his purchasing power over other men's labor, for the two are identical. With the rise of property income this coincidence is broken. Now real income varies solely with the ability to command other men's *products*. But as labor is irksome, everyone strives to save himself "toil and trouble" and to impose it upon others (p. 30). In one sense, what is purchased with products is still the "toil and trouble" of others. And so, an increase of real income means not merely more purchasing power over goods, but more purchasing power over labor. What is true of individual income is true of aggregate income: the wealth (read: income) of a nation is measured by the number of wage units commanded by the whole product.

This seems to be the gist of Smith's reasoning. Capital accumulation by producing a positive change in the labor-index, means an increase in subjective welfare. A standard of measurement, however, must itself be invariable to accurately reflect changes in the things being measured. On the face of it, the wage unit fails to meet this condition: it varies with every change in the price of wage-goods and in the demand and supply of labor. But supposing for the moment that money and real wages do remain the same. In what sense would this provide an invariant standard of subjective welfare? Clearly, in the sense that we could then assume that the average disutility of labor per unit of effort is the same for all individuals at all times: "Equal quantities of labour, at all times and places, may be said to be of equal [esteem] value to the labourer" (p. 33).[6]

This is surely a heroic assumption. A constant outlay of subjective sacrifice per man hour implies unit elasticity of supply of effort, or unit elasticity of demand for income in terms of effort. This is a poor assumption for an analysis concerned with welfare apraisals in the long run: a falling effort-price of income in a growing economy is itself a major element in the improvement of welfare.

Fortunately, the validity of this assumption can be tested by its consequences. The effort-price of income must be expressed in terms of an operational standard of measurement. The first difficulty is that of selecting a representative money wage unit. In the chapter on relative wages (Book I, chapter 10) Smith had shown that, despite differences in the hourly wage rates of different occupations, perfect competition does tend to equalize monetary returns to units of disutility of labor; the market does reduce the various types of labor to a common standard. Therefore, in principle, a representative money wage unit can be constructed.[7] The second difficulty is that of selecting a stable value-coefficient to express real wages. Smith argues that for calendar periods of moderate length a nominal wage unit in terms of silver will prove satisfactory owing to the relative stability in the value of silver "from year to year" and even "for a half a century or a century together" (p. 35). However, for longer periods a corn-wage would be more suitable: the price of corn fluctuates sharply in the short run and rarely in the same direction, or with the same amplitude, as money wages (pp. 36, 74, 75, 83, 85) but "from century to century" corn prices are remarkably stable" (pp. 36-7, 477, 482). The reason for this is that cost-reducing improvements in agriculture are "more or less counterbalanced" by the rising price of cattle, "the principal instruments of agriculture" (pp. 187, 219-24, 240). And since corn is "the basic subsistence of the people," the money price of corn governs money wages in the long run: "from century to century, corn is a better measure than silver, because from century to century, equal quantities of corn will command the same quality of labour more nearly than equal quantities of silver" (pp. 37, 187, 476).[8] The argument is complete: the wage unit in real terms and in money terms, i.e., the wages of common labor measured in corn, is invariant through time and reflects an invariant disutility of labor.

Smith did not doubt that "at all times and places, that is cheap which costs little labour to acquire." And so, as output per man hour rises, the "real prices" of goods should fall relative to corn, meaning they will command less labor. Likewise, the number of wage units commanded by the total product year after year should tend downward. This is reasonable enough since the labor commanded by commodities is the reciprocal of labor's purchasing power over real income. However, this line of reasoning is in direct contradiction to Smith's positive index of subjective welfare. The contradiction is due to the fact that the positive index assumes constant real wages and constant returns to techno-logical progress. Actually, Smith believed that an increase of population would raise output per man by extending the scope of the division of labor; and this tendency alone implies that every addition to output will command less additional wage units. Or, as Ricardo would say, an increase in welfare may mean an increase in "riches" or a fall in "value." An increase of riches is what we would now call "capital widening," an increase in output without a change in the capital and labor coefficients. Whereas a fall in value denotes a rise in the average productivity of labor, or, in Smith's language, a fall in the amount of labor commanded per unit of output.

Ricardo dismissed riches per se as irrelevant to economic welfare. This is a defensible position. But both Smith and Ricardo do agree essentially in treating "value" as an inverse index of the average productivity of labor and therefore of economic welfare. Ricardo regards welfare as a matter of minimizing human effort per unit of output while Smith regards it as a matter of maximizing labor's *potential* purchasing power over real income. But Smith's standard, just because it is tied more explicitly to subjective income, rests upon a greater number of dubious assumptions. If, for example, real wages vary through time, the entire argument breaks down. Commodities may command less labor simply because money wages have risen or because prices of wage-goods have fallen. The resulting effect upon investment, and hence upon the trend of wage units commanded by total output, will be very different in the two cases. This difficulty disappears only if both real and money wages tend to remain constant in the long run. This is the source of Ricardo's disagreement with Smith. In Ricardo's system, capital accumulation spells a rising price of corn; real wages remain unaltered but money wages rise with corn prices; this is what causes rents to rise and profits to fall.

"Dr. Smith's error throughout his whole work," Ricardo declared, "lies in supposing that the value of corn is constant."[9] It would have been a simple matter to have shown that Smith's belief in the stability of corn prices "from century to century" is irrelevant to the analyses of such policy measures as the Corn Law of 1815 – Ricardo's purpose was, after all less ambitious than Smith's. This Ricardo failed to do. By assuming that Smith was concerned with Ricardian questions, he filled his *Principles* with a series of misguided attacks on Smith's standard.[10] It would take a monograph to unravel Ricardo's criticisms; Malthus's prolix but perverse defense of Smith's measure would provide some entertaining chapters. But we have done with it here.

III

Properly understood, there is nothing wrong with Smith's labor-standard. It is simply that Smith applied it indiscriminately. Actually, as has been pointed out, modern methods of making international comparisons of economic welfare per head are nothing but applications of Smithian welfare economies. For instance, Soviet living standards may be compared with American living standards by asking how many hours of work, rewarded at the going rate, would be required to buy specific articles at current prices in each of the two countries. This procedure assumes, among other things, that the disutility of labor in the U.S.S.R. is the same as in the U.S.A. Or, in real earnings may be compared in terms of a given basket of wage goods valued at constant dollar prices (Colin Clark's International Units), which involves similar assumptions. No one will deny that these methods ought to be supplemented by comparisons of the productivity of labor and of capital – and of personal income distribution, an aspect of welfare which the classical economists completely neglected – before secure pronouncements can be made about economic welfare. As soon as this is understood, the controversy between Ricardo and Smith on the proper "standard of value" takes on the character of so many great battles in intellectual history: a conflict between two poorly expounded half-truths.

Notes

1.   *Works of David Ricardo*, P. Sraffa and M.H. Dobb, eds. (Cambridge, Eng.: Cambridge University Press, 1951), I, p. 14; K. Marx, *Theories of Surplus Value*, translated by G.A. Bonner and E. Burns (London: Lawrence & Wishart, 1951), pp. 108-16. But see the incisive comment by J.S. Mill, *Principles of Political Economy*, W.J. Ashley, ed. (London: Longmans, Green and Co., 1909), p. 568.

2.   See M. Bowley, *Nassau Senior and Classical Economics* (New York: Augustus M. Kelly, 1949) pp. 67-71; J.A. Schumpeter, *History of Economic Analysis* (New York: Oxford University Press, 1954), pp. 180-8; H.M. Robertson and W.L. Taylor, "Adam Smith's Approach to the Theory of Value." *Economic Journal*, June 1957; H. Myint, *Theories of Welfare Economics* (Cambridge, Mass., 1948), chapter 2.

3.   Only physical output is considered because services, being non-durable, are incapable of being accumulated. With the important exception of the transmission of knowledge, this is true enough but what difference it makes is another matter.

4.   A similar argument is used in Book II, chapter 5 to show that equal quantities of capital with equal rates of turnover "put in motion" more labor in agriculture than in manufacturing because in agriculture the value of the product is sufficient to pay rent in addition to wages and profits. This is obviously wrong if rent is an intramarginal return, as Ricardo was quick to see (*Works*, I, pp. 76-9). But elsewhere Ricardo contradicts himself, unwittingly adopting Smith's standpoint (*ibid.*, p. 350, 429).

5.   All subsequent references are to the Cannan edition of *The Wealth of Nations* (New York: Modern Library, 1937).

6.   Once this is granted, it can be said that when labor temporarily receives more wage-goods "it is their [esteem] value which vaies, not that of the labour which purchases them" (p. 33). This remark, which has puzzled so many commentators, is perfectly logical in its context.

7.   One could object here and argue the the relevant question is whether the wage structure is rigid through time.

8.   The whole of the famous "Digression concerning the Variations of the Value of Silver during the Course of the Four last Centuries" is devoted to justifying the notion of the long run constancy of corn-wages. But it is difficult to know whether this is anything but a simplifying

assumption. At one place Smith remarks upon the lack of time series data on money wages in contrast to the regularly recorded series of corn prices. The fact alone, he suggests, forces us to resort to corn prices "not as always exactly in the same proportion as the current prices of labour, but as being the nearest approximation which can commonly be had to that proportion" (p. 38).

9.   *Works of David Ricardo*, I, p. 374.

10.   Ricardo's favorite method is to construct a numerical example to show that Smith's measuring rod cannot distinguish between "a rise in the value of labour" and "a fall in the value of things . . . on which wages are expended." A single illustration will suffice to indicate the character of the critique. (*Ibid.*, pp. 19-20; see also pp. 103-4, 306.) Suppose that labor is paid in corn and consumes ½ bushel of corn per week, trading the rest for other goods. Now corn falls in price. Labor receives more corn but yet can buy less of other goods which have not varied in price (despite changes in relative prices, the composition of the market basket remains the same).

Wages in corn	Corn prices per bu.	Money wages	Expend. on corn	Expend. on other goods
1 bu.	80s.	80s.	40s.	40s.
1¼ bu.	40s.	50s.	20s.	30s.

In this case, Ricardo alleges, Smith would have to say that labor has risen in value because "his standard is corn, and the labourer receives more corn for a week's labour," whereas he should have said that the value of labor had fallen because labor's real wages have decreased. Obviously, the criticism is unfair. Ricardo ignores the fact that Smith's standard is meant to be employed for long run comparisons, and a huge long run at that. Naturally if the price elasticity of demand for corn is zero and the cross-elasticities of demand for all consumption goods are also zero, a fall in corn prices associated with a fall in money wages may leave the laborer worse off. But what of the repercussions of the fall in real wages? Population growth will slacken, Smith might have replied, the demand for corn will fall off, corn prices will rise, followed by money wages, etc.

61

Adam Smith's *Moral Sentiments* as Foundation for his *Wealth of Nations*

A.L. Macfie

Source: *Oxford Economic Papers*, Vol. 11, October, 1959, pp. 209-28.

I

The year 1959 marks the second centenary of Adam Smith's *Theory of Moral Sentiments*. This work, though highly esteemed in his day, has since been eclipsed by its mighty successor, to such an extent that it has tended to be regarded as an early rather academic exercise, in some respects difficult to reconcile with the more experienced work. An anniversary seems a proper time to reconsider the connexion between the two works as indicated by their actual contents.

Today we should expect the link between a book on Ethics and one on Economics to be found in utility. But here this is not so. For in neither book does Utilitarianism or utility play an important part. How far Adam Smith believed in Utilitarianism as an ethical creed is a subject for separate ethical treatment. Enough to show that its influence on the *Moral Sentiments* was sufficiently minor to prove that this theory had to explicit influence on the *Wealth of Nations*, and we can content ourselves with giving some Smithian arguments to show that this was so. This indeed is not surprising when one remembers what slight treatment utility gets in the economic work as a basis of value theory. One of Smith's most inadequately balanced statements is surely the notorious sentence: 'The things that have the greatest value in use have frequently little or no value in exchange; and, on the contrary, those which have the greatest value in exchange have frequently little or no value in use.' The hoary examples are equally tendentious. A damaging neglect of demand theory inevitably resulted.

In the *Moral Sentiments*, however, Smith was obliged to consider Utilitarian ethics, and he does so explicitly in his criticism of Hume's utility theory. That 'ingenious and agreeable philosopher' had held that we approve of an object's utility simply because of the pleasure we know or believe it yields. Utility corresponds to pleasant consequences. Smith comments on this: 'It is not the view of this utility or hurtfulness which is either the first or principal source of our approbation or disapprobation. . . . For first of all, it seems improbable that the approbation of virtue should be a sentiment of the same kind as that by which we approve a convenient or well-contrived building; or that we should have no other reason for praising a man than that for which we commend a chest of drawers.'[1] Then again, 'The sentiment of approbation always involves in it a sense of propriety quite distinct from the sense of utility.' The proper estimate of this 'sense of propriety' he indeed claims as his own invention: 'That this fitness, this happy contrivance of any production of art should often be more valued than the very end for which it is intended; and that the exact adjustment of the means for obtaining any conveniency or pleasure should frequently be more regarded than that very conveniency or pleasure, in the attainment of which their whole merit would seem to subsist, has not, so far as I know, been taken notice of by any body. That this is however very frequently the case, may be observed in a thousand instances, both in the frivolous and in the most important concerns of human life.'[2] He goes on to define his theory more positively by equating the sense of propriety to 'beauty', the beauty of the 'well-contrived machine', such as provides 'a thousand agreeable effects', whereas a rusty, jarring machine would be 'necessarily offensive'. Utility then is no more than a means, or mediate good; and this we can accept as sufficient basis for economic science. We need not therefore describe Adam Smith's positive ethical position. Suffice it to say that in the *Moral Sentiments* the position is eclectic, with a distinct bias towards the modified Stoicism typical of Cicero, and almost conventional in the Enlightenment. His account of the different 'systems of virtue' concludes: 'The only difference between it ("that theory which places virtue in utility") and that which I have been endeavouring to establish is, that it makes utility and not sympathy or the correspondent affection of the spectator the natural and original measure of this proper degree ("of all the affections").'[3] Clearly, Adam Smith was not trying to establish the ethical primacy of utility.

This becomes even more specific in his treatment of the 'pleasures of wealth and greatness', in which the economist might surely expect to find utility recognized as the source of economic endeavour. Yet, in the crucial passage in the *Moral Sentiments*, utility is not mentioned as a motive. What we find is this: 'The pleasures of wealth and greatness . . . strike the imagination as something grand and beautiful and noble, of which the attainment is well worth the toil and anxiety which we are so apt to bestow on them.' This, however, he at once dubs a 'deception', though it remains the force 'which rouses and keeps in continual motion the industry of mankind'. For here we confront the 'capacity of the ("proud and unfeeling landlord's") stomach' which 'bears no proportion to the immensity of his desires'.[1] Hence the rich 'consume little more than the poor, and in spite of their natural selfishness and rapacity . . . they divide with the poor the produce of all their improvements'; 'so they are led by an invisible hand . . . without intending it, without knowing it, to advance the interest of society, and afford means to the multiplication of the species'.[4]

This 'deception' theory, which is here part of the *ethical* theory of the *Moral Sentiments*, is a tricky one. If we look at the 'pleasures of wealth and greatness' alone, in isolation, it then appears that they are vain. They deceive us. Indeed, 'in ease of body and peace of mind, all the different ranks of life are nearly upon a level, and the beggar who suns himself by the side of the highway possesses that security which kings are fighting for'.[4] On this score, taken alone, then, the more satisfying aims for individuals should be 'security, ease of body, peace of mind', as against 'the palaces and economy of the great'. But in fact this is not the whole story. We have also to think of the 'beauty of the arrangement', 'the order, the regularity and harmonious movement of the *system*'. It is here that the 'deception' finds its justification. For in the system, the 'deception' is seen as necessary 'to raise and keep in motion the industry of mankind'. It is the dynamo of progress, necessary if the multiplying people are to be fed. So the 'pleasures of wealth and greatness' are at once not 'the real happiness of life', as contrasted with 'the real satisfaction which these things are capable of affording', and they are also a 'deception', 'contemptible and trifling', if we accept them as in any sense real or final. But we realize their true function if we climb to a higher, almost metaphysical level. For there we see their true usefulness in the purposes of the invisible hand, which in its benevolence 'advances the interests of society'. These 'deceptive pleasures' find their justification or utility in the beauty of the system.[5]

This doctrine of luxury spending has of course an important place in early economic theory, where it supplies much of the force we today ascribe to 'investment'. What is here important is the fact that this theory, and the almost theological view of the invisible hand behind it, are exactly carried over from the *Moral Sentiments* into the *Wealth of Nations*. Certainly, there, as seems proper, the ethical overtones are damped down. The 'deception' becomes 'an end which was no part of his intention. Nor is it always the worse for the society that it was no part of it',[6] in respect of efficiency. The individual motive itself becomes 'the uniform, constant and uninterrupted effort of every man to better his condition'[7] (surely in no sense a 'deception'). So the analysis is now properly pushed no further than the economic level. But the invisible hand here remains to control the individual conflicts and excesses of competition, and to safeguard the public good throughout healthy competition. Such is his faith.

Utility is also considered by Smith in its social reference, as usefulness to the 'great machine'. The inadequacy of this as general social theory will be considered later. Here we may note an explicit statement on the adequacy of utility as a social bond. 'Society', he says, 'may subsist among different men, as among different merchants, from a sense of its utility, without any mutual love or affection.' But it cannot 'subsist among those who are at all times ready to hurt and injure one another'. So prior to utility must come justice. 'Justice . . . is the main pillar that upholds the whole edifice.'[8] For benevolence cannot be forced, whereas utility *depends* on justice being enforced. So utility can never dispense with justice, though the opposite can hold. We see the utility to society of the death penalty for a sleeping sentry – "an unfortunate victim who indeed must, and ought to be devoted to the safety of numbers'.[9] But the final sanction is 'the justice of God'. 'Our sense of the ill-desert [of injustice] pursues it, if I may say so, even beyond the grave, though the example of its punishment there cannot serve to deter the rest of mankind.'[10] What then is the essential social cement? An early description is this: 'Man, it has been said, has a natural love of society . . .: the orderly and flourishing state of society is agreeable to him, and he takes delight in contemplating it.'[11] The specific social bond is here for Smith a felt one. It is sympathy, one of the seminal sources in the *Moral Sentiments*, to which we must next turn.

II

Sympathy is important because an economic theory must be based on some assumptions as to the social bond, and for Smith sympathy was the effective cement of society. The *Moral Sentiments* in fact begins on this note – that sympathy is an emotion. 'Pity and compassion are words appropriated to signify our fellow-feeling with the sorrows of others. Sympathy, though its meaning was perhaps originally the same, may now, however, without much impropriety, be made use of to denote our fellow-feeling with *any passion whatever*.'[12] Sympathy is therefore essentially fellow-feeling, a feeling for others through 'putting ourselves in their situation', a 'very illusion of the imagination'.[12] Smith therefore at once attacks 'those who are fond of deducing all our sentiments from certain requirements of self-love'.[13] For that sympathy is in no way selfish he constantly insists. The clearest argument is perhaps that near the end of the book, where he deals with 'those authors who deduce from self-love the interest which we take in the welfare of society'.[1] Discussing the 'virtue of Cato' and the 'villainy of Cataline', he insists that 'Sympathy cannot in any sense be regarded as a selfish principle.' 'The idea, in short, which those authors were groping about, but which they were never able to unfold distinctly, was that *indirect sympathy* which we feel with the gratitude or resentment of those who received the benefit or suffered the damage resulting from such opposite characters.'[13] Indeed, when I imagine your distress, I do not merely imagine what I should suffer if I were really in your position. 'I consider what I should suffer if I were *really you* . . . My grief is therefore entirely upon your account, and not in the least upon my own.' So he moves to the characteristic conclusion: 'A man may sympathize with a woman in child-bed, though it is impossible that he should conceive himself as suffering her pains in his own proper person.'[14]

Sympathy is then an emotion, and an unselfish emotion. To the modern mind, however, this does not appear sufficient to establish it as the cement of actual societies. Though it might so instinctively bind a flock of sheep, it could hardly create the wealth of concrete social activities and institutions which for us constitute societies. Here, the most reasonable view, on his written word, seems to be that while Smith realized that sympathy was not enough, he was not in fact able to transmute it into a specific theory of social life. He did show that he understood *how* sympathy alone was not enough, for, in effect, though not in consciously offered theory, he did trace how *rational* sympathy (including *proper* self-regard) produced the effective actual institutions of society. But his *explicit* description of society was held in detachment from this inductive line of thought. This explicit view was that common in the eighteenth century, and handed down from the seventeenth (and indeed from the Stoics) that society was a 'great machine', with God as the 'All-wise Architect and Conductor'.[15] This uncriticized dogma successfully prevented him from working out a more adequate explicit theory. On the inductive side, however, especially in the *Wealth of Nations* there is ample detail to show how he might have grown to such a theory in a more favourable climate, if he had worked out his ideas as to how social sympathy actually develops in real societies. The most important of these we must now trace.

First, then, Smith insists that we must *approve* of the 'affection from which the action proceeds' when we sympathize: we must 'regard the person towards whom it is directed, as its proper and suitable object'. Now, 'approval', judgements of what is appropriate, cannot be made by mere emotion. They are bound to be rational.[16] Our sense of propriety reflects Smith's constant emphasis on the 'fitting' as one essential in the good. But the fitting can be described only by reason and in relation to a situation. Smith himself makes this general point. 'Our moral faculties are by no means, as some have pretended, upon a level in this respect with the other faculties and appetites of our nature . . . No other faculty or principle judges of any other.'[17] 'Any' is the vital word. And that this judgement occurs in the form of reason appears in these further quotations. We have already noted how he defines 'virtue'. Here, he describes 'sympathy or the *correspondent* affection of the spectator' as 'the natural and original measure of (the) proper degree of all the affections'[18] in which virtue consists. Here we need merely insist that the idea of the 'spectator' *adds* something – something more than the 'affection' alone. The further essence or facet is in fact judgement, and Smith's constant 'impartial' in his regular phrasing emphasized just this. Without sympathy, reason may be inhuman and powerless. But without the 'impartial spectator', without reasoning judgement, sympathy is dumb. It is therefore unfruitful; it alone could not search out the 'many inventions' of social institutions or of justice or economy.[19] Alone, it could merely feel. The practical act, like the act of artistic creation, is a complex unity. Feeling and thought, like colour and form, are aspects of this unity. To suggest that we can finally separate them, or explain the act by any one alone, is the major (and constant) error that the merely analytic intelligence commits. Smith's freedom from this type of intellectual aridity is possibly his greatest asset. It is the source of his realism – how, we must next consider.[20]

The way in which sympathy acts to create social opportunities, duties, and institutions works through its social reflection in public opinion. Thus, through its reasoning side, it establishes a proper code of social behaviour. Referring to resentment or revenge, Smith says: 'There is no passion, of which the human mind is capable, concerning whose justness we ought to be so doubtful, concerning whose indulgence we ought so carefully to consult our natural sense of propriety, or so diligently to consider what will be the sentiments of the cool and impartial spectator.'[21] Again, 'Magnanimity, or a regard to maintain our own rank and dignity in society, is the only motive which can ennoble the expressions of this disagreeable passion. This motive must characterize our whole style and deportment.'[21]

One passage which expresses this important realization of the formation through social experience of standards and institutions, 'the general laws of morality', appears in the chapter 'Of the Nature of Self-deceit, and the Origin and Use of General Rules' (pt. iii, ch. iv). 'Nature', he says, 'has not abandoned us entirely to the delusions of Self-love. Our continual observations upon the conduct of others, insensibly lead us to form to ourselves certain general rules concerning what is fit and proper either to be done or to be avoided.'[22] In this way social customs influence us through the 'impartial spectator' the 'man within the breast', and the 'self-deceit' which causes 'the partial views of mankind with regard to the propriety of their own conduct' is overcome. On this there follows a passage which surely must have inspired Burns's

> O wad some Pow'r the giftie gie us
> To see oursels as others see us!

(For Burns treasured his copy of the *Moral Sentiments*.) Smith's prosaic version is 'If we saw ourselves in the light in which others see us, or in which they would see us if they knew all, a reformation would generally be unavoidable.' It is submitted these passages prove conclusively that for Smith the approval of what is at least useful, what is appropriate, what probably is good or virtuous, takes place through the faulty and gradual operation of individual consciences guided and formed by social experience and institutions on particular issues. As well as being emotional, as is sympathy, as well as being intuitive, as would be a moral sense, it must be rational, and so guided by rationalized social rules. At least, we listen to public opinion: 'We hear everybody about us express the like detestation against (some actions of others which shock all our natural sentiments).' Of course, a highly important development of these social institutions takes place in economic life; and in dealing with the 'prudent man' of the *Moral Sentiments*, I shall later quote the explicit reference to 'oeconomy' in the earlier book. This is indeed the moral basis on which he founds his economic man theory in the *Wealth of Nations*.

III

The special fact that this essay seeks to establish will now be clear. It is that while sympathy is the essential social sentiment for Smith as for Hume (who coupled it with utility), for Smith sympathy is always *united with reason*, with the operation of the impartial spectator; and that, on a broad estimate, it seems true to say that Smith specially stressed the rational rather than the emotional side. Reason links the emotion with impartiality or conscience. Feeling will not make you 'well-informed' or 'impartial'. Only reason can do that – the practical reason.[23]

Here we meet a modern difficulty in the interpretation of Smith. Today we tend to *analyse* propositions. It was Smith's special genius to hold together different propositions under one formula which he used to explain social life. We, when we see 'sympathy' and 'impartial spectator' linked together, tend to stress the difference between the ideas and their functions. Adam Smith, on the contrary, saw them as two aspects of one practical working function which emerged in practical judgements based on experience. I am not contending that Smith's method is better than analytic procedures, far less that it is faultless. Consistency was not his shining virtue. The contention merely is one of fact – this is what Smith's method was. The rational element in his argument needs special stress, because without it we fail to see the link between our social feelings and the actual growth of judicial and economic systems. When we consider the relevance of the 'prudent' man, who in the *Wealth of Nations* appears as Mill's 'economic man', we shall see that Smith did give the prudent man a *rational* place in his system of the moral sentiments, and we shall realize that only reason could reveal and define this place. If so, it would indeed be in his emphasis on the 'impartial' that Smith's originality in ethics would consist. Hume had worked out the social functions of sympathy, as had other eighteenth-century thinkers. The 'impartial spectator', as Smith used it, is all his own. Smith wishes a more positive role for reason, as the builder of social institutions. If, then, Hume lit the destructive spark which helped to inspire the Kantian reconstruction, Smith may well have contrived in his 'impartial spectator' the revealing light which led to the *Critique of Practical Reason*.[24]

It may be useful here to collect the various ideas which, pieced together, go to show the kind of social theory that Adam Smith might have evolved had the thought and facts of his times been propitious to such a theory. Such a selection introduces the risk of bias; but I think it will be agreed that the theory and politics of the eighteenth century did not permit of an explicit theory of *society* as in some sense a *living human organism*, such as today we require as a minimum. The explicit theories of the seventeenth and eighteenth centuries from Hobbes to Bentham and his school are based on the natural rights of the *individual*; but these theories are political rather than social, legalistic rather than biological or evolutionary. Smith inevitably accepts this background. Explicitly he also repeats the mechanistic social theory of the seventeenth century. This is the view that human society is an 'immense machine'. 'Human society, when we contemplate it in a certain abstract and philosophical light, appears like a great, an immense machine, whose regular and harmonious movements produce a thousand agreeable effects.'[25] This view is linked with his description of God as 'the all-wise Architect', the engineer with his hands on the controls of the 'whole machine of the world', again a seventeenth-century, almost Newtonian picture.

Now, I should not assert that this theological type of theory has no influence on Smith's practical thought about man in society. It has obvious influence through his doctrines of order and harmonious adjustments of individual interests by the 'invisible hand', where necessary. But I should assert that it supplies no more than a very general theological framework, which Smith in no way reconciled with his inductive approach. In contrast, we should recognize Smith's realization that any more or less mechanical view of harmony was simply inadequate to explain the process by which men in society develop their moral rules and economic practices in the actual world. This follows from the famous passage on 'the man of system' who

> is apt to be very wise in his own conceit, and is often so enamoured with the supposed beauty of his own ideal plan of government, that he cannot suffer the smallest deviation from any part of it . . . He seems to imagine that he can arrange the different members of a great society with as much ease as the hand arranges the different pieces upon a chess-board. He does not consider that the pieces upon the chess-board have no other principle of motion besides that which the hand impresses upon them; but that in the great chess-board of human society, every single piece has a principle of motion of its own, altogether different from that which the legislature might choose to impress upon it . . . Some general, and even systematical, idea of the perfection of policy and law may no doubt be necessary for directing the

views of the statesman. But to insist upon establishing, and upon establishing all at once, and in spite of all opposition, everything which that idea may seem to require, must often be the highest degree of arrogance. It is to erect his own judgement into the supreme standard of right and wrong.[26]

Here we have at once the exposure of any claim by any man, or even 'legislature', to assume the functions relevant only to perfect wisdom, and the implied case for individual liberty as against such human tyrannies. It shows proper realization of human imperfection as well as of rich individual differences. It exposes the totalitarian. The system of the Great Artificer may be appropriate to God. It is *hubris* for any human body. The individual is no mere piece of machinery. At the practical level, the method and purpose of individuals living in society cannot be explained by merely mechanical or logical thinking. Yet Smith always looks at society in his inductive thinking from the angle of the individual.

If so, must we then conclude that Adam Smith did not have an adequate social *theory*? So far as this mechanical or theological line goes, I should say he had not. And so far as he followed the political theory of legalistic individual rights, clearly that theory must accept the constructive criticism of more recent times. But I should hold that there is also an *implicit* social theory which develops through his treatment of sympathy and the impartial spectator, and that this in fact is the theory which directs and dominates all Smith's thought. It is not self-conscious; it is not offered or argued as a theory of society. It is rather reflected and inspired by the stream of his inductive thought about the nature of individual life in society. It appears in his views about justice; utility is not enough, as a social framework. Justice 'follows the culprit beyond the grave where utility to society is irrelevant'. More concretely, social conduct and theory must take account of public opinion; they therefore reflect 'the man of real constancy and firmness, the wise and just man who has been thoroughly bred in the great school of self-command, in the bustle and business of the world . . . He has never dared to forget for one moment the judgement which the impartial spectator would pass upon his sentiments and conduct.'[27] Still more concretely, this inductive social theory is implied in the view of the impartial spectator as the growing-point of sympathy in human conduct, the constructive logical force through which human institutions are built. Sympathy is the emotion, reason the operative method of the social act, both expressed through individual persons. Such a view could stand as a fair representative of much modern social theory. And while in Smith's work it is merely the working leaven, as such a leaven it is the vital dynamic of his thought, explicit or no.

IV

Perhaps the acid test of this interpretation is to be found in Smith's theory of the individual. Did it permit of social harmony? Can it show how the individual can be mediated into an adequate social life? If not, the mere success in evolving institutions, customs, and rules will not be enough to justify the claim that it is a true *social* theory. It might merely support a robber society, or a generalized claim to self-interest, linking men through a rather narrow utilitarian social theory. And this, of course, is very usually the conclusion that has been drawn by those considering the economic man of the *Wealth of Nations* alone. It has indeed been argued that the theory of the economic man there is in direct conflict with that of the prudent man in the *Moral Sentiments*.[28] If this is so, then the *Wealth of Nations* has simply cut adrift from the ethical position of the *Moral Sentiments*. I shall argue that there seems to be no evidence for this unlikely view, certainly unlikely in such an integrated character as Smith. It might still, however, be the case that the doctrine of the prudent man in the *Moral Sentiments* does reflect a narrowly utilitarian position. Here again, I shall answer that this is simply not so, because the doctrine of the prudent man is in fact there very carefully fitted into his theory of virtue, which includes his social theory, and which is certainly not a utilitarian theory. It is indeed just in social life and in the creation of good social customs that the individual, even when he does not fully intend this, finds his own 'property' and happiness.

First, then, as to the supposed conflict between the two books. I should agree that there would be conflict if the prudent man and the economic man were understood as merely seeking their own interest, and as against this there were no other theory of reconciliation than a supra-rational 'invisible hand' or 'great machine' – truly a *deus ex machina*. For then, on the rational level, a conflict would be potentially universal. But it has been the argument here that there is such a reconciling theory, one worked out on a purely inductive humane pragmatic level through examining the process by which the laws of justice and the institutions of economic life are developed. Within the treatment of the sympathetic and impartial spectator, Smith's treatment of the prudent man seems a crucial and telling example of the way in which he tried to cope with the main difficulty in all social theories, the obstinate selfishness of the individual. If this is to be done convincingly, one must take the individual in all his narrowness, and show how his limited view of his own interest, and even his freedom to act harmfully, can work to the net benefit of society. This, it is argued, is just what can be done if we follow our texts and accept the view of sympathetic impartiality described.[29] Once again, the evidence has to be pieced together. For, just because his explicit theory of society was inadequate, Smith did not reach a satisfactory theory of the individual in society. But we have a clear argument as to the prudent man's service to society in the *Moral Sentiments*, and also for the economic man in the *Wealth of Nations*.

The argument arises in the *Moral Sentiments* in the interesting *progressive* analysis of 'vanity' and 'pride', of prudence and self-love, and of the self-interest of the *Wealth of Nations*. As to vanity, we should note how fundamental a determinant of human action it seemed to Smith. Two from the many possible quotations must suffice. 'From whence then', he asks, 'arises that emulation which runs through all the different ranks of men, and what are the advantages we propose by the great purpose of human life which we call *bettering our condition*?[30] To be observed, to be attended to, to be taken notice of with sympathy, complacency and approbation, are all the advantages which we can propose to derive from it. It is the vanity, not the ease or the pleasure, which interests us.'[41] Then, there is that shrewd definition of the purpose of education: 'The great secret of education is to direct vanity to proper objects.'[32] From this it might be deduced that vanity is wholly useless, selfish, and frivolous. But this, emphatically, is not Smith's view; he shows very clearly how vanity itself has a social function and regard, being itself derived from sympathy. Men desire 'to stand in that situation which sets them most in the view of general sympathy and attention. And thus, place, that great object which divides the wives of aldermen, is the end of half the labours of human life.'[33] 'Compared with the contempt of mankind, all other external evils are easily supported.'[34] But, further, vanity can and does develop into a relatively *worthy* sentiment when it is allied to the desire for the esteem of others. Vanity so motived Smith considers capable of modified approval, as pride; not in itself– for in itself it is a vice,[35] but because it is capable of development into magnanimity. 'The desire of the esteem and admiration of other people, when for qualities and talents which are the natural and proper objects of esteem and admiration, is the real love of true glory; a passion which, if not the very best passion of human nature, is certainly one of the best. Vanity is very frequently no more than an attempt prematurely to usurp that glory before it is due.'[36] But justified pride and magnanimity are certainly precious social virtues, essential links between the personal and the social advantages. 'That degree of self-estimation, therefore, which contributes most to the happiness and contentment of the person himself, seems likewise most agreeable to the impartial spectator.'[37] The word 'degree' should be noted. For it *is* a question of degree, especially where excess of pride is anti-social. So the psychological basis may be merely individual: 'Every man, as the Stoics used to say, is first and principally recommended to his own care, and every man is certainly, in every respect, fitter and abler to take care of himself than any other person.'[38] But this start is built up into a 'golden mean' theory of that degree of self-interest which also best serves society.

Here then we have the picture of the prudent man, of whom *homo oeconomicus* of the *Wealth of Nations* is just the economic facet. Especially I wish to stress, as showing how the second book is founded on the first, that in his account of the prudent man in the *Moral Sentiments*, Adam Smith quite explicitly underlines his economic side. This occurs in his first treatment (in pt. vi, sect. i). 'In the steadiness of his industry and frugality, in his steadily sacrificing the ease and enjoyment of the present moment for the probable expectation of the still greater ease and enjoyment of a more distant but more lasting period of time, the prudent man is always both supported and rewarded by the entire approbation of the impartial spectator, and of the representative of the impartial spectator, the man within the breast' – in sum by informed public opinion, and by his own conscience: thus the teacher of moral philosophy, not economics, in the early 1750's. In broader terms, prudence is the balancing virtue, as is temperance in Greek ethics. It is the mediating virtue in individual conduct, the base colour which best brings out the qualities of the individual colours, if there in proper measure; so also for economy, the right proportion of factors or goods for proper production or consumption.[39] Prudence can therefore operate between the more ordinary as well as the highest claims, and it borrows its elevation from the level of its material. When it refers only to health or fortune or rank, it commands no more than a 'cold esteem'. But it can also operate on the 'more splendid virtues', valour, benevolence, justice. 'This superior prudence . . . necessarily supposes the art, the talent, and the habit of disposition of acting with the most perfect propriety . . . It necessarily supposes the utmost perfection of all the intellectual and of all the moral virtues. It is the best head joined to the best heart.'[40] Here certainly the prudent man is at once his own and society's best friend. In a final reference (pt. vii, sect. ii, ch. ii, 'Of those systems which make Virtue consist in Prudence') the comparison of prudence to the epicurean virtue of temperance is carried through, though for Smith prudence has a wider range of material. 'Temperance, in short, was, according to the epicurean, nothing but prudence with regard to pleasure.'[41]

It is, however, in his criticism of those who regard benevolence as the supreme virtue that we see the typical Smithian common-sense regard for the facts. For 'this system seems to show the contrary defect, of not sufficiently explaining from whence arises our approbation of the inferior virtues of prudence, vigilance, circumspection, temperance, constancy, firmness'. 'Regard to our own private happiness and interest appear [*sic*], too, upon many occasions very laudable principles of action. The habits of oeconomy, industry, discretion, attention and application of thought are generally supposed to be cultivated from self-interested motives, and at the same time are apprehended to be very praiseworthy qualities which deserve the esteem and approbation of everybody.'[42] Lack of proper self-regard 'would undoubtedly be a failing'. 'Carelessness and lack of oeconomy are universally disapproved of, not however as proceding from a want of benevolence, but from want of proper attention to the objects of self-interest.' The 'proper' is the vital word. It links with 'the *proper* degree of all the affections', which Smith regards as the right system, so long as 'sympathy or the correspondent affection of the spectator' is made the 'natural and original measure of this proper degree'.[43]

Here then, it is submitted, we have a theory of the prudent man, of self-love, which is carefully fitted into the theory of society, as operative through the working of sympathy and reason constructing the detail of moral rules and economic institutions as essential guides to appropriate action. The prudent man may respect social opinion as one of his highest criteria. In his personal career he therefore seeks to find his own happiness through earning social esteem. In this way self-interest can dovetail with society's benefit (though wherein that benefit may consist is a deeper question). And in this prudent self-love, the *Moral Sentiments* explicitly mentions the *economic* interest, indeed mentions it first, and so presumably of primary importance. This, it is submitted, gives us sufficient proof that the economic man of the *Wealth of Nations* is himself assumed by Smith to be a servant of society, so far as he is truly prudent, or acts appropriately. If this is so, far from there being any clash between the two books, the later one gives merely a particular development of the broader doctrine in the first. The economic man is the prudent man in the economic sphere. So the economic man also is under the sway of social sympathy and the impartial rulings of the informed spectator.

V

If this view of the *Moral Sentiments* is correct, what conclusion follows as to its connexion with the *Wealth of Nations*? It would appear that the *Wealth of*

Nations is simply a special case – the economic case – of the philosophy implicit in the *Moral Sentiments*. It works out the economic side of that 'self-love' which is given its appropriate place in the developed ethical system of the earlier book. For self-love is there an essential element in virtue, or in the good life in society.

This seems to be the obvious view. Adam Smith was a man of stable integrated character, not subject to deep intellectual doubts or fissures. It is quite unlikely that such a man would write two books over the same period, the one adopting virtue, propriety, rational sympathy as the final human good, the other insisting on the social value of a self-interest which could with any truth be equated to selfishness. The 'over the same period' should be remembered. There were five editions of the *Moral Sentiments* between 1759 and 1789. In them, the alterations were not extensive. But in the sixth and final edition of 1790 the corrections and additions were considerable.[44] Yet there is no hint that Smith himself thought there was any conflict of doctrine between the two books. If we accept this, it follows that, if any conflict there is, it arises from the view either that the *Moral Sentiments* did in fact condemn 'self-love', or that the doctrine of self-love (or interest) in the *Wealth of Nations* in fact advocates selfishness. The former, we have seen, is the reverse of the truth – self-love is carefully and positively valued.[45]

As to the latter argument, it is here asserted that the two main principles which span the crucial breach between the individual and the social interest are *the same* in the *Moral Sentiments* and the *Wealth of Nations* – the latter simply reproducing the former. These principles are that of the invisible hand, or Natural Harmony, and that of the system of natural liberty of the individual, or the right to justice. The central importance of 'the obvious and simple system of natural liberty' is well described in the *Wealth of Nations* (ii. 180). But it should be noted that Smith at once adds the second 'duty' of the 'sovereign', that of 'protecting, as far as possible, every member of the society from the injustice or oppression of every other member of it, or the duty of establishing an exact administration of justice'. This recognizes the inevitable clashes that must arise from individual liberties. Does it not also install the 'sovereign' as here representing the 'invisible hand' in the everyday world? If so, the considerable controlling duties given to the State in Book V naturally follow. The invisible hand passages[46] are indeed almost identical in logic; though, as one would expect, that in the *Wealth of Nations* is worked out economically, in the strategic respect of capital accumulation and direction. The *Wealth of Nations* also elaborates the 'deception' idea: 'Nor is it always the worse for the society that it (the individual's intention) was no part of it (the end). By pursuing his own interest he frequently promotes that of the society more effectually than when he really intends to promote it. I have never known much good done by those who affected to trade for the public good.' 'The statesman who should attempt to direct private people in what manner they ought to apply their capitals' is equally criticized. It should be noted, however, that it is the passage in the *Moral Sentiments* which gives the specific source for economic theory and action: the 'capacity of the human stomach' passage, which 'obliges' distribution of his surplus by the landlord, and so gives scope for economic exchange.[47] This line of argument has, of course, a rich history; and it is reproduced in almost identical terms and effect in Book I, Chapter XI of the *Wealth of Nations* ('of the Rent of Land').[48] The connecting link could hardly be more explicit.

The argument as to Natural Liberty is, as one would expect, much more fully analysed in the *Moral Sentiments*. In the *Wealth of Nations* it is rather an assumed and accepted standard of judgement. The *Moral Sentiments* argument is a reflection of the God-directed structure of the universe and of society. Through his intended liberty, and so far as he carries out the dictates of justice, the individual at once best serves his own purposes and his proper function in society. Here Smith's models are Stoic, though he criticizes the 'perfect apathy'[49] of Stoicism, and indeed himself proposes a more positive role for natural liberty in his theory of self-love.[50] The argument is the same in both works. What the *Wealth of Nations* does show up is the width of the large unbridged gap between the social and the individual interest, for it is specially obvious in economic affairs. The invisible hand passage in the *Wealth of Nations* is indeed introduced[51] in an unduly dogmatic passage, by the natural harmony argument: 'Every individual is continually exerting himself to find out the most advantageous employment for whatever capital he can command. It is his own advantage, indeed, which he has in view. But the study of his own advantage naturally, or rather necessarily, leads him to prefer that employment which is most advantageous to the society.' This is a constant theme in the *Wealth of Nations* – the inadequate benevolence of the 'butcher, the brewer, or the baker' is only the *locus classicus*. The spring and source of economic activity is constantly described as the 'desire of bettering our condition, a desire which, though generally calm and dispassionate, comes with us from the womb, and never leaves us till we go into the grave'.[52] This is the economic form which the energy of self-love takes. Its political form is even more important, as the claim for justice or personal liberty.

While Smith's self-love theory is certainly crucial, it equally certainly does not imply an unduly high estimate of men's moral quality. Smith constantly harps on human inadequacies – 'the coarse clay of which the bulk of mankind is formed'.[53] Nor are his strictures confined to 'the bulk of mankind'. Could anything be more savage than this: "All for ourselves and nothing for other people, seems, in every age of the world, to have been the vile maxim of the masters of mankind.'[54] Or again, 'A revolution of the greatest importance to the public happiness was in this manner brought about by two different orders of people who had not the least intention to serve the public. To gratify the most childish vanity was the sole motive of the great proprietors. The merchants and artificers, much less ridiculous, acted merely from a view to their own interest, and in pursuit of their own pedlar principle of turning a penny wherever a penny was to be got.'[55] If the clay is as coarse as all that (fortunately it is not) all the wisdom of the Greatest Artificer would be in vain. More than 'a deception' would be needed. Yet the last Stoic quotation shows that this very exaggeration underlines the firmness with which he grasped the central doctrine of democracy, the sacred right to be wrong. The true line of criticism seems to me to be rather than put by James Bonar.[56] With Smith, 'God's in his Heaven, all's right with the world' is too easily assumed, in view of his very realistic estimate of human nature. Thus in effect it is almost impossible to understand in any detail just how the 'deception' of individuals can work out to social benefit, or on what principle liberty can discern the right social path, or when or how it may be merely negative, offering a 'free-for-all', and when and how it may light the path for creative progress. The *logical* rationalization of self-love is certainly given in the *Moral Sentiments*. But one should not expect a convincing reflection in the *Wealth of Nations*. For this would need to be on the philosophical level. The *Wealth of Nations* keeps to economics.

It is, however, vital to remember that these convictions as to the right function of self-love are reflected and assumed in the *Wealth of Nations*, though in the second work a mere reference to them at the start is considered a sufficient explicit link. The *Wealth of Nations* begins on the Division of Labour. But this is itself traced farther back: 'it is this same trucking disposition which originally gives occasion to the division of labour' (a fact upon which modern thought has cast legitimate doubt). But this itself is not Smith's ultimate economic propensity, as is sometimes assumed. This 'propensity to truck, bargain and exchange'[57] is itself probably 'the necessary consequence of the faculties of reason and speech'; and also 'man has almost constant occasion for the help of his brethren, and it is in vain to expect it from their benevolence only. He will be more likely to prevail if he can interest their self-love in his favour . . . Give me that which I want, and you shall have this which you want.'[57] So self-love is the definite source in the *Wealth of Nations* of exchange activity. And this is vital. For it is just because the self-interest of the *Wealth of Nations*[58] has been identified in isolation with selfishness that the latter work has so often been described as in opposition to the former. But when it is realized that the same theory of self-love holds for both, and that it includes the virtue of economy, which is in principle as much stressed in the *Moral Sentiments* as in the *Wealth of Nations*, then this suggestion of inconsistency disappears.

A final paragraph is no place to begin describing the eighteenth-century doctrines of self-love. Some dogmatism will be allowed, for the general theory is well known. Briefly, self-love was regarded by all the eighteenth-century thinkers as at least one basic, final, and abiding motive in individual action: only benevolence could with some writers challenge precedence. There is, of course, a wide range between Hobbes and, say, Butler. But all accepted our wider self-interest as a natural, indeed *the* natural approach to the study of ethical behaviour. In this galaxy Smith approaches very near to Butler, especially in his emphasis on conscience, though he adds insights of his own through the impartial spectator. Here then we have the source of confusion between the eighteenth century and today. They regarded proper self-love as obligatory and admirable; we tend to equate it with selfishness.[60] The issue has been vividly analysed by Erich Fromm.[60] He argues that our thought has gone wrong here because 'self-interest' has been accepted in a too exclusively subjective sense: 'Self-interest was no longer to be determined by the nature of man and his needs; correspondingly, the notion that one could be mistaken about it was relinquished and replaced by the idea that what a person *felt* represented the interest of his self was necessarily his true self-interest.'[61] And he contrasts the 'objective approach' of Spinoza: 'To him, self-interest, or the interest "to seek one's profit" is identical with virtue.'[61] Now, our argument has underlined throughout the *objective* element which Smith gave to his view of individual activity in society, producing moral rules and conventions and social institutions. So the arguments for a merely selfish interpretation of self-love are least applicable to him. True, Smith does say we are led by 'nature' to benefit society by a deception. But the deception does not imply that he thinks we always act from positively selfish motives. It only (truly) describes the limitations of scope and vision in the *understanding* of the ordinary man. It is then a wise dispensation that 'nature' should so induce us. The prime personal factor binding individuals in society is, however, the emotional one. 'Man, it has been said, has a natural love of society . . . The orderly and flourishing state of society is agreeable to him, and he takes delight in contemplating it.'[62]

Smith's rather original broadening of the 'self-love' analysis was very possibly confirmed by his criticism of Mandeville's 'private vices, public benefits' argument.[63] For he insists that Mandeville's paradox holds water only if we regard *asceticism* as the standard of private virtue. In fact, here as elsewhere, we should seek the 'golden mean'. Mandeville's private vices may well be justifiable indulgences necessary to social progress. To Mandeville, passions are evil. To Smith they are natural, but to be duly restrained. And the positive agent in restraint he finds, not in any revulsion from due self-love and developing wealth, but in the growth of moral rules and social institutions to control them appropriately, through the slow working of informed sympathy. Here, surely, Smith was broadly right. Criticism should be directed rather to the considerable inconsistencies that remain in what is after all a broad, free sketch, with many unfilled spaces. This theory of the individual can indeed be specially recommended today; for we are open to bias here, when so often the approach is from the assumed primacy of society's claim. We do well to study this cool account of the individual's value and function.

Notes

1. *Moral Sentiments*, pt. iv, ch. ii. In the sequel, *M.S.* will stand in the footnotes for the *Theory of Moral Sentiments*, and *W.N.* for the *Wealth of Nations*. The editions referred to are Alex. Murray's (1872) reprint of the *Essays of Adam Smith* for the *Moral Sentiments*, and to the Everyman edition for the *Wealth of Nations*.
2. *M.S.*, pt. iv, ch. i, pp. 158-9.
3. Ibid., pt. vii, sect. ii, ch. iii, p. 271.
4. Ibid., pt. iv, ch. i, pp. 162-3.
5. Utility for Smith, as for Hutcheson, was utility for it. In this way it differs from self-interest and partakes in beauty and fitness: in this sense only, the 'deception' has utility.
6. *W.N.*, vol. i, p. 400.
7. Ibid., p. 306.
8. *M.S.*, pt. ii, sect. ii, ch. iii, p. 79.
9. Ibid., p. 83.
10. Ibid., p. 84.
11. Ibid., p. 80.
12. Ibid., pt. i, sect. i, chs. i, ii, p. 13 – italics mine.
13. *M.S.*, pt. vii, sect. iii, ch. i, p. 281 – italics mine.
14. Ibid. – italics mine.
15. Ibid., sect. ii, ch. i, p. 255, and pt. vii, sect. iii, ch. iii, p. 290.
16. Here, however, different interpretations can be taken. Quotations showing that Smith stressed the objective side of approval are given later. But it should here be noted that he continually refers to approval and disapproval as *feelings*, and therefore presumably subjective. This leads to a

totally different view of the *Moral Sentiments*. A clear exposition of it will be found in *Polity and Economy: an Interpretation of the Principles of Adam Smith* (1957), by Joseph Cropsey. This stimulating work advocates the consistency of Smith's two major works, as is done here, but on different grounds. Dr. Cropsey traces the mechanical psychological 'passions' or 'Motions' as the controlling force behind human motivation in the *Moral Sentiments* and from this he logically deduces a line of economic determinism in the *Wealth of Nations* – as Marx himself did. This mechanical psychology is certainly common in the eighteenth century, and Dr. Cropsey's argument is at least a sound corrective to any undue softening of the hard-headed Smithian outlook. But the opposing theory based on sympathy and the impartial spectator is at least as prevalent throughout the *Moral Sentiments*. Criticism supporting the latter view will be found in L. Bagolini, 'La Simpatia nella Morale e nel Diretto', J.N. Prior, 'Logic and the Basis of Ethics', and J.N. Findlay, 'Values in Speaking' (*Philosophy*, vol. 25).

17.   *M.S.*, pt. iii, ch. v, p. 145.

18.   Ibid., pt. vii, sect. iii, ch. iv, p. 271 – my italics.

19.   Here are some quotations to illustrate this fundamental Smithian idea. 'We endeavour to examine our own conduct as we imagine any fair and impartial spectator would examine it. If upon placing ourselves in his situation, we thoroughly enter into all the passions and motives which influenced it, we approve of it, by sympathy with the approbation of this supposed equitable judge' (ibid., pt. iii, ch. i, p. 101). Or again, stating the rational side, 'Bring a man into society, and he is immediately provided with the mirror he wanted before.' But the mirror is never passive. 'When I endeavour to examine my own conduct . . . I divide myself into two persons . . . The first is the judge, the second the person judged of' (ibid.). The essence of this is mediate judgement, the 'impartial spectator's' judgement being the 'correspondent' rational aspect of sympathy. Similarly, 'It is not the soft power of humanity, it is not that feeble spark of benevolence which Nature has lighted up in the human heart, that is thus capable of counteracting the strongest impulses of self-love. It is a stronger power . . . It is reason, principle, conscience, the inhabitant of the breast, the man within, the great judge and arbiter of our conduct. . . . The natural misrepresentation can be corrected only by the eye of this impartial spectator . . .' (ibid., ch. iii, p. 120). Again, criticizing the view that we have an internal intuitive or 'moral sense' which pronounces actions right or wrong, he insists that it is through experience in social life, and with reference to social rules that we form these judgements.

20.   The artist Braque suggests an analogy to the relation between Smith's sympathy and the impartial spectator, when he writes: 'Colour and form make their effect simultaneously, though they have nothing to do with each other.' (Quoted in Dora Vallier, 'Braque, La Peinture et Nous', in *Cahiers d'Art*, 1954).

21.   *M.S.*, pt. i, sect. ii, ch. iii, p. 36.

22.   Ibid. The passages in this paragraph occur at pt. iii, ch. iv, p. 139.

23.   The fact that for Smith sympathy and reason were two facets of the one activity is specially obvious in this summary statement: 'Whatever judgement we can form concerning (our sentiments and motives) . . . must always bear some secret reference, either to what are, or to what on a certain condition, would be, or to what, we imagine, ought to be the judgement of others. We endeavour to imagine our conduct as we imagine any other fair and impartial spectator would examine it. If, upon placing ourselves in his situation, we thoroughly enter into all the passions and motives which influenced it, we approve of it, by sympathy with the approbation of this supposed equitable judge' (*M.S.*, pt. iii, ch. i, p. 100). Again, concluding his estimates of the 'ancient' and 'some modern systems' according to which virtue consists in various forms of propriety or 'acting according to the truth of things', or in 'that of my Lord Shaftesbury . . . maintaining a proper balance of the affections', he concludes: 'None of these systems either give, or even pretend to give, any precise or distinct measure by which this fitness or propriety of affection can be ascertained or judged of. That precise and distinct measure can be found nowhere but in the *sympathetic feelings of the impartial and well-informed spectator*' (ibid., pt. vii, sect. ii, ch. i, p. 259. My italics).

Reference may here be made to two learned American writers, whose so scholarly appreciations themselves underline the tendency to underestimate the 'impartial spectator', the rational element. They are Dr. O.H. Taylor in his *Economics and Liberalism*, pp. 70 et seq., and Glenn R. Morrow in *Adam Smith 1776-1926*. The emphasis of both is strongly on the emotional side of sympathy, e.g. in the development of justice. But sympathetic feelings alone could not build systems of law; justice also needs brains; the impartial judge is the architect of just institutions.

24.   The possible connexion between Adam Smith and Kant has frequently been noted,

especially by German commentators. A. Oncken, for instance, produced, *A. Smith and I. Kant* (1877) and *Das A. Smith Problem* (1898), in the latter of which he suggests Smith as 'ein Vorläufer Kant's', in respect of the *Moral Sentiments*.

25.   *M.S.*, pt. vii, sect. iii, ch. i, p. 280.

26.   *M.S.*, pt. vi, sect. ii, ch. ii, p. 207.

27.   Ibid., pt. iii, ch. iii, p. 127.

28.   L. Bagolini, op. cit., gives a useful bibliography of the two opposed views here – that Smith's two books are complementary, or in conflict – at pp. 95 et. seq.

29.   I am not of course suggesting that the impartial spectator – or public opinion at its best even – are always right; obviously they are not. But this is the way in which societies rub along, and, we hope, slowly improve. This is Smith's temper; he was far from having our conceit of ourselves.

30.   A key phrase also in the *Wealth of Nations*. My italics.

31.   *M.S.*, pt. i, sect. iii, ch. ii, p. 48.

32.   Ibid., pt. vi, sect. iii, p. 230.

33.   Ibid., p. 55.

34.   Ibid., p. 56.

35.   Ibid., p. 226: '[Vanity] always, and [pride] for the most part, involve a considerable degree of blame.'

36.   Ibid., p. 230. This description of vanity is surely very shrewd.

37.   Ibid., p. 232.

38.   Ibid., sect. ii, ch. i, p. 193.

39.   I have developed this comparison between economy and temperance (or prudence for Smith) in *Economic Efficiency and Social Welfare*, pp. 114-18.

40.   *M.S.*, pt. vi, sect. i, p. 191.

41.   Ibid., pt. vii, sect. ii, ch. ii, p. 262.

42.   Ibid., ch. iii, p. 269.

43.   Ibid., pp. 270, 271. This doctrine is developed in pp. 273, 274.

44.   Cf. *Moral Sentiments*, advertisement to 6th edition; and Rae, *Life of Adam Smith*, ch. xxxi.

45.   We may here note that a similar situation arises as to Smith's *Lectures on Justice, Police, Revenue and Arms*. In the latter, the link with the *Moral Sentiments* is mentioned only once – at the outset. There, the two principles 'authority and utility' are stated as those 'which induce men to enter into civil society' (*Lectures*, p. 9). Commenting on the continuing influence of 'superior wealth' in 'contributing to confer authority', Smith then remarks: 'This principle ["the strong propensity of (the poor) to pay (the rich) respect"] is fully explained in the *Theory of Moral Sentiments*, where it is shown that it arises from our sympathy with our superiors being greater than with our equals or inferiors.' Sympathy is therefore the force behind authority and utility. Thereafter, the treatment of justice becomes at once legalitic, the language technical, as we might expect. This, it is submitted, is in exact analogy with the *Wealth of Nations*. Both are applied science in relation to the *Moral Sentiments*, the one in Jurisprudence, the other in Economics. Yet no one has suggested that the *Lectures* conflict in principle with the *Moral Sentiments*. Is it not always the case that an author writes on different topics in a different manner and language? Could not a similar situation be found in the different works of John Stuart Mill, or Herbert Spencer, or Henry Sidgwick? Do not both the *Lectures* and the *Wealth of Nations* trace specific lines of development in the social workings of rational sympathy, in the institutions of law and economy? There seems no obvious reason to expect more coherence than appears.

46.   *M.S.*, pt. iv, ch. i, p. 162; *W.N.*, vol. i, p. 400.

47.   Ibid., p. 162.

48.   *W.N.*, vol. i, p. 150.

49.   *M.S.*, pt. vii, sect. ii, ch. i, p. 259. 'Apathy' has of course Stoic origin.

50.   Smith speaks with obvious approval of the 'Ancient Stoics' opinion' that 'the vices and follies of mankind made as necessary a part of [God's] plan as their wisdom or their virtue; and by that eternal art which educes good from ill, were made to tend equally to the prosperity and perfection of the great system of nature' (ibid., pt. i, sect. ii, ch. iii, p. 35).

51.   *W.N.*, vol. i, p. 398.

52.   *W.N.*, vol. i, p. 305.

53.   *M.S.*, pt. iii, ch. v, p. 143.

54.   *W.N.*, vol. i, p. 367.

55.   Ibid., p. 369.

56.   *Philosophy and Political Economy*, pp. 177 et seq.

57.   *W.N.*, vol. i, pp. 12, 13, Cf. *Lectures*, pp. 160, 171, where 'the self-love of his fellows' and 'the principle to persuade' are given as the sources of the 'propensity to barter'.

58.   Constantly there given its economic expression as 'the uniform, constant and uninterrupted effort of every man to better his condition' (i. 306).

59.   To say it all depends on how high a view you take of the 'self' is too easy as a general solution, though obviously the higher that view the less place for selfishness. But probably we are the hypocrites here, the eighteenth century the realists. The reason for this change is, however, probably mainly historical. It stems from the emotional stresses arising out of the Reformation. So far as the individual was regarded as essentially and originally selfish, indeed predestined to sin, the equation of self-love with selfishness was almost inevitable. It only reflects the general Puritan reaction (if we can use Puritan in a broad, loose way) to pleasure-seeking, as contrasted with that of Roman Catholicism. No doubt Puritans would think the latter rather cynical, whereas Catholics would stress their own realism, and suggest hypocrisy in the other view. However this may be, these growing tensions seem responsible for our tendency simply to misinterpret doctrines of appropriate self-love, such as Smith gives us.

60.   *Man for Himself*, especially ch. iv, sect. 1.

61.   Fromm, op. cit., pp. 134, 133. Smith himself refers to this personal feeling. His 'fallacious sense of guilt', *M.S.*, pt. ii, sect. iii, ch. iii, p. 98, has almost a Freudian ring, especially as he illustrates by 'Oedipus and Jocasta'.

62.   Ibid., sect. ii, ch. iii, p. 80.

63.   Cf. Bonar, op. cit., pp. 154, 171 and reference to *M.S.* there given.

Some Institutional Aspects of the *Wealth of Nations*

N. Rosenberg

Source: *Journal of Political Economy*, Vol. 18 (6), December 1960, pp. 557-70.

Perhaps as a result of the increasingly formal nature of economics as an academic discipline, the institutional content and preoccupations of Adam Smith's *Wealth of Nations* have suffered prolonged neglect. The following syllogistic restatement, by Wesley Mitchell, may be taken as representative of contemporary formulations of Smith's central argument:

> First, every individual desires to increase his own wealth; second, every individual in his local situation can judge better than a distant statesman what use of his labor and capital is most profitable; third, the wealth of the nation is the aggregate of the wealth of its citizens; therefore, the wealth of the nation will increase most rapidly if every individual is left free to conduct his own affairs as he sees fit.[1]

The view which will be presented here is not that this syllogism is wrong, as an interpretation of Smith's views, but that it is uninteresting. By jumping directly from the conception of man as a rational creature to the policy recommendation of laissez faire and all that, it completely short-circuits much of the real substance of Smith's work. By visualizing the human agent as engaged in the effort to maximize a single, unambiguous magnitude, two aspects of Smith's book and the crucial importance of the interplay between them are ignored: (1) his much more elaborate conception of the *conflicting* forces which impel the human agent to action and, as a direct result, (2) his sustained inquiry into the ultimate impact, in terms of human action and its welfare consequences of different kinds of institutional arrangements. It is the purpose of the present paper to examine the interrelationships between these two sets of forces.

We begin, then, by adding what Smith regarded as certain essential components of human behavior to the traditional image of the relentless pursuit of material gain.

In addition to the well-known "constant, uniform and uninterrupted effort of every man to better his condition," Smith attached great importance to the belief that the generality of mankind is intractably slothful and prone to indolence. A major counterbalance to the desire for and the pursuit of wealth, therefore, is a love of ease and inactivity. "It is the interest of every man to live as much at his ease as he can . . ."[2]

A critical corollary of this position is that, although it is the desire for wealth which prods and lures mankind to put forth his greatest efforts, the *attainment* and possession of wealth are regarded by Smith as almost universally corrupting. For, once such wealth has been acquired, man naturally gives vent to his desire for ease. "The indolence and vanity of the rich"[3] is fully as important a force in Smith's system as is the desire for riches itself. For "a man of a large revenue, whatever may be his profession, thinks he ought to live like other men of large revenues; and to spend a great part of his time in festivity, in vanity, and in dissipation."[4]

Thus the considerable wealth of the large landlord virtually disqualifies him from supervising the efficient operation of his estate. His background and opulence render him incapable of devoting unremitting attention to details, of making those marginal calculations which are so essential to efficiency.[5] Elsewhere, in speaking of landlords, Smith refers to "that indolence, which is the natural effect of the ease and security of their situation."[6]

Perhaps even more disastrous, because of its effects on capital accumulation, is the effect of high profits upon the business class:

> The high rate of profit seems every where to destroy that parsimony which in other circumstances is natural to the character of the merchant. When profits are high, that sober virtue seems to be superfluous, and expensive luxury to suit better the affluence of his situation.[7]

Although he does not spell it out, there seems to be some rate of profits which may be regarded as optimum from the point of view of achieving the maximum rate of economic growth. Higher profits are clearly regarded as desirable up to some level, since they constitute both the major source and the major incentive for the accumulation of capital. Beyond this unspecified optimum, however, "parsimony . . . that sober virtue seems to be superfluous." Thus Smith opposes monopoly not only because it results in resource misallocation. Monopoly has the equally insidious effect of retarding capital accumulation, since easily earned profits result in prodigality.[8] Indeed, as will be seen below, the conflicting forces which motivate man to act really establish an optimum level of income in all economic activities.

Finally, and most important, Smith regards it as a strategic component of the human personality that man is naturally deceitful and unscrupulous and will quite willingly employ predatory practices so long as such practices are available to him. "Such, it seems, is the natural insolence of man, that he almost always disdains to use the good instrument, except when he cannot or dare not use the bad one."[9]

Given these human characteristics, it is plain that the mere absence of external restraints and the freedom to pursue self-interest do not suffice, in Smith's view, to establish social harmony or to protect society from "the passionate confidence of interested falsehood."[10] What are required, above all, are institutional mechanisms which *compel* man, in his "natural insolence," "to use the good instrument."

What the usual emphasis on self-interest and individual freedom overlooks is that such self-interest can be pursued in innumerable antisocial ways. It is not sufficient to answer that Smith assumed a competitive framework in his analysis and policy recommendations, because such a framework is not sufficiently specific. Atomistic competition, absence of collusion, and mobility of resources are not nearly sufficient to establish the linkage between un-hampered pursuit of self-interest and social well-being. Smith himself clearly realized this. Indeed, large portions of his *Wealth of Nations* are specifically devoted to analyzing the nature of the appropriate institutional framework.

Failure to stress the relationship between Smith's broader conception of human nature and the institutional order with which he was so much preoccupied leads to the creation of unnecessary problems of interpretation and "reconcilia-tion." Thus we have recently been told that

> Smith's reliance on moral sentiments as pre-requisites of any workable system of competition has often been lost sight of and even denied by later generations of economists who preferred to popularize Smith's reference to the invisible hand as evidence of his glorification of selfishness. Nothing could be further from the truth. It is unthinkable that a moral philosopher of the stature of Adam Smith, who published *The Theory of Moral Sentiments* in 1759, would have abandoned his conceptions of the moral laws governing human behavior in 1776 when he published *The Wealth of Nations*, without making such a change of view explicit. It is, therefore, imperative that *The Wealth of Nations* be read in conjunction with the earlier *Theory of Moral Sentiments* in order to understand that Smith presupposes the existence of a natural moral law as a result of which the prudent man was believed to be anxious to improve himself only in fair ways, i.e., without doing injustice to others.[11]

It will be shown below that such an interpretation is not only totally incorrect but does a considerable injustice to the subtlety and sophistication of Smith's argument.

A neglected theme running through virtually all of the *Wealth of Nations* is Smith's attempt to define, in very specific terms, the details of the institutional structure which will best harmonize the individual's pursuit of his selfish interests with the broader interests of society. Far from assuming a "spontaneous" identity of interests (in the mere absence of government restrictions) or of being "blind to social conflicts,"[12] Smith was obsessed with the urge to go beyond the ordinary market-structure definition of competition and to evaluate the effectiveness of different institutional forms in *enforcing* this identity.

The ideal institutional order for Smith is one which places the individual under just the proper amount of psychic tension. The individual applies himself with maximum industry and efficiency when the reward for effort is neither too low (slaves, apprentices) nor too great (monopolists, large landowners).[13] However, more complicated than the *intensity* dimension of individual effort is the matter of the *direction* into which this effort is channeled. Smith is, in effect, searching for the appropriate definition of an institutional order which will eliminate zero-sum (or even negative-sum) games. It is the function of institutional arrangements to cut off all avenues (and they are many) along which wealth may be pursued without contributing to the welfare of society. Such a goal in practice requires a careful balancing of incentive, of provision of opportunity to enlarge one's income, against the need to minimize the opportunities for abuse, i.e., possibilities for increasing one's income in an antisocial fashion.

A central, unifying theme in Smith's *Wealth of Nations*, then, is his critique of human institutions on the basis of whether or not they are so contrived as to frustrate man's baser impulses ("natural insolence") and antisocial proclivities and to make possible the pursuit of self-interest *only* in a socially beneficial fashion. Indeed, it will become apparent below that Smith's basic argument applies to the whole spectrum of social contrivances and is not restricted to economic affairs. The question is, in each case, whether institutions do, or do not, harness man's selfish interests to the general welfare. This is, of course, the basis of Smith's critique of mercantilism.

The violence of Smith's polemic against mercantilism lay in the fact that it enabled merchants to better their condition in a manner which did not contribute to the nation's economic welfare. As a result of the dispensation of monopoly grants, of the arbitrary bestowal of "extraordinary privileges" and "extraordinary restraints" upon different sectors of industry by the government, the individual merchant was able to enrich himself without at the same time enriching the nation. For, as Smith clearly recognizes, the pursuit of one's economic self-interest is not necessarily confined to the economic arena. When it spills over into the political arena, it leads to actions which detract from, rather than add to, the economic welfare of society. By contrast, the competitive order which Smith advocated was an institutional arrangement which was characterized, negatively, by the absence of all special privilege and sources of market influence and, positively, by the all-pervasive and uninhibited pressures of the market place. The price system, as Smith saw it, was an intensely coercive mechanism. Its decisive superiority as a way of organizing economic life lay in the fact that, *when it was surrounded by the appropriate institutions*, it tied the dynamic and powerful motive force of self-interest to the general welfare. Its free operation would, in most cases, leave the individual producer no alternative but to pursue his economic interests in a manner conducive to the national welfare.[14]

The secondary literature on Adam Smith has devoted considerable attention to the ways in which the establishment of a free-market network will promote economy effiency. But the emphasis has been primarily on the allocative efficiency of the free market and too little on the ways in which appropriate institutions contribute to the productivity of the human agent as a factor of production – a matter of supreme importance to Smith. Appropriate institutions increase both the *motivation* and the *capacity* of the human agent, whereas inappropriate institutions detract from these things.

Thus Smith opposes apprenticeship laws not only because they impede the mobility of labor between industries but also because they constitute institutional arrangements which pervert the incentive to industry and hard work. During his apprenticeship the young man perceives (correctly) that there

apprenticeships.

is no connection between his effort and his reward (as would exist, e.g., under piecework), and habits of slothfulness and laziness are therefore encouraged:

> The institution of long apprenticeships has no tendency to form young people to industry. A journeyman who works by the piece is likely to be industrious, because he derives a benefit from every exertion of his industry. An apprentice is likely to be idle, and almost always is so, because he has no immediate interest to be otherwise . . . A young man naturally conceives an aversion to labour, when for a long time he receives no benefit from it . . . But a young man would practise with much more diligence and attention, if from the beginning he wrought as a journeyman, being paid in proportion to the little work which he could execute, and paying in his turn for the materials which he might sometimes spoil through awkwardness and inexperience.[15]

Smith had much to say, of course, about the whole complex of institutions surrounding the ownership and cultivation of the land. His condemnation of such feudal relics as the laws of entail and primogeniture, which impeded the free marketability and therefore the optimum employment of land, is well known. Here, too, however, his search is for the most appropriate institutional scheme. Indeed, all of Smith's historical discussion of systems of land tenure (especially Book III, chap. 2) constitutes a highly interesting account of how specific legal and traditional arrangements in Europe have impeded economic progress by failing to provide proper and necessary incentives to landlord and tenant.[16]

The excessive wealth of the great landlord renders him incapable of efficient operation of his estate.[17] However, so long as large estates continue to exist, their most efficient mode of operation poses a serious problem. To place the operation of the land in the hands of a hired agent would be to sever completely the linkage between self-interest and social welfare which the union of property ownership and self-management ordinarily provides. Under such an arrangement,

> the country . . . would be filled with idle and profligate bailiffs, whose abusive management would soon degrade the cultivation, and reduce the annual produce of the land, to the diminution, not only of the revenue of their masters, but of the most important part of that of the whole society.[18]

The larger the unit of ownership under a single proprietor, the greater the abuses we may expect from the "negligent, expensive, and oppressive management of his factors and agents."[19] As a logical extension of this argument, Smith observes that

> the crown lands of Great Britain do not at present afford the fourth part of the rent, which could probably be drawn from them if they were the property of private persons. If the crown lands were more extensive, it is probable they would be still worse managed.[20]

Where lands were tenant-operated, Smith attached great importance to all arrangements, either legal or customary, which assured a close relationship between personal diligence and reward. Thus Smith regards long leases and security against arbitrary eviction as decisive in accounting for English achievements, which he felt contrasted so favorably with those of her Continental neighbors:

> There is, I believe, no-where in Europe, except in England, any instance of the tenant building upon the land of which he had no lease, and trusting that the honour of his landlord would take no advantage of so important an improvement. Those laws and customs so favourable to the yeomanry, have perhaps contributed more to the present grandeur of England, than all their boasted regulations of commerce taken together.[21]

The ideal unit of agricultural organization, of course, is the small proprietorship, which represents a fusion of all the Smithian virtues:

> A small proprietor . . . who knows every part of his little territory, who views it all with the affection which property, especially small property, naturally inspires, and who upon that account takes pleasure not only in cultivating but in adorning it, is generally of all improvers the most industrious, the most intelligent, and the most successful.[22]

Within this context, Smith's well-known opposition to the joint-stock company should occasion no surprise, nor should it be treated, as it occasionally is, as a quaint ("pre-industrial") archaism on his part. Whatever advantages the corporate form or organization might bring, Smith regarded the offsetting disadvantages as decisive. The divorce of ownership and management and the consequent loss of incentive to diligence and efficiency are precisely the same objections that he raises to the management of large estates by persons other than the owners:

> The trade of a joint stock company is always managed by a court of directors. This court, indeed, is frequently subject, in many respects, to the controul of a general court of proprietors. But the greater part of those proprietors seldom pretend to understand any thing of the business of the company; and when the spirit of faction happens not to prevail among them, give themselves no trouble about it, but receive contentedly such half yearly or yearly dividend, as the directors think proper to make to them.[23]

Moreover, all the ordinary incentives to economize, naturally existing in the owner-operated firm, are lost upon the managers of a joint-stock company. Smith makes it perfectly clear that he would object to the adequacy of recent attempts to measure the effectiveness of competitive forces by the use of industry (or product) concentration ratios. For he regards bigness itself, in the *absolute* and not only the relative sense, as objectionable. Joint-stock companies destroy the incentive to efficiency *within* the individual firm:

> The directors of such companies, however, being the managers rather of

other people's money than of their own, it cannot well be expected, that they should watch over it with the same anxious vigilance with which the partners in a private copartnery frequently watch over their own. Like the stewards of a rich man, they are apt to consider attention to small matters as not for their master's honour, and very easily give themselves a dispensation from having it. Negligence and profusion, therefore, must always prevail, more or less, in the management of the affairs of such a company.[24]

If an "unremitting exertion of vigilance and attention . . . cannot long be expected from the directors of a joint stock company,"[25] the mercantile projects of princes hold out even smaller prospects of success. Such projects

> have scarce ever succeeded. The profusion with which the affairs of princes are always managed, renders it almost impossible that they should. The agents of a prince regard the wealth of their master as inexhaustible; are careless at which price they buy; are careless at what price they sell; are careless at what expence they transport his goods from one place to another. Those agents frequently live with the profusion of princes, and sometimes too, in spite of that profusion, and by a proper method of making up their accounts, acquire the fortunes of princes.[26]

Thus Smith is constantly searching out the impact of specific institutional forms upon the human actor. Given his basic conception of human motivations and propensities, the specific kinds of behaviour which we may expect of any individual will depend on the way the institutions surrounding him are structured, for these determine the alternatives open to him and establish the system of rewards and penalties within which he is compelled to operate. Indeed, Smith not only directs some very harsh remarks at human hypocrisy but clearly implies that, once the institutional framework is specified, human behavior becomes highly predictable. After an extensive criticism of the self-seeking behavior of the servants of the East India Company, he states:

> I mean not, however, by any thing which I have here said, to throw any odious imputation upon the general character of the servants of the East India Company, and much less upon that of any particular persons. It is the *system* of government, *the situation in which they are placed*, that I mean to censure; not the character of those who have acted in it. *They acted as their situation naturally directed*, and they who have clamoured the loudest against them would, probably, not have acted better themselves.[27]

Although it would occur to few people to look to Smith for guidance in the conduct of government business, there is much useful instruction in such matters in the *Wealth of Nations* (Book V). The general lesson which has always been drawn from Smith– especially by those who have clearly neglected to read him (or Viner[28]) – has concerned the very limited number of functions which a government can "appropriately" perform. Of much greater interest for our present purposes are the rules laid down or implied by Smith as to how the government ought to organize the conduct of its affairs, for here Smith touches, at great length, upon the subject matter of this paper.

The guiding principle in the organization of public affairs may be stated briefly: "Public services are never better performed than when their reward comes only in consequence of their being performed, and is proportioned to the diligence employed in performing them."[29] But this statement is neither so obvious nor so platitudinous as it may sound, for the establishment of the optimum arrangements in accordance with this principle is an extraordinarily difficult task and even today (perhaps one should say "especially today") is seriously neglected. Although reward should be "proportioned to the diligence employed," care must be taken that such diligence can be exerted only in socially beneficial directions. Here again it is the direction, rather than the mere intensity, of human effort that is crucially important. For, as Smith points out, in legal proceedings the income of attorneys and clerks of court had indeed been proportioned to their diligence. But, unfortunately, this diligence had been defined and measured for remunerative purposes in a too strictly quantitative sense, i.e., in terms of the number of pages of their written output. As a result,

> in order to increase their payment, the attornies and clerks have contrived to multiply words beyond all necessity, to the corruption of the law language of, I believe, every court of justice in Europe. A like temptation might perhaps occasion a like corruption in the form of law proceedings.[30]

The administration of justice is, indeed, rife with examples of the difficulties involved in devising techniques which effectively link the pursuit of self-interest with the public welfare. Although present arrangements leave much to be desired, anything which tends to reduce the financial interest of the lawyer in the case of his client is studiously to be avoided. "Lawyers and attornies, at least, must always be paid by the parties; and, if they were not, they would perform their duty still worse than they actually perform it."[31]

Yet the administration of justice in the broader sense ought *never* to be conducted primarily with respect to financial considerations, most especially where the sovereign himself exercises judicial authority. For this establishes a highly improper liaison with self-interest which leads to the flagrant abuse of justice, rather than its promotion:

> This scheme of making the administration of justice subservient to the purposes of revenue, could scarce fail to be productive of several very gross abuses. The person, who applied for justice with a large present in his hand, was likely to get something more than justice; while he, who applied for it with a small one, was likely to get something less. Justice too might frequently be delayed, in order that this present might be repeated. The amercement, besides, of the person complained of, might frequently suggest a very strong reason for finding him in the wrong, even when he had not really been so.[32]

The exact methods devised for the remuneration of judges are, therefore, of considerable importance. Fixed salaries, while limiting possibilities for corruption, are likely to lead to indolence and neglect, whereas allowing the judges to establish and to collect fees, out of which they are to derive their incomes, increases the possibility that the pursuit of self-interest will lead to corrupt practices. Since, at the same time, it is desirable that the law courts should defray the expenses of their operation and that the judiciary should be completely independent of the executive branch, Smith proposes a carefully contrived system whereby fees are independently determined and standardized, means of payment precisely defined and publicly recorded, and payment to the judges withheld until proceedings are completed. Under these circumstances, Smith is hopeful, judges will have practically no alternative but to mete out justice in a fair and expeditious manner.[33]

The strong feelings which Smith harbored against "that insidious and crafty animal, vulgarly called a statesman or politician," are too well known to require elaboration. They represented the *fons et origo* of the many perversions and extravagances which Smith identified with "the Mercantile System." More important, however, is the fact that Smith regards politicians and government officials as a class of men peculiarly insulated not only from the ordinary pressures of the market but from any other institutionalized compulsion which engages the pursuit of their selfish interests with the public welfare. At the same time, the opportunities and devices typically available for enriching themselves directly at the expense of the public he regards as myriad. Just as in the case of the servants of the East India Company, however, it must be emphasized that Smith condemns not politicians per se but the institutional framework within which politicians typically find themselves.

On the question of the functions which may appropriately be undertaken by governments, Smith makes several highly interesting observations, indicating that his antigovernment bias was, in substantial measure, a reflection of the currently limited possibilities for engaging the "interested diligence" of public officials upon the efficient operation of government undertakings. For example, Smith cites approvingly the mercantile projects carried out by small European governments. His invidious comparisons with the government of England turn, not on a matter of principle, but upon the almost certain incapacity of the British government to engage successfully in similar undertakings, in contrast with the established efficiency of the (small) governments of Venice and Amsterdam:

> The orderly, vigilant, and parsimonious administration of such aristocracies as those of Venice and Amsterdam, is extremely proper, it appears from experience, for the management of a mercantile project of this kind. But whether such a government as that of England; which, whatever may be its virtues, has never been famous for good oeconomy; which, in time of peace, has generally conducted itself with the slothful and negligent profusion that is perhaps natural to monarchies; and in time of war has constantly acted with all the thoughtless extravagance that democracies are apt to fall into; could be safely trusted with the management of such a project, must at least be a good deal more doubtful.[34]

Similarly, although cautioning that much of the information available concerning events in Asia was derived from such unreliable sources as the accounts of "stupid and lying missionaries," Smith concedes that roads and canals may be operated by Asian governments with a high degree of efficiency. This is because, in such places as China and Indostan, the primary source of revenue to the sovereign is derived from a land-tax or land-rent. Under these circumstances, it is in the direct interest of the sovereign to provide and maintain the most efficient possible network of transportation facilities.[35] It is highly improbable, however, "during the present state of things," that any European government could provide such transport facilities with any degree of efficiency because their self-interests are not similarly engaged by their sources of revenue:

> The revenue of the sovereign does not, in any part of Europe, arise chiefly from a land-tax or land-rent. In all the great kingdoms of Europe, perhaps, the greater part of it may ultimately depend upon the produce of the land: But that dependency is neither so immediate, nor so evident. In Europe, therefore, the sovereign does not feel himself so directly called upon to promote the increase, both in quantity and value, of the produce of the land, or, by maintaining good roads and canals, to provide the most extensive market for that produce.[36]

What is involved here, therefore, is not only the matter of administrative competence or efficiency but also the absence of institutional arrangements so instructed as to engage the motive and interests of those concerned.

Smith's shrewd perception of the impact of different organizational arrangements upon the individual pursuit of wealth appears in the distinction that he draws between the operation of roads and canals. Canals, he argues, may more properly be left in private hands than roads. This is because the interested diligence of the canal-owner requires the canal to be maintained, or it will become impassable through neglect and therefore cease entirely to be a source of revenue. Highways, on the other hand, deteriorate by degrees and, although entirely neglected, may still remain passable. If private persons are allowed to collect such tolls, the roads will therefore suffer considerable neglect, since such persons will lack the personal incentive to maintain them.[37]

Smith's search for an institutional scheme which will establish and enforce an identity of interests between the public and private spheres even carries over into his discussion of the nation's military establishment. After an extended discussion of the changing technology of warfare and its consequences for the organization of a nation's military establishment, he concludes: "It is only by means of a standing army . . . that the civilization of any country can be perpetuated, or even preserved for any considerable time."[38] The obvious threat which such a standing army poses to republican principles, "wherever the interest of the general and that of the principal officers are not necessarily connected with the support of the constitution of the state,"[39] is to be remedied by insuring that military leadership is recruited only from among those classes whose self-interest is indissolubly linked with the support of the existing government. Thus,

> where, the sovereign is himself the general, and the principal nobility and gentry of the country the chief officers of the army; where the military force is

placed under the command of those who have the greatest interest in the support of the civil authority, because they have themselves the greatest share of that authority, a standing army can never be dangerous to liberty.[40]

Smith's further exploration of this general theme is richly developed in his discussion of religious and educational institutions (Book V, chap. 1, Arts. 2d and 3d). Although Smith raises strong social and political objections to the accumulation of wealth and power by ecclesiastical institutions, he argues that such accumulation almost certainly destroys their effectiveness as "institutions for the instruction of people of all ages" as well. For members of the clergy are likely to be most zealous and industrious as teachers of religious doctrine if they "depend altogether for their subsistence upon the voluntary contributions of their hearers."[41] If they are independently endowed, if their interested diligence, in other words, is not made dependent on public assessment of the effectiveness of their performance, they are likely to become negligent and slothful in the fulfilment of their duties. It is this situation which prompted Smith to make such frequent disparaging references to clergy of "ancient and established systems . . . reposing themselves upon their benefices" and to the "contemptuous and arrogant airs" displayed by "the proud dignitaries of opulent and well-endowed churches," etc.[42]

But, although Smith is opposed to the "independent provision" of the clergy, he does not advocate the alternative of leaving them to the free pursuit of their interested diligence. For the extreme tensions under which the clergy would then be placed would tempt them to adopt reprehensible practices which they might otherwise not choose, were the compulsions less great. Such a policy would lead to deceitful appeals to a naïve, credulous, and superstitious public and wholesale exploitation of the gullibility of the latter – in effect, unfair ecclesiastical practices.[43] Thus the special circumstances surrounding the usual functions of the clergy lead Smith to amend somewhat his general maxim: "In every profession, the exertion of the greater part of those who exercise it, is always in proportion to the necessity they are under of making that exertion."[44] The difficulty here is that extreme necessity is not only likely to maximize effort and to overcome the natural indolence of the clergy but to influence the direction of that effort in socially disagreeable ways. Here again Smith's concern is not only with the maximization of effort but with the more subtle dimensions of human behavior.

It is of considerable interest to the argument of this paper to note that, although Smith is highly critical of almost every religious order with which he deals, he does single out at least one important exception. Reference is made to the very high praise indeed which Smith accords to the Presbyterian clergy:

> There is scarce perhaps to be found any where in Europe a more learned, decent, independent, and respectable set of men, than the greater part of the presbyterian clergy of Holland, Geneva, Switzerland, and Scotland.[45]

And, further:

> The most opulent church in Christendom does not maintain better the

uniformity of faith, the fervour of devotion, the spirit of order, regularity, and austere morals in the great body of the people, than this very poorly endowed church of Scotland.[46]

One may, if one wishes, dismiss this major exception as originating in a source of bias too obvious to be worth recording. But this would be doing much less than jutice to the scope of Smith's argument and to the fact that this judgment is consistent, at least in Smith's eyes, with criteria which he develops and employs elsewhere. Smith seems to feel that the mode of payment devised for the Presbyterian clergy struck just that optimum balance between underpayment, which drove the mendicant orders to that excessive and misplaced zeal which Smith likened to a plundering army,[47] and overpayment from large independent endowments, which was so often responsible for indolence, negligence, and "contemptuous and arrogant airs." The consistency of Smith's judgment and the generality of his argument are perfectly clear in the closing paragraph of the section devoted to the clergy:

> The proper performance of every service seems to require that its pay or recompence should be, as exactly as possible, proportioned to the nature of the service. If any service is very much under-paid, it is very apt to suffer by the meanness and incapacity of the greater part of those who are employed in it. If it is very much over-paid, it is apt to suffer, perhaps, still more by their negligence and idleness. A man of a large revenue, whatever may be his profession, thinks he ought to live like other men of large revenues; and to spend a great part of his time in festivity, in vanity, and in dissipation. But in a clergyman this train of life not only consumes the time which ought to be employed in the duties of his function, but in the eyes of the common people destroys almost entirely that sanctity of character which can alone enable him to perform those duties with proper weight and authority.[48]

Smith's devastating remarks respecting the state of education are often treated as a mere *curiosum*. In fact, however, Smith's critique of educational institutions – especially universities – is entirely consistent with the general principles which have been referred to in this paper. Because of special privileges and independent endowments, England's great universities in particular lack the appropriate institutional mechanisms which link the pursuit of self-interest on the part of the faculty to the need to perform satisfactorily their professional duties. This is especially the case where the colleges are not only heavily endowed[49] but where also (*mirabile dictu!*) the teachers themselves constitute the governing body.[50] Under such a self-perpetuating arrangement the incomes of teachers bear virtually no relation to their proficiency as either scholars or pedagogues. This sham is intensified in those cases where class attendance is made obligatory and students are unable to exercise their consumer sovereignty by awarding their fees to instructors of greatest competence. In those cases where the instructor derives his entire income from endowments, the connection between effort and reward is completely ruptured, and the situation is hopeless. For even if the teacher is naturally energetic and constitutionally incapable of a life of total quiescence, his energies will be channeled into directions *other* than that of scholarship, since the marginal private gains in such pursuits have been effectively set at zero.[51] The result is, inevitably, a total and shameful neglect of learning.[52]

The situation, mercifully, is not so bad in the public schools, which "are much less corrupted than the universities." The principal reason for the difference, as might be expected, is that "the reward of the schoolmaster in most cases depends principally, in some cases almost entirely, upon the fees or honoraries of his scholars."[53]

The central argument of this paper may be restated as follows: Smith's *Wealth of Nations* provided the first systematic guide to the manner in which the price mechanism allocated resources in a free-market economy, and the book has been justly celebrated for this unique achievement.[54] At the same time, however, Smith was very much preoccupied with establishing the conditions under which this market mechanism would operate most effectively. His conception of human behavior allowed for the free operation of certain impulses, motivations, and behavior patterns which were calculated to thwart, rather than to reinforce, the benificent operation of market forces, and Smith was therefore very much concerned with providing an exact, detailed specification of an optimal institutional structure. Later generations of economists have virtually ignored this aspect of Smith's analysis both by oversimplifying his conception of human behavior and by merely invoking, without examination, a competitive economy. The result has been a neglect of some of the most fruitful and suggestive aspects of Smith's analysis and a distortion of the broader implications of his argument. The present paper represents a partial attempt to restore this balance.

Recent concern among economists with problems of economic development and with specific areas of government policy formulation suggests a resurgence of interest in the incidence of different institutional forms upon economic behavior.[55] Although the *Wealth of Nations* is certainly not the last word on this subject, its analytical framework still constitutes a most useful point of departure.

Notes

1.   Wesley Mitchell, *The Backward Art of Spending Money*, Augustus M. Kelley, Inc., New York, 1950, p. 85; see also his *Lecture Notes on Types of Economic Theory* Augustus M. Kelley, Inc., New York, 1949, Vol. I, chap. 5.

2.   Adam Smith, *The Wealth of Nations*, p. 718. Subsequently referred to as "*Wealth*." All references are to the Cannan edition which was reissued in the Modern Library Series (New York: Random House, 1937).

3.   *Wealth*, p. 683.

4.   *Ibid.*, p. 766.

5.   *Ibid.*, pp. 363-64.

6.   *Ibid.*, p. 249.

7.   *Ibid.*, p. 578.

8.   *Ibid.*, pp. 578-79.

9.   *Ibid.*, p. 751. Smith's generally low estimate of humanity is subjected to an entertaining, tongue-in-cheek, treatment in a recent article by Arthur H. Cole, "Puzzles of the 'Wealth of Nations,'" *Canadian Journal of Economics and Political Science*, XXIV (February, 1958), 1-8.

10.   *Wealth*, p. 463.

11.   K. William Kapp, *The Social Costs of Private Enterprise* (Cambridge, Mass.: Harvard University Press, 1950), pp. 28-29. Smith's general skepticism and reluctance to attach too much force to the unalloyed operation of humanitarian motives, even where it might appear most appropriate, is neatly conveyed in the following quotation: "The late resolution of the Quakers in Pennsylvania to set at liberty all their negro slaves, may satisfy us that their number cannot be very great. Had they made any considerable part of their property, such a resolution could never have been agreed to" (*Wealth*, p. 366).

12.   "A sunny optimism radiates from Smith's writing. He had no keen sense for social disharmonies, for interest conflicts . . . On the whole, it is true to say that he was blind to social conflicts. The world is for him harmonious. Enlightened self-interest ultimately increases social happiness" (Gunnar Myrdal, *The Political Element in the Development of Economic Theory* [London: Routledge & Kegan Paul, Ltd., 1953], p. 107).

13.   The manifest impossibility of acquiring and enjoying wealth is, of course, completely stultifying to economic efficiency: "The experience of all ages and nations, I believe, demonstrates that the work done by slaves, though it appears to cost only their maintenance, is in the end the dearest of any. A person who can acquire no property, can have no other interest but to eat as much, and to labour as little as possible. Whatever work he does beyond what is sufficient to purchase his own maintenance, can be squeezed out of him by violence only, and not by any interest of his own" (*Wealth*, p. 365).

On the other hand, as already cited: "A man of a large revenue, whatever may be his profession, thinks he ought to live like other men of large revenues; and to spend a great part of his time in festivity, in vanity, and in dissipation" (*ibid.*, p. 766).

14.   For Smith's own qualifications of this proposition see Jacob Viner, "Adam Smith and Laissez-Faire," chap. v of J.M. Clark *et al., Adam Smith, 1776-1926: Lectures To Commemorate the Sesquicentennial of the Publication of "The Wealth of Nations"* (Chicago: University of Chicago Press, 1928). I wish to acknowledge my intellectual indebtedness to Viner's masterly analysis of Smith.

15.   *Wealth*, pp. 122-23.

16.   For a recent treatment of the same problem, bearing numerous parallels to Smith's argument, see United Nations, *Land Reform: Defects in Agrarian Structure as Obstacles to Economic Development* (New York: United Nations, Department of Economic Affairs, 1951).

17.   *Wealth*, pp. 363-64.

18.   *Ibid.*, p. 784.

19.   *Ibid.*, p. 775.

20.   *Loc. cit.* So strongly did Smith feel about the importance of maintaining the union between ownership and management that he actually suggested a form of discriminatory taxation, contrived in such a manner "that the landlord should be encouraged to cultivate a part of his own land" (*ibid.*, pp. 783-84).

21.   *Ibid.*, pp. 368-69. Elsewhere, Smith observes: "Some leases prescribe to the tenant a certain mode of cultivation, and a certain succession of crops during the whole continuance of the lease." With typical sarcasm he attributes this arrangement to "the landlord's conceit of his own superior knowledge (a conceit in most case very ill founded)" (p. 783).

22.   *Ibid.*, p. 392. Notice, however, that Smith regards it as an important virtue of the cultivating landlord that he can afford to bear the costs of experimentation. "The landlord can afford to try experiments, and is generally disposed to do so. His unsuccessful experiments occasion only a moderate loss to himself. His successful ones contribute to the improvement and better cultivation of the whole country" (*ibid.*, p. 784).

23.   *Ibid.*, p. 699.

24.   *Ibid.*, p. 700.

25.   *Ibid.*, p. 713.

26.   *Ibid.*, p. 771.

27.   *Ibid.*, pp. 605-6 (italics mine). The importance of institutional determinants of human behavior is reinforced, in Smith's view, by his belief that natural, inborn differences among men are not very significant and are typically exaggerated (see *ibid.*, pp. 15-16).

28.   Viner, *op. cit.*

29.   *Wealth*, p. 678.

30.   *Ibid.*, p. 680. Had the Russians read their Smith with nearly the same diligence as they did their Marx, they might not now be so plagued with problems perfectly analogous to, but far more

serious than, "the conveyances of a verbose attorney."

"Orders from above have an entirely different effect from that desired by the planners themselves. Thus they plan output in tons in many ministries (including heavy machine-building and iron and steel) so that the factories concentrate on the heavier goods within each item of the assortment (product-mix) a specified in the plan. They plan output of textiles by length and not area, so that factories produce narrower cloths than their looms will take in order to boost their output figures. They plan geological surveys in metres drilled and not in tons of minerals discovered, so that you can fulfil the plan by doing unnecessary drilling. The output of each factory is planned in wholesale prices as well as in physical terms; and as wholesale prices include the cost of raw materials, factories concentrate on those items which use more raw materials and less labour, again in order to boost their output figures" (R.W. Davies, "Industrial Planning Reconsidered," *Soviet Studies*, April, 1957, p. 428).

31.   *Wealth*, p. 677.

32.   *Ibid.*, p. 675.

33.   *Ibid.*, pp. 677-81. The system of paying fees to courts of law, Smith argues, has led in the past to competition among different courts of justice which had highly beneficial consequences. The competition for litigation led not only to an expansion in the jurisdiction of courts originally set up for specific purposes, such as the court of exchequer, but also, as a direct consequence, to a swift and impartial justice. Even more interesting is the suggestion that such intercourt competition was a dynamic force in changing the law itself and in leading to the emergence of new legal concepts, such as the highly important writ of ejectment. Smith reports that "the artificial and fictitious writ of ejectment, the most effectual remedy for an unjust outer or dispossession of land," was invented by the courts of law to regain a considerable amount of litigation which had been temporarily lost, in this competitive process, to the court of chancery (*ibid.*, p. 679).

34.   *Ibid.*, p. 770. Of course, Smith insists that, wherever possible and appropriate, the administration of smaller (local) units of government is to be preferred to that of larger, national units (*ibid.*, p. 689).

35.   *Ibid.*, p. 688; see also pp. 789-90.

36.   *Ibid.*, pp. 688-89.

37.   *Ibid.*, p. 684. In a discussion of the appropriate investment criteria for underdeveloped countries, Albert Hirschman recently made a proposal whose inner logic was strikingly similar to that underlying Smith's distinction between the operation of roads and canals: "Priority should be given to investments, industries, and technical processes which either hardly require maintenance or *must* have maintenance because its absence carries with it a very high penalty, i.e., leads to accidents or immediate breakdown rather than to slow deterioration in the quantity and quality of output. The fact that the performance of the airlines in Columbia is excellent, that of the railroads mediocre, and that of the roads outright poor can be explained in terms of this criterion: nonmaintenance would lead to certain disaster in the case of airplanes, but roads can be left to deteriorate for a long time before they finally disappear, and railroads occupy a somewhat intermediate position from this viewpoint." (Albert Hirschman, "Economics and Investment Planning: Reflections Based on Experience in Columbia," in *Investment Criteria and Economic Growth* (Cambridge, Mass.: Center for International Studies, Massachusetts Institute of Technology), p. 48; see also Albert Hirschman, *The Strategy of Economic Development* (New Haven, Conn.: Yale University Press, 1958), pp. 139-43.

38.   *Wealth*, p. 667.

39.   *Ibid.*, p. 667.

40.   *Ibid.*, pp. 667-68.

41.   *Ibid.*, p. 740.

42.   *Ibid.*, pp. 741 and 762. A further consequence of large endowments and benefices, to which Smith attached considerable inportance, is that, by their competitive attractions, they draw superior talents out of universities and into the church. "After the church of Rome, that of England is by far the richest and best endowed church in Christendom. In England, accordingly, the church is continually draining the universities of all their best and ablest members" (*ibid.*, p. 763; see also pp. 762-64).

43.   See *ibid.*, pp. 742-43, for the extended quotation from Hume's *History of England* which Smith apprrovingly inserts.

44.   *Wealth*, p. 717.

45.   *Ibid.*, p. 762.

46.   *Ibid.*, p. 765.

47.   *Ibid.*, p. 742: "The mendicant orders derive their whole subsistence from (voluntary) oblations. It is with them, as with the hussars and light infantry of some armies: no plunder, no pay."

48.   *Ibid.*, p. 766.

49.   "The endowments of schools and colleges have necessarily diminished more or less the necessity of application in the teachers. Their subsistence, so far as it arises from their salaries, is evidently derived from a fund altogether independent of their success and reputation in their particular professions" (*ibid.*, p. 717).

50.   Perhaps it should be added that, in Smith's opinion, the control of a university by some "extraneous jurisdiction" (bishop, governor, minister of state) was likely to be ignorant and capricious in nature – as in the French universities (*ibid.*, pp. 718-19).

51.   "If he is naturally active and a lover of labour, it is his interest to employ that activity in any way, from which he can derive some advantage, rather than in the performance of his duty, from which he can derive none" (*ibid.*, p. 718).

52.   "In the university of Oxford, the greater part of the public professors have, for these many years, given up altogether even the pretence of teaching" (*ibid.*, p. 718). And, more generally: "The discipline of colleges and universities is in general contrived, not for the benefit of the students, but for the interest, or more properly speaking, for the ease of the masters. Its object is, in all cases, to maintain the authority of the master, and whether he neglects or performs his duty, to oblige the students in all cases to behave to him as if he performed it with the greatest diligence and ability" (*ibid.*, p. 720).

53.   *Ibid.*, p. 721.

54.   Cf., however, the reservations expressed by Schumpeter, to whom nothing, except Walras' *Elements*, appears to have been sacred (J.A. Schumpeter, *History of Economic Analysis* [New York: Oxford University Press, 1954], pp. 184-86).

55.   Cf., for example, W.A. Lewis, *The Theory of Economic Growth* (Homewood, Ill.: Richard D. Irwin, Inc., 1955), esp. chap. iii, and the masterly analysis of the American patent system in Fritz Machlup, *An Economic Review of the Patent System* (Study No. 15 of the Subcommittee on Patents, Trademarks and Copyrights of the Committee on the Judiciary, U.S. Senate [Washington: Government Printing Office, 1958]).

63

The First Spanish Edition of *The Wealth of Nations*

R.S. Smith

Source: *South African Journal of Economics*, Vol. 35, September 1967, pp. 265-8.

Writing from Munich in December, 1792, Sir John Macpherson told Edward Gibbon that the Spanish government had "permitted an extract of Adam Smith's *Wealth of Nations* to be published, though the original is condemned by the Inquisition."[1] The 'extract' was a 300-page book, published at the Royal Press 'by superior order.'[2] Labelled a 'Compendium,' the work was an expurgated translation of Condorcet's synopsis of the *Wealth of Nations*.[3] The translator, Carlos Martínez de Irujo, not only suppressed or garbled parts of Condorcet's work but failed to identify the original as the work of Smith.

It was not the English text but a French translation which the Inquisition banned on March 3, 1792. Macpherson thought it 'curious' that the *Wealth of Nations* should be condemned for "the lowness of its style and the looseness of the morals which it inculcates." Actually, the censors objected that the book, "beneath a captious and obscure style, favours tolerance in religion and is conducive to naturalism."[4]

John Rae expressed surprise that within two years after banning the *Wealth of Nations* the Inquisition permitted the publication of a Spanish translation. Unaware that the proscription applied to the French edition, he surmised that a "change must have speedily come over the censorial mind."[5] In fact, the 'censorial mind' was plural: the Royal Council of Castile, the Royal Academy of History, and the Inquisition all had a hand in deciding that the expurgated Spanish translation avoided the errors which won the French translation a place in the Index.[6]

Smith's first (and until 1956, *only*) Spanish translator was José Alonso Ortiz, a lawyer and professor of canon law and theology at the University of Valladolid.[7] In 1792 Ortiz came to Madrid with a translation of the eighth (sic) edition of the *Wealth of Nations*. (Undoubtedly, he used the fifth edition; why he thought it was the eighth, I do not know). The translation, Ortiz affirmed, was purged of 'various offensive propositions'; and he deleted an entire article (Book V, ch. 1, pt. iii, art. iii) in which "the author favours tolerance in religious matters, so that the translation contains nothing which could lead to error or laxity on religious or moral grounds." In February, 1793, he advised the President of the Supreme Council of the Inquisition that he had submitted his manuscript to the Council of Castile. Government approval of Martínez de Irujo's *Compendio* seemed to strengthen the argument that Spaniards should have an opportunity to read a direct (but censored) translation of "a work of such great value in economic matters." Ortiz appealed to the Inquisition to review his manuscript promptly and approve its publication.[8]

The Inquisition agreed to appoint two censors to compare Ortiz' work with the offensive French translation, but no appointment had been made when he renewed his petition in April. Meantime, the Council of Castile, accepting the advice of censors appointed by the Academy of History, had granted permission to publish the Ortiz translation.[9] To obviate all doubts Ortiz again requested the Inquisition's approval.

On May 2 the Inquisition commissioned Father Manuel de San Vicente and another priest of his choice to examine the French and Spanish translations. (Curiously, it was never suggested that Ortiz's translation be collated with the English text; the French version was repeatedly referred to as the 'original'.) Father San Vicente and Father Gabriel de Santa Ana reported on May 28 that the Ortiz translation of the work of Scith (sic) was indeed "purged of the causes for which the original work was prohibited." They noted specifically his 'correction' of Smith's observation (Book I, ch. 4) that "the avarice and injustice of princes and sovereign states, abusing the confidence of their subjects, have by degrees diminished the real quantity of metal, which had been originally contained in their coins." According to the Spanish translator, "sometimes out of necessity, other times for lack of experience, neglect, or bad advice, and on other occasions for reasons of state not well understood, some princes and sovereign states have commonly decreased gradually the real quantity of metal which the coins used to contain." Similarly, the censors concluded that Ortiz had 'revised' the chapter on prices (Book I, ch. 6) "in terms quite different from the original . . . correcting its doctrine so that in the translation there is no proposition against which can be levied the censure accorded at this point to the propositions in the original." Nevertheless, the Inquisition wanted Father Antonio de la Santisima Trinidad, who had censured the French translation, to review Ortiz' work; but this idea was abandoned because of Fray Antonio's absence from Madrid.

None of the deliberations of the Inquisition were communicated to Ortiz, who on July 31 complained bitterly that he was forced to remain in Madrid awaiting a decision which should be easy to reach since only 'purely economic points' were involved. The Inquisition had already designated two new censors, Father Tomás Muñoz and Father Luis Garcia Benito, to review the manuscript. They agreed that the translation contained nothing objectionable except the expression "interest, or lawful usury" (*interes, o usura licita*). The word 'lawful' was not only unnecessary but "a little dangerous, principally because no distinction is made between moderate and immoderate usury, between what is prohibited and what is permitted by civil law, between what is fixed and what is not regulated by public authority."

The Inquisition then asked Father San Vicente to comment on this point. He replied that Ortiz had correctly differentiated interest, wages, and rent, and that nothing remained to censure. The Inquisition, however, sided with Muñoz and Benito and required Ortiz to substitute "usury or yield on money" for Smith's "interest or the use of money" and to write "interest on money, or usury understood in this manner" for the original "interest of money". The manuscript was returned to Ortiz on October 22, 1793, and the following year his translation was published in Valladolid.[10]

Although the Academy of History reviewed four manuscript volumes of Ortiz' work, the Inquisition's censors commented on the fact that they had seen only one volume, corresponding to not quite all of Smith's Book I. They supposed that the rest of the manuscript would be submitted for criticism, but there is no evidence that the Inquisition ever passed on the text of Books II-V. This anomaly, if it is anomalous, may be explained by the government's decision to expedite the publication of certain works without the clerical imprimatur. In his memoirs Manuel de Godoy boasts of his 'great services' to literature, science, and the arts and mentions economics and political science as objects of his 'preferential attentions'. He then cites Smith's *Wealth of Nations* and Hume's *Political Discourses* among the many books which were published "at the expense of or with the aid of the government."[11] Ortiz' first edition (but not the second) contains a flowery dedication to the Prince of Peace, who encouraged him because of his (Godoy's) desire to spread "throughout the nation the deepest understanding of civil economy."

The second 'corrected and improved' edition, like the first, falls short of representing the author's thoughts faithfully. In the preface Ortiz admits to the suppression of "some details, but very few, either because they are irrelevant to our nation or hardly in keeping with the holy religion we profess." The omissions, he asserted, did not 'adulterate' the fundamentals of Smith's work: an impartial comparison with the original would convince the reader that the expurgation was inconsequential. Although he advised the censors of the omission of an entire article in Book I, he failed to mention this fact in the preface; and at no point in the text did he give notice of the deletions, revisions, free translation, and gratuitous additions to the original *Wealth of Nations*. The result, as Beltran observes, was a 'mutilated' version of Smith's immortal work.[12]

Surprisingly, more than a century later, when José M. Tallada undertook to edit a new Spanish edition of the *Wealth of Nations*, he used the Ortiz translation and made only unimportant orthographical and grammatical revisions.[13] At long last Amando Lázaro Ros gave the Spanish-speaking world a complete and accurate translation (Madrid, 1956), and Gabriel Franco and Manuel Sánchez Sato brought out a second unexpurgated Spanish version (Mexico, 1958). Both follow the Cannan edition, and Franco and Sánchez reproduce Cannan's notes.

Notes

1. *The Miscellaneous Works of Edward Gibbon, Esq.*, II (London, 1814), 479.

2. *Compendio de la obra inglesa intitulada Riqueza de las naciones* (Madrid, 1792 and 1803, and Palma de Mallorca, 1814).

3. First published as "Recherches sur la nature et les causes de la richesse des nations," *Bibliothèque de l'homme public*, III (Paris 1790), 108-216, and IV (1790), 3-115.

4. The handbill posted by the Inquisition in Seville (March 4, 1792) includes *Recherches sur*

la nature et les causes de la richesse des nations (specifically, the London edition of 1788) in a long list of 'Prohibited' works but not in the shorter list of titles "Prohibited even for those who have permission," i.e., to read prohibited texts. A copy of this handbill is found in the Servicio Historico Militar, Madrid, *Coleccion documental del Fraile*, tomo 863, fol. 152.

5.   *Life of Adam Smith* (London, 1895), pp. 360-361.

6.   Where it remained, at least until 1842 (*Indice general de los libros prohibidos* |Madrid, 1844|, p. 318).

7.   Alonso Ortiz' interest in English literature had already led him to translate poems of Ossian (*Obras de Ossian, poeta del siglo tercero en las montañas de Escocia*; Valladolid, 1788) and Alban Butler's *Lives of the Saints* (*Vida de los padres, mártires y otros principales santos*; 13 vols., Valladolid, 1789-91). Narciso Alonso Cortes identifies him as a "lawyer, from Granada" (*Diario Pinciano* |facsimile edition, Valladolid, 1933|. p. v). That Alonso Ortiz was more interested in economics than in theology is suggested not only by his two editions of the *Wealth of Nations* but by the intervening publication of a substantial treatise on money and credit: *Essayo economico sobre el sistema de la monedapapel y sobre el credito publico* (Madrid, 1796).

8.   Unless otherwise noted, the source for the remainder of this paper is the manuscript "Expediente de calificaion de la obra de Adam Smith intitulada Investigacion de la naturaleza y causas de las riquezas de las naciones traducidas en castellano y expurgado por el Lic.*do* d.*n* Jose Alonso Ortiz" (Archivo Historico Nacional, Madrid, *Inquisicion*, egajo 4484, no. 13). I have to thank the Servicio Nacional de Microfilm for a filmcopy of this document.

9.   Between 1746, when the Council of Castile first called on the Academy of History to review manuscripts submitted for publication, and 1792, the Academy examined 822 titles and rejected more than one-fourth (*Memorias de la Real Academia de la Historia*, I [Madrid, 1796], xcviii-c). There were three separate decisions on Ortiz' manuscript, but only two censors are named, Father Jose Banqueri and Don Casimiro Ortega (*Boletin de la Real Academia de la Historia*, XXXV |Madrid, 1899], 412-413).

10.   *Investigacion de la naturaleza y causas de la riqueza de las naciones, escrita en ingles por el Dr. Adam Smith, y traducida al castellano por el Lic. D. Josef Alonso Ortiz, con varias notas y ilustraciones relativas a España* (4 vols., Valladolid, 1794). There was a second "corrected and improved" edition: 4 vols., Valladolid, 1805-1806.

11.   *Principe de la Paz, Memorias*, I (*Biblioteca de autores españoles*, tomo 88; Madrid, 1956, pp. 197-297).

12.   Lucas Beltran, *Historia de las doctrinas economicas* (Barcelona, 1961), p. 97. I have pinpointed some of Ortiz' mutilations in "The Wealth of Nations in Spain and Hispanic America." *Journal of Political Economy*, LXV (1957), 102-125.

13.   *Investigacion de la naturaleza y causas de la riqueza de las naciones* (3 vols., Barcelona, 1933-34, 1947).

64

Smith's Travels on the Ship of State

G.J. Stigler

Source: *History of Political Economy*, Vol. 3 (2). Fall 1971, pp. 265-77.

The *Wealth of Nations* is a stupendous palace erected upon the granite of self-interest. It was not a narrow foundation: "though the principles of common prudence do not always govern the conduct of every individual, they always influence that of the majority of every class or order."[1] The immensely powerful force of self-interest guides resources to their most efficient uses, stimulates laborers to diligence and inventors to splendid new divisions of labor – in short, it orders and enriches the nation which gives it free rein. Indeed, if self-interest is given even a loose rein, it will perform prodigies:

> The natural effort of every individual to better his own condition, when suffered to exert itself with freedom and security, is so powerful a principle, that it is alone, and without any assistance, not only capable of carrying on the society to wealth and prosperity, but of surmounting a hundred impertinent obstructions with which the folly of human laws too often incumbers its operations; though the effect of these obstructions is always more or less either to encroach upon its freedom, or to diminish its security (2: 49-50 [508]).

This very quotation neatly summarizes the basic paradox which forms our subject.

The paradox is simply this. If self-interest dominates the majority of men in all commercial undertakings, why not also in all their political undertakings? Why should legislators erect "a hundred impertinent obstructions" to the economic behavior which creates the wealth of nations? Do men calculate in money with logic and purpose, but calculate in votes with confusion and romance?

To ask such a question is surely to answer it. A merchant who calculated closely the proper destination of every cargo, the proper duties of every agent, the proper bank to negotiate each loan – such a merchant would calculate also the effects of every tariff, every tax and subsidy, every statute governing the employment of labor. Indeed no clear distinction can be drawn between commercial and political undertakings: the procuring of favorable legislation *is* a commercial undertaking.

The widely read, widely traveled, superlatively observant author of the *Wealth of Nations* need not be told so obvious a thing as that self-interest enters also political life. A list of instances in which legislation is explained by the interests of several economic groups is compiled in Table 1. The list is incomplete in two respects. Some references have no doubt been overlooked, and none is included unless Smith explicitly mentioned the interests which were served. Often Smith did not cite the economic interests which supported a law because the identity was self-evident. When the Statute of Labourers fixed wage rates in order to deal with the "insolence of servants," Smith does not even bother to mention the probable role of employers in obtaining the legislation, probably because it was self-evident.

Even an incomplete list, however, is sufficient to document the extensive role of self-interest in economic legislation. The merchants and manufacturers are singled out for the unusual combination of cupidity and competence which marks their legislative efforts. Few other economic groups are absent from the list: the great landowners jostle the parisimonious local county's magistrates and the debtors in the queue for favorable legislation, and even the sovereign is ardent in the pursuit of his private interests.

A shorter list can be compiled of policies which have been obtained by economic classes under the mistaken understanding that they are beneficial. The main examples are these:

(1) Attempts to increase the pay of curates have simply drawn more candidates into the clergy (I, 146 [130-31]).

(2) The bounty on exports of corn, first passed in 1688, has not appreciably benefited the farmers or landowners because it raises money wages (I, 219 [196-97], 418-19 [371-72]; II, 15-20 [480-84]).[2]

(3) The practice of primogeniture has lost its onetime role of achieving security of property, and injures the landowner (I, 408-9 [362-3]).

(4) The institution of slavery is uneconomic, but panders to pride (I, 411-12 [365-66]).[3]

(5) Laws against forestallers, engrossers, etc., serve only to appease popular prejudice (II, 33-41 [493-501]).

Even such mistaken uses of political power are testimony to the pursuit of self-interest in the formulation of public policy.

So far, however, we have established only two propositions in Smith's discussion of legislation:

A. Sometimes (often?) economic legislation is passed at the request of economic groups who hope to benefit by the legislation.

B. On occasion a group is mistaken in the consequences of the legislation and receives no benefit or even positive harm from its legislative program.

The first proposition is platitudinous. The second proposition is probably of wholly minor scope: some of Smith's examples are simply wrong (in particular, the corn export subsidy surely benefited landowners) and others (such as

Table 1. Economic Classes and Their Political Behavior

Political Behavior	Beneficiary Class	Reference
1. Debasement of currency	Sovereign: to reduce debts	I, 31 |27-28|, 38 |34|
2. Prohibition of combinations of workmen	Employers	I, 75-76 |66-67|
3. Usury laws	Sovereign: to reduce debt service	I, 102 |90|
4. Exclusive privileges of corporations	Members of corporations (guilds)	I, 133 ff. |119 ff.|
5. Statute of apprenticeship	Members of corporations	I, 150 |134|
6. Settlement law (poor law)	Local communities	I, 151 f. |135 f.|
7. Wage-fixing laws	Employers	I, 158, f. |141-42|
8. Opposition to turnpikes	Counties near London	I, 165 |147-48|
9. Prohibition on planting of new vineyards	Vineyard owners	I, 172-73 |154-55|
10. Restriction on planting of tobacco	Tobacco farmers	I, 176-77 |157-58|
11. Bounty on corn exports	Agricultural class	I, 219 |197|
12. Protection of woolen trade	Woolen trade	I, 256 |230-31|
13. Protection of hides	Leather trade	I, 258-59 |232-34|
14. Legal tender of paper money	Debtors	I, 347 |310-11|
15. Primogeniture	Landowners	I, 408 |361-62|
16. Varieties of tariffs	Protected industries	I, 474 |420| II, 96-97 |550-51|
17. Abolition of seignorage	Bank of England	II, 62 |519|
18. Colonial policy	Merchants	II, 87-88 |541-43| 129 |579-80|
19. Selection of "enumerated" commodities	Merchants and fishermen	II, 91-92 |546-47|
20. Free importation of raw materials	Manufacturers	II, 161 |609|
21. Grants to regulated companies	Merchants	II, 255 |691|
22. Defeat of Walpole's tax reforms	"Smuggling Merchants"	II, 412 |833|
23. Exemption of home brewing from tax	Rich consumers	II, 421-25 |840-45|
24. Use of debt to finance wars	Avoid taxpayer revolt	II, 455 |872|
25. Raising value of currency	Debtors in rome	II, 468-69 |883-84|
26. Abolition of slavery in Pennsylvania	Quakers had few slaves	I, 412 |366|

primogeniture) do not receive a convincing explanation. In any event, men make mistakes in economic life – witness the South Sea Bubble – so why not occasionally also in political life?

A much stronger proposition, one would have thought, appropriately came from the premier scholar of self-interest:

   C. All legislation with important economic effects is the calculated
   achievement of interested economic classes.

Appropriate or not, Smith implicitly rejected the use of self-interest as a general
explanation of legislation. The rejection manifested itself in various ways.
   1. The most important evidence is that for most legislation no group is
identified which could have fostered the law and would benefit from it. The most
important area of this neglect is the discussion of taxation (II, 349-440 [779-
858]). Each tax is described, its incidence explained, and its merits and
demerits assessed – with hardly ever an explanation of why such a tax exists. As
we shall see, this omission of consideration of the political bases of taxes had
serious effects upon Smith's policy proposals.
   2. Puzzles in legislation are posed where none would exist if Smith had
considered systematically the role of self-interest in legislation. Consider the
example of laws forbidding payment of wages in kind. Smith observes that
"Whenever the legislature attempts to regulate the differences between masters
and their workmen, its counsellors are always the masters. When the regulation, therefore, is in favour of the workmen, it is always just and equitable; but it
is sometimes otherwise when in favour of the masters" (I, 158-59 [142]). Smith
illustrates this conclusion by the just and equitable laws forbidding truck wages.
   What a puzzling event! The legislature, creature of the masters, deprives the
masters of the opportunity (which Smith says they sometimes exercised) to
defraud their workmen with overpriced goods. Surely Smith's puzzle is
connected with the fact that a legislature dominated by the agricultural class
passed a law forbidding truck wages in certain nonagricultural industries
(textiles, iron, apparel).[4]
   Other examples are at hand. The laws forbidding the lower classes to wear
fine textiles (I, 271-72 [245]) surely were not designed simply to keep them
from wearing clothing that was "much more expensive" – one is entitled to
suspect the support of the manufacturers of cheaper raiment. The prohibition
on banks of the issue of small bank notes was more likely calculated to
discourage entry into banking than to keep bank notes in knowledgeable hands
(I, 343-45 [307-08]). A much more skeptical eye would have been turned to
arguments such as the one that absolute governments treat slaves more kindly
than republican states (II, 99-100 [553-54]).
   3. Smith gave a larger role to emotion, prejudice, and ignorance in political
life than he ever allowed in ordinary economic affairs. The mercantile policies
directed to the improvement of the balance of trade with particular countries
have their origin in "national prejudice and animosity" (I, 497 [441]). The
legislation against corn traders is so perverse as to lead Smith to compare it to
laws against witchcraft (II, 41 [500]); indeed, "the laws concerning corn may
every where be compared to the laws concerning religion" (II, 48 [507]). In fact
all unwise economic legislation from which no politically strong constituency
drew benefits must be nonrational legislation.
   The agricultural classes, the classes with preponderant political power in
Smith's England, are singled out for their benevolence and stupidity:

   When the public deliberates concerning any regulation of commerce or police, the proprietors of land never can mislead it, with a view to promote the interest of their own particular order; at least, if they have any tolerable knowledge of that interest. They are, indeed, too often defective in this tolerable knowledge. They are the only one of the three orders whose revenue costs them neither labour nor care, but comes to them, as it were, of its own accord, and independent of any plan or project of their own. That indolence, which is the natural effect of the ease and security of their situation, renders them too often, not only ignorant, but incapable of that application of mind which is necessary in order to foresee and understand the consequences of any public regulation (I, 276-77 [249];[5] also I, 455-56 [402-3]).

Yet Smith notes often enough legislation which has been procured by the agricultural classes for their own interests (I,416, [369], 443 [394]; II, 91, [545], 425 [844-45]).[6]

Little attention is paid to the political process, and that little is tantalizingly diverse. In some respects the sovereign is an incompetent manager. He cannot conduct a trading enterprise:

Princes, however, have frequently engaged in many other mercantile projects, and have been willing, like private persons, to mend their fortunes by becoming adventurers in the common branches of trade. They have scarce ever succeeded. The profusion with which the affairs of princes are always managed, renders it almost impossible that they should. The agents of a prince regard the wealth of their master as inexhaustible; are careless at what price they buy; are careless at what price they sell; are careless at what expence they transport his goods from one place to another (II, 343 [771]).

Again, "the persons who have the administration of government [are] generally disposed to reward both themselves and their immediate dependents rather more than enough" (II, 395 [818]). Only the post office, Smith states in a rare moment of inverted clairvoyance, can be successfully managed by "every sort of government." In general, monarchies are conducted with "slothful and negligent profusion" and democracies with "thoughtless extravagance," but aristrocracies such as Venice and Amsterdam have "orderly, vigilant and parsimonious administration" (II, 342 [770]).

Yet on other occasions Smith views political behavior in perfectly cold-blooded, rational terms. The discussion of the "recent disturbances" which constituted the American revolution provides a striking example:

Men desire to have some share in the management of public affairs chiefly on account of the importance which it gives them. Upon the power which the greater part of the leading men, the natural aristocracy of every country, have of preserving or defending their respective importance, depends the stability and duration of every system of free government. In the attacks which these leading men are continually making upon the importance of one another, and in the defence of their own, consists the whole play of domestic faction and ambition. The leading men of America, like those of all other countries, desire to preserve their own importance. They feel, or imagine, that if their assemblies, which they are fond of calling parliaments, and of considering as equal in authority to the parliament of Great Britain, should be so far degraded as to become the humble ministers and executive officers of that parliament, the greater part of their own importance would be at an end. They have rejected, therefore, the proposal of being taxed by parliamentary requisition, and like other ambitious and high-spirited men, have rather chosen to draw the sword in defence of their own importance (II, 136-37 [586]).

Smith shrewdly proposed to draw these leaders away from "peddling for the little prizes" in the "paltry raffle of colonial faction" by giving representation to the colonies in Parliament, where dazzling prizes might be won by ambitious colonists in the "great state lottery of British politics."[7]

In general, however, Smith's attitude toward political behavior was not dissimilar to that of a parent toward a child: the child was often mistaken and sometimes perverse, but normally it would improve in conduct if properly instructed.

The canons of taxation illustrate both the attitude and the fundamental weakness of Smith's position. Here are the maxims:

1. The subjects of every state ought to contribute towards the support of government, as nearly as possible, in proportion to their respective abilities; . . .
2. The tax which each individual is bound to pay ought to be certain, and not arbitrary.
3. Every tax ought to be levied at the time, or in the manner, in which it is most likely to be convenient for the contributor to pay; . . .
4. Every tax ought to be so contrived as both to take out and to keep out of the pockets of the people as little as possible, over and above what it brings into the public treasury of the state (II, 350-51 [777-79]).

Many of the specific taxes Smith proceeds to examine fail to meet one or more of these criteria, and many reforms are accordingly proposed.

A Chancellor of the Exchequer would have found these rules most peculiar. If adopted, they would obtain for him at least the temporary admiration of the professors of moral philosophy, but this is a slender and notably fickle constituency on which to build a party. The two basic canons of taxation are surely rather different:

1. The revenue system must not imperil the political support for the regime.
2. The revenue system must yield revenue.

Smith's maxims touch on aspects of a revenue system which are relevant to its productivity and acceptability – not always in the direction he wished – but they form a wholly inadequate basis for judging individual taxes.

One may give – for generations economists have given – advice lavishly without taking account of the political forces which confine and direct policy. In the absence of knowledge of these political forces, the advice must often be bad and usually be unpersuasive. Why tell the sovereign that free trade is desirable, if one has no method of disarming the merchants and manufacturers who have obtained the protectionist measures? Why tell the French sovereign to abandon the *taille* and capitations and increase the *vingtièmes*, when only a revolution could dislodge the tax-favored classes?[8] Why believe that better turnpikes await only the appointments of a better class of commissioners (II, 248 [684-85])?

The contrast between Smith's discussions of political reform and other reforms is instructive. The dons of Oxford, he says, grossly neglect their duties of instruction. Does he preach to each don a moral reform, seeking a pledge of diligence and good sense? Smith would have considered such a remedy to be silly: the teacher is intelligently pursuing his interest, which is "to live as much at his ease as he can" because his income is independent of his efforts (II, 284 [718]). A system of remuneration based upon effort and achievement, not a weekly sermon, would bring about the changes Smith wishes.

In the political sense no corresponding search is made for the effective principles of behavior. Therefore reforms must be effected, if effected they can be, by moral suasion. At best this is an extra-ordinarily slow and uncertain method of changing policy; at worst it may lead to policies which endanger the society. Of course erroneous and undesirable public policies arise out of failures of comprehension as well as out of the efforts of self-serving groups, but there is little reason to accept Smith's implicit assumption that the main source of error is ignorance or "prejudice." Yet Smith's only remedy for erroneous policy is sound analysis, and that remedy is appropriate only to a minority of objectionable policies.

It may appear that Smith's failure to apply the organon of self-interest to political behavior requires no explanation. Political science had been a normative literature for 2300 years before Smith wrote and has continued to remain normative to the present day. The great Bentham, who did apply a theory of utility-maximizing behavior to political as well as other social phenomena, never stirred an inch beyond preaching, to see how well his theory actually explained legislation – and that is why his great organon remained sterile.

Yet it is uncomfortable to explain Smith's failure by the failure of everyone else, for he is a better man than everyone else. His ability to examine the most pompous and ceremonial of institutions and conduct with the jaundiced eye of a master economist – and the evident delight he took in such amusement – is one of the trademarks of his authorship. The "uniform, constant, and uninterrupted effort of every man to better his condition" (I, 364 [326]) – why was it interrupted when a man entered Parliament? The man whose spacious vision could see the Spanish War of 1739 as a bounty and who attributed the decline of feudalism to changes in consumption patterns how could he have failed to see the self-interest written upon the faces of politicians and constituencies? The man who denied the state the capacity to conduct almost any business save the postal – how could he give to the sovereign the task of extirpating cowardice in the citizenry? How so, Professor Smith?

A Postscript on Failures of Self-Interest

It is in the political arena that Smith implicitly locates the most numerous and consistent failures of self-interest in guiding people's behavior, but this is not the only place where self-interest fails. Since the effective working of self-interest is so central to Smith's work, it may be useful to sketch the nature of the failures he described.

Every failure of a person to make decisions which serve his self-interest may be interpreted as an error in logic: means have been chosen which are inappropriate to the person's ends. Nevertheless it is useful to distinguish several categories of failure, all of which are found in the *Wealth of Nations*.

Class I: The individual knows the "facts" but fails to anticipate the consequences of his actions. The occasional behavior of the landlord is an example in Smith's book. He points out more than once that "improvements, besides, are not always made by the stock of the landlord, but sometimes by that of the tenant. When the lease comes to be renewed, however, the landlord commonly demands the same augmentation of rent, as if they had been all made by his own" (I, 162 [144-45]; also I, 414 [367-68]). The landlord is shortsighted in his greed: he removes the incentive to the tenant to make improvements which would yield more to tenant and landlord than the going rate of return. Hence there exists a system of rents which would make both tenant and landlord better off. This superior form of tenancy does not require the cooperation of any third party – only clear reasoning and a little inventiveness in writing a lease are necessary. The failure of self-interest to be served arises out of a failure to reason correctly.

The following are additional examples of the failure of individuals to reason correctly:

(1) The apprenticeship system does not give appropriate incentives to the apprentice to be diligent in his work (I, 137 [122]).
(2) Only a landlord can work no-rent land because he demands a rent from others (I, 184 [165]).
(3) The crown lands would be more valuable if they were sold off (II, 348 [775-76]).

One important subclass of failures due to imperfect knowledge involves the future: future gains are overestimated, or future costs underestimated. Examples are these:

(1) The possible gains are overestimated relative to the possible losses in risky ventures (I, 119 [106]; I, 124 [111]).
(2) Workers do not anticipate in seasons of plenty the higher prices of provisions in seasons of scarcity (I, 83 [74]).
(3) Workmen paid by the piece are "very apt to overwork themselves, and ruin their health and constitution in a few years" (I, 91 [81-82]).
(4) In the absence of usury laws, lenders will deal with "prodigals and projectors" (who will be unable to repay the loans?) (I, 379 [339]).

Class II: In an important range of situations, the employer or master is unable to control his agents so they will act in his interest. Among the examples are these:

(1) Slaves are often managed by a "negligent or careless overseer" (I, 90 [81]).
(2) Monopoly is the great enemy of good management (I, 165 [147]; II, 154 [602]).
(3) The East India Company's employees trade only in their own interest (II, 155 [603]; also II, 265 [700]).

Smith does not explain why *all* agents or employees do not display the same tendency to self-serving conduct, and it may be that this charge is made only against institutions which he objects to also on other grounds.

Class III: In the production of what is now called a public good, self-interest does not lead the individual to supply the correct amount of the good. Smith gives the example of the inadequate preparation by the individual citizen for war (II, 219 [658]). This is not so much a failure of self-interest as it is a failure of individual action.

The first class of (nonpolitical) failures is much the most important in the *Wealth of Nations* if importance is measured by number and variety of examples. A good number of these failures are due to incomplete factual information, and it would only be anachronistic to lament Smith's failure to discuss the problem of the optimum investment of the individual in the acquisition of knowledge. The implicit charge of inadequate analysis of known facts, it should be observed, is made against all classes: the greedy landlord, the impetuous laborer, the negligent employer, the shortsighted lender. No principle is apparent by which one can distinguish these failures from the many decisions which effectively advance these various persons' self-interests: the decisions are not especially subtle or especially demanding of information. One could make a fair case, I believe, that every alleged failure was nonexistent or of negligible magnitude. The high priest of self-interest, like all other high priests, had a strong demand for sinners.

Notes

Mr. Stigler is Walgreen Professor of American Institutions at the University of Chicago.
   1.   *The Wealth of Nations*, ed. Cannan (London: Methuen, 1961), 1: 313 [279]. Page references to the Modern Library edition, disfigured by a vulgar preface, are given within brackets.
   2.   There is a related argument on the taxation of necessaries (II, 402-5) [824-27].
   3.   Hence the institution serves self-interest, but not production.
   4.   We need not explore the reason truck wages were preferred in some trades: George Hilton's explanation does not appear to be completely general; "The British Truck System in the Nineteenth Century," *Journal of Political Economy*, June 1957.
   5.   The laborers are no better: "But though the interest of the labourer is strictly connected with that of society, he is incapable either of comprehending that interest, or of understanding its connexion with his own." (I, 277 [249]).
   6.   In an interesting reversal of the argument, Smith argues that when tenants possess the vote, their landlords treat them better! (I, 414-15 [368]).

7.   The retention of the unprofitable colonies by Great Britain is attributed to the interests of the administration-bureaucracy (II, 131-32 [581-82]). For a lesser example of the explanation of political behavior by interests of the sovereign, see II, 252-53 [688-89].

8.   And Smith so recognized: II, 437 [855-56].

65

Adam Smith's Conception of Self-Interest in Economic and Political Affairs

A.W. Coats

Source: *History of Political Economy*, Vol. 7 (1), Spring 1975, pp. 132-6.

In a stimulating recent paper, George Stigler commented on the apparent inconsistency between Adam Smith's emphasis on the role of self-interest in economic affairs and his reluctance to apply the same principle to political behavior. By assigning "a larger role to emotion, prejudice, and ignorance in political life than he ever allowed in economic affairs," Stigler declared, Smith created unnecessary "puzzles" which would not have arisen had he "considered systematically the role of self-interest in legislation." Although Smith sometimes discussed political behavior in "perfectly cold-blooded, rational terms," his fundamental attitude was paternalistic – i.e., didactic but hopeful. He made no search for the "effective principles" of political conduct, assuming implicitly that the main source of error in public policies was ignorance or prejudice; and Stigler concluded by asking why Smith failed to grasp the true importance of self-interest in politics and legislation.[1]

The purpose of this note is to suggest that self-interest, especially if interpreted "in perfectly cold-blooded, rational terms," is an inadequate and misleading basis from which to evaluate Smith's account of politics and the legislative process. As Stigler has shown, Smith revealed numerous "failures" of self-interest in both economic and political affairs, and there seems to be no reason why this should be either surprising or paradoxical, given Smith's conception of self-interest. Indeed, Smith's views on this point are a good deal more subtle and complex than historians of economics have generally assumed, and there is no inherent reason why self-interest should function as effectively in the political arena as in the marketplace.

Like many other historians of economics, Stigler has concentrated exclusively on *The Wealth of Nations*, the most economic of Smith's works, in which man's self-interested pursuit of economic gain occupied the center of the stage. Yet *The Wealth of Nations*, considered in isolation, conveys a misleading and one-sided impression of Smith's attitude to human nature and conduct, and it must be supplemented and corrected by reference to his other writings, especially *The Theory of Moral Sentiments*. Although learned commentators have long disagreed as to the exact interpretation of self-interest and the roles of reason and emotion in Smith's account of human psychology, a narrowly rational and atomistically individualistic interpretation is no longer tenable. As Viner observed at the close of his distinguished career:

> The important thing for the interpreter of Smith is to note how low down in this scale |of psychological traits and ethical values| reason enters into the picture as a factor influencing social behavior. The sentiments are innate in man: that is, man is endowed with them by providence. Under normal circumstances, the sentiments make no mistakes. It is reason which is fallible. Greatest of all in degree of fallibility is the speculative reason of the moral philosopher, unless the legislator is on a still lower level. Man, however, tends to attribute to the human reason what is really the wisdom of the Author of Nature as reflected in the sentiments.[2]

Even in the economic sphere, according to Smith, the basis of man's conduct was instinctual rather than rational; viz., the instinct to "truck, barter and exchange"; and while his treatment of the relationship between self-interest and the social sympathies is too complex to be summarized briefly, it was certainly not narrowly individualistic. Indeed, as Gladys Bryson remarked thirty years ago, in Smith's works "there sometimes seem to be no individuals at all, so organic is the relation of person to person conceived to be";[3] and very recently, in this journal, Ralph Anspach argued that Smith regarded the "auto-pleasures" as less important than "sympathy-pleasures" in the social and political spheres.[4] Whether he considered that sympathy or any other species of fellow feeling actually influenced market behavior is still a matter of dispute, partly because his references to this matter are obscure.[5] But we are less concerned at present with the psychological origins and nature of human behavior than with the character of the judgmental process in different spheres, and here we must introduce a further complication mentioned by Smith himself. The chain of connections between men's motives and their consequences is directly affected by the prevalence of illusion or self-deceit, which operates in the economic sphere to induce men to grossly overrate the advantages of wealth and rank. As is well known, Smith maintained that when men in fact promote the public good they generally do so indirectly and unintentionally, while pursuing their own individual aims; and these unintended consequences of individual purposive action occur in the social and political, as well as the economic realm.[6] Smith stated that merchants and manufacturers were usually well aware of their own interest, were effective in achieving it, and rarely professed to be acting for the public good. In political affairs, however, men often do genuinely believe themselves to be acting for the public good, and it is therefore appropriate to note Smith's warning that the individual seeking his own interest "frequently promotes that of the society more effectually than when he really intends to promote it."[7] This is but one of the significant differences between economic and political affairs, a matter to which we must now turn.

In comparing Smith's treatment of economic and political matters it is clear that the subjective differences in human behavior patterns are less important than objective differences in the activities themselves; and it is the nature of these activities that explains the comparative weakness and ineffectiveness of self-interest in politics. According to Stigler, failures of self-interest fall into three broad categories:

(a) cases where the individual knows the facts but fails to anticipate the consequences of his action;
(b) cases where the individual employer is unable to control his agents so they will not act in his interest; and
(c) cases where self-interest does not lead the individual to supply the correct amount of a commodity or service; i.e., with so-called "public goods."

As already noted, the combined operation of the individual's capacity for self-deceit – "this fatal weakness of mankind, is the source of half the disorders of human life" – and his inability to foresee the broader consequences of his actions might be considered a sufficient explanation of any number of failures. But in the political sphere there are difficulties additional to those encountered in the marketplace. For example:

(i) The individual's inability to know his "true" self-interest may occur because political interests often cannot be specified as precisely as economic interests; the measuring rod of money is absent, or at least less generally prevalent, and political interests tend to be multi-faceted rather than single-faceted.
(ii) Even when a person knows his true interest, the relationship between ends and means is often more obscure in politics than in commercial matters; in other words, the political process is more difficult to comprehend than market transactions, the rules of the political game are more complex and less well-defined than the mechanistic operation of market forces.
(iii) When the poltical process is completed, the individual participant or observer may find it more difficult to decide whether he has actually attained his objective(s), because political outcomes more often tend to emerge as multiples rather than singletons; not all the ingredients of the package are equally welcome, and the absence of a convenient measuring rod complicates the task of weighing up the gains and losses.

These schematically presented differences between political and economic processes are obvious enough; and they may suggest reasons why Smith's works lack a clear-cut conception of political equilibrium comparable to the concept of economic equilibrium elaborated in *The Wealth of Nations* and the suggestions of social equilibrium embodied, though not fully worked out, in *The Theory of Moral Sentiments*.

Failures of the kind encountered in category (b) need not be considered separately; the reasons already given – i.e., (i) to (iii) above – indicate why they are somewhat more likely to occur in political affairs. Category (c) failures, on the other hand, deserve more careful consideration in view of the special circumstances of collective action of the type commonly encountered with public goods and political processes. Leaving aside the possibility that individuals may frequently act less rationally in political than in economic affairs, as Mancur Olson has shown, where group action is involved the assumption of rational self-interested behavior on the part of individuals cannot correctly be generalized without reference to the size of the group and the attendant circumstances:

> It does *not* follow, because all of the individuals in a group would gain if they achieved their group objective, that they would act to achieve that objective, even if they were all rational and self-interested. Indeed, unless the number of individuals in a group is small, or unless there is coercion or some other special device to make individuals act in their common interest, *rational self-interested individuals will not act to achieve their common or group interests.*[8]

In the case of a "latent" group, for example,

> if one member does or does not help provide the collective good, no other member will be significantly affected and therefore none has any reason to react ... Accordingly, large or "latent" groups have no incentive to act to obtain a collective good because, however valuable the collective good might be to the group as a whole, it does not offer the individual any incentive to pay dues to any organization working in the latent group's interest, or to bear in any other way any of the costs of the necessary collective action.[9]

It would be a trifle far-fetched to suggest that Smith had fully grasped this point, though he was very sensitive to the influence of small group actions by monopolizing merchants and manufacturers. Yet at times he also seemed aware of the wider implications of the case as, for example, when he observed in the *Lectures*:

> It is the sense of public utility, more than of private, which influences men to obedience. It may sometimes be for my interest to disobey, and to wish government overturned, but I am sensible that other men are of a different opinion from me, and would not assist me in the enterprise. I therefore submit to its decision for the good of the whole.[10]

This passage, taken in conjunction with Olson's analysis and the suggestions contained in Stigler's paper, indicates that Adam Smith's account of the legislative process and political action generally would repay further study. It seems clear that Smith's commentators have paid insufficient heed to these aspects of his work.

Notes

A.W. Coats, author of the first article to appear in HOPE, vol. 1, no. 1, is head of the Department of Economic and Social History in the University of Nottingham.

1. George J. Stigler, "Smith's Travels on the Ship of State," *History of Political Economy* 3 (1971): 270, 269, 271, 274.

2. Jacob Viner, *The Role of Providence in the Social Order: An Essay in Intellectual History* (Philadelphia, 1972), pp. 78-79. For other accounts of the interdependence of feeling and reason in Smith see A.L. Macfie, *The Individual in Society* (London, 1967), e.g., pp. 63-67, 92, 95-96; and T.D. Campbell, *Adam Smith's Science of Morals* (London, 1971), pp. 65-66.

3. Gladys Bryson, *Man and Society: The Scottish Inquiry of the Eighteenth Century* (New York, 1968; originally published in 1945), p. 160.

4. Ralph Anspach, "The Implications of the Theory of Moral Sentiment for Adam Smith's Economic Thought," *History of Political Economy* 4 (1972): 180, 186.

5. Cf. Jacob Viner, "Adam Smith," in *International Encyclopedia of the Social Sciences*, 5 (New York, 1968): 325; and Anspach, p. 196. According to some commentators, "Smith suggests that the social order becomes possible by virtue of the restraints which individuals impose upon themselves" (Cf. Andrew Skinner, editor's introduction to *The Wealth of Nations*, Harmondsworth, 1970, p. 17); others, however, emphasize the importance of economic and institutional constraints. Cf. Nathan Rosenberg, "Some Institutional Aspects of the *Wealth of Nations*," *Journal of Political Economy* 68 (1960): 557-70.

6. For an extended discussion of this point see Louis Schneider, *The Scottish Moralists on Human Nature and Society* (Chicago, 1967), pp. xxix.xli. and lxii-lxv.

7. *The Wealth of Nations*, ed. Edwin Cannan (London, 1904), 1:421.

8. Mancur Olson, *The Logic of Collective Action: Public Goods and the Theory of Groups* (Cambridge, Mass., 1965), p. 2. I am indebted to Mark Blaug, who drew my attention to this analysis.

9. Ibid., pp. 50-51. Olson's argument is, of course, too subtle to be presented here in detail.

10. Adam Smith, *Lectures on Justice, Police, Revenue and Arms*, ed. Edwin Cannan (Oxford, 1896), p. 10.

66

Adam Smith's *Wealth of Nations*

D. White

Source: *Journal of the History of Ideas*. 37, 1976, pp. 715-20.

Adam Smith, *An Inquiry into the Nature and Causes of the Wealth of Nations*, edited by R.H. Campbell and A.S. Skinner; textual editor, W.B. Todd; 2 vols., Clarendon Press, Oxford, 1976. Pp. 1080, $62.50.

Andrew S. Skinner and Thomas Wilson, eds., *Essays on Adam Smith*, Clarendon Press, Oxford, 1975. Pp. 647, £15.

Although nearly every western European country had a great outburst of creative energy during the eighteenth century, none is more remarkable than Scotland. Recently united with Britain politically, and even more recently culturally and economically, tiny Scotland produced an amazing number of outstanding figures in politics, economics, education, engineering, philosophy, and literature (to use modern categories that for the most part had no technical definitions in the eighteenth century). Leaving the literary people aside, most educated people would recognize the name of David Hume but not those of Adam Ferguson, Frances Hutcheson or Thomas Reid who enjoyed an equal reputation among their contemporaries. Most likely, only scholars would know Lord Monboddo, James Oswald, Lord Kames, or Joseph Black to name some of the better known personages of what has been called the "Scottish Renaissance." If none of these men are exactly household names, there is one eighteenth-century Scotsman who probably is. I refer, of course, to Adam Smith.

Why is Adam Smith so famous and particularly why is the bicentennial of the first edition of *Wealth of Nations* being celebrated with lectures, conferences, and the publication of his complete works in an elaborate and costly edition?[1] The answer to this rhetorical question is not exactly simple. Some parts of the answer are not difficult. Rightly or wrongly, Adam Smith has been enshrined as the patron saint of the free enterprise system. Without Karl Marx, and particularly the Russian Revolution, the name of Adam Smith would probably be no less obscure than those of the gentlemen mentioned above. It is also true that Smith's position seems to be secure, in textbooks at any rate, as the "Father of Political Economy." Certainly *Wealth of Nations* was an influential book

140

and a genuinely popular one. Reading Smith's windy periods today, it is rather difficult to appreciate why his contemporaries admired his literary style, as well as his opinions, but they obviously did. *Wealth of Nations* went through five editions in Smith's lifetime, totaling over 5000 copies. The first edition sold out in six months.[2] T.H. Buckle in his *History of Civilisation in England* (1857) mentions that *Wealth of Nations* was cited favorably in Parliament no fewer than thirty-seven times between 1783 and the turn of the century. Further, it is possible that the Tory government of Lord North appointed Smith, a Whig, to the lucrative position of Commissioner of Customs for Scotland because of the inspiration for new taxes North got from *Wealth of Nations*.[3]

R.H. Campbell and A.S. Skinner in their immensely valuable introduction to *Wealth of Nations* argue, rightly I think, that Smith's importance lies in the unique appeal he had to Englishmen of the eighteenth century. As they say, "the attraction of the WN was not that it was a tourist's guide to the subsequent course of industrialization, but that it had a command of the institutional structure of the time sufficiently convincing to demonstrate its contemporary relevance."[4] Smith was writing about the economic conditions of Britain as they existed during the third quarter of the eighteenth century, conditions that were unique to Britain at that time and foreign to an industrialized Britain of a later time. I shall return to this point later.

If *Wealth of Nations* was uniquely a tract for the times, Adam Smith was personally very much a man of the times. The intellectual world of the eighteenth century was a small one in two senses. In the one sense it was small enough for a man of talent to master almost all of it. The volume of *Essays* under review here, gives Smith two hats to wear. There is the Adam Smith of *Wealth of Nations* (sixteen essays, 309 pages) and the Adam Smith of the *Theory of Moral Sentiments* and everything else (fourteen essays, 294 pages). Of course Smith himself would have accepted only one hat, that of moral philosopher, a field which included almost all existing knowledge outside of natural philosophy, theology, and classical literature. Although it is true that Smith, in terms of publication, spent most of his time writing and revising *Wealth of Nations*, his original aim was apparently to incorporate the whole of moral philosophy into his writing as he had in his teaching.

Adam Smith's personal collection of books (some three thousand volumes) give further indication of the breadth of his learning. Almost half were in foreign languages (Latin, Greek, French, and Italian). In subject matter Smith's library contained Latin and Greek classics; literature and art; law and politics; economics and history and science and philosophy. The only things conspicuously absent were theology and prose fiction.[5] His leisure reading, particularly during his latter years, was primarily in the Greek poets. The range of Smith's learning would have been remarkable at any time but it was less conspicuous during the eighteenth century when versatility and catholicity of taste was the rule among intellectuals.

Adam Smith's world was also small physically, that is, in terms of his personal contacts. As we have seen, Smith read almost everything except theology and prose fiction. He also knew personally or exchanged ideas by letter with most of the important intellectuals of his generation. As I have already pointed out, the Scotland of his day was filled with stimulating people, all of whom he seems to have known intimately. Also it seems that Scotsmen of his day were determined to join the rest of the world at large. Other than trying to get rid of their accent (always a problem), the principal way they did it in this context was by the formation of clubs for self improvement and the mutual dissemination of ideas. While Smith was teaching at Glasgow he was a member of the Political Economy Club founded by the famous banker Andrew Cochrane. This club must have been important to Smith's practical education for the basis of Glasgow's flourishing trade was the importation of tobacco from the colonies and its trans-shipment to England and Europe. This under the benevolent protection of the Navigation Acts. But Glasgow also suffered from the mercantilistic policies of the British government because it imported flax and iron under onerous conditions. Notably, Glasgow manufacturers had to import expensive Swedish iron rather than the cheaper colonial product. (I should also point out that later, as Commissioner of Customs, Smith came into daily contact with what he regarded as the evil effects of mercantilism.) He was also a founder of a club at Glasgow, the Literary Society. At Edinburgh he was a member of no less than five clubs or societies. In London, he was a member of the famous Literary Club. In addition to these more or less formal organizations he was a member at various times of numerous dining groups whose rationale was conversation rather than food. His own Sunday night suppers in Edinburgh were famous for their distinguished company.

Outside of Scotland, Smith was several times a visitor to London for extended periods. As tutor to the Duke of Buccleugh he spent three years abroad, mostly in France, where as usual he rubbed shoulders with everyone. During the several months he spent in Paris, his connection with the Duke of Buccleugh and his own reputation as the author of the *Theory of Moral Sentiments* gave him entrance to all the famous literary *Salons*. More important for the future, this was ten years prior to the publication of *Wealth of Nations*, he became intimate with Quesnay, Turgot, and other *philosophes* of a physiocratic persuasion.

All of this raises the issue of Smith's originality. Obviously he did not exist in an intellectual vacuum. He personally knew many of his like-minded contemporaries and had read the rest. Further, as Skinner points out in his introduction to the *Essays*,[6] all of Smith's writings were informed by a set of propositions that were not specifically his but rather the common property of the "enlightened" men of his generation. They are: (1) the study of human nature is prior in time and importance; (2) the experimental method of Newton is the proper way to study man; and (3) human nature was and had been everywhere the same. To these I should like to add another characteristic mental attitude that Smith shared with his contemporaries. That is his belief in a pattern in the affairs of men; a belief in rigid stages of human development. In *Wealth of Nations* that belief is explicit in Smith's famous four-stage theory of economic development, but I believe it is implicit in the *Theory of Moral Sentiments*.

Adam Smith himself was very sensitive to the charge that his ideas were patterned after those of others. It seems clear that Smith did learn much from his teacher Francis Hutcheson, as he certainly did from his friend David Hume.[7] Montesquieu, Quesnay, Turgot, and many other *philosophes* provided him with inspiration and sometimes direct examples.[8] It is well known, for example, that the famous opening passage of *Wealth of Nations* on the division of labor comes from the *Encyclopédie* of 1755. However, although *Wealth of Nations* was not published until 1776, Smith always claimed that the basic ideas of *Wealth of Nations* were in his mind and in his lectures at least from the beginning of his tenure at Glasgow. Dugald Stewart, his earliest biographer, cites a statement of Smith's to this effect and found confirmation from some of his early students who remembered hearing "the doctrine of natural liberty" from him.[9] In fact what is probably the best statement on this subject comes from Dugald Stewart, a distinguished economist in his own right. He remarked that *Wealth of Nations* served the purpose "of an elementary treatise on political economy." "The skill and comprehensiveness of mind displayed in his arrangement, can be judged of by those alone who have compared it with that adopted by his immediate predecessors. And perhaps, in point of utility, the labour he has employed in collecting and methodising their scattered ideas, is not less valuable than the results of his own original speculations: for it is only when digested in a clear and natural order, that truths make their proper impression on the mind, and that erroneous opinions can be combated with success."[10]

The work of Adam Smith is of enormous historical importance and worth studying for that reason alone. But is there more than that? Does Adam Smith have any utility today? Of course the time is past when one learned economics from *Wealth of Nations* or even begins the serious study of economics by reading it. And only the most serious students of the eighteenth century are likely to read the *Theory of Moral Sentiments* or the fragments of the works he left unpublished during his lifetime. In the economic field, however, he has sometimes been treated as a contemporary authority or, more often than not, chided for not foreseeing the future. For example, he has been taken to task for his neglect of women, for failing to notice the so-called Industrial Revolution, for his overemphasis on agriculture, and for his harsh treatment of the mercantilists. He has even been taken to task for not mentioning Sir James Steuart's *Principles of Political Oeconomy* (1767), a mercantilist treatise, and for distracting attention from the Physiocrats.[11] The point in both cases is that the dominance of *Wealth of Nations* obscured works which are now seen to have greater relevance to modern economic conditions.

The present editors of *Wealth of Nations* will have none of this anachronistic treatment of Smith. At several points in their introduction they point out that the source of its popularity and influence was precisely its contemporary relevance. Agriculture *was* the chief source of wealth during the third quarter of the eighteenth century. Commerce was second (principally the re-export of colonial tobacco, sugar, and Indian cotton) while manufacturing may have been in a temporary decline in terms of relative importance. Smith wrote before the mechanisation of the cotton industry, the growth of the factory system, and the large accumulations of capital via the joint stock company. To quote Campbell and Skinner again: "to search the WN for examples of the institutional structure that was to emerge later in a more advanced industrial economy is to search for qualities which it cannot possess except fortuitously."[12]

Now to turn directly to this new edition of *Wealth of Nations* and its associated volume of essays. Some readers are going to ask if a new edition was really necessary, particularly at the price involved. Of course the present volumes are a part of a complete new edition of the works of Smith so the only alternative to a new edition would have been to republish the fine edition of Edward Cannan. However, I am going to suggest that this edition is well worth while. First of all, W.B. Todd has given us the most accurate edition of *Wealth of Nations* that is practically feasible. He collated forty-nine printed copies of editions one through six and has included in his apparatus all variant readings. There is a concordance to the Methuen edition of 1930 and the Modern Library edition of 1937. There are three textual schedules of accidental readings, excluded variants, and line-end hyphenation. Textually we have here a bibliographer's joy. I only have one small complaint. Throughout the text there are numerals enclosed in brackets. They are in two series which overlap the two volume format of this edition: 2 through 518 and 2 through 464. I can find no clue in the textual introduction or the apparatus as to what they mean.

From the point of view of general scholarship the chief virtue of this new edition is the general introduction and the notes to the text. In both, R.H. Campbell and A.S. Skinner provide a valuable overview to the work of Smith as a whole by explaining the inter-relationships among them in the general introduction and by giving cross-references between *Wealth of Nations* and the others in the notes. In other respects the notes are extremely helpful in explaining the text and in providing bibliographic references.

Essays on Adam Smith is one of the companion volumes in the Glasgow edition of the works of Adam Smith; the other is a much-needed biography which unfortunately was not in print at the time of this writing. These thirty essays, covering everything from rhetoric to technical economic analysis, are indeed a tribute to the wide-ranging genius of Adam Smith. Indeed, it would take an Adam Smith to review them all. For that reason, as well as limitations of space, I shall mention only the ones that might be of particular interest to readers of this Journal.

In Part I, devoted to the philosophical and political aspects of Smith's thought, readers will be immediately drawn to W.P.D. Wightman's essay on "Adam Smith and the History of Ideas." The title is a bit of a misnomer for Wightman deals primarily with the *History of Astronomy*. He does remind us, however, that Smith, despite his self-acknowledged debt to the "Newtonian" method, retains a lot of the deductive analysis of Descartes. J. Cropsey, in "Adam Smith and Political Philosophy," makes two important points. First of all, he emphasizes Smith's debt to Locke in his attempt to reconcile the duties of moral virtue with the rights of nature. Secondly, Cropsey points out that Smith anticipated many of the Marxian criticisms of capitalism, notably, the preponderance of economic influence on human affairs, the primacy of labor in the process of production, and, more generally, that "the engine of progress was the ignoble desires and strivings of man, channelled through the economic institutions of production and distribution. . ." Both A.S. Skinner in "Adam Smith: an Economic Interpretation of History" and D. Forbes in "Sceptical Whiggism, Commerce, and Liberty" emphasize Smith's conception of liberty as the fortuitous product of economic development. And although Smith identified the growth of personal freedom with the historical development of the

Whig interest, Forbes calls Smith a "sceptical" Whig because he, like Hume, rejected the "idols" of the "vulgar" Whig position (e.g., the contract theory of government).

Part II of the *Essays* deals with the subject matter of the *Wealth of Nations* and is primarily, but not exclusively, economic in nature. Of particular interest is R.L. Heilbroner's essay on "The Paradox of Progress: Decline and Decay in *The Wealth of Nations*," which argues that Smith's economic and social philosophies are incompatible with one another. This is in contrast to the essays by W. Eltis, "Adam Smith's Theory of Economic Growth" and by G.B. Richardson, "Adam Smith on Competition and Increasing Returns," which are much more optimistic than Heilbroner's essay concerning the fate of the working class and the effects of increasing concentration on competition respectively. Finally, I would like to call attention to the essay by Mark Blaug, "The Economics of Education in English Classical Political Economy: A Reexamination." Blaug argues that Smith, in contradistinction to the "classical" political economists, gave much more weight to the role of education in respect to the public good.

I have one concluding remark concerning this volume of essays. The Glasgow editors obviously felt that a companion volume of this nature was appropriate to their series. I tend to disagree for the simple reason that these essays are so worth reading that there is a danger that they will be neglected in this format. I believe they would have found a wider audience by being published in scholarly journals as indeed some of them have been.

Notes

1. The Glasgow Edition of the *Works and Correspondence of Adam Smith*.
2. W.B. Todd, "The Text and Apparatus," WN I, 61-64.
3. John Rae, *Life of Adam Smith* (London, 1895), 327ff.
4. General Introduction, WN, I, 50.
5. H. Mizuta, *Adam Smith's Library* (Cambridge, 1967).
6. *Essays*, 8.
7. *Essays*, 14.
8. General Introduction, WN, I, 22.
9. Rae, *Life of Adam Smith*, 60-65, 215-16.
10. *Ibid.*, 62.
11. For a fuller treatment of this subject: Clyde Dankert, *Adam Smith: Man of Letters and Economist* (Hicksville, N.Y., 1974), 241-49.
12. General Introduction, WN, I, 50.

67

The Wealth of Nations 1776–1976

E. Roll

Source: *Lloyds Bank Review*, 119, January 1976, pp. 12-22.

According to temperament, all human history, perhaps especially the history of ideas, can be looked at in two ways. To some, it will be a continuous development without any break: a seamless garment. To others, it will be a series of seemingly unconnected but massive events, the haphazard appearance of great individuals responsible for gigantic leaps in man's imagination. For some, it will be a slow, laborious building of stone upon stone by many humble workers. For others, progress will be identified with Moses, Jesus and Mohammed, with Smith, Marx and Keynes, with Ptolemy, Newton and Einstein.

For the origin of political economy as a modern discipline, the first view can certainly be supported by much evidence. It is true that the classical system of economics associated with the name of Adam Smith, and the beginning of the era of industrial capitalism which it accompanied, had been in the making for nearly a hundred years before *The Wealth of Nations*. In the field of political and economic thought, North had inveighed against the remaining shackles of mercantilist ideas and restrictive regulations of trade; Locke and Hume, in philosophy, both general and political, had exemplified that liberal spirit that was later to find its clearest expression in the writings of the French philosophers; Petty had wrestled with the problem of value a century before Adam Smith; and the French Physiocrats had almost succeeded in building a self-consistent system of the circulation of wealth well before 1776.

Nevertheless, one would have to be peculiarly unimaginative, indeed insensitive, not to see the last quarter of the eighteenth century as one of the great watersheds in the evolution of human society. In 1775, James Watt, that strange, curmudgeonly genius, joined with the worldly industrialist Matthew Boulton to make steam engines by factory methods: as symbolic a partnership between science and business – and in as crucial an era of enterprise at that time – as could not possibly be bettered even if it had been contrived as fiction. Fourteen years later, the French Revolution unleashed forces of social and political change to transform society that were to go on working right up to the present day. In between, there was that *annus mirabilis* 1776.

And what a year it was! On 9 March there appeared without the fanfare of literary lunches or any other of the paraphernalia that today would greet the publication of a potential best-seller *An Enquiry into the Nature and Causes of the Wealth of Nations*, by Adam Smith. Some months later (traditionally, on 4 July, though the precise date is in dispute among scholars) there was signed at Philadelphia the Declaration of Independence. It may seem odd, at first sight, to couple the two large quarto volumes of sober and intricate argument by a Scottish moral philosopher with the short resounding call to arms of Thomas Jefferson. But the family connection is so powerful that it is right to begin by joining them in this bicentennial celebration.

The nexus is most obvious in those parts of the book in which Adam Smith discusses specifically colonial trade with America and the East Indies and, in particular, monopoly in that trade. Consider, for example, these passages: 'The monopoly of the colony trade, therefore, like all the other mean and malignant expedients of the mercantile system, depresses the industry of all other countries, but chiefly that of the colonies, without in the least increasing, but on the contrary diminishing, that of the country in whose favour it is established.' Or, 'to promote the little interest of one little order of men in one country, it [monopoly] hurts the interest of all other orders of men in that country, and of all the men in all other countries.' And in advocating voluntary separation of the American colonies from Britain, he says 'by thus parting good friends, the natural affection of the colonies to the mother country, which, perhaps, our late dissensions have well nigh extinguished, would quickly revive.' Of Adam Smith, at least, Jefferson's complaint that the British brethren had 'been deaf to the voice of justice and consanguinity' was not true.

But, more fundamentally, the essential spirit that inspired Adam Smith was the same as that on which the new republic was to be founded. There is in both the appeal to the 'natural order' or the 'laws of nature.' The proposition that the pursuit of happiness is one of the inalienable rights of man is close to the whole approach of Smith's earlier work, *The Theory of Moral Sentiments*; and the principle that 'all men are created equal' is not far removed from Smith's view that 'the difference of natural talents in different men is, in reality, much less than we are aware of ... The difference between ... a philosopher and a common street porter, for example, seems to arise not so much from nature, as from habit, custom, and education.'

In these matters, the relation between the individual and society and their respective rights and duties in the broadest sense, Adam Smith was very much in the spirit of the age. He believed, as the naturalist school of philosophy from the Greek Stoics to Hobbes and Locke had believed, that these relations were in large measure (though by no means exclusively) subject to the actions of natural forces which spontaneously produced a harmonious pattern and that the, largely unimpeded, operation of these forces would automatically best promote the interests of each individual consistently with those of others. It will be important presently to examine more closely the precise meaning of this doctrine, its application to the economic sphere and, in particular, the relevance of the conclusions drawn from it to the problems of today. But, first, a few words about the man, about his contribution to the science of economics and about his role in the evolution of economic policy.

Adam Smith the Man

Adam Smith was fifty-three when his great work was published. By that time, this son of a Scottish Judge Advocate, who had been educated at the Universities of Glasgow and Oxford, had been a professor for thirteen years, during which time he published *The Theory of Moral Sentiments* and had travelled for two years in France as tutor to the Duke of Buccleuch, from whom he received a substantial pension. Soon after the publication of *The Wealth of Nations* he became a Commissioner of Customs, which he remained until his death in 1790. He was the first truly academic economist and it was from his time onwards that the progress of economics becomes increasingly the result of academic work. His lectures during his thirteen years as a professor, partly through the medium of the closely-related *Theory of Moral Sentiments* (in many respects containing the philosophical foundations of *The Wealth of Nations*), were clearly elements in the process of evolution which culminated in the latter work. Dugald Stewart, Smith's early biographer, thought the lectures lost. Happily, this proved not to be so, for in 1895 Edwin Cannan was given to examine, and in 1896 published, a set of notes of Smith's lectures on *Justice, Police, Revenue and Arms* which contained much that was to be further elaborated in *The Wealth of Nations*. And in 1958 Professor Lothian discovered, and five years later published, a set of much earlier lectures by Smith on *Rhetoric and Belles Lettres*, which, though barely relevant to his economic ideas, give a fuller idea of the range of his interests and intellect.

An extraordinarily wide range it turns out to be. We already know from Dugald Stewart of his knowledge of languages and literature, ancient and modern, of his wide circle of acquaintances and friends among the outstanding minds of his time. These aspects of his personality are emphasized particularly by a reading of the *Rhetoric* lectures. He was a man of very wide culture: an eighteenth-century intellectual *par excellence* for whom the advances in economic reasoning were intimately linked with, indeed part and parcel of, speculations in political and social philosophy as well as in a large variety of other disciplines. (Smith may not in later life have been as interested in the natural sciences as were other contemporary thinkers but it is perhaps relevant to note that it is reported that, while a student at the University of Glasgow, mathematics and natural philosophy were his favourite pursuits.) It may be a sign of maturity that two hundred years after *The Wealth of Nations* much of economics is not only more abstract, but often highly mathematical, and certainly not as accessible to the average educated reader as was and is Smith's *opus*. But it is certainly regrettable, and perhaps of even deeper significance, that not many of its practitioners can display the same width of interests and knowledge as the founder of the science!

Smith's Place in Economics

The advances in economics proper associated with Adam Smith are so well known that a relatively short recapitulation should suffice. There is, first, the general approach and method of treatment. No one before Adam Smith had attained anything like the same level of systematic and consistent analysis in which, despite the regular use of examples and illustrations from the real world, a high degree of abstraction prevails. For the first time, economics becomes recognizable as an independent discipline, indeed as a science, self-conscious and self-confident; and while its affiliation to social philosophy is still clearly visible, it has now come of age and is ready to lead a life of its own. The plan of the work, the broad sweep of its reasoning, the skilful appeal, amidst intricate theoretical argument, to homely analogies the truth of which was universally accepted, demonstrate a mastery of the subject unequalled before and explain the immediate acclaim which greeted the book and the influence which it had on policy.

Although not entirely followed in subsequent economic treatises (notably Ricardo's *Principles*, the other pillar of the classical system) the structure of the book had a great influence on all later writers. Book One deals in the main with what today would be called static analysis: production, exchange and distribution. Book Two contains the more dynamic parts, the nature of capital and capital accumulation. Book Three continues the dynamic analysis and does so largely on the basis of historical and descriptive material rather than abstract reasoning. Book Four, entitled "Of Systems of Political Oeconomy", contains the celebrated and devastating attack on mercantilism. It takes apart not only the individual devices of the mercantilist state, but criticizes the whole system in a manner which has not been surpassed to this day, though, no doubt, the examples used and the language in which the attack is formulated are presented in a more up-to-date manner in recent 'free-trade' literature. Book Five deals with the 'public sector', that is, as it was then defined. It contains both a detailed analysis of public expenditure and the means of meeting it, revenue from taxes and otherwise. It is here, perhaps, even more than either in the theoretical chapters on the nature of exchange and of markets or in those attacking mercantilism that Adam Smith's theory of economic policy becomes clear and that the opponents of state intervention can find most ammunition for their views.

In terms of the subsequent progress of pure economic theory, however, it is in the earlier parts of the work that the major contributions can be found. Here I would say it is not so much the theory of value that is path-breaking, for it has been shown that Smith had important forerunners, that much of the analysis is somewhat muddled and that it was Ricardo who was to give the specifically 'classical' theory its clearest expression. One could also argue (and I would be disposed to do so) that, in the light of the history of the subject during the last two hundred years, the dominant place which value occupied for so long at the core of economic theory was not wholly beneficial and that the shift of focus in recent decades is advantageous. It must, however, be remembered that the great attention paid to value by Smith stemmed from his desire to put at the centre of economic thinking labour as the creator of value, the division of labour as the means for making labour more productive (thus more creative of value) and the market as the means both for making division of labour possible and for determining its extent. This, indeed, was his greatest achievement and the imperfections in the elaboration of the theory of value weigh very little in the balance.

The other, related, great achievement was the emphasis on wealth as a flow rather than as a static fund. The very first sentence of the introduction sets a tone which is different from that of earlier writers or of the contemporaneous French Physiocrats.

> The annual labour of every nation is the fund which originally supplies it with all the necessaries and conveniences of life which it annually consumes, and which consist always either in the immediate produce of that labour, or in what is purchased with that produce from other nations.

It may be noted in passing that the next sentence carries the implication, as seen by Edwin Cannan, that the nation's welfare is to be measured as an average or *per caput* index rather than as an aggregate. Though it was some 150 years before the national income analysis and, later, the GNP measurement matured, here, in embryo is a decisively new approach.

There is, however, much more to be found in *The Wealth of Nations* that was new and was to prove of lasting value for economics. There is, for example, the analysis of wages and wage-differentials contained in the theory of net advantages and in the doctrine of non-competing groups which, though elementary now, is still an accepted part of the theory on the subject. There are, as I have already mentioned, the detailed critical discussions on tariffs and other restrictive devices in international and domestic trade which subsequent analysis has much refined but by no means displaced. There are also the celebrated four canons of taxation – equality, certainty, convenience and economy – which will evoke the emphatic, if wistful, agreement of every modern taxpayer.

But whatever its contribution to pure economic theory, the epoch-making character of *The Wealth of Nations* derives from its bearing on public policy. In this regard, Adam Smith was, as a later economist and historian of economic thought, Wesley Mitchell, recognized, 'one of the makers of modern history', his book being noteworthy above all for its criticism of 'the principles of a civilization which was passing', and for laying down 'the principles of a civilization that was coming into being'. To this aspect, I now turn.

Prescriptions for Policy

The essential character of Adam Smith's social philosophy from which, via his economic analysis, his prescriptions for economic policy are derived is simple enough. The whole of medieval society and in large measure that of early commercial and industrial capitalism had been based upon a complex system of rules and regulations, defining, often in meticulous detail, the rights and duties of individuals not only in regard to the wider aspects of human and social existence, but more particularly in the economic sphere. The mercantile system, especially, made the business of industry and trade one for regulation by the state either directly or through the delegated authority of guilds and privileged companies. This system was already in a process of rapid breakdown when Smith wrote. For new forms of production based on new technical inventions were demonstrating the incompatibility of old economic relationships with the new productive powers. The steam engine, the power loom, the spinning jenny required a wider, freer and more flexible social and economic (and eventually political) framework if their potentialities were to be fully exploited.

In *The Wealth of Nations*, Adam Smith, though he did not begin with this, provided a brilliant critique of the absurdities to which the strict regulation of business activity under the mercantilist system led, culminating in the great demonstration of the doubly harmful nature of the colonial system (to metropolis and colony alike) and its political consequences, to be shortly most vividly exemplified by the Declaration of Independence. But it was not enough to show up the follies of particular restrictive devices and of the whole system of state regulation. Smith was a philosopher; moreover, the whole spirit of the age tended towards comprehensive explanations and 'system-building'. The attack on mercantilism had, therefore, to be based on a rational exposition of the superiority of a different economic system, and this, in turn, on a social philosophy which could be generally accepted as being in accord with the prevailing human understanding and with universal aspirations in these matters. Not surprisingly, therefore, the attack on mercantilism comes after the analysis of the virtues of a market economy and of the social philosophy with which it has a close family tie.

Smith believed, as had his teacher Francis Hutcheson, in the natural order. In essence, it means a belief in what is natural as against what is contrived. There is a natural order which if allowed to assert itself without let or hindrance would soon show its superiority over any order resting on artificially created man-made laws. It must be remembered that in *The Theory of Moral Sentiments* Smith had already expounded the mainsprings of human actions which in their balanced operation explain how a natural order can exist. They were: self-love balanced by sympathy, ie love of one's neighbour, the desire to be free, a sense of propriety, a habit of labour and a propensity to exchange. Let there be no interference with the free play of these forces and each individual will be 'led by an invisible hand to promote an end which was no part of his intention'. Applied to the economic sphere, 'it is not from the benevolence of the butcher, the brewer, or the baker that we expect our dinner, but from their regard to their own interest'. All the prescriptions, however recondite, for freeing domestic industry and trade and international commerce from direction and restriction ultimately stem from this simple principle. More generally, though he applied it in particular to the restriction of imports, Smith's basic approach was to equate economic statesmanship with the principles underlying prudent conduct by the 'master of a family'. These, he claimed, 'can scarce be folly in that of a great Kingdom'.

Perhaps because his natural order philosophy was founded in much the same pragmatic approach as that of the English utilitarian school generally, thus less 'mystical' than that of the Physiocrats in France (who were moreover handicapped by a similar 'mystical' belief in the superiority of agriculture), Smith became a more effective opponent of mercantilism and a more successful advocate of the policy of *laissez-faire*. With extraordinary rapidity his advocacy of the free market (to give the greatest scope to division of labour), of competition (which would always assert itself provided monopolistic positions were not supported by the state) and of unimpeded international commerce gained ground intellectually and helped the new industrial classes to achieve in large measure that emancipation from mercantilist shackles for which they were striving.

It would, nevertheless, be a mistake (which is often tacitly made) to think that *The Wealth of Nations* ushered in an era of unlimited *laissez-faire* – a golden age of economic freedom which was brought to an end by some kind of intellectual fall from grace. It is more than doubtful whether anywhere and for any length of time anything like a true system of *laissez-faire* has ever existed and whether it has been more than, according to taste, a chimera or a platonic ideal towards which one is urged constantly to strive. This is not the place to trace the growth – which was not long delayed – of all the interventionist measures of the hundred and fifty years following Adam Smith. The fact is that interventionism of one kind or another has spread and that, with very limited exceptions indeed, both in duration and in geographical extent, the free market as Smith envisaged it has continued to be a distant ideal. Why this should be so is a difficult question which cannot be examined here. What seems to have become increasingly apparent is that the progress of universal suffrage and political democracy in the widest sense is incompatible with a *laissez-faire* economy, despite the fact that both went hand-in-hand in their infancy. What is more appropriate in this bicentenary year is to examine the relevance of those tenets of economic policy associated peculiarly with Adam Smith and *The Wealth of Nations* to the conflicting views on these matters held today.

Any Lessons for Today?

It is always tempting to try to guess what some great writer of the past would say were he alive today. It is equally tempting to cull from his writings passages that seem strongly to support one particular point of view. But, apart from the well-known ability of those of evil intent to cite scripture, there are great hazards in yielding to these temptations. On the face of it, these hazards should be at a minimum where Adam Smith is concerned. The case he made for the free market and against intervention seems so obvious and so emphatic that it is natural for the extreme advocates of these views to claim him as a powerful ally. If the essence of the 'Keynesian revolution', which has so much influenced present-day economic thought, is to draw a distinction between what is rational economic conduct of the individual (or the individual enterprise) and the proper management of the aggregates of the economy by the state, would the man who equated prudence in the family with that in the kingdom not repudiate much of today's thought – and the action based on it? Or would he accept Keynes's own verdict (expressed in 1945 when defending the Anglo-American financial arrangements) that it was right to 'combine the advantages of a freedom of commerce with safeguards against the disastrous consequences of a *laissez-faire* system which pays no regard to the preservation of equilibrium and merely relies on the eventual working out of blind forces.' Would he agree that what Keynes aimed at was 'to use what we have learnt from modern experience and modern analysis, not to defeat, but to implement the wisdom of Adam Smith'?

No decisive answer to these questions is possible. There is a great deal to be found in *The Wealth of Nations* to delight the heart of any opponent of the 'welfare state', of 'hand-outs', of public as against private enterprise or of the financing of public works out of the general tax revenue, to say nothing of import duties or other restrictions on trade. No doubt, on the evidence of Book Five, there is not much of present public expenditure (and the public sector borrowing requirement that goes with it) that would escape his criticism; though his reference to the Post Office as 'perhaps the only mercantile project which has been successfully managed by, I believe, every sort, of government' and which produces 'a large profit' will evoke a wry smile in the modern reader.

Nevertheless, care is necessary in making these interpretations, quite apart from the fact that Adam Smith is not available to give evidence himself. In counselling care, I cannot base myself on much in Adam Smith's own words. There is hardly anything to be found except in the well-known cases of defence and education in which 'authority' in the shape of the state or otherwise is explicitly allowed to do what unimpeded market forces might not, though there is a hint in one place of a derogation in favour of new developments that might not otherwise take place (a hint of the 'infant industry' argument?). On trade unions one would hardly expect any trace of modern thought; indeed in the quarter century following *The Wealth of Nations*, the Combination Laws were made even more stringent than they had been before.

There are, nevertheless, passages which show that Adam Smith was not particularly confident about the beneficence of the aims of individuals when left to themselves. Landlords 'love to reap where they have not sowed'; and those who live from profits, who have a better knowledge of their own interest than the landlord has of his, have an interest which 'is never exactly the same with that of the public, who have generally an interest to deceive and even to oppress the public, and who accordingly have, upon many occasions, both deceived and oppressed it'.

But if we are to be, as I believe we should be, somewhat wary about invoking the authority of Adam Smith in the advocacy of an extreme *laissez-faire* attitude, this is not, and cannot in the nature of things be, on account of any specific disclaimer or qualification in Adam Smith's work itself. He was a child of his time. His objective was aggressive: to destroy what remained– and a great deal did – of an antiquated system that put severe constraints upon the development of society's productive powers resulting from the ingenuity and venturesomeness of the new men who were building the new industrial age. In so doing, despite the more extensive use of the language of the natural law philosophers than was common among other English writers and despite many ambiguities, he was, I believe, in the main moved by a practical motive; and even he had, therefore, to defend his policy precepts by reference to the positive good they wrought (that is to say by the utilitarian principle) than exclusively by their conformity to a providential scheme of things.

Lionel Robbins – surely a sensitive as anyone can be on this point – has shown that the utilitarian (English) tradition (not as clearly visible in Adam Smith as in Bentham and Hume) regarded all laws and rights – indeed all social arrangements – as man-made and, therefore, to be judged according to their effects on human happiness. That happiness – for the individual – was the supreme objective and every human institution was merely a means towards its achievement. Bentham, though most of his work was after *The Wealth of Nations*, epitomizes the utilitarian spirit and its liberal implications best. Yet Bentham, in both his political and economic writings, pours scorn on the undiluted natural law philosophy. It is perhaps symbolic that Bentham's *Fragment on Government* also appeared in 1776. And in that work, as indeed in many others, Bentham consistently took the view that the individual interest must be *made* to harmonize with that of others in order to produce the greatest happiness of the greatest number and that, as he said in another place, natural rights were 'simply nonsense'. It is perhaps not too fanciful to see in the special emphasis on the natural order that is to be found in Adam Smith, in contrast to almost any other of the great figures of the utilitarian and radical movements of the age, the need to establish economics as a science by making it rely on certain 'natural laws' akin to those of the natural sciences; to demonstrate a certain *Gesetzmässigkeit*, as the Germans were to call it, in economic phenomena, since, if this were absent, it would prove much more difficult, if not impossible, to regard economics as a scientific discipline. Such an approach would not necessarily rule out the intervention of human agency for certain defined purposes, supporting, or at times running counter to, the 'natural' course which economic tendencies might take. Indeed, Lionel Robbins has shown that the whole classical school was much less doctrinaire about the 'agenda' of state action than is often believed.

That Adam Smith, were he alive today, would be highly suspicious of those who are prepared to ignore the important part which 'the market' could play in the proper ordering of economic affairs, there can be little doubt. It is understandable that, given the widespread attack on the value of the market mechanism, many should be tempted, paraphrasing Wordsworth, to say 'Adam Smith! thou should'st be living at this hour: England hath need of thee'. But it is not likely, in my view, that Smith would endorse an exclusive reliance on market forces in all cases, particularly when the democratic process has put power into the hands of different groups to adapt the operation of these forces so as to favour sometimes one and sometimes the other group. We would certainly be praying for the presence of one whose good sense and broad humanity would be of inestimable value amid the shrill clamour of divergent views which are vying for our support. But we should, I think, do so without illusion. Undoubtedly, if he were alive today, Adam Smith would have some very crushing things to say about those who would deprive our economy of the benefit of a smoothly-working market mechanism. But I believe that he would not be among those who would empty our mixed economy of all its interventionist ingredients. Above all, I suspect, that were Keynes also alive today, those two great thinkers, whose principal works are one hundred and sixty years apart, would find much common ground in respect of the broad principles that should guide the management of the economy.

Note

Sir Eric Roll, after a distinguished career in academic and public life, is now Chairman of S G Warburg & Co Ltd, and has written widely on economics and on the history of economic thought.

68

The Adam Smith Nobody Knows

R.L. Heilbroner

Source: *Journal of Portfolio Management*, Vol. 2 (4), Summer 1976, pp. 65-6.

Here is a great voice from the past who turns out to be a great critic of the present.

It is the bicentennial of our patron saint, Adam Smith – or rather of his magnum opus, the *Wealth of Nations*. Few books have weathered the years so well; fewer, I suspect, have so long a life still before them. Yet there is a danger in Smith's eminence. It is that, like so many great men, his books have become permanently relegated to that select library of which we all know the titles but no longer bother to read the contents. Who has not heard of Plato's *Republic*, Machiavelli's *Prince*, Dante's *Inferno*? Who has read them?

So it is with the *Wealth of Nations*, universally admired, universally unread. Most of us regard the book as a long disquisition in favor of a free economy, which indeed it is, but we ignore or forget (or simply never knew) that there is much more in Smith than that. A treasury of shrewd observations about social behavior, individual and mass psychology, history, and human nature speak to us in contemporary tones, even when the economic analysis is outmoded or quaint.

In what follows I have taken the liberty of assembling a few less well-known passages that show Smith in his many-sided roles.[1] In their cadenced 18th Century prose they will not lend themselves to skimming, but they are worth reading slowly, at your leisure, for the pleasure they will afford.

On Risk

The over-weening conceit which the greater part of men have of their own abilities, is an ancient evil remarked by the philosophers and moralists of all ages. Their absurd presumption in their own good fortune, has been less taken notice of. It is, however, if possible, still more universal. There is no man living who, when in tolerable health and spirits, has not some share of it. The chance of gain is by every man more or less over-valued, and the chance of loss is by most men under-valued, and by scarce any man, who is in tolerable health and spirits, valued more than it is worth. (p. 107)

On Lotteries

That the chance of gain is naturally over-valued, we may learn from the universal success of lotteries. The world neither ever saw, nor will ever see, a perfectly fair lottery; or one in which the whole gain compensated the whole loss; because the undertaker could make nothing by it. In the state lotteries the tickets are really not worth the price which is paid by the original subscribers, and yet commonly sell in the market for twenty, thirty, and sometimes forty per cent advance. The vain hope of gaining some of the great prizes is the sole cause of this demand. The soberest people scarce look upon it as a folly to pay a small sum for the chance of gaining ten or twenty thousand pounds; though they know that even that small sum is perhaps twenty or thirty per cent more than the chance is worth. In a lottery in which no prize exceeded twenty pounds, though in other respects it approached much nearer to a perfectly fair one than the common state lotteries, there would not be the same demand for tickets. In order to have a better chance for some of the great prizes, some people purchase several tickets, and others, small shares in a greater number. There is not, however, a more certain proposition in mathematics, than that the more tickets you adventure upon, the more likely you are to be a loser. Adventure upon all the tickets in the lottery, and you lose for certain; and the greater the number of your tickets, the nearer you approach to this certainty. (p. 108)

On Imperial Pretensions [a few minor emendations indicated by brackets][2]

The rulers of [the United States] have, for more than a [decade], amused the people with the imagination that they possessed a great empire on the west side of the [Pacific]. This empire, however, has hitherto existed in the imagination only. It has hitherto been, not an empire but the project of an empire; not a gold mine, but the project of a gold mine; a project which has cost, which continues to cost, and which, if pursued in the same way as it has been hitherto, is likely to cost, immense expense . . . It is surely now time that our rulers should either realize this golden dream, in which they have been indulging themselves, perhaps, as well as the people; or that they should awake from it themselves, and endeavor to awaken the people. If the project cannot be completed it ought to be given up. (pp. 899-900)

On the Mixed Economy

The natural effort of every individual to better his own condition, when suffered to exert itself with freedom and security, is so powerful a principle, that it is alone, and without any assistance, not only capable of carrying on the society to wealth and prosperity, but of surmounting a hundred impertinent obstructions with which the folly of human laws too often incumbers its operations . . . (p. 508)

On Tariff Lobbying [with emendations once again in brackets]

Commerce, which ought naturally to be, among nations, as among individuals, a bond of union and friendship, has become the most fertile source of discord and animosity. The capricious ambition of [presidents] and ministers has not, during the present and the preceding century, been more fatal to the repose of [America and] Europe, than the impertinent jealousy of merchants and manufacturers. The violence and injustice of the rulers of mankind is an ancient evil, for which, I am afraid, the nature of human affairs can scarce admit of a remedy. But the mean rapacity, the monopolizing spirit of merchants and manufacturers, who neither are, nor ought to be, the rulers of mankind, though it cannot perhaps be corrected, may be very easily prevented from disturbing the tranquillity of anybody but themselves. (p. 460)

On Economic Equality

Wherever there is great property, there is great inequality. For one very rich man, there must be at least five hundred poor, and the affluence of the few supposes the indigence of the many . . . Civil government, so far as it is instituted for the security of property, is in reality instituted for the defence of the rich against the poor, or of those who have some property against those who have none at all. (pp. 670, 674)

On Labor and Capital

We rarely hear, it has been said, of the combinations of [managers], though frequently of those of workmen. But whoever imagines, upon this account, that [managers] rarely combine, is as ignorant of the world as of the subject. [Managers] are always and everywhere in a sort of tacit, but constant and uniform combination, not to raise the wages of labor above their actual rate . . . We seldom, indeed, hear of this combination, because it is the usual, and one may say, the natural state of things which nobody ever hears of.

On Mass Production

In the progress of the division of labour, the employment of the far greater part of those who live by labour . . . comes to be confined to a few very simple operations, frequently to one or two. But the understandings of the greater part of men are necessarily formed by their ordinary employments. The man whose whole life is spent in performing a few simple operations . . . has no occasion to exert his understanding, or to exercise his invention in finding out expedients for removing difficulties which never occur. He naturally loses, therefore, the habit of such exertion, and generally becomes as stupid and ignorant as it is possible for a human creature to become. (p. 734)

This is More Than Economics

Is this economics? Not, of course, in the current analytic sense, although there is plenty of analysis in Smith. But it is the stuff on which economics is built. In its telling estimates of the manner in which wish tinctures judgment, ambition overrules reason, self-interest evades restraint, profit seeking guides policy, riches feed on poverty (who would have thought to find *that* in Smith!) labor and capital interact, we have the raw material from which economic science is made.

I need hardly say that these few quotes hardly do justice to the 900 aphorism-laden pages of the *Wealth*. Perhaps, however, they will serve to do justice to Smith by making of his bicentennial an occasion for actually going back and reading him, not merely to enjoy a great voice from the past, but to benefit from a great critic of the present.

Notes

1. Page references are from the Modern Library edition.
2. Without brackets, this selection referred to Great Britain's vain attempt to retain its "empire" across the Atlantic.

69

The Bicentenary of Adam Smith[1]

T.W. Hutchison

Source: *Economic Journal*, Vol. 86, September 1976, pp. 481-92.

I

Anniversaries – especially when they reach some impressive round figure – seem to be receiving more and more attention from editors and programme-planners for the media, who, voracious for ideas to fill space and time, keep the horizon scanned for any promising birthdays which may be looming up. Naturally academics, too, in these hard times, are keenly on the look-out for any opportunity of raising the wind for some celebratory get-together, or for an expensive new edition or collection of essays. Apart from its other (trans-atlantic) connections, '76 is obviously one of the most celebrated and celebratable years in the economist's century (though '83 with its Marx-Keynes double-header should offer some unusual possibilities). Equally obviously, Glasgow – so far as cis-Atlantic political economy is concerned – has first claims on '76. In fact, the University of Glasgow has commissioned a complete edition of Adam Smith's *Works and Correspondence* to celebrate the Bicentenary. This edition is to appear in six parts, with two associated volumes, one of essays on Smith (here under review) and the other a new life by I.S. Ross. The celebrations could not possibly take a worthier or more valuable form than this. All scholars should be profoundly grateful that such a major intellectual need is at last being met. It should now, or soon, really become possible to get much nearer than previously to seeing Smith and his work "whole", or as near as we are ever likely to be able to do this (which, because of irreparable gaps in basic material, and a certain elusiveness in Smith as a person, may never be all that near).

II

The leading expositors of the English classical version of the history of political economy, such as, primarily, McCulloch, and incidentally, but very influentially, J.S. Mill, assigned to Smith the role and title of the supreme founding father of the subject – (Marx, incidentally, described Petty as "the founder of modern political economy"). Four editions of *The Wealth of Nations*, those of Playfair, Buchanan, Wakefield, and McCulloch himself (now hardly looked at) appeared in the opening decades of the nineteenth century. But at some points the treatment of Smith was apt to strike a rather patronising note when very high claims were being advanced as to the remarkably rapid scientific progress which had taken place in the period, since *The Wealth of Nations*. As J.S. Mill puts it in the Preface (1848) to his *Principles*, he was seeking to produce a work:

> Similar in its object and general conception to that of Adam Smith but adapted to the more extended and improved ideas of the present age . . . *The Wealth of Nations* is in many parts obsolete, and in all, imperfect. Political Economy, properly so called, has grown up almost from infancy since the time of Adam Smith.

It was only during what is called the "neo-classical" period with the development of more systematic scholarly standards (and perhaps, fleetingly, more intellectual modesty) that the modern study of Smith can be said to have got under way. First, there was the work of German historical economists, notably Hasbach, Leser, and Oncken. "Das Adam-Smith Problem", about which they were much concerned—that is, the contrasts or even contradictions, between *The Theory of Moral Sentiments* and *The Wealth of Nations* – is today mostly regarded as exaggerated or even imaginary (though quite enough "Adam-Smith problems" remain). But at least these Germans were on the right track in looking at Smith's work *as a whole*, and in regarding him as primarily a philosopher. In England, apart from Bagehot's brilliant essays, it was not until the 'nineties, and the turn of the century, that the basic works appeared which until today have provided most of the main foundations of our knowledge and understanding of Smith's work on political economy: that is, Bonar's catalogue of his library (1894); Rae's life (1896); and Cannan's editions of the *Lectures* (1996) and *The Wealth of Nations* (1904).

Since about the beginning of the century major importance could probably only be claimed for Scott's biographical work, with his publication of the "Early Draft" (1937), and for the discovery of the *Lectures on Rhetoric and Belles Lettres* (1963). There have been quite a number of interesting and informative articles and lectures (led by the Chicago sesquicentennial volume) which have discussed various particular aspects or sectors of Smith's work; and recently Smith's philosophy, and other writings, seem to have been attracting much more attention. But there has been nothing corresponding to the interest and opportunities opened up by the splendid complete editions of Ricardo and J.S. Mill, or to the new and lively interest in Malthus aroused by Keynes. So, for some decades, Smith's work has, *comparatively*, been falling behind, in spite of many interesting partial or detailed contributions, in respect of the kind of profound and comprehensive attention which it requires.

This gap, or delay, with regard to Adam Smith, may have been due, in part to the "multi-", as well as the "cross-disciplinary" character of his work (to adopt the slightly disgusting contemporary terminology). However, this has not prevented the highly "*multi*-disciplinary" work of J.S. Mill from obtaining its due setting from Toronto, or even from a start being made on Bentham. But the lack of a complete edition has been all the more serious, just because of the intensely *cross*-disciplinary element in Smith's different works, now regarded as "belonging" to different university departments. J.S. Mill's writings are, of course, extensively *multi*-disciplinary, but although a knowledge of his logic, or of his political essays, or his autobiography, may enrich somewhat one's understanding of his *Principles of Political Economy*, this latter book can be quite adequately understood and appreciated without any or much acquaintance with Mill's other writings. But to a quite different degree, an understanding of what *The Wealth of Nations* is really about, if it is not to be seriously impoverished or superficial, essentially requires a considerable acquaintance with *The Theory of Moral Sentiments*, as well as with *The Lectures* and other works. So this Glasgow edition will, for the first time, make possible, or much more feasible or convenient, the kind of comprehensive study which Smith's work deserves and requires.

It remains to be seen how far further comprehensive studies may lead to any clarifications or solutions with regard to the considerable range of gaps, mysteries and puzzles, which can be found in Smith's life and work. First, there are the biographical gaps. As Professor Mossner has wondered, *just what was Smith doing* in his six years in Oxford? Did he make no mark there at all? And precisely how did it develop that after returning home, apparently a somewhat disgruntled graduate student of 23, he emerged only three or four years later as the brilliant young Edinburgh lecturer, promptly awarded a major chair at the age of 28? Then there are intriguing questions about his political influence in his later years. For example, how far was the sometimes slightly whimsical C.R. Fay justified in (apparently) suggesting that it was Smith's logical, professorial advice, insisting that colonists should pay taxes, which in 1766 impelled Townshend to the measures which led on to the Revolution ten years later?[2]

Then there are the puzzles, and even mysteries, in his writings or thought. For example, there is the treatment of "use", utility, and value in that curious but crucial paragraph in chapter 4 of Book I (though, as we shall note, Professor Samuel Hollander does not see any puzzle or difficulty here). More profound and even more insoluble, perhaps, are the puzzling contrasts between what Professor Heilbroner, in his stimulating essay on "Decline and Decay in *The Wealth of Nations*", calls the brighter and darker side of Smith's politico-economic vision: the contrast, that is, between the expansive, progressive optimism, and the long-run prospect of running down into an apparently pretty dismal stationary state: and the further well-known contrast in the treatment of the division of labour as a great driving force of economic progress on the one hand, and towards cultural degradation (and "alienation") on the other hand – with the mass of the population (labouring by hand, and brain too, presumably) in danger of becoming "as stupid and ignorant as it is possible for a human creature to become" – with only state-financed education to ward this off.

Great though the stimulus which this splendid bicentenary edition should impart to their study, a considerable degree of fascinating elusiveness, ambiguity, and even mystery, seems likely (perhaps fortunately) always to remain with regard to Smith and his work.

III

With Cannan's admirable edition comparatively easily and cheaply available, *The Wealth of Nations* (though its Bicentenary is the occasion for this edition) is the work of Smith which seems least in need of a new scholarly edition. But certainly the two new volumes eclipse Cannan's in the sheer sumptuousness of their physique.

Extraordinary pains have been taken by Professor W.B. Todd of the University of Texas to establish the text.[3] Forty-nine copies in seven libraries around the world have been checked and collated, and a shorthand code has been devised for referring to them all. The tables of "Corresponding Passages" with regard to the 1930 and 1937 editions of Cannan is a useful inclusion at the end of each volume. A rather prominent feature is the numbering of paragraphs, which at some points produces – possibly appropriately – a somewhat Biblical appearance. But some people might have preferred that *the titles of chapters*, and not only their numbers, should appear at the top of the right-hand pages (as in the Cannan edition).

The annotation and critical apparatus is on a much larger scale – especially for about the first fifty pages – than in the Cannan edition (or in the Sraffa edition of Ricardo, or the Bladen-Robson edition of J.S. Mill's *Principles*). Three, or even four different types of notes or "data" (as Professor Todd calls them) may appear at the bottom of a page, or on the bottom half of a page, below the text. First, there may be Smith's own references (of which there are very few) attached to which may be extensions, or additions to Smith's notes by the editors. Below these will come the textual variations, in code; and finally the editors' own comments. These comprise cross-references within *The Wealth of Nations*, references to Smith's other writings, and parallels with other writers. Also, "comment has been made on matters of historical fact where this might be of benefit to the modern reader" (p. v). Here is an extract where all the various types of annotation come together in a few lines (which does not happen often). The passage is from chapter iv "Of the Origin and Use of Money":

> 5 Different metals have been made use of by different nations for this purpose. Iron was the common instrument of commerce among the antient Spartans; copper among the antient Romans[9]; and gold and silver among all rich and commercial nations.[10]
>
> 6 Those metals seem originally to have been made use of for this purpose in rude bars, without any stamp or coinage. Thus we are told by Pliny,* upon the authority of ᶜTimaeusᶜ an antient ᵈhistorian,ᵈ that till the time of Servius Tullius, the Romans had no coined money . . .

"9" and "10" indicate notes by the editors citing a cross-reference, and references to the two editions of the *Lectures* and to Cantillon. (*) indicates one of Smith's own references to Pliny, the passage being then quoted in English translation by the editors. The pairs of "c"s and "d"s indicate alternative readings in other editions (for example, "author" instead of "historian").

Doubtless much useful and interesting information is made available below the text. But it might be held that to deserve to get on to *the same page*, and compete for the reader's eye and attention with Adam Smith's own words, any notes, or "data", surely ought to have to justify themselves in terms of a pretty high degree of urgency and importance.

In some ways one of the most crucial paragraphs in *The Wealth of Nations* is that (No. 13) towards the end of the chapter which we have just mentioned (I. IV. p. 45), dealing with the concepts of value-in-use and value-in-exchange, and the water-and-diamonds paradox. Here ten-and-a-half lines of large-print text occasion some fifty-five lines of small-print annotation. Now it is certainly useful to have briefly quoted, or summarised, Smith's other treatments of the paradox of value, elsewhere in *The Wealth of Nations* and in the two versions of the *Lectures*. It is also significant to have references to Plato, Pufendorf, Harris, Cantillon, and Mandeville. An excellent quotation is provided from John Law, and finally quite a lengthy one from Francis Hutcheson. But the interpretation and appraisal of this crucial paragraph is a matter of some controversy, about which, of course, entire essays or articles could be (and have been) written. For those who take the view that in *The Wealth of Nations*, especially in this paragraph – though not in *The Lectures* – Smith departed significantly from Hutcheson's treatment of "use", "utility", and value, it could seem misleading that the quotation from Hutcheson was not prolonged to include another sentence or two which could be regarded as clinching this significant departure, or contrast, between Hutcheson and Smith.

Possibly this merely means that one cannot please everybody. But clearly unless a very tight rein is kept on the citation of references, cross-references, parallels or contrasts, the extent of the annotation, on the same page as Smith's own text, may result in the latter getting rather swamped by the former.

Obviously the tastes and needs of different kinds of readers may vary widely. This is presumably an edition for readers already pretty familiar with *The Wealth of Nations*, who wish to ponder and analyse closely particular passages, especially the opening five chapters of Book I, after which the rate of annotation considerably diminishes. Such readers will find here much richly rewarding material. But someone reading this great book for the first or second time may feel that they can make more rapid, uninterrupted progress in Cannan's edition.

It might have been very helpful if the Introduction could have summarised the lessons or conclusions emerging, as the editors saw them, from their immense labours on the text and on the notes. It could have been highly interesting to have had some general pointers, or examples, regarding the significance of all the textual variations so carefully collated. It might also have been instructive to have had the editors' conclusions regarding how far all their work on the notes may fill out, or possibly alter, the not-very-clear picture available of Smith's sources and his indebtedness to earlier authors. A first impression seems to suggest that perhaps this indebtedness was rather more detailed and extensive than has previously been realised. But this could be mistaken.

Volume I is opened by an informative and erudite sixty-page "General Introduction", by Professor R.H. Campbell and Mr Andrew Skinner, devoted to summaries of Smith's previous writings, notably the remarkable *Essay on Astronomy*, *The Theory of Moral Sentiments*, and the new set of *Lectures on Jurisprudence*. Following this, some main themes in, or about, *The Wealth of*

Nations, are taken up under such headings as "Economic Theory and the Exchange Economy", "The Role of the State", "The Institutional Relevance of *The Wealth of Nations*" and "Smith's Use of History".

There is only one remark in this Introduction which moves this reviewer to sharp protest, that is the statement (p. 18) that Smith's "economic analysis involves a high degree of abstraction". Of course any "analysis", indeed any putting of pen to paper, *must* involve *some* degree of abstraction. But compared with the subsequent development of economic analysis, especially since Ricardo, Smith's work involves *a markedly low or lower* degree of abstraction. It is not so much that (as the editor continues):

> In his economic work Smith was concerned only with some aspects of the psychology of man and in fact confined his attention to the self-regarding propensities.

There is a sense in which this is not untrue. But the point is that in *The Wealth of Nations*, as in fact is stated later (p. 38) in the Introduction. Smith is referring to "*different areas* of human experience", as compared with *The Theory of Moral Sentiments*. What Smith is doing is not indulging in a high degree of abstraction in terms of a particular *aspect* of human behaviour, but focusing on a particular *area*, in terms of a realistically *low* degree of abstraction. "*Areas*" of human experience shade into one another in the real world, and often cannot, without much arbitrariness, be sharply marked off from one another as clearly as "aspects" can be defined in terms of precise abstract assumptions. That is why Smith's work lacks the "rigour" and "precision" obtainable (at a perhaps fatally high cost) by much higher degrees of abstraction than he employed. Anyhow, however much mileage may be obtainable from this distinction between "aspects" and "areas", it should be insisted that compared with subsequent, post-Ricardian economic analysis, Smith operates at a comparatively very low, rather than a very high, level of abstraction.

IV

The *Essays on Adam Smith* is a companion volume to *The Works*, in the same impressive and sumptuous format. The 640-odd pages contain 30 essays, *plus* an Introduction and a Conclusion. The volume is divided into two roughly equal parts, the first (with 14 essays and an introduction) being "mainly concerned with the broadly 'philosophical' and political aspects of Smith's contribution", and the second (comprising 16 essays and a conclusion) being concerned "with the subject-matter (by no means entirely economic) of *The Wealth of Nations* itself" (p. i). Seven of the pieces have been published before, two having been extracted from books. The volume therefore has something of the nature of a book of readings by living writers. The essays certainly range widely, and partly, at some points, even beyond Smith himself, with contributions on Montesquieu and Hume (from Chamley) and on the Classical Economists and Education (from Blaug). However, though there is a considerable concentration in some areas, such as Capital, Growth and Profits with five essays, other areas are very thinly covered, for example distribution, which is only represented by a distinguished paper from Professor Rees on "Compensating Wage Differentials". The scope and method of *The Wealth of Nations*, receives very little attention in this volume, though Smith's work, in this respect, is unique in its balance and comprehensiveness, differs profoundly from that of his Ricardian successors, and possesses significant implications for the nature of his policy conclusions. The lack of attention to this subject, incidentally, contrasts markedly with the celebratory discussion of 1876 by the Political Economy Club of London which was largely devoted to methodological debate.

V

Since it is hardly practicable to discuss all the 32 papers in this volume, or even to re-paraphrase the brief summaries provided at the beginning of each half, we may drastically reduce the problems of selection, more or less at a stroke, by concentrating on Part II, that is on the essays concerned with the subject-matter of *The Wealth of Nations*. An apology is due to the contributors to Part I, and also to those to Part II whose essays are not, or only very briefly, referred to. But as an exception with regard to Part I, we might pick out the only article by an economist, that is Professor George Stigler's paper, "Smith's Travels on the Ship of State". Professor Stigler complains here of Smith's rejection of self-interest as a general explanation of *political* activity, as contrasted with his general emphasis on it in explaining *economic* activity. It seems possible that Professor Stigler's complaint may be rather too sharply drawn, partly because self-interest does not, according to Smith, always dominate everybody's economic activities, for example those of landlords. But this is a very stimulating paper, with a challenging, clearly perceived and sharply focused theme, forcefully expounded, with an impressive array of detailed evidence and illustration brought together in a brief compass.

Turning to Part II, this is opened by Professor Samuel Hollander's essay on "The Role of Utility in *The Wealth of Nations*" (extracted from his recent book). Professor Hollander is concerned to refute the criticisms directed by P.H. Douglas, Kauder, Taylor and Robertson, Schumpeter and others, against Smith's treatment of utility and value. First, there is an historical point regarding the treatment of utility and demand by Smith's predecessors (and even by himself in *The Lectures*) and how far Smith crucially departed from this, or seriously changed the emphasis, in *The Wealth of Nations*.

As regards this historical question, it seems doubtful whether the generalisation can be sustained (against the writings of de Roover) that the Scholastics generally placed greater emphasis upon costs than upon demand and utility.[4] But it is not necessary, at this point, to go back to the Scholastics and argue over such a massive generalisation. It is simply relevant to point up the contrast with Francis Hutcheson, with regard to the definition of utility or "use". For Hutcheson employs a comprehensive concept of use, or utility which includes that of giving "any satisfaction, by prevailing custom or fancy, as a method of ornament or distinction . . . for this will cause a demand as well as natural use".⁵ Smith, on the other hand, in *The Wealth of Nations* maintains that "utility", which "may be called 'value in use' ", is *not necessary at all* for "the greatest value in exchange". Smith is thus amputating the utility concept, in a manner rejected by most economists before and since, so as to confine it to a kind of "biological", or (as P.H. Douglas called it) "moralistic" utility. This drastic alteration in definition is quite unnecessary to make the familiar point (which Hutcheson made) that there is no relation or correspondence between market values and biological or "moralistic" usefulness. Professor Hollander seems to try to defend Smith by refusing to accept what he actually wrote, when he (Hollander) refers to "Smith's 'so-called' rejection of utility as a possible cause of value".⁶ It was "so-called" by Adam himself when he first defined "utility" so as to render it totally unnecessary for exchange value.

Smith's treatment of utility and value had vast historical consequences. Moreover, his biological, "moralistic", or objective concept of utility has very dangerous implications. How, or by what authority, is it to be decided, in terms of such a definition, which items of my food or clothing have "utility", and which, have none, and are merely ornamental, non-basic, or perhaps even frivolous, so that I could reasonably be deprived of them? Smith himself would have recoiled in horror from such implications: but he left them there for others to pick up.

Next, Mr M.H. Dobb contributes an article on "Ricardo and Adam Smith", which is far more about the former than the latter. Almost needless to say, Mr Dobb introduces his usual rather dogmatic insistence regarding what must be "the key to the determination of prices" – (an arbitrary and perhaps meta-physical conception in itself). He goes on to maintain that a theory of distribution must be derived from some "social datum", in turn depending "on socio-economic institutions (e.g. property-ownership and its distribution)". Except that Walras does not, of course, deal in dogmatic, one-way "keys", but in general interdependence, this conception is somewhat similar to that of Walras, who separates distribution from the pricing of factor services in his *Social Economics*, and proceeds to advocate the nationalisation of land. Returning, fleetingly, to Adam Smith, Mr Dobb concludes:

> It is a commonplace that Ricardo shared with Smith the characteristic of being *par-excellence* a theorist of perfect competition.⁷

This seems a strange commonplace, at least as far as Smith is concerned. It seems to be comprehensively contradicted in the next paper but one, which is perhaps the most discerning in this part of the volume, that is, Mr. G.B. Richardson's paper on "Adam Smith on Competition and Increasing Returns". Mr Richardson points out that Smith's concept of competition, and of the working of the economic system was

> very different from that implicit in the formal models employed by modern equilibrium analysis . . . His theory of economic evolution presumes the general prevalence of increasing returns. Nowadays, on the other hand, economists employ a model – perfect competition – which postulates universally diminishing returns to scale, it being presumed that increasing

returns must tend to concentration and eventual monopoly.[8]

Mr. Richardson observes that Adam Smith "did not appear in the least troubled by the thought that competition and increasing returns might not be able to coexist". He proceeds to emphasise an interesting comparison with Chamberlin's theory of monopolistic competition, which in important respects "corresponds much more closely to Smith's vision than does the perfectly competitive model".[9]

Professor Albert Rees's paper on "Compensating Wage Differentials" concludes that this concept "has been a hardy device for generating fruitful hypotheses about wage structure". Professor Rees contributes the following perceptive *aperçu* regarding Smith's method as contrasted with that of his successors:

> The concept of net advantage or net satisfactions did not arise as a way of covering up deficiencies in the predictive power of a theory of monetary maximization. On the contrary, the concept of net advantage is the original one, and lapses into a theory of monetary maximization came later, as a result of the difficulties of measuring non-monetary factors.[10]

In other words, Smith was not concerned with such "rigorous" abstractions as the maximisation of some arbitrarily precise (and/or empty) maximand, but with setting out the more important motives or considerations of real-world people.

Five papers follow on various aspects of capital, profits, and growth, by Professors Marian Bowley ("Some Aspects of the Treatment of Capital in *The Wealth of Nations*"), Rosenberg ("Adam Smith on Profits – Paradox Lost and Regained"), Spengler ("Adam Smith and Society's Decision-Makers"), Lowe ("Adam Smith's System of Equilibrium Growth"), and Mr Eltis ("Adam Smith's Theory of Economic Growth").[11]

Next, in his paper on "Adam Smith and the Theory of International Trade", Professor Arthur Bloomfield defends Smith's contribution and also (like Mr Richardson in the general domestic case) significantly contrasts Smith's method with that of his successors. He discerns "a dynamic approach to the gains from trade that was to be neglected by the later classical economists".[12]

The treatment of the monetary and banking framework, assumed to implement the smooth functioning of Smith's simple system of natural liberty, is certainly one of the less satisfactory aspects of *The Wealth of Nations*. What the framework of monetary and banking policies and institutions might be, which would assure the smooth, satisfactorily self-adjusting operation of the economy in macro-economic terms, is not at all clearly or fully spelt out. On this subject, excellent and effectively complementary papers are forthcoming from Professor Douglas Vickers on "Smith's Theory of Money", and from Professor S.G. Checkland on "Adam Smith and the Bankers".

Professor Vickers is not being unduly ungenerous when he argues: "In the matter of the theory of money *The Wealth of Nations* does not deserve high praise."[12] This is especially so (as Professor Vickers is best qualified to point out) if one compares Smith's treatment of money with that of his great predecessors, Cantillon, Hume, and Steuart.

Professor Checkland's contribution is very helpful and learned in his discussion of Smith's treatment of Scottish banking. He concludes that Smith's assumption that the banks acting in aggregate would "provide an optimal money supply or an effective approximation to it", was not justified by the conditions of the time:

> In the light of banking conditions in the Scotland of Adam Smith's time not to speak of the years to follow when matters approximated even less to his assumption, his view of banking omitted important aspects of reality which, if properly attended to, might have damaged his view of economic processes.[13]

This "view of economic processes", or, in other words, Smith's macro-economics, was, of course, what came to be known as the "classical" model in the Keynesian sense – of which Adam Smith was the great originator, and J.B. Say and James Mill comparatively unimportant elaborators.

Next comes Professor R.L. Heilbroner's very stimulating essay – already referred to – on "The Paradox of Progress: Decline and Decay in *The Wealth of Nations*". Professor Heilbroner is concerned to explore what he calls the "insufficiently examined dark side of Smith's thought".[14] He emphasises the apparently very dismal kind of "stationary state" for which it seems society is eventually destined:

> The condition of the working class has been reduced to a Malthusian precariousness. The employer of moderate means ekes out a modest livelihood; a few men of great wealth live from their interest. The position of the landlord, prefiguring the conclusion of Ricardo, is presumably of all classes the most improved.[15]

In addition to this, with the extension of the division of labour there will be the "alienation" problem, though here the darker prospects would have seemed to be relieved by the immense hopes which Smith, as a man of the Enlightenment, placed in education. Such darker possibilities as these, however, have to be reconciled with the "sense of confidence and promise" which, on the surface at any rate, seems to pervade Smith's work. Professor Heilbroner sees as applying to Smith's thought, Peter Gay's proposition that "the question of the lower orders is the great unexamined political question of the Enlightenment".[16]

In the next essay, however, on Adam Smith and Alienation, Professor E.G. West denies that the "serious cultural and human hazards" entailed in the advancement of the division of labour resembled at all closely the "alienation" which Marx accused "capitalism" of fostering. Professor West does not seem to regard as so serious this "darker" side of Smith's ideas about the social and economic future. But he does quote the interesting passage in which Smith seems to envisage a kind of cultural polarisation between the fascinating, richly various prospects for the philosophical few to contemplate, and the contracted perspectives of the many:

In a civilised state, on the contrary, though there is little variety in the occupations of the greater part of individuals, there is an almost infinite variety in those of the whole society. These varied occupations present an almost infinite variety of objects to the contemplation of those few, who, being attached to no particular occupation themselves have leisure and inclination to examine the occupations of other people. The contemplation of so great a variety of objects necessarily exercises their minds in endless comparisons and combinations, and renders their understandings, in an extraordinary degree both acute and comprehensive.[17]

Though the extraordinarily "acute and comprehensive" understandings of Smith's fellow philosophers of the eighteenth century may indeed be admired, this is not how things have worked out two hundred years later. Those who earn their living (like economists) by examining (hardly at leisure) "the occupations of other people", find their vision restricted and narrowed by the intellectual division of labour into much more limited perspectives than Smith himself would have approved.

Professor Alan Peacock provides an enlightening review of "The Treatment of the Principles of Public Finance in The Wealth of Nations", demonstrating that: "Adam Smith treated issues in public finance which receive close attention in the current literature with a good deal more sophistication than is often found to-day."[18]

Professor Blaug's re-examination of the "Economics of Education in English Classical Political Economy" starts from the charge that most of the existing literature on this subject "is unfortunately contradictory if not downright misleading".[19]

Professor Blaug's paper is only initially concerned with Adam Smith, whose views on this subject do not, for the most part, seem to have been closely followed by his classical successors. Professor Blaug points out Smith's serious concern with the great unsolved problem, as regards universities especially, of "how should we reward teachers so as to induce them to perform their tasks with maximum efficiency?" Professor Blaug adds: "It is interesting to ask oneself how British university teaching is now evaluated."[20]

As Professor Blaug points out, Adam Smith, of course, had a very direct and hard-headed answer to this problem.

Finally, in "Some Concluding Reflections", Professor T. Wilson claims that "the essays in this volume on Adam Smith have reviewed the range and shown the subtlety of his system of thought".[21]

This claim is justified. Professor Wilson also finishes off by pointing to what may be one of the central questions which this new edition may assist in illuminating, that is the relations between the ideas in *The Theory of Moral Sentiments* and in *The Wealth of Nations*. This sounds rather like "Das Adam-Smith problem" of the German historical economists. But it is not that the relations between these two works and their ideas – or with regard to the other writings of Smith – need be seen as at all seriously inconsistent: it is simply necessary to realise how richly significant these relations are, and that progress in understanding and interpreting Adam Smith requires further elucidation of their precise nature. Anyhow, there are quite enough important and intriguing problems outstanding regarding Smith and his work, the study of which will be encouraged and assisted by this splendid new Glasgow edition of his complete writings. So no more valuable way of commemorating the Bicentenary could have been devised.

Notes

    1.   A review-article of two publications:

An Inquiry into the Nature and Causes of the Wealth of Nations. By Adam Smith, Edited by R.H. Campbell, A.S. Skinner and W.B. Todd. (Oxford: Clarendon Press, 1976. Volume 2, pp. vii + 537. £25 for the set.)

Essays on Adam Smith. Edited by A.S. Skinner and T. Wilson (Oxford: Clarendon Press, 1975. Pp. xvi + 647, £15).

    2.   "I submit, though the temple fall on me as I say it, that in the last analysis it was professorial advice which lost us the first empire" (C.R. Fay, *Adam Smith and the Scotland of his Day*, 1956, p. 116).

    3.   For an account, see vol. I, pp. 61-6.

    4.   See page 314.

    5.   *System of Moral Philosophy* (1755), vol. II, pp. 53-4.

    6.   p. 315 n.

    7.   p. 335.

    8.   p. 354.

    9.   In his "Concluding Reflections" Professor T. Wilson observes that although the existence of competition was a "crucial" part of the "proper environment" for Smith: "This need not indeed be 'perfect' competition in the special sense accorded to the expression in the nineteen-thirties. But what is required is rivalry and workable competition" (p. 604).

   10.   p. 337.

   11.   p. 473.

   12.   p. 484.

   13.   p. 523.

   14.   p. 524.

   15.   p. 529.

   16.   p. 538.

   17.   p. 552.

   18.   p. 554.

   19.   p. 568.

   20.   p. 569.

   21.   p. 600.

70

Adam Smith and *The Wealth of Nations*

T.W. Hutchison

Source: *Journal of Law and Economics*, Vol. 19 (3), October 1976, pp. 507-28.

I

Since I first received your flattering invitation to contribute a lecture on Adam Smith to this very distinguished bicentennial celebration, my sense of inadequacy has been much deepened by the recollection that this bicentenary of the publication of *The Wealth of Nations* is also the fiftieth anniversary of the sesquicentennial commemoration held here in Chicago in 1926. On that occasion a series of lectures was given on "Adam Smith and *The Wealth of Nations*" by Hollander, J.M. Clark, Douglas, Viner, and others which still contains much of the best commentary and criticism available on its great subject.[1] I cannot hope to emulate the scholarship and judgment of 1926 regarding the topics which were then so magisterially discussed. I can only explore the possibility that in the fifty intervening years, with their turbulent and sometimes appalling politico-economic experiences, and with the transformation of economics as a subject, there may have been opened up (or forced upon the attention) vistas, angles, or perspectives which provide insights into Smith's work not readily discernible or relevant for our distinguished predecessors in 1926.

There are also reasons at this bicentenary for recalling briefly the celebrations of *1876* and, in particular, "the grand dinner and special discussion" held by the Political Economy Club of London, with Mr. Gladstone presiding. As a London daily newspaper stated at the time, the centenary celebration of 1876 in Britain did not "coincide with an auspicious moment in the history of the science which Adam Smith founded."[2] In fact, the first centenary took place at a time in Britain especially – not so much elsewhere – of fundmental challenge and uncertainty. Rather suddenly, in the late sixties, the doctrines of classical political economy in respect of theories, policies, and methods (which had achieved in Britain such an extraordinary dominance over the subject and which had enjoyed such confidence and prestige among the articulate public and political elite) were shaken by fundamental criticisms and lost rapidly in credibility. By 1876 little firm consensus had emerged regarding the nature and methods of the subject. Therefore, to a large extent the centenary celebration in London consisted of conflicting claims and opposing interpretations regarding the methods and significance of *The Wealth of Nations*. Fifty years later in 1926, in spite of institutionalist criticisms in the United States, there was not so much fundamental uncertainty and challenge but indeed something like comparative "normalcy" or a lull before the storm. On the other hand, at this bicentenary – though the scale and many other aspects are of course very different – one can discern certain broad, if distant, parallels with the state of the subject in Britain a hundred years ago. It could, therefore, again have become relevant at this juncture to start by focusing on rather fundamental questions of the scope and method of *The Wealth of Nations*. Such questions often are – and certainly are in Smith's work – significantly related to the treatment of policy issues, and they have not received as much attention as other less significant aspects of Smith's work nor as much as their unusual and, in some ways unique, features deserve.

II

Sometimes with very great men who have some outstanding deed or epoch-making achievement to their name, it is possible to look at their previous life simply as a preparation, brief or lengthy, leading up to the fulfillment of their supreme historic task. In the second half of the eighteenth century there was, as Smith himself was definitively to demonstrate, a great historic work to be written on political economy, one which would pull together and systematise the subject, lay down new or reformed principles of perennial significance (or at any rate valid) for decades to come, and at the same time instigate a long revolution in economic policy just at the juncture when England was about to enter upon one of the most crucial phases in her, or any other country's, economic history. What better intellectual grounding for the person destined to produce this supreme work could then have been found anywhere in the world than in Francis Hutcheson's Moral Philosophy class (reading Grotius at fifteen)[3] in Glasgow from 1737 to 1740? As Smith claimed decades later – though surely he would have maintained that it held also in his student days:

> In the present state of the Scotch universities, I do most sincerely look upon them as, in spite of all their faults, without exception the best seminaries of learning that are to be found anywhere in Europe. They are, perhaps, upon the whole, as unexceptionable as any public institutions of that kind, which all contain in their very nature the seeds and causes of negligence and corruption, have ever been, or are ever likely to be.[4]

The next stage for our historic author-to-be was Oxford – a sharp contrast with Glasgow in educational terms – where, as *The Wealth of Nations*, of course, tells us ". . . the greater part of the public professors have, for these many years, given up altogether even the pretence of teaching."[5] We have strangely little knowledge of how Smith spent these six years (except that he evidently was not taught anything). W.R. Scott maintained that "the Oxford of his time gave little if any help towards what was to be his life-work."[6]

On the other hand, even if Oxford was not exactly ideal for this purpose, it was surely invaluable for Smith to obtain some direct, firsthand acquaintance with the social, political, and economic institutions of England (to which, indeed, significant tributes are paid in *The Wealth of Nations*). For though philosophically somewhat in the shade compared with Scotland and France, mid-century England was, as we just noted, approaching a supremely important passage in her and the world's economic development. *The Wealth of Nations* was probably significantly enriched by its observant author's firsthand experience of English life and society at this stage.

Then, coming home to Scotland again to emerge remarkably rapidly as a successful young lecturer and be rewarded with a major chair at twenty-eight, what could have been more valuable for our future master than, *first*, the closest friendship with (as Adam Smith himself called David Hume) "by far the most illustrious philosopher and historian of the present age,"[7] who, in his *Political Discourses* of 1752, was about to contribute significantly to emerging revolutionary ideas on political economy? And *secondly*, what could have been more stimulating and fruitful than the contacts with the merchants of Glasgow – doubly important for a scholarly philosopher in imbuing his work with a vitally realistic, practical, concrete power? For as John Rae tells us: "It was amid the thickening problems of the rising trade of the Clyde, and the daily discussions they occasioned among the enterprising and intelligent merchants of the town, that he grew into a great economist."[8]

Meanwhile there followed a longish period of teaching and lecturing, in part on political economy, to foster a solid mastery of the subject. For, as *The Wealth of Nations* explains:

> To impose upon any man the necessity of teaching, year after year, any particular branch of science, seems, in reality, to be the most effectual method of rendering him completely master of it himself. By being obliged to go every year over the same ground, if he is good for any thing, he necessarily becomes, in a few years, well acquainted with every part of it: and if upon any particular point he should form too hasty an opinion one year, when he comes in the course of his lecture to re-consider the same subject the year thereafter, he is very likely to correct it.[9]

Very likely, and up to a point; but these learning-by-teaching processes seem sometimes to be liable to a kind of diminishing returns or exhaustion of investment opportunity. So after a dozen years, as Lord Keynes appreciated: "At the age of forty-one (just at the right moment, neither too soon nor too late)" Smith "launched himself on the great world,"[10] notably making contact in the salons of Paris with the leading "economists" of France, where at the same time he had an instructive view of the French economic policies of that day – policies later likened by Walter Bagehot to "a sort of museum stocked with the most important [economic] errors."[11] Finally our future author returns home once more, endowed with the financial resources enabling him to concentrate for most of a decade on the composition of his masterpiece published in 1776.

In spite of some teleological overemphasis, there is clearly much that is valid in the foregoing account from the point of view of a modern economist. It sets out the main intellectual sources, experiences, and ingredients which went into the making of *The Wealth of Nations*. But one thing about it is entirely out of focus: Smith himself would never for one moment have entertained (even in his later years, after 1776, when *The Wealth of Nations* was bringing him such resounding and rewarding success) an interpretation of his intellectual career as having been centred round, or dominated by, political economy – even in the broadest possible sense of the term.

For Adam Smith was in fact, and undoubtedly always considered himself to be, a philosopher in a highly comprehensive sense – not as interested in epistemology as Locke, Berkeley, and Hume but penetrating much more deeply into social and legal philosophy and the psychology of ethics. Smith remained a philosopher from the beginning to the end of his life. He would never have regarded his work as a whole as primarily economic. He thought of economics – or political economy – as only one chapter, and not the most important chapter, in a broad study of society and human progress which involved psychology and ethics (in social and individual terms), law, politics, and the development of the arts and sciences.[12] Smith did not merely start life with a youthful enthusiasm for philosophy and then narrow down his interests in his maturity to become an economist. Fortunately for our subject, as it turned out, he did devote a decade or so of his prime years to political economy (using up, perhaps, quite a lot more scarce time than he had originally intended in completing his work in that particular section of his vast field). But having finished *The Wealth of Nations*, Smith moved on (or back) to the history and philosophy of law and of the progress of the arts and sciences. When he lamented in his last days that "he had done so little," Smith did not, of course, mean that he had planned but failed to complete further volumes on political economy (as Alfred Marshall originally planned a multi-volume *Principles of Economics* which, very unfortunately for the subject in the twentieth century, was never completed in the form originally intended). What Smith, with excessive modesty, was lamenting was that he had not completed more than a small part (which fortunately included the politico-economic part) of his original vast philosophical-historical plan.[13] Therefore, that *The Wealth of Nations* played such an important role in establishing political economy as an independent subject is one of those felicitous, unintended, and quite unplanned outcomes to which Smith himself assigned such an important and often beneficient role in human affairs. In his own celebrated words Smith himself was "led by an invisible hand to promote an end which was no part of his intention,"[14] – the end, that is, of establishing political economy as a separate, autonomous discipline.

Moreover, it is not simply that Smith held that an 'Inquiry," and the conclusions thereof, into the wealth of nations or the progress of opulence must be regarded as a subordinate part of a far more comprehensive whole. There is, in fact, at every important point *within* his "Inquiry," a constant interpenetration between factors of economics and political economy and those of law, morals, psychology, and politics.

One of the most important themes of Smith's vast, uncompleted lifework seems to have been centred around the idea of human progress, or the progress of society.[15] In fact, as Walter Bagehot in his essay of 1876 illuminatingly observed regarding *The Wealth of Nations*:

> It was not the exclusive product of a lifelong study . . . on the contrary, it was in the mind of its author only one of many books, or rather a single part of a great book, which he intended to write . . . he spent his life accordingly, in studying the origin and progress of the sciences, the laws, the politics, and all the other aids and forces which have raised man from the savage to the civilised state . . . he investigated the progress of opulence as part of the growth and progress of all things . . .
>
> . . . the last way in which he regarded Political Economy was as a separate and confined speciality; he came upon it as an inseparable part of the development of all things, and it was in that vast connection that he habitually considered it.[16]

But, it may well be asked what interest for economists today have Smith's apparently vast intellectual ambitions regarding the intended scope of his lifework and the somewhat limited and subordinate place of *The Wealth of Nations* in that intended work? Are Smith's comprehensive intellectual concepts more than a rather magnificent "period" museum specimen of eighteenth-century intellectual design, which in any case Smith himself came nowhere near to completing, and which is quite obsolete and irrelevant in scale for the tasks of 1976?

Of course it can be validly claimed that for nearly two centuries the concentration and specialisation carried through by successive generations beginning with Ricardo and Senior has largely paid off, in spite of objections advanced from time to time by historical, Comtian, Marxist, and institutionalist critics. But this specialisation in political economy and economics has depended to a large extent on the assumption of a fairly stable social and political environment which would not too seriously or irregularly interfere with economic processes – processes which, therefore, could be studied more or less in isolation. This assumption of a stable framework (or what Pigou about fifty years ago was describing as a "stable general culture")[17] permitted the development of classical and neo-classical political economy in Britain; and, indeed, there may always be plenty of more narrow and specifically economic questions which will not require the kind of comprehensive social and historical setting envisaged by Adam Smith. But to the extent that the assumption of a more or less stable social framework – and the kind of specialisation in economics which it permits – *may be* becoming significantly less valid than it used to be, there may well be reasons for regarding Smith's conceptions of the scope of the subject and its close interrelationships and interpentration with other fields (especially that of law) not simply as an obsolete, unpractical, intellectually unfeasible irrelevance of no more than period interest for economists today in 1976. What at least might be concluded is that Adam Smith would not have neglected nor underestimated the legal, social, and social-psychological factors in our contemporary economic problems (for example, the problem of inflation) just because such factors may be outside what have more recently come to be regarded as accepted professional or departmental frontiers.

III

Conceptions of the scope of the subject are naturally related to conceptions regarding methods, and in turn are related to the kind of conclusions regarding policy which are considered intellectually feasible or justified. The combination and balance of methods employed in *The Wealth of Nations* have been as rarely followed by subsequent economists as have Smith's comprehensive conceptions of the scope and of the wide-ranging interdependencies of social and economic enquiry. There was surely some justification for the claim of the historical economist Thorold Rogers at the centenary celebration a hundred years ago, that there was ". . . nothing more significant than the difference of the process by which Adam Smith collected his inferences, and that by which his followers or commentators have arrived at theirs."[18]

In fact, following the James Mill-Ricardo methodological revolution, the comprehensiveness and balance of methods deployed in *The Wealth of Nations* has hardly ever been regained in a general work on the subject of major stature. It is a tribute to the remarkable balance which Smith achieved that he has been both acclaimed and criticised from both or all sides in subsequent methodological debates. But there is certainly a most striking contrast with the Ricardian methods which later obtained such prestige.[19] For the bulk of the text of *The Wealth of Nations* consists of descriptive and historical material. As one of Smith's recent successors at Glasgow has noted:

> . . . he was rather a rich inductive thinker than a rigidly local system-builder . . . though he was both. He had the modesty and wisdom always to give true weight to the facts . . . [He had a] genius for choosing and using factual data. He was at home in facts. He enjoyed ferreting them out, and giving them their proper weights.[20]

Sixty years after the appearance of *The Wealth of Nations*, Nassau Senior, in formulating the viewpoint established by the Ricardian methodological revolution, was to complain of "the undue importance which many economists have ascribed to the collection of facts."[21]

According to Senior, the science of political economy apart from its multifarios applications, was not, *avide de faits*. Adam Smith emphatically was *avide de faits*, and overwhelmingly demonstrated his avidity, and the conception of the subject which this avidity implied, in *The Wealth of Nations*.

In his *Lectures on Rhetoric and Belles Lettres*, Smith is reported as referring to "abstract and speculative reasonings, which perhaps tend very little to the bettering of our practice."[22] In fact, in *The Wealth of Nations* "abstract reasonings" are kept on a very tight rein. Smith is certainly not one for taking off into the Ricardian stratosphere of "strong cases" or extreme, arbitrary abstractions. Of course Smith employed a "system," as he called it, by which he meant an abstract, deductive model. But he sharply denounced "the man of system" who indulges in what Viner called

> over-attachment to and exaggeration of the applicability to concrete issues without qualification of abstract and therefore at its best partial and

incomprehensive theorising . . .

. . . he [Smith] very much doubted that abstraction could provide either understanding of the real world or, by itself, safe guidance for the legislator or statesman.[23]

When Smith wanted to use a simple case for its illustrative value, he seldom invented an abstraction. He sought to go back in history and find a factual illustration in a simpler kind of economy, such as the hand-to-mouth hunting and fishing economy which is so frequently referred to from the first page onwards in *The Wealth of Nations*. How far Smith's history, or sometimes what has been called his "conjectural history," was always accurate is beside the point methodologically. Smith did not consider that students of society or the wealth of nations could, or should, seek to compensate very far for their inability to experiment by setting up abstract models.

Smith was methodologically comprehensive. Though sharing much of the intellectual confidence of his age, he realised that significant social and philosophical truth, including economic truth, was always a *very* scarce commodity and especially so in relation to the extravagant needs for it implicitly postulated by, though often not explicitly understood to be an essential prerequisite for, the plans and projects of reformers and revolutionaries. So the student of society, or of the economy, cannot afford to overlook *any* method by which some grain of truth, however insubstantial and fragmentary, may be picked up. As John Neville Keynes said of Smith, "He rejected no method of enquiry that could in any way assist him in investigating the phenomena of wealth."[24]

In fact, Smith employed methods which recently have been powerfully denounced by some philosophers and economists. For Smith was an historical economist not only in the sense that he was empirical, but in that the theme of *progress through natural stages of development* runs all through his *Inquiry into the Nature and Cause of the Wealth of Nations*. Smith was in fact – with Adam Ferguson and Smith's pupil John Millar – a leader of the Scottish historical school,[25] and they might well be described as proto historicists. Smith did not claim to have discovered "laws" of economic development or indeed *any* economic laws, and so might not be describable as a historicist in the fullest sense. But especially in the often rather neglected Book III of *The Wealth of Nations*, "Of the Natural Progress of Opulence," Smith seeks to lay down "the natural course of things" or an "order of things which necessity imposes in general," though he allowed that this natural course or order could be "inverted" by misconceived government policies.

Of course, as with most methods (including, for example, quantitative methods) "historicist" procedures, as Sir Karl Popper has demonstrated, have been grossly misused, and widely exaggerated claims have been made on their behalf. But if one is interested in different kinds of economy existing at different times and places and their different actual and potential levels of development, then one cannot afford fastidiously to dismiss "historicist" concepts, questions, and methods, however uncertain and unreliable. Though the economist should test and scrutinise results or predictions with the utmost feasible strictness, he cannot dismiss in advance *any* method which may yield some fragment of insight – and certainly not just because such a method is not employed in what are called the most "mature" natural sciences such as physics.

Therefore, even more definitely than with regard to the scope of the subject, there may seem in 1976 to be important lessons to be found in the methodological comprehensiveness and balance of Smith's *Inquiry*, which has in this respect virtually never been emulated in a book of general principles of major importance. Though John Stuart Mill made something of an attempt,[26] and Marshall discerned and wrestled with the problem of meshing history and analysis in an exposition of general principles, no one has really been able to put it all together again with the balance and comprehensiveness achieved in *The Wealth of Nations*.

IV

Adam Smith's *Inquiry*, with its abundantly marshalled empirical and institutional data, evidence, and illustration, with its sometimes extensive historical digressions (for example, on silver, or on the corn trade, or on the Bank of Amsterdam), and with its exhaustive surveys of institutions (for example, especially educational institutions), is all eventually held together securely but flexibly by the thread provided by a single *type* of model or "system": what Smith called "the simple system of natural liberty," or what we might call the freely competitive, self-adjusting market model. The conditions for "natural" values and prices, wages, profits and rents having been analysed out, the model is applied generally (but not dogmatically, universally, or exclusively) both to domestic and foreign trade as well as to the allocation of particular resources and to their accumulation and employment in the aggregate. Moreover, Smith uses his simple system of natural liberty as a historically "dynamic" model in that it is concerned not only with a static criterion or ideal condition but with the *progress* of the economy – an essential part of Smith's central theme. What Smith's *Inquiry* is primarily about is how the simple system starting from individual initiative allocates, accumulates, and reallocates resources *via* free markets so as to release and stimulate more effectively than any other "system" the economic forces which make for progress. The essential unique contribution of "the simple system" is this vital and attractive complementarity between individual freedom and the economic progress of society.

This assertion of the simple "system," or the free-market model, in such broad, general terms (but not universally or exclusively) provides one of the main grounds for maintaining that Smith's *Inquiry* marks an epoch in the history of economic thought or even a revolution in the subject (in a justifiable sense of a recently often unjustifiably overworked term). For it was Adam Smith who really generalised the theory of market self-adjustment as operating effectively by and large – though with several and, in some cases, important exceptions – throughout the economic cosmos, domestically and internationally, micro-economically and macro-economically. Of course, others before Smith had discerned self-adjusting forces at work in particular sectors and had also sometimes urged that in some areas these forces should be allowed to work themselves out free of government intervention: for example, Gervaise and Hume for international trade, North, Mandeville, and Josiah Tucker for domestic markets, or with regard to labour or capital markets. But it was Smith who asserted the "system," or model in general terms, as a general answer regarding most economic processes of a natural or normal kind. It must also be emphasised that for Smith self-adjustment was not assumed as a hypothetical abstraction, but was asserted as an imprecise and qualified, but in principle refutable, empirical theory regarding how particular market processes actually tended to work out. Smith was asserting that market processes worked out in general – given some reasonably simple specifiable and practically feasible conditions – in a very different way from what had mostly been stated or implied in previous economic writings.

In *The Wealth of Nations* there are two great economic forces making for economic progress, which depend in their turn on the psychological factor of the individual's striving to better his condition and on a favourable legal framework (especially regarding property and land tenure). The first of these two great economic forces is the division of labour. It has been justifiably asserted that the initial and basic proposition of Smith's *Inquiry*, that the division of labour depends on the extent of the market, "is one of the most illuminating generalisations which can be found anywhere in the whole literature of economics."[27]

What might be called Smith's micro-economics and international economics are concerned with how free competitive markets allow the division of labour to contribute with its full force to economic progress; while his macro-economics shows how, under his simple system of natural liberty, individual frugality can be fully implemented in the progress of the economy.

Of course, as we have already emphasized, Smith does not assert the empirical validity of the "simple system" in dogmatic, unqualified, or universal terms. In the mass of historical evidence and illustration – which it is an essential part of Smith's method to bring to bear and to assign its due weight – a variety of qualifications and exceptions are to be found, certainly in the microeconomic and international applications of the simple system or model.

In the first place Smith emphasises the basic preconditions to be satisfied, such as a favourable legal and property framework. It was laws and customs relating to land tenure which "have perhaps contributed more to the present grandeur of England, than all their boasted regulations of commerce taken together."[28] Smith is, of course, also constantly emphasising (and denouncing) the striving after monopoly and the persistence of monopolies and restrictive practices, which "may sometimes last for many years," or "for whole centuries together," and which are based sometimes on "particular accidents" and sometimes on "natural causes," as well as government legislation.[29]

The important qualifications and exceptions, which Smith cites to the beneficent working of his simple system, are well known.[30] They include, notably, defence and shipping; justice; public works (a potentially capacious category); and building methods and standards. Smith is even prepared to allow the government to fix or limit the rate of interest (for which he was logically rebuked by Jeremy Bentham). As regards foreign trade, he was ready to support an export duty on wool and moderate import duties for the purposes of revenue and retaliation or bargaining.

V

There is one feature of Smith's microeconomics which had very important consequences in the subsequent history of economic thought and about which some disagreements have appeared in recent years: this is his labour and cost-of-production analysis of value. Recently there have been some denials (of what, following several leading authorities, I myself would maintain) that Smith's treatment of value (1) marked a significant shift of emphasis as compared with his predecessors and (2) involved a serious *under*-emphasis or confusion regarding the role of utility and demand.[31]

At any rate, it hardly seems deniable that Smith's initial assertion in a crucial passage that goods which may possess the greatest value in exchange may have *no* "value in use," or "utility," was highly confusing. This proposition of Smith has been defended by maintaining that he must have meant by "value in use" and "utility," not what has been meant by economists before and after his time (that is desiredness – or satisfying a want of whatever kind), but that he must rather have meant a kind of objective, biological, or moralistic usefulness. But this attempt at an explanation must be countered by observing (1) that Smith is changing the meaning of the term "use" or "utility" as compared with his predecessors (for example, Francis Hutcheson),[32] (2) that in any case this usage is economically irrelevant and need not have been adopted simply to make the point Smith may have wished to make – that is, the familiar point that economic values are not "objective," moralistic, or biological values.

Seen in proportion and perspective in the whole vast setting and sweep of *The Wealth of Nations*, this seems a rather petty analytical point, or "a little local difficulty," regarding the dissection of which Smith himself might have felt some impatience. But historically his treatment of value and the new shift of emphasis which he introduced in that consequential paragraph at the end of Chapter IV of Book I[33] (along with his unusual definition of utility and value-in-use) had a very significant influence on orthodox theorising for the next century until Jevons, and provided a starting point for the labour theory of value and exploitation of Marx. In fact, Smith's treatment of value and his objective concept of utility were certainly not helpful to his own major purpose, that of establishing the case for economic freedom which requires – or is much assisted by – a value analysis which gives a full role to subjective utility and individual choice and demand. Smith's objective biological or "moralistic" concept of utility contains possible implications from which Smith himself would have recoiled in horror: that is, that there are objective biological or moral questions or "utilities" which experts of one sort or another may be qualified to instruct us about. Moreover, the "objective" labour and cost analysis of value can lead, and has in fact led, in the totally opposite direction to that of Smith's supreme message regarding economic freedom. This is why those economists who have so enthusiastically supported Stalinist and similar types of planning are so bitterly opposed to the subjective value analysis of the "neo-classicals" (and many pre-Smithians) which recognises that value is rooted in subjective, individual choices. To obliterate such implications they are prepared to proceed to extreme lengths in terms of oversimplification (or "strong cases") in order to construct an analysis of value which precludes or extrudes any awkward role for individual utility or freedom of choice and demand. We must therefore agree strongly with Professor P.H. Douglas' conclusion in his lecture of fifty years ago that historically it turned out to be highly unfortunate that Smith shifted the emphasis, along with a crucial definition, in the analysis of value from the scarcity approach developed by his predecessors Pufendorf, Carmichael, and Hutcheson along the road which led to Ricardo, Marx (and Stalin).[34]

VI

The second of the two major economic factors by or through which progress is promoted is that of saving, investment, and accumulation. Smith's stress on the role of capital accumulation in promoting economic progress has even been described as the greatest innovation in *The Wealth of Nations*, and there are clearly some grounds for such a claim. But Smith's point is not simply the importance of accumulation but how, within the simple system of natural liberty, individual frugality and initiative in free markets will be fully and smoothly implemented and converted into capital accumulation and the economic progress of society without any intervention of government. It is the "simple system" which enables the frugal man, concerned simply to "better his own conditions," almost inevitably to be a public benefactor. Throughout his macroeconomics, in both his analysis of saving and investment and his treatment of money, Smith holds to the logic of his "simple system" and its implications for government policy in a highly, though not absolutely, consistent manner (apart from his incongruous approval of a maximum rate of interest).

Smith's macroeconomics (that is, both what Schumpeter called the Turgot-Smith saving-and-investment theory, as well as his treatment of money and the money supply) represent a sufficiently sharp novelty and contrast, compared with most of what had gone before, as also fully to deserve the description "revolutionary."[35] There had been only a few intimations previously of the new, unconditionally pro-saving model in the writings of one or two of Smith's predecessors (for example, in Francis Hutcheson's notable denunciation of Mandeville's eulogy of luxury spending, as well as, of course, in Turgot's *Réflexions*).[36]

We noted the flexibility and qualifications with which Smith applies his "simple system" in the fields of microeconomics and international trade. But his macroeconomics, on the other hand, is the one major area where he applies this system without sufficient regard to qualifications and exceptions or to the necessary conditions, which very much need specifying, with regard to the monetary and banking framework.

First, there is Smith's bald, unqualified assertion about saving and investing that, "What is annually saved is as regularly consumed as what is annually spent, and nearly in the same time too." Consequently, ". . . every prodigal appears to be a public enemy, and every frugal man a public benefactor."[37]

Secondly, there is Smith's treatment of the money supply. He seems at times to suggest that it is simply a crude fallacy of "the mercantile system" to be concerned about the money supply any more than, say, the wine supply:

> We trust with perfect security that the freedom of trade, without any attention of government, will always supply us with the wine which we have occasion for: and we may trust with equal security that it will always supply us with all the gold and silver which we can afford to purchase or to employ, either in circulating our commodities, or in other uses. . . . Upon every account, therefore, the attention of government never was so unnecessarily employed, as when directed to watch over the preservation or increase of the quantity of money in any country.[38]

At some points it seems that Smith is implying that his "simple system" of competitive freedom can and will always be so flexible as to adjust satisfactorily to any variations in the money supply. Elsewhere Smith seems to recognize that a growing economy needs a growing money supply, while pointing out in the "Digression on Silver" that the world supply of precious metals, or international liquidity, may be extremely uncertain and unreliable.[39] However, Smith seems also to assume that, internally, if the quantity of gold and silver is not maintained in a country, then paper money will automatically be created to the appropriate amount without giving rise, apparently, to any serious problems of central regulation.

Of course, the monetary and banking conditions required for the reasonably smooth working of Smith's "simple system" can be worked out. But Smith did not get very far towards this. His rather cavalier treatment generated a long-persistent over-optimism, first regarding the intellectual and practical difficulties of devising and implementing, *through governments*, a satisfactory framework of monetary and banking rules and institutions, and secondly, regarding the seriousness of defects in these rules, or in their implementation, for economic stability. With regard to money and macroeconomics, Smith did not adequately develop the conditions and qualifications for his simple system which the less "revolutionary" but more perceptive insights on these subjects of his greatest friend, David Hume, or of his eclipsed rival, Sir James Steuart, might have suggested.

VII

Smith's intellectual horizons in *The Wealth of Nations* ranged with tremendous spaciousness in time and place, and with regard to levels of development, over every variety of society, economy, and human specimen from the primitive savage to the eighteenth-century Scotsman. Geographically, there is hardly any major area of the world, except Australia, nor any significant period of history, which Smith does not call upon at some point for evidence and illustration. Peoples and countries literally from China to Peru, not omitting the

Tartars and the Hottentots, and including, of course, frequently and at length the ancient Greeks and Romans, all have their contribution to make to the empirical or historical comprehensiveness of *The Wealth of Nations*. When Smith declares what "are the two greatest and most important events recorded in the history of mankind," he does not include a fundamental invention, a decisive battle, a great political declaration or religious revelation: the two most important events in the history of mankind are for Smith, "The discovery of America and that of a passage to the East Indies by the Cape of Good Hope," that is, two vast extensions of the market – and the second of Smith's greatest historic events is not even an extension in area but an improvement of the means of communication.[40]

These vast extensions of the world market had in Smith's day given rise to the most important process or problem in international politico-economic relations of the period, that of colonisation. Colonisation as Smith saw it was essentially the expression in the international arena of the constant mercantile striving after monopoly. If according to Clausewitz war was the continuation of foreign policy by other means, then according to Smith colonisation was the continuation of monopolisation by other means. Nothing is more passionately and constantly condemned throughout *The Wealth of Nations* than this monopolistic drive, both generally and in its particular manifestation in colonial policies:

> To prohibit a great people . . . from making all that they can of every part of their own produce, or from employing their stock and industry in the way that they judge most advantageous to themselves, *is a manifest violation of the most sacred rights of mankind.*[41]

The colonial policies of Britain, according to Smith, were "less illiberal and oppressive" than those of other countries. At home, also, the bad effects of monopoly had been countered especially by

> that equal and impartial administration of justice which renders the rights of the meanest British subject respectable to the greatest, and which, by securing to every man the fruits of his own industry, gives the greatest and most effectual encouragement to every sort of industry.[42]

But her colonial policies were nevertheless, in Smith's estimation, causing Britain herself very serious harm:

> . . . the whole system of her industry and commerce has thereby been rendered less secure; the whole state of her body politic less healthful, than it otherwise would have been. . . . Under the present system of management, therefore, Great Britain derives nothing but loss from the dominion which she assumes over her colonies.[43]

If his cherished plan of a federal union or commonwealth of the colonies and mother country was unattainable, then (though it was vain, Smith believed, to hope that this would be conceded), it would be preferable for Britain to abandon gradually but completely the restrictions on colonial trade and to give up altogether authority over her colonies (and in the first place over those in North America):

> By thus parting good friends, the natural affection of the colonies to the mother country, which, perhaps, our late dissensions have well nigh extinguished, would quickly revive. It might dispose them not only to respect, for whole centuries together, that treaty of commerce which they had concluded with us at parting, but to favour us in war as well as in trade, and, instead of turbulent and factious subjects, to become our most faithful, affectionate, and generous allies . . .[44]

In the very last paragraph of *The Wealth of Nations* Smith repeats the demand that "if any of the provinces of the British empire cannot be made to contribute towards the support of the whole empire," then it was surely time for Great Britain to give up her "project of an empire." In that case, in the very last sentence and last words of the book Smith instructs his country "to accommodate her future views and designs to the real mediocrity of her circumstances."[45] Commenting in *1876*, Walter Bagehot found this "a strange passage, considering all that has happened since, and all the provinces we have since taken."[46] In *1976*, on the other hand, perhaps these famous last words do not seem so "strange."

VIII

Smith once described his treatment of economic policy in *The Wealth of Nations* as a "very violent attack upon the whole commercial system of Great Britain."[47]

Moreover, when he delivered that attack, it was from what was still a heretical or minority point of view. As Walter Bagehot said a hundred years ago,

> It is difficult for a modern Englishman, to whom "Free Trade" is an accepted maxim of tedious orthodoxy, to remember sufficiently that a hundred years ago it was a heresy and paradox. The whole commercial legislation of the world was formed on the doctrines of Protection.[48]

But if Smith could be violent in denunciation and revolutionary in policies and objectives, he tended to be moderate and gradualist regarding timing and methods. As an empirical and historical economist and as something of a historical relativist, Smith does not resort to abstract, absolute optima and maxima in his criticisms and appraisals of economic institutions and policies (which highly abstract criteria can be and often are used in such misleading and question-begging ways). In *The Theory of Moral Sentiments* Smith's approach to policy-making even bears a somewhat conservative cast in that he urges "the man whose publick spirit is prompted altogether by humanity and benevolence" to be prepared to bear with the faults and injustices of the existing order of society:

> ... he will content himself with moderating, what he often cannot annihilate without great violence. When he cannot conquer the rooted prejudices of the people by reason and persuasion, he will not attempt to subdue them by force ... He will accommodate, as well as he can, his publick arrangements to the confirmed habits and prejudices of the people, and will remedy, as well as he can, the inconveniences which may flow from the want of those regulations which the people are averse to submit to. When he cannot establish the right, he will not disdain to ameliorate the wrong; but, like Solon, when he cannot establish the best system of laws, he will endeavour to establish the best that the people can bear.[49]

It is here that Smith's methodological approach implies an attitude to policy differing very significantly from the narrowly abstract, a priori, deductive *laissez-faire* of Quesnay and Ricardo. For Smith accuses Quesnay of irrelevantly and misleadingly applying the criteria of absolute or perfect optimality in imagining that an economy and polity

> would thrive and prosper only under a certain precise regimen, the exact regimen of *perfect* liberty and *perfect* justice. . . .

> If a nation could not prosper without the enjoyment of *perfect* liberty and *perfect* justice there is not in the world a nation which could ever have prospered.[50]

IX

It was noted earlier how Smith was able, plausibly and validly, to make the complimentarity of freedom and economic growth a central theme of *The Wealth of Nations*, and also how attractive a message is which proclaims that more of each of two highly valued *desiderata* are obtainable, so that it is unnecessary to sacrifice one of them to obtain more of the other. But there can be no doubt as to which of this happily complementary pair Smith would have chosen if he had felt forced to do so.[51] Smith was at least ambiguous about the significance of an increase in wealth as a value or objective. While greater wealth for a society had a part in rendering it more civilised and more free or was an indicator of social progress, regarding individuals at any rate,

> In ease of body and peace of mind, all the different ranks of life are nearly upon a level, and the beggar, who suns himself by the side of the highway, possesses that security which kings are fighting for.[52]

This belief perhaps explains why Smith does not seem to show much interest in policies concerned with the distribution of wealth or income. Anyhow, Smith would always have put freedom first and would surely have done so more than ever today when we are so often faced with the paradox that tremendous technical progress, and in some respects higher material living standards, seem to be accompanied rather by more insidious threats to freedom than a greater abundance of it. Smith valued economic freedoms not simply because he believed that they promoted a more rapid growth of GNP per head, but *for their own sake*, because they were a kind of freedom which many ordinary people highly value and an essential component of civil freedom. The paradox has recently been pointed out how today – in some countries at any rate – we have the most strident demands and assertions regarding many new kinds of cultural and social "liberation" combined with a disdain, or even a concentrated hostility, towards economic freedoms.[53] For Smith's great enemy, monopoly, is more than ever on the march, in ever more powerful forms. The monopolisers of one type of another seem often to be aided both by the trend of technology, which gives new opportunities or pretexts for their encroachments, as well as by the upsurge of centralised government expenditure by democratic governments, which Smith himself referred to as "the thoughtless extravagance that democracies are apt to fall into."[54]

In some countries at any rate, Smith's description of monopolists seems truer than ever today:

> Like an overgrown standing army they have become formidable to the government, and upon many occasions intimidate the legislature. The member of parliament who supports every proposal for strengthening this monopoly is sure to acquire not only the reputation of understanding trade, but great popularity and influence. . . . If he opposes them, on the contrary, and still more if he has authority enough to be able to thwart them, neither the most acknowledged probity, nor the highest rank, nor the greatest public services, can protect him from the most infamous abuse and detraction, from personal insults, nor sometimes from real danger, arising from the insolent outrage of furious and disappointed monopolists.[55]

Today indeed the monopolists and monopolisers of types almost unknown to Smith are certainly as insolent, outrageous, and furious as ever, but unfortunately they do not seem so often to be disappointed. It is just this dangerously adverse trend, discernible here and there, which makes all the more precious today the message of *The Wealth of Nations* and which makes the cause of the economic freedom for which it stands all the more vital. But this cause was not fought for by Adam Smith and cannot with full effect be fought for today from the narrow base of modern economics. *The Wealth of Nations* was not founded on abstractions, nor on the particular abstraction of economic actions and processes from their historical interdependence and interpendence and interpenetration with social, legal, and political actions and processes. Smith's case for his "simple system of natural liberty" was constructed on a much broader base than that provided by modern economics or even that provided by the nineteenth-century classical political economists *or* by their socialist critics such as Karl Marx. Smith's case was built not only on economic analysis or political economy (though, of course, it included much of these). Smith's case was built on a comprehensive *View of Man* and of the kind of social and economic institutions man was capable of sustaining; and this view was based in turn on a study of individual and social psychology, on moral, social, and political philosophy, and on the comprehensive study of history and comparative institutions. That is the kind of broad foundation on which Smith built his case: on a view of man much more subtle, flexible, comprehensive, and realistic than that possessed by any of his classical, neo-classical, or Marxist successors.

Today the case for freedom expounded in *The Wealth of Nations* two hundred years ago can only be sustained on the kind of full, broad foundations on which Adam Smith constructed that case. In conclusion, we are entitled at least to contemplate the possibility – however we may assess the probability – that in 2026 when here in Chicago our successors will be commemorating again this great, perennially valuable work, economists may by one route or another have found their way back to the comprehensive foundations so superbly laid by Adam Smith in 1776.

Notes

1.   John Maurice Clark et al., Adam Smith, 1776-1926: Lectures to Commemorate the Sesquicentennial of the Publication of "The Wealth of Nations" (1928) [hereinafter cited as Smith Lectures].

2.   See Political Economy Club, Revised Report of the proceedings at the Dinner of 31st May, 1876 (1876); also T.W. Hutchison, A Review of Economic Doctrines 1870-1929, at 1-6 (1953), quoting the Pall Mall Gazette, June 1, 1876.

3.   See W.R. Scott, Adam Smith: An Oration 6 (Glasgow Univ. Pub. no. 48, 1938).

4.   See the letter from Adam Smith to William Cullen, September 20, 1774, reproduced in full in 1 An Account of the Life, Lectures and Writings of William Cullen, M.D. 473 (John Thomson and William Thomson ed. 1859).

5.   Adam Smith, An Inquiry into the Nature and Causes of the Wealth of Nations 718 (Edwin Cannan ed. 1937) [hereinafter cited as Wealth].

6.   William Robert Scott, Adam Smith as Student and Professor 40 (Glasgow Univ. Pub. no. 46, 1937).

On the other hand, Sir George Clark has maintained: "Adam Smith is still by common consent the greatest of economic historians, as he is the greatest of economists, and we shall not do well if we tamely acquiesce in the belief that the six years which he spent without interruption in Oxford contributed little to the formation of his mind. It is to be hoped that one of the present fellows of Balliol will publish what he knows about the remarkable coincidence between the books referred to in the footnotes to *The Wealth of Nations* and the books which are known to have been in the college library when its future author was in residence." (See G.N. Clark's inaugural lecture of 1932 reprinted in The Study of Economic History (N.B. Harte, ed. 1971). This suggestion does not so far seem to have been followed up.

7.   Wealth 742.

8.   John Rae, Life of Adam Smith 87 (Jacob Viner ed. 1965). In a letter from Sir Thomas Munro to Kirkman Finlay, Aug. 15, 1825, in James Finlay & Company Limited: Manufacturers and East India Merchants 1750-1950, by James Finlay & Co. 8 (1951) he wrote: "I remember . . . about the time of the appearance of *The Wealth of Nations*, that the Glasgow merchants were as proud of the work as if they had written it themselves; and that some of them said it was no wonder that Adam Smith had written such a book, as he had had the advantage of their society, in which the same doctrines were circulated with the punch every day." Doubtless the influence of the Glasgow merchants on Smith was not *all* in one direction or only of the kind they claimed. They may also have provided him with material for his attacks on "mercantile" practices and ideas. But a powerful realistic influence they almost certainly had, in one direction or another.

9.   Wealth 764.

10.   [Book Review], 3 Econ. Hist. 33 (1938). Regarding coincidences between Smith and

Keynes, it is incorrect that they were both certainly born on June 5th. What we know is that Smith was *baptised* on that day. But they did publish their major works at almost exactly the same age: Smith at a few days *over* and Keynes at a week or two *under*, 52 years and 9 months.

11.   Walter Bagehot, Adam Smith as a Person, in Biographical Studies 247, 264 (Richard Holt Hutton ed. 1881).

12.   A number of earlier and more recent writers have recognized this point. For example James Bonar: "Adam Smith undoubtedly started with the purpose of giving to the world a complete social philosophy." (Philosophy and Political Economy in Some of Their Historical Relations 149 (3d ed., 1922)). A.L. Macfie wrote: ". . . he himself would not have regarded his work as primarily economic. For him it was broadly social, fitting into that title the political as well as the psychological and ethical aspects of individuals living in societies. . . . They in the eighteenth century thought of economics only as one chapter (not the most important) in a general theory of society involving psychology and ethics, social and individual, law, politics, and social philosophy as well" (The Individual in Society 13, 16 (1967)). Again, Glenn R. Morrow, in his Chicago lecture of 1926, maintained of *The Wealth of Nations*: "This an economic work? It is far more than that; it is a history and criticism of all European civilization . . . a philosophical work." (Adam Smith: Moralist and Philosopher, in Smith Lectures 157). More recently Professor J. Ralph Lindgren has very strongly insisted that "all who are at all familiar with Smith's life and writings recognize that he was a philosopher by profession and that all his writings were conceived and executed as works of philosophy: (J.R. Lindgren, The Social Philosophy of Adam Smith, at ix (1973)).

13.   See Smith's letter of Nov. 1, 1785, to the Duc de la Rochefourcauld, reproduced in 6 Econ. J. 165 (1896); also Dugald Stewart's account, "prefixed" to Adam Smith, Essays on Philosophical Subjects at xciii-xciv (1795); and the preliminary "Advertisement" to Adam Smith, The Theory of Moral Sentiments, at v-vi (1817 ed.).

14.   Wealth 423.

15.   See Duncan Forbes, "Scientific" Whiggism: Adam Smith and John Millar, 7 Cambridge J. 643-70 (1955). As Mr. T.D. Campbell points out, the theme of progress is not so prominent in The Theory of Moral Sentiments. But we would suggest that there too it is significantly present. See T.D. Campbell, Adam Smith's Science of Morals 80n (1971).

16.   Walter Bagehot, *supra* note 11, at 248-50; and Adam Smith and Our Modern Economy, in Economic Studies 129 (Richard Holt Hutton ed. 1894).

17.   A.C. Pigou, The Economics of Welfare 21 (3d ed. 1929).

18.   Political Economy Club, *supra* note 2, at 32.

19.   See Henry J. Bittermann, Smith's Empiricism and the Law of Nature, 48 J. Pol. Econ. 487, 504 (1940): "Smith's work is not deductive in the sense that the term could be applied to, say, the major works of Ricardo and Senior. The bulk of Smith's text consists of descriptive, historical, and statistical data, with a few inferences from 'conjectural history.' There are some deductions from definition and arguments supported only by common knowledge or casual observation, which give parts of the work an abstract tone. But Smith had argued that valid generalizations could be reached only by induction from observation, and he tried to apply this technique."

20.   A.L. Macfie, *supra* note 12, at 13, 139.

21.   Nassau W. Senior, An Outline of the Science of Political Economy 6 (1836).

22.   Adam Smith, Lectures on Rhetoric and Belles Lettres 37 (J.M. Lothian ed. 1963).

23.   See 2 Adam Smith, Theory of Moral Sentiments, *supra* note 13, at 59-60; Jacob Viner, Guide to John Rae's Life of Adam Smith, in John Rae, Life of Adam Smith 33 (Jacob Viner ed. 1965); and Jacob Viner, Adam Smith, in 14 Int'l Encyclopedia of the Social Sciences 327 (David L. Sills ed. 1968).

24.   John Neville Keynes, The Scope and Method of Political Economy 10 (1890). Smith's readiness to use different methods was not, of course, accompanied by any fervent professional overconfidence regarding actual results. On the subject of quantitative methods, Schumpeter castigated Smith for remarking that he placed "not much faith in Political Arithmetick" or in the "exactness" of its "computations": ("It was the inspiring message, the suggestive program, which wilted in the wooden hands of the Scottish professor. . . . A. Smith took the safe side.") After the pretentious over-confidence regarding "the quantitative revolution," which has taken place since Schumpeter was writing (with its marvellous results for economic policies), it may be possible today to discern more intellectual merit in the sobering attitude of someone who was ready to "take the safe side." (See Joseph A. Schumpeter, History of Economic Analysis 212 (1954); and Wealth

501.)

25.   See Roy Pascal, Property and Society, The Scottish Historical School of the Eighteenth Century, 1 Modern Q. 167 (1938); and Ronald L. Meek, Smith, Turgot, and the "four Stages" Theory, 3 Hist. Pol. Econ. 9-27 (1971).

26.   See John Stuart Mill, Principles of Political Economy, at xxviii (W.J. Ashley ed. 1909): "It appears to the present writer that a work similar in its object and general conception to that of Adam Smith, but adapted to the more extended knowledge and improved ideas of the present age, is the kind of contribution which Political Economy at present requires. *The Wealth of Nations* is in many parts obsolete, and in all, imperfect. Political Economy, properly so called, has grown up almost from infancy since the time of Adam Smith. . . . No attempt, however, has yet been made to combine his practical mode of treating his subject with the increased knowledge since acquired of its theory, or to exhibit the economical phenomena of society in the relation in which they stand to the best social ideas of the present time, as he did, with such admirable success, in reference to the philosophy of his century."

27.   Allyn A. Young, Increasing Returns and Economic Progress, 38 Econ. J. 527, 529 (1928).

28.   Wealth 369.

29.   Wealth 60-61.

30.   See Jacob Viner's essay, Adam Smith and Laissez Faire, in Smith Lectures 116-55.

31.   See Samuel Hollander, The Economics of Adam Smith 133-43 (1973); and Marian Bowley, Studies in the History of Economics Theory Before 1870, at 110-32 (1973).

32.   Hutcheson defines "use" as "not only a natural subserviency to our support, or to some natural pleasure, but any tendency to give any satisfaction, by prevailing custom or fancy, as a matter of ornament or distinction" (2 Francis Hutcheson, System of Moral Philosophy 53-54 (1755)).

33.   Wealth 28-29.

34.   See Paul H. Douglas, Smith's Theory of Value and Distribution, in Smith Lectures 77-115. I would agree with the recent summary of Professor Denis O'Brien: "Adam Smith laid the foundation for classical value theory. What he did, and the way he did it, were to prove extremely important because he seems deliberately and consciously to have rejected the value theory which he inherited. He inherited a subjective value theory: and instead of developing this he largely substituted for it a cost of production theory . . . The dismissal of utility as a determinant of value is justified by reference to the 'diamonds and water' paradox although, as we have seen, Smith solved this in his *Lectures*. It is interesting to see that Smith so far purges his analysis of the subjective elements as to redefine utility. As understood by Hutcheson and Smith's other predecessors, utility was subjective; and this was also the view adopted by the other Classical economists from Ricardo onwards. But for Smith 'having utility' meant not being productive of subjective satisfaction but having objective usefulness." (Denis O'Brien, The Classical Economists 78-80 (1975)). On the other hand, I cannot quite follow Professor O'Brien's explanation of Smith's having to "rework his value theory," in this way, between the *Lectures* and *The Wealth of Nations*, because in the latter work he had a distribution theory and in the former he did not, Smith could have followed the line taken soon after by J.B. Say in terms of "relative productive contribution."

It seems, however, to go too far to assert as does Professor R.L. Meek that: "It cannot be too strongly emphasised that any approach to the problem of the determination of value from the side of utility and demand (as opposed to that of cost and supply) would have been regarded by him [Smith] as quite alien to the general outlook of *The Wealth of Nations*. Smith makes it perfectly clear that in his opinion demand has nothing directly to do with the determination of exchange value" (Ronald L. Meek, Studies in the Labour Theory of Value 73 (2nd ed. 1973)). Certainly in his work on the labour theory Professor Meek seeks to emphasise and demonstrate very strongly the continuity and direct line of descent from Ricardo to the leading (and "uniquely authoritative") modern exponent of the labour theory, J. Stalin, to whom is assigned the place in history of being the single major contributor, after Marx's death, to the labour "theory" of value.

35.   As Sir John Hicks has noted: "It is generally recognized (Keynes himself recognized) that in the age of Adam Smith there was an 'anti-Keynesian Revolution'; that it was at this period that the 'classical' doctrine of savings and investment (using 'classical' in Keynes' sense) took shape. But it does not seem to be so generally appreciated that the main agent of the 'Revolution' was Adam Smith himself. More, I think, would have been made of his responsibility if it had not seemed to be out of character; Smith was not at all a dogmatically minded man, and that he should be the source of such dogmatism! How is it to be explained? It is not simply the reaction against Mercantilism;

Hume was equally against Mercantilism, but Hume's Essay on Money is not 'anti-Keynesian' in the way that Smith's is. I believe that it is to be explained – that the whole change is to be explained – if we attribute it to the power of a model." (John Hicks, Capital and Growth 41-42 (1965)).

36.   See T.W. Hutchison, Berkeley's *The Querist* and its Place in the Economic Thought of the Eighteenth Century, 4 Brit. J. Philos. of Sci. 52-77 (1953); and Terence W. Hutchison, Keynes und die Geschichte der klassischen Nationalökonomie, 17 Z. Für Nationalökonomie 393 (1957).

37.   Wealth 321, 324.

38.   Wealth 404-406.

39.   Wealth 181, 188, 207, 281, 304.

40.   Wealth 590.

41.   Wealth 549 (emphasis added).

42.   Wealth 576.

43.   Wealth 571, 581.

44.   Wealth 582. Of course Smith's first preference in colonial policy was for a union or commonwealth involving both representation for, *and taxation of*, the colonists. In fact C.R. Fay seems to have gone so far as to place an immense responsibility on Smith for having pressed on Townshend in 1766 the case for American taxation: ". . . in the last analysis it was professorial advice which lost us the first empire." (Adam Smith and the Scotland of his Day 116 (1956)).

45.   Wealth 900.

46.   Walter Bagehot, *supra* note 11, at 275.

47.   Letter from Adam Smith to Andreas Holt, Oct., 1780, in William Robert Scott, *Supra* note 6, at 281-84.

48.   Walter Bagehot, *supra* note 16, in Economic Studies 128 (Richard Holt Hutton ed. 1895).

49.   2 Adam Smith, Theory of Moral Sentiments, *supra* note 13, at 59. Smith returned to the comparison with the laws of Solon in Wealth 510 with regard to the prohibition of wheat exports: ". . . this law . . . though not the best in itself, it is *the best which the interests, prejudices, and temper of the times would admit off*." (emphasis added).

50.   Wealth 638 (emphasis added).

51.   "Smith may be understood as a writer who advocated capitalism for the sake of freedom, civil and ecclesiastical." (Joseph Cropsey, Polity and Economy: An Interpretation of the Principles of Adam Smith 95 (1957)).

52.   1 Adam Smith, Theory of Moral Sentiments, *supra* note 13, at 249. Just before this quotation (*id.* at 244-45) comes the marvellous passage on the rat race and gracious living (cited by George J. Stigler: see Five Lectures on Economic Problems 3 (1949)): "The poor man's son, whom heaven in its anger has visited with ambition, when he begins to look around him, admires the condition of the rich. He finds the cottage of his father too small for his accommodation, and fancies he should be lodged more at his ease in a palace. He is displeased with being obliged to walk afoot, or to endure the fatigue of riding on horseback . . . To obtain the conveniences which these afford, he submits in the first year, nay in the first month of his application, to more fatigue of body, and more uneasiness of mind than he could have suffered through the whole of his life from the want of them. He studies to distinguish himself in some laborious profession. With the most unrelenting industry he labours night and day to acquire talents superior to all his competitors. He endeavours next to bring those talents into publick view . . . For this purpose he makes his court to all mankind; he serves those whom he hates, and is obsequious to those whom he despises. Through the whole of his life he pursues the idea of a certain artificial and elegant repose which he may never arrive at, for which he sacrifices a real tranquillity that is at all times in his power, and which, if in the extremity of old age he should at last attain to it, he will find to be in no respect preferable to that humble security and contentment which he had abandoned for it. It is then, in the last dregs of life, his body wasted with toil and diseases, his mind galled and ruffled by the memory of a thousand injuries and disappointments which he imagines he has met with from the injustice of his enemies, or from the perfidy and ingratitude of his friends, that he begins at last to find, that wealth and greatness are mere trinkets of frivolous utility, no more adapted for procuring ease of body or tranquillity of mind, than the tweezer-cases of the lover of toys. . ."

53.   See Samuel Brittan, Capitalism and the Permissive Society (1973).

54.   Wealth 770.

55.   Wealth 438. With regard to professional-academic monopolies, the remarkable letter to William Cullen of 1774, *supra* note 4, at 473, should be remembered: "Had the Universities of Oxford and Cambridge been able to maintain themselves in the exclusive privilege of graduating all

the doctors who could practice in England, the price of feeling the pulse might by this time have risen from two and three guineas, the price which it has now happily arrived at, to double or triple that sum; and English physicians might and probably would, have been at the same time the most ignorant and quackish in the world." The letter is also found in John Rae, *supra* note 8, at 273-80.

71

Sources and Contours of Adam Smith's Conceptualized Reality in the *Wealth of Nations*

H.E. Jensen

Source: *Review of Social Economy*, Vol. 34 (3), December 1976, pp. 259-74.

This paper is based on a simple twofold thesis. Firstly: in writing the *Wealth of Nations*, Adam Smith founded the paradigm of classical political economy which served later nineteenth-century economists as a basis and framework for their own research. Secondly: the formal economic models and theories contained in Smith's paradigm emanate from a specific "conceptualized reality" which he embedded in the same paradigm.

I use the term paradigm in Thomas S. Kuhn's sense of "recognized scientific achievements that for a time provide model problems and solutions to a community of practitioners." [Kuhn, p. viii] Provisionally, I define Smith's conceptualized reality as his idealized image of the socioeconomic order.[1]

Because of space constraints and the primacy which I assign to the conceptualized reality in Smith's paradigm, the present study is restricted to an inquiry into the sources and nature of this reality. In order to place this entity in its proper setting, the following schematic outline of Smith's paradigm is provided.

I. Schematic Outline of Smith's Paradigm

Smith was policy oriented because of his "interest . . . in social reform." Consequently, he developed his analytical apparatus in order to solve "live economic problems . . ." [Stigler, p. 56] As a result, the foundations of his formal analysis are charged with values whereas his economic model and theories *per se* are relatively objective technical means to normative ends.

Smith's paradigm may therefore be visualized as a continuum of inter-connected constituents whose normative and positive contents vary inversely along the entire paradigm spectrum. Thus starting with those components that are predominantly normative in content, the matrices of the Smithian paradigm may be classified and ordered as follows.

1) A visionary preamble which contains the principal ideological basis of the paradigm. [Schumpeter, pp. 41, 42] 2) A conceptualized reality which gives direction to Smith's analysis by virtue of the problems it contains and the cause

and effect relationships it harbors. 3) An economic model built by Smith out of a limited number of judgmentally selected elements which he abstracted from the conceptualized reality. 4) A set of theories, or " 'laws' of the model" [Harre, p. 60] which Smith formulated on the basis of assumptions deduced from the same reality. 5) A formal analysis of the behavior of the model performed by Smith through manipulation of its variables by means of the tools of his theory. 6) A number of conclusions drawn by Smith on the basis of his explanatory and predictive analysis.

Thus the conceptualized reality is a fundamental component of Smith's paradigm. But what are the nature and character of this reality? And what ingredients did he use when he constructed this stylized image of the world around him? The beginning of an answer to these questions must be sought in Smith's vision of the good society of the future.

II. Smith's Visionary Preamble

Even a cursory reading of the *Wealth of Nations* will reveal that this work is predicated on the proposition that the study of socioeconomic problems "is and must be determined by valuations" in the sense of "ideas about how reality . . . ought to be . . ." [Myrdal, 1968, p. 32, and 1958, p. 71] Such valuations may, therefore, be conceived of as a "Vision" which constitutes "a preanalytic act that supplies the raw material for the analytic effort" of the architect of a paradigm. Hence a vision is "ideological almost by definition. It embodies the picture of things as we . . . wish to see them." This picture is not selected at random, however. It is disclosed by the particular "light" in which one sees "things." [Schumpeter, pp. 41, 42]

The light in which Smith saw things as they ought to be in the socioeconomic order of the future emanated largely from the ideology of the Enlightenment. The picture which this light revealed to the author of the *Wealth of Nations* shows an ideal society which is characterized by the following chief features.

In the first place, it is a "well-governed state" which has reached a high level of affluence. Secondly, it is a community distinguished by social justice because its institutions "make nearly the same distribution of the necessaries [and conveniencies] of life, which would have been made, had the earth been divided into equal portions among all its inhabitants . . ." Thirdly, in Smith's ideal society of the future, there is "perfect liberty" for individuals to make their own economic decisions. Finally, Smith's vision includes a world order in which all nations, including emancipated colonies, are parts of a "liberal system" of free trade which functions as a reciprocating foreign-trade engine of global economic growth. [*M.S.*, pp. 354, 350, and *Wealth*, pp. 78-79, 56, 506, 559, 581, 462, 464][2]

A. Smith's Ultimate and Instrumental Goals

The *Wealth of Nations* is a monument to Smith's faith in the possibility of transforming his contemporary society of poverty and monopoly into a state that would resemble that of his envisioned ideal society, *if* proper reforms and policies were instituted. [*Lectures*, pp. 222-236, and *Wealth*, pp. 437-438] It was, therefore, his ultimate social goal to attain such a transformation gradually; and it was this goal that stimulated him to undertake his economic research.

The social transformation desired by Smith had to follow a path, however. Given the disparity in opulence between his ideal society and his actual contemporary society and his conviction that no society can be "happy, of which the far greater number of the members are poor and miserable," Smith *selected* economic growth as the relevant path to follow. [*Wealth* pp. 79, 81 lvii; Cf., Spengler, 1959] This objective might therefore be called Smith's instrumental goal inasmuch as he fancied that his ultimate goal of social transformation would be achieved through secular increases in per capita real income.

Once he had defined his instrumental goal, Smith had no difficulty in conceiving of those problems for which he had to find solutions if his fundamental goal were to be achieved. As he saw it, these problems manifest themselves in the guise of "impediments. . . [to] the . . . progress of opulence." [*Lectures*, p. 222] Conceivably, such obstacles to growth might appear in many specific forms. But however defined, they must occur in a particular socioeconomic setting. Consequently, Smith's identification of what he deemed to be *the* problems of growth was conditioned by the way in which he conceived of the structure, organization and processes of the socioeconomic reality in which they are embedded.

The actual reality in which Smith lived could not, however, "be 'known' [to him] in the same way as natural objects get to be 'known'." [Kecskemeti, p. 31] Hence the reality with which he was concerned is a conceptualized one in the sense that it "consists of the mental constructs . . . [which he] built . . . out of his percepts and concepts of the real realm . . ." [Spengler, 1960, p. 7]

III. Categoric Inputs for Smith's Process of Reality Conceptualization

Smith's conceptualized reality may be viewed, therefore, as the output of an intellectual process of conceptualization in which he used a variety of inputs. In terms of their sources, however, these inputs may be divided into two broad categories: hypothetical-theoretical and empirical.

The former inputs Smith drew from a contemporary fund of theories concerning human motivations, faculties and behavior; theories which he extended and fused together to form his own master theory of human nature. [*M.S.*] He then used this master theory as a mold for the casting of a number of specific faculties and behavioral propensities which he imputed purposefully to the actors in his economic drama. In so doing, he made their responses to external stimuli uniformly predictable.

These stimuli emanate from the facts of Smith's conceptualized reality. But "what is a fact . . . is a very subjective thing." [Samuelson, p. 739] Hence what appear as stimulating facts in the Smithian reality are the forms and shapes which his chosen empirical data [*Wealth*, pp. 356-396] assumed when he saw them through the "selecting grid" [Stark, p. 108] of his master theory and its underlying ideology.

One set of facts is constituted of a number of institutional "constants" [Lowe,

p. 168] which mold the individual's social experience with the aid of certain faculties, such as his innate "powers of perception" and "reason." [*M.S.*, pp. 508, 502] Another set of facts is comprised of those alternatives in the economic and moral realms among which each person makes choices as directed by a bundle of behavioral propensities which Smith's chief mentor, Francis Hutcheson, identified as "Springs of Actions." [Hutcheson, p. 136] Significantly, the experience, behavioral propensities and faculties of each of the actors in the Smithian reality interact in such a manner that, as a group, they make decisions under conditions of certainty. [*M.S.*, p. 360]

By endowing the economic actors in his conceptualized reality with such capabilities, Smith laid the foundation for his deductive, predictive economic theories in the *Wealth of Nations*. The following are some of the relevant portions of that psycho-philosophic theory he employed in this endeavor.

IV. Foundations of Smith's Program for Human Behavior in His Conceptualized Reality

According to Smith, man and society are integral parts of a macrocosmic "theatre of nature" which the "Author of Nature has established for the happiness and perfection of the world . . . [and] mankind . . ." By happiness, Smith meant a state of personal "security and contentment, . . . ease of body and peace of mind . . ." [*Principles*, p. 45, and *M.S.*, pp. 284, 343, 351] He was convinced, however, that such feelings could not be generated in the absence of a minimum real income and that an expansion of happiness above this threshold level would largely be a function of an increase in "riches . . ., contrived to produce . . . conveniencies to the body . . ." Only in such a state of growth would man be able to experience a gain in "real satisfaction" without a corresponding increase in the "disagreeableness" of productive efforts. [*M.S.*, pp. 346, 347, and *Wealth*, p. 100] To Smith, this would be tantamount to an expansion of happiness because "[p]leasure and pain are the great objects of desire and aversion . . . [and] these are distinguished . . . by immediate sense and feeling." [*M.S.*, p. 504]

The desire for "utility" is, therefore, one of those "secret motive[s]" which the author of nature has "implanted . . . in the human breast" as a means to the achievement of "happiness of all" men, or the attainment of the "greatest Happiness for the greatest Numbers," as Hutcheson had put it earlier. [*M.S.*, pp. 338, 341, 238, 241; Hutcheson, p. 177] Hence it was the human want for satisfaction which Smith selected as the chief motivating agent for the purely economic behavior of the actors in his hypothetical reality.

A. Economic Instincts

As a motive for economic action, the desire for utility is grounded in "self-love." [*Wealth*, p. 14] Thus as consumers, human beings are selfishly interested in acquiring those material things that "prevent their wants, . . . gratify their wishes, and . . . amuse and entertain their . . . desires." These enjoyments constitute "the *real* satisfaction which all these things are capable of affording . . ." [*M.S.*, pp. 347, 347-348; emphasis added]

Aside from the desire for food, which is "limited . . . by the narrow capacity of the . . . stomach," the individual's aggregate wants for durable and non-durable consumer goods "seem to be altogether endless." But his purchasing power has a "boundary." Furthermore, its acquisition is irksome because the "real price of everything, . . . is the toil and trouble of acquiring it." Hence the consumer has to make choices. He does so with the aid of his natural faculty of "reason" and the therefrom derived "propensity to truck, barter, and exchange one thing for another." [*Wealth*, pp. 164, 30, 13]

Smith's language seems to imply that he believed that the consumer is capable of ordering his preferences. Thus he observed that the individual distinguishes among articles of different degrees of "agreeable[ness]" and that those "qualities, which are the ground of *preference*, and which give occasion to pleasure and pain, are the causes of many . . . demands . . ." [*Lectures*, p. 159; emphasis added]

But in addition to equipping "mankind with an appetite" for real satisfaction, the "great director of nature" has also "endowed . . . [its members] with an appetite for the *means* by which alone this end can be brought about, for their *own sakes*, and independent of their tendency to produce it." This second type of appetites manifests itself in the form of a craving for "riches." [*M. S.*, pp. 168, 346; emphasis added].

In Smith's opinion, the satisfaction of this craving is a "deception," [*M. S.*, p. 348] however, because its achievement does not, in itself, contribute anything to welfare in the form of real satisfaction. Smith's choice of words notwithstanding, there is no indication that he attributed the origin of the human desire for wealth to a devious act of trickery on the part of the author of nature. On the contrary, Smith hailed the craving as one of those natural "means adjusted with the nicest artifice to the ends which they are intended to produce," namely human welfare and happiness. And the pursuit of the deceptive "pleasures of wealth" serves these ends admirably because it "is this deception which rouses and keeps in motion the industry of mankind." Hence "it is well that nature imposes upon us in this manner." [*M. S.*, pp. 191, 348]

Thus by making human beings "value the means more than the end," nature has provided mankind with a motive to save and invest in "those enormous and operose machines, [that are] contrived to produce" the outputs that yield real satisfaction. Hence the desire for deceptive satisfaction is a means to the achievement of that purpose which Smith judged to be "the sole end . . . of all production . . . [namely] Consumption . . ." [*M. S.*, pp. 352, 346, and *Wealth*, p. 625]

Even the poor dedicate themselves "for ever to the pursuit of wealth," but to no avail. Their acquisitive instinct and natural capacity to "abstain from present pleasures[s]" of consumption, by the exercise of "self-command," are rendered impotent by their poverty. [*M. S.*, pp. 342, 360, 343] And the majority of landlords and professional people do not save because of the emphasis on ostentatious consumption in their subcultures. [*Wealth*, pp. 314-318] Hence the socially important function of capital formation through saving is carried out by "undertakers" of business who view additions to real satisfaction as less desirable than increases in deceptive satisfaction. They do so in consequence of their attainment of a comfortable level of living, often based on inherited commercial wealth, and by virtue of the fact that they are under the sway of a self-command that is nurtured into unusual strength by their *milieu*. [*Wealth*, pp. 381, 671-673, 736-738] Thus although the undertakers' desires for satisfaction are endless, these desires are compartmentalized into wants for real satisfaction and wants for deceptive satisfaction in such a fashion that the latter exercise a restraining influence on the former.

The members of the business community are, therefore, in a unique position to activate the following behavioral propensities which Smith found to be residing in all human beings.

> The qualities most useful to ourselves are first of all superior reason and understanding, by which we are capable of discerning the remote consequences of all our actions, and of foreseeing the advantage or detriment which is likely to result from them: and secondly, self-command, by which we are enabled to abstain from present pleasure or to endure present pain, in order to obtain a greater pleasure or to avoid a greater pain in some future time. [*M.S.*, p. 360]

If, however man is to exercise his economic propensities in such a fashion that happiness may be increased by the means of economic growth, the individual must be able to make decisions in "perfect liberty." This may spell anarchy and chaos, however, so that the "immense fabric of human society . . . crumble[s] into atoms." [*Wealth*, p. 56, and *M.S.*, p. 190]

Fortunately, Smith found that man is also endowed with a sense of "natural justice." [*M.S.*, p. 548]

B. Sense of Justice

Like his economic propensities, man's sense of justice is rooted in one of those "original and immediate instincts" with which he has been endowed by the director of nature. The instinct in question is an unselfish one, however, because it manifests itself as a principle in man's "nature, which interest[s] him in the fortune of others, and render[s] their happiness necessary to him, though he derives nothing from it except the pleasure of seeing it." Hence Smith labeled this instinct "sympathy," by which he meant a "fellow-feeling with any passion whatever." [M.S., pp. 168, 1, 6]

Such a fellow-feeling arises in consequence of an "imaginary change in situation" with another person. Thus "we enter as it were into his body and become in some measure him, and thence form some idea of his sensations, and even feel something which . . . is not altogether unlike them." This imaginary situation transfer is accomplished by a special attribute, namely an "impartial spectator" who resides within each person. In his dissertation on justice, Smith was therefore concerned with the following parties: an aggrieved person who feels "resentment" because he has "received . . . [a] provocation"; the "agent" or actor who made the provocation, and the impartial spectator of a third person who, "upon bringing the case home to himself," is also excited to feel resentment against the perpetrator; a resentment which Smith called "sympathetic resentment" by virtue of its origin in the spectator's fellow-feeling with the victims's resentment. [M.S., pp. 36, 2-3, 148, 143, 68, 159,

22, 170]

Consequently, any member of the human race "appears to deserve . . . punishment, who . . . is to some person or persons the natural object of a resentment which the breast [i.e., the spectator] of every reasonable man is ready to adopt and sympathise with." [*M.S.*, pp. 148-149] The feeling of sympathetic resentment is one of "those original principles in human nature, of which no further account can be given," however. [*Wealth*, p. 13] What can be accounted for, according to Smith, is the way in which such resentments contribute to the formation of a moral code of natural justice.

This code has come about in consequence of man's ability to discover, with the aid of his reason, "those general rules of justice by which we ought to regulate our actions . . ." Hence these rules are "founded upon experience of what, in particular instances, our moral faculties . . . approve, or disapprove of." And once they have been "established by the concurring sentiments of mankind, we . . . appeal to them as the standards of judgment . . ." [*M.S.*, pp. 502, 266, 268]

But experience also shows that self-command, which prompts man to follow the rules of justice, is not of equal strength in all persons. And those in whom it is weakest tend to provoke, harm and injure their fellow men. [*M.S.*, New Edition (1966) pp. 349-388] Consequently, if society relied on a system of *laissez faire* in the administration of justice, it "would become a scene of bloodshed and disorder, every man revenging himself at his own hand whenever he fancied he was injured." It was for these reasons that the members of society had given their government a monopoly on the administration of justice. [*M.S.*, pp. 547, 547-548]

This theory of justice supplied Smith with the relevant inputs when he established those governmental and legal institutions in his conceptualized reality which prevent the oppression of one person by another; protect the right to property, and define, formulate and enforce the rules for free economic intercourse. [*M.S.*, p. 269, and *Wealth*, pp. 651, 862] In so doing, he created a social environment in which the acquisitive instinct can play its natural role as the "dynamo of progress." [Macfie, p. 211] By spurring saving and investment, this instinct mobilizes "the productive powers of labour" with the result that such labor is turned into a "fund which . . . supplies . . . [the community] with all the necessaries and conveniencies of life which it annually consumes . . ." [*Wealth*, pp. 5, 1vii]

C. Smith's Lookingglass

It may therefore be concluded that the "lookingglass" in which Smith saw that reality which he analyzed in the *Wealth of Nations* was one that reflected his own values and theory of human motivations, behavior and capacities. But as he pointed out himself, such "looking-glasses. . . [can be] deceitful, and by the glare which they throw over the face, conceal from the *partial* eyes of the person many deformities which are obvious to every body besides." [*M.S.*, pp. 260-261; emphasis added] Some of the deformities which Smith purposefully did not see in his lookingglass were those which he accused the mercantilist policy makers of having built into the actual British economy of his time. [*Wealth*, pp. 398-626] In other words, the reality with which Smith was concerned is an idealized one which he constructed through a fusion of his value-loaded theory of human behavior with those empirical data which he saw as economic facts when he viewed them through the lenses of the very same theory.

V. Major Contours of Smith's Conceptualized Reality

Stark scarcity is the overriding problem of that reality which Smith constructed for the purpose of economic analysis. Its economic actors have not brought scarcity upon themselves through irrational misallocation or wasteful under-utilization of available resources, however. [*Lectures*, pp. 222-223, and *Wealth*, pp. 58-60, 268, 321, 407, 508] They are poor because of their society's dearth of capacity to produce. To "increase . . . [its] riches" is therefore "the great object of the political economy" of the Smithian reality. [*Wealth*, p. 352]

Given his philosophic orientation, Smith had no doubt about the source of such a potential increase in wealth. In his hypothetical reality, man himself is the agent of growth.

A. Man and Growth

According to Smith, labor consists of a stock of differentiated human capital which has been accumulated by its possessors for the purpose of enhancing their earning capacity through specialization. [*Wealth*, pp. 7, 101, 265-266] One such specialized occupation is that of the inventor. Among the inventors, "those who are called "philosophers," or scientists, are of special importance, however. That is so because it is their trade "not to do anything, but to observe every thing; and . . . upon that account, [they] are often capable of combining together the powers of the most distant and dissimilar objects." [*Wealth*, p. 10] Although the scientists may pursue their study "for its own sake,"[3] their inventions are acquired by alert businessmen because the economic application of an "invention" will increase the "productive powers of the same number of labourers" in their shops. [*Principles*, p. 50, and *Wealth*, pp 7, 326]

Once an investment in an invention has proved profitable for its undertaker, it is copied by other businessmen, however. "There are many commodities, therefore, which . . . come to be produced by so much less labour than before, that the increase of its price is more than compensated by the diminution of its quantity." [*Wealth*, p. 86] This gradual increase in investment leads to a secular expansion of employment opportunities. [*Wealth*, p. 326] And these opportunities will be realized because of the growth of the labor supply which the accelerating investments engender. They do so by making the "reward of labor" increasingly "liberal" which stimulates a lowering of the marriage age and an increase in the number of children. In other words, "the demand for men, like that for any other commodity, necessarily regulates the production of men . . ." [*Wealth*, p. 80]

Thus investments in inventions by innovators and the duplication of such investments by imitators have a dual effect: the "number of . . . productive labourers" is increased and "the productive powers of . . . [these] labourers" are enhanced. The resultant rise of per capital real income is experienced by the working population in the form of a reduction in the "real price of manufacturers" and other goods. [*Wealth*, pp. 326, 248]

Extensive and intensive economic growth is, therefore, the stuff of which social progress is made. And it is the faculty of labor that creates this progress. But inasmuch as the "workmen stand in need of . . . materials . . . [tools], wages and maintenance," they depend on the capitalist for such supplies. The price they pay for these accommodations consists of a "share . . . in the produce of their labour" which goes to the capitalists. Hence, "profit makes a . . . deduction from the produce of . . . labour . . ."[*Wealth*, p. 65]

This, of course, makes the capitalist "unproductive" *qua* accumulator. [*Wealth*, p. 639][4] Nevertheless, the capitalist is indispensable. Through his saving, he "puts into motion an additional quantity of industry [i.e., human efforts] which gives an additional value to the annual produce" of the economy. Hence "[p]arismony, and not industry, is the immediate cause of the increase of capital" and output. [*Wealth*, p. 321]

The real income of the aristocracy, government officials, rentiers and professional people is likewise deducted from the output of productive workers. Hence the institutions of Smith's conceptualized reality function in such a manner that "the whole annual produce of . . . labour . . . [is] parcelled out" as wages, profits, rent, interest and taxes. [*Wealth*, pp. 65, 314-315, 52, 777]

This "parcelling out" is accomplished primarily through exchange operations in the private sector. Consequently, Smith devised the following market structure for his conceptualized reality.

B. Market Structure

In accordance with his theory of justice, Smith's market structure exists within the framework of a government monopoly on the administration of justice which is designed to prevent the oppression of one person by another; to protect the right to property; to enforce contracts and adjudicate conflicts, and to regulate the relations between creditors and debtors. [*Wealth*, pp. 651, 862] Consequently, every man, "as long as he does not violate the laws of justice, is left perfectly free to pursue his own interest in his own way, and to bring his industry and capital into competition with those of any . . . order of men." [*Wealth*, p. 651]

By competitors, Smith meant "rivals" who are engaged in "eager competition" involving "active price responses" in the form of bids, counterbids and bargaining. [*M.S.*, pp. 60, 56; McNulty, p. 397] This concept of aggressive competition, Smith formulated through a synthesis of his theory of assertive human behavior and his observations of those contemporary British markets where the "corporation [or guild] spirit has never prevailed . . ." [*Wealth*, p. 126] On the basis of this synthesis, Smith constructed a market sytem with the following principal features.

In most markets for goods, there are numerous buyers and several firms which are operated by their owners. Hence both buyers and sellers act in accordance with Smith's theory of economic behavior. [*Wealth*, pp. 342-343, 713, 715, 55-60] The degree of homogeneity of products depends on the producers' place on the vertical continuum of production. Thus the outputs of extractive industries are perfectly homogeneous whereas some nondurable consumers' goods and most producers' and consumers' durables are more or less differentiated. Furthermore, there may be only two or three producers of a given custom-made durable good in a particular local market. [*Wealth*, pp. 11, 58, 59, 164, 246, 430, 492, 498][5]

In spite of the existence of some degree of product differentiation in certain trades and an occasional appearance of industrial concentration in local markets, monopolistic power is conspicuous by its absence in Smith's *conceptualized* reality.[6] As a matter of fact, the smaller the number of firms in a given market and the more differentiated their products, the fiercer is their rivalry. That is so because the operators of such firms view each other as "dangerous rivals" or "enemies," rather than as potential partners in collusion. Consequently, they feel compelled "to have recourse to . . . competition . . . for the sake of self-defence." [*Wealth*, pp. 461, 147] Moreover, any attempt at entering into some "sort of tacit . . . combination" will be defeated by the intermarket mobility of information and factors of production. [*Wealth*, pp. 66, 62]

In the Smithian reality, the labor market is likewise competitive. This is due to the fact that "the demand for those who live by wages . . . is continually increasing" in consequence of the capitalists' search for profit. Hence "every year furnishes employment for a greater number . . . than the year before" and the "workmen have no occasion to combine in order to raise their wages" when such raises come about naturally. And if the employers should attempt to enter into a "combination . . . not to raise wages, . . . [t]he scarcity of hands occasions a competition among masters, who bid against one another, in order to get workmen . . . ." Consequently, any attempt to establish a monopsonistic cartel is rendered impossible by the profit-spurred process of economic growth. [*Wealth*, p. 68]

Thus in this, as in all other matters pertaining to the expansion and use of resources, the institutions of Smith's conceptualized reality constitute an efficient system for the exploitation of those economic instincts with which he endowed the actors in his economic drama. That is, by virtue of being permitted to follow his natural propensities under conditions of perfect liberty in a society of law and order, the individual actor is "led by an invisible hand to promote an end which was no part of his intention," namely that of rendering "the annual revenue of the society as great as he can." [*Wealth*, p. 423]

VI. Conclusions

Given his concept of the economic reality and its problems, the analytical task before Smith was to explain and predict under what conditions this reality could be propelled along the high road of economic growth toward the state of his envisioned ideal society.

Smith's first step in this endeavor was to build a model of his conceptualized reality by the use of a limited number of constants and variables abstracted from this reality. The constants consist of those institutions and economic classes that form the social structure of the said reality: private property, competitive markets, capitalists, workers, landlords, and so on. The ultimate dependent variable in Smith's model is per capita real income and the ultimate independent variables are saving and investment.

Next, Smith formulated and used a number of economic theories for the purpose of explaining and predicting the behavior of his model; theories which are based on assumptions deduced from his hypothetical reality, such as the predictability of human behavior. As a perusal of the *Wealth of Nations* will reveal, Smith's major theories are: a theory of value, a theory of market prices, and a theory of capital formation closely integrated with a theory of distribution. In concert, these theories form Smith's sweeping general theory of economic growth.

The conclusions Smith reached on the basis of his analysis of the behavior of his model persuaded him that optimal economic growth in the real world could be achieved only if the actual economy were organized *a la* his conceptualized reality. This was the message which he transmitted to statesmen and men of affairs. But he also left a message, or two, for the practitioners of economics.

Firstly, he convinced a group of early nineteenth-century economists that the problems he analyzed were of importance. At the same time, he provided these economists with a theoretical system that was provisional and "open-ended." [Kuhn, p. 10] Hence they were challenged to improve upon this system in order to make the theoretical solutions of the received Smithian problems less ambiguous. Once David Ricardo *et al.* accepted Smith's problems and preliminary solutions, his body of doctrine became a paradigm.

Secondly, Smith furnished latter-day architects of economic doctrines with a schema for the construction of their own individual paradigms. Thus the founders of neoclassicism and Keynesianism followed the pattern of Smith's paradigm when they constructed their own bodies of doctrine: vision, conceptualized reality,[7] model, and theories. But neoclassicism and Keynesianism are paradigms in their own right by virtue of the distinctness of the respective conceptualized realities, models and theories contained therein and because of their acceptance by identifiable groups of practitioners.

Smith's most enduring contribution to economics is therefore in the form of the schema for the construction of economic paradigms which he left for others to follow when they became aware of new economic problems which cried for solution because they were no part of a hitherto accepted paradigm.

Notes

The author is indebted to Barry Dunman, Edna Gott, Dana Nelson Stevens and two anonymous referees for valuable criticism and comments. Partial financial support from the College of Business Capital Gifts Endowment is gratefully acknowledged.

1. I use the term "conceptualized reality," rather than "conceptualized model," because I view the former as the substitute for world reality and consider the model as an abstraction of the conceptualized reality.

2. Most of Smith's vision and conceptualized reality is found in *The Theory of Moral Sentiments*. Thus this work is truly a foundation for the *Wealth of Nations*. [Cf., Anspach and Macfie]

3. In spite of this, Smith seems to have been of the opinion that economic considerations, in addition to the pleasure of discovery, are instrumental in steering individuals into science. [Cf., *Wealth* pp. 264-265]

4.   Although he used this term primarily with reference to unproductive service workers, Smith was of the opinion that the capitalist is productive only in his capacity of entrepreneur. But his "labour of inspection and direction" can easily be routinized and "committed to some principle clerk." [*Wealth*, p. 49]

5.   Smith's reference to a local duopoly pertains to the grocery business. [*Wealth* p. 342] It is implified in his discussion, however, that similar situations occur in manufacturing.

6.   That is so because he had removed the mercantilist "deformities" from his conceptualized reality in order to demonstrate theoretically that competition is superior to the actual monopolistic system in England which he scorned so acidly in the *Wealth of Nations*. [pp. 128-129, 437-438]

7.   For pertinent observations on the part of some of these founders, cf., Jevons, pp. 202-204; Keynes, 1936, pp. 372-384; Marshall, pp. 1-5 (and Keynes, 1925, pp. 5-12, 16-17); Walras, pp. 40, 60, 71, 79, and Stigler, pp. 56-57.

References

Anspach, Ralph, "The Implications of the *Theory of Moral Sentiments* for Adam Smith's Economic Thought," *Hist. Polit. Econ.*, Spring 1972, *4*, 176-206.

Harre, Rom. *The Principles of Scientific Thinking*, Chicago, 1970.

Hutcheson, Francis. *An Inquiry into the Original of our Ideas of Beauty and Virtue*, 2nd ed., New York, 1971.

Jevons, W. Stanley. *The Principles of Economics and Other Papers*, London, 1905.

Kecskemeti, Paul, "Introduction," in Karl Mannheim. *Essays on the Sociology of Knowledge*, London, 1952, pp. 1-32.

Keynes, John Maynard, "Alfred Marshall, 1842-1924," in A.C. Pigou (ed.). *Memorials of Alfred Marshall*, London, 1925, pp. 1-65.

———. *The General Theory of Employment, Interest and Money*, New York, 1936.

Kuhn, Thomas S. *The Structure of Scientific Revolutions*, 2nd ed., Chicago, 1970.

Lowe, Adolph. *On Economic Knowledge*, New York, 1965.

Macfie, A.L., "Adam Smith's *Moral Sentiments* as Foundation for his *Wealth of Nations*," *Oxford Econ. Pap.*, Oct. 1959, n.s., *11*, 209-228.

Marshall, Alfred. *Principles of Economics*, 8th ed., London 1956.

McNulty, Paul J., "A Note on the History of Perfect Competition," *J. Polit. Econ.*, Aug. 1957, Part I, *75*, 395-399.

Myrdal, Gunnar. *Value in Social Theory*, New York, 1958.

———. *Asian Drama*, Vol. I, Pantheon ed.; New York, 1968.

Samuelson, Paul A., "Theory and Realism: A Reply," *Amer. Econ. Rev.*, Sept. 1964, *54*, 736-739.

Schumpeter, Joseph A. *History of Economic Analysis*, New York, 1954.

Smith, Adam. *An Inquiry into the nature and Causes of the Wealth of Nations*, New York, 1937.

———. *Lectures on Justice, Police, Revenue and Arms*, New York, 1964.

———. "The Principles Which Lead and Direct Philosophical Enquiries: Illustrated by the History of Astronomy," in J. Ralph Lindgren (ed.). *The Early Writings of Adam Smith*, New York, 1967, pp. 30-109.

———. *The Theory of Moral Sentiments*, New York, old edition, 1971; new edition, 1966. (All citations are to old edition except where indicated.)

Spengler, Joseph J., "Adam Smith's Theory of Economic Growth," *Southern Econ. J.*, Apr. 1959, *35*, 397-415, Part I; July 1959, *36*, 1-12, Part II.

———. "The Problem of Order in Economics Affairs," in Joseph J. Spengler and William R. Allen (eds.). *Essay in Economic Thought*, Chicago, 1960, pp. 6-34.

Stark, W. *The Sociology of Knowledge*, London, 1958.

Stigler, George J. *Essay in the History of Economics*, Chicago, 1965.

Walras, Léon. *Elements of Pure Economics*, Homewood, 1954.

72

The Just Economy: The Moral Basis of the *Wealth of Nations*

L. Billet

Source: *Review of Social Economy*, Vol. 34 (3), December 1976, pp. 295-315.

He is certainly not a good citizen who does not wish to promote by every means in his power, the welfare of the whole society of his fellow citizens. [*M.S.*, 339][1]

The *Wealth of Nations* is a profoundly political work in the richest and deepest sense. It is pervaded by a concern with justice and injustice, with the conflict between private and public interest, and with the problem of liberty and coercion. These are questions which arise from the very nature of political community. Ideas and ideals of justice, liberty and the public interest provide the essential framework for this most famous of inquiries into the nature and causes of the wealth of nations; they delineate its purpose and give it unity and force. It is little noted that Smith referred to his own system as the "liberal plan of equality, liberty, and justice," [*Wealth*, 628] the "natural system of perfect liberty and justice," [*Wealth*, 572] and the system of "natural liberty and justice." [*Wealth*, 141] The better known phrases "system of natural liberty" and "perfect liberty" are clearly derivations.

The *Wealth of Nations* is, in fact, fundamentally concerned with the question, 'what is a just economy?' This central theme of Smith's treatise has been neither adequately recognized nor emphasized by scholars and commentators on his political economy. The *Wealth of Nations* is rarely considered to be essentially related to the problem of justice,[2] although it is usually acknowledged that Smith thought law and order or a proper administration of 'justice' was necessary in order to attain the stability and security conducive to the accumulation of wealth and economic progress.[3] Many hold that the *Wealth of Nations* is concerned solely with the acquisition of riches – a 'how to get rich' book for society, which neglects the larger moral and political questions of economic order.[4] Yet Smith's work, which is so important a part of our political-economy tradition cannot be properly understood without comprehension of the notions of morality and justice which guide it. Because morality and justice have not been seen to guide the *Wealth of Nations* and because Smith's views have been misunderstood, distorted and identified with purposes and interests he would have opposed, his ideas have, in large part, become cliché expressions for economic analyses and enterprise stripped of all moral concern, insensitive to the requirements of justice and even symbolic of injustice and exploitation.

For example, in the introduction to the most widely known contemporary edition of the *Wealth of Nations*, it is stated that Smith "gave a new dignity to greed and a new sanctification to the predatory impulses . . . he rationalized the economic interests of the class that was coming to power . . ." [*Wealth*, xxxii] This view is both too generous an attribution to Smith and a complete misreading of his thought. No one can give dignity to greed or sanctify predatory impulses. To the contrary, Smith argues for the market economy as a means of enhancing and diffusing well being and restraining man's anti-social impulses. [*Wealth*, 460, Rosenberg, p. 560]

To argue that Smith saw man as essentially "homo-economicus" or to accept Marx's accusation that Smith saw man "as merchant" really does violence to Smith's view of human nature. [Grampp, West, pp. 102-03] The idea that the *Wealth of Nations* is a defense of "capitalists" and "capitalism" or "exploitation" is simply false. What is true is that "he saw, as economists half a century after him had become almost incapable of seeing, that economic processes are, and must be, at last, incidents of larger moral processes." [Small, p. 201]

In order to better comprehend the nature of Smith's political economy as well as its potential significance for today, one must analyze the conception of morality and justice which underlies it. One must also ask why, for Smith, social justice implies 'liberty' in the sphere of economic activity. This essay aims to demonstrate that 1) justice is the critical link between Smith's social philosophy and his political economy, and 2) that justice is *the* organizing concept for the *Wealth of Nations* and the moral basis for the emphasis on liberty.

I. Moral Philosophy, Jurisprudence, and Political Economy

The wisdom of every state or commonwealth endeavors, as well as it can, to employ the force of the society to restrain those who are subject to its authority from hurting or disturbing the happiness of one another. The rules which it establishes for this purpose constitute the civil and criminal law of each particular state or country. The principles upon which those rules are or ought to be founded, are the subject of a particular science, of all sciences by far the most important, but hitherto, perhaps, the least cultivated – that of natural jurisprudence. [*M.S.*, 319]

"It has always appeared somewhat strange," remarked Edwin Cannan, the famous 19th century editor of Smith's work, "that the publication of the *Wealth of Nations* should have been regarded by Adam Smith as a partial fulfillment of a promise to give an account of the general principles of law and government." [*Lectures*, xxxii] Cannan felt that the mystery of Smith's reference to the *Wealth of Nations* as a work on polity was solved when the lecture notes of one of Smith's students was discovered which clearly showed the explicit basis and origins of the *Wealth of Nations* in the part of Adam Smith's moral philosophy course which treated of jurisprudence or "the theory of the general principles of law and government." [*Lectures*, 3] What seems more strange, however, is that Cannan and others were so puzzled by Adam Smith's statement regarding the political nature of his treatise. That Smith considered the *Wealth of Nations* as an aspect of his concern with jurisprudence [Morrow, pp. 59-60] reflects perfectly his own understanding of the character of economic science as a part of political and social inquiry. In the light of Smith's self-conscious and well known ambition to do comprehensive social science, it is necessary to explore the way in which his 'economic' treatise was a partial account of the general principles of law and government.

Smith stated in the *Wealth of Nations* that he considered the most appropriate framework for the orderly pursuit of knowledge to be the three part division of philosophical inquiry which he identified with the ancient Greek thinkers; physics or natural philosophy, ethics or moral philosophy, and logic. "This general division seems perfectly agreeable to the nature of things." [*Wealth*, 723] Like the ancient thinkers, Smith considered moral philosophy as the science concerned with human nature and the connecting principles of social life. [*Wealth*, 724]

> Wherein consisted the happiness and perfection of a man, considered not only as an individual, but as the member of a family, of a state, and of the great society of mankind, was the object which the ancient moral philosophy proposed to investigate. In that philosophy, the duties of human life were treated of as subservient to the happiness and perfection of human life. [*Wealth*, 726]

Smith shared his investigative aim with the ancients and viewed moral philosophy as "by far the most important of all the branches of philosophy." [*Wealth*, 726]

In order to view the human condition through a perspective appropriately and rationally termed "moral" philosophy, one must assume, as both Adam Smith and the older Greek thinkers did, that the "connecting principles" of human social relations and the "happiness and perfection" of mankind are essentially moral in character; that is to say, resting on ideas about 'right' and 'wrong'. For Smith, unlike Hobbes,[5] morality derives from a genuinely social aide of human nature, a "general fellow-feeling which we have with every other man, merely because he is our fellow creature," [*M.S.*, 130] which "naturally" (without force or fear) inclines mankind to society. He further argues that society is impossible without appropriate rules by which human relations may be governed. "Our moral faculties" Smith said, "were given us for the direction of our conduct in this life." [*M.S.*, 233] They are uniquely concerned "to judge, to bestow censure or applause upon all the other principles of our nature." [*M.S.*, 234] Norms and rules make community possible; all human societies are, therefore essentially based on accepted notions of right and wrong, i.e., moral communities.

It is primarily in his earlier treatise on morality that Smith most explicitly argues for the unique importance of justice among all the "rules of morality" for understanding the nature of human society and government. "Justice," he asserts, "is the main pillar that upholds the whole edifice [of society.] If it is removed, the great, the immense fabric of human society . . . must in a moment crumble into atoms." [*M.S.*, 125]

> Society may subsist, though not in the most comfortable state, without beneficence; but the prevalence of injustice must utterly destroy it. [*M.S.*, 125]

Since, for Adam Smith, the rules of justice are the foundation of social order, the central matter of political inquiry (jurisprudence) and of political life is the question of justice. The study of political or civil society necessarily involves the aim of understanding the "rules of natural jurisprudence." [*M.S.*, 501] Jurisprudence is viewed as one major branch of moral philosophy, the other being ethics proper. So the *Wealth of Nations* is most appropriately referred to as a work on jurisprudence or the "theory of the general principles which ought to run through and be the foundation of, the laws of all nations," [*M.S.*, 503] with particular respect to the production and distribution of the "comforts and conveniencies" of human living.

For Smith, the idea of justice binds the study of economy to the study of political order. The proper place for 'economics' within the hierarchy of social inquiry corresponds to its actual place in the context of social life. Just as political life is an aspect of moral order so economic life is a part of political order and necessarily the object of law and government. Economic science is a part of political inquiry and "political economy, or of the nature and causes of the wealth of nations," is a "branch of the system of civil government." [*Wealth*, 643]

The pivotal role of justice in the *Wealth of Nations* is demonstrated further by Smith's comments at the end of the *Theory of Moral Sentiments* referring to his projected work on "natural jurisprudence" of which his political economy is a part. "Every system of positive law," he argues, "may be regarded as a more or less imperfect attempt towards a system of natural jurisprudence, or towards an enumeration of the particular rules of justice." [*M.S.*, 501]

> . . . in no country do the decisions of positive law coincide exactly, in every case with the rules which the natural sense of justice would dictate. Systems of positive law, therefore, though they deserve the greatest authority, as the records of the sentiments of mankind in different ages and nations, yet can never be regarded as accurate systems of the rules of natural justice. [*M.S.*, 502]

Justice is also the key moral notion in applied economy which aims to establish or reform the institutions most immediately related to improving the material conditions of human life. Political economy, in the practical sense, aims at a just economy in a just society, i.e., one in which the well being of all would advance in the fairest and most appropriate, if imperfect, manner. The *Wealth of Nations* is predicated on the view that economic liberty is most conducive to "that universal opulence which extends itself to the lowest ranks of the people." [*Wealth*, 11] This was an undoubted good in Adam Smith's mind. It was a central aim of political economy as he understood it and the moral basis of his concern with economic 'efficiency.' Smith aimed at a more extensive, a more equal and a more just possession and use of goods.

> No society can surely be flourishing and happy, of which the far greater part of the members are poor and miserable. It is but equity . . . that they who feed, clothe and lodge the whole body of the people, should have such a share of the produce of their own labour as to be themselves tolerably well fed, clothed and lodged. [*Wealth*, 79]

Opulence, however, was not for Smith either the sole or the highest good and his vision of a good society was not based on the endless pursuit of wealth. He believed that, for most men, a certain level of material security and comfort was a necessary prerequisite to the flowering of higher virtues. This view is somewhat reminiscent of Marx who argued that man could be himself only after "the productive forces have also increased . . . and all the springs of cooperative wealth are flowing more abundantly." [Marx, p. 388] "Before we can feel much of others," Smith suggests, "we must in some measure be at ease ourselves. If our misery pinches us very severely, we have no leisure to attend to that of our neighbour," [*MS*, 297] and therefore, "it is among civilized nations [that] the virtues which are founded on humanity are more cultivated . . . and the mind is more at liberty to unbend itself and indulge its natural inclinations in all these particular respects." [*MS*, 297]

Acquisitiveness or the pursuit of riches *per se* by individuals or nations is neither advocated nor admired either in the *Moral Sentiments* or in the *Wealth of Nations*. The sympathy in the latter work with the striving or ordinary men to "better their condition" is justified in the former work as an expression of prudent self-regard, or "the care of the health, of the fortune, of the rank and reputation of the individual, the objects upon which his comfort and happiness in this life are supposed principally to depend." [*MS*, 311] This is a valid endeavor, Smith argues, and "proper prudence" is a genuine, if lower case, virtue, "an amiable and agreeable quality, yet it never is considered as one either of the most endearing or of the most ennobling of the virtues." Prudence, "commands a certain cold esteem, but seems not entitled to any very ardent love or admiration." [*MS*, 316]

Although an appropriate prudence is respected, if not admired, the pursuit of riches and power is strongly denigrated as contradictory to virtue and wisdom, and as a positive danger and leading source of corruption to man's moral sentiments.

> To feel much for others, and little for ourselves . . . to restrain our selfish, and to indulge our benevolent affections, constitutes the perfection of human nature; and can alone produce among mankind that harmony of sentiments and passions in which consists their whole grace and propriety. [*MS*, 27]

In this context "wealth and greatness are mere trinkets of frivolous utility, . . . more troublesome to the person . . . than all the advantages they can afford him are commodious." [*MS*, 261] "If we consider the real satisfaction which all these things are capable of affording . . . it will appear in the highest degree contemptible and trifling." [*MS*, 263] Man sometimes realizes or glimpses this truth when he is discouraged, ill, or in old age.

> Power and riches appear then to be, what they are, enormous and operose machines contrived to produce a few trifling conveniencies to the body, consisting of springs the most nice and delicate, which must be kept in order with the most anxious attention, and which, in spite of all our care, are ready every moment to burst into pieces, and to crush in their ruins their unfortunate possessor. They are immense fabrics which it requires the labour of a life to raise, which threaten every moment to overwhelm the person that dwells in them, and which, while they stand, though they may save him from some smaller inconveniences, can protect him from none of the severer inclemencies of the season . . . They keep off the summer shower, not the winter storm, but leave him always as much, and sometimes more, exposed than before to anxiety, to fear, and to sorrow; to diseases, to danger, and to death. [*MS*, 262-63]

The pursuit of wealth above a moderate plenty is not only based on self-deception and ignorance as to how little it can contribute to human happiness, but the false admiration for wealth and power is the great corrupter of man's higher moral sentiments and desires.

> The disposition to admire, and almost to worship, the rich and the powerful, and to despise, or, at least, to neglect, persons of poor and mean condition, . . . is . . . the great and most universal cause of the corruption of our moral sentiments. That wealth and greatness are often regarded with the respect and admiration which are due only to wisdom and virtue; and that the contempt, of which vice and folly are the only proper objects, is often unjustly bestowed upon poverty and weakness, has been the complaint of moralists in all ages. [*MS*, 84]

Smith not excepted.

The *Wealth of Nations* is not about 'riches' but about comfort and conveniencies. It is not urging 'acquisition' but betterment. It speaks not to greedy or avaricious man but to just and prudent man and it aims not at accumulation for its own sake, but at civilization, material and moral progress.

Hopefully, the preceding discussion has also shed some light on the well known controversy in Smithian scholarship regarding what appear to be conflicting attitudes towards 'wealth' in his two major works. Smith is severely critical of the pursuit of wealth and power in his work on morality and yet maintains a positive attitude toward wealth in his political economy. The supposed contradiction can be resolved when one realizes that in the *Wealth of Nations* his sympathy towards "bettering one's condition" expresses the preoccupation of political economy with the subsistence and comfort of the masses, and that he has *already* provided in his earlier book an explicit and comprehensive critique of 'riches' and the pursuit of power, aimed at admonishing the rich and enlightening the receptive. Furthermore, as Macfie [pp. 59-81] has argued, Smith's notions of 'prudence' and 'self-love' are the same in both his works. Also, since Smith saw a number of editions of the *Moral Sentiments* through to press in the years after the publication of the *Wealth of Nations*, it would seem very unlikely that the two books represent fundamentally contradictory views on so important a subject as his attitude towards wealth, though they provide quite different contexts for its discussion.

II. Justice

> To hurt in any degree the interest of any one order of citizens, for no other purpose but to promote that of some other, is evidently contrary to that justice and equality of treatment which the sovereign owes to all the different orders of his subjects. [*Wealth*, 618]

What is justice and why is justice ultimately "natural"? For Smith, justice is natural in the sense that it flows directly from human nature. Justice is "original" in man and conceptions of justice do not merely express the dominant notions of the day or of a class. Man comes to justice and is concerned with justice essentially by being "himself." Justice is an expression of mankind's "strong fellow-feelings with the injuries that are done to their brethren." [*MS*, 45] Because human nature is its source, justice serves as a standard for evaluating society and class interests, not as a 'reflection' of them. For Smith, who sharply disagreed in this matter with his friend Hume, justice is not fundamentally utilitarian [Lindgren, pp. 16-17, 75] though it is in fact eminently helpful and useful to the individual and society. [*MS*, 127-132, 270-71] Justice arises from sources deeper in man than those related to calculations of social consequences, to social utility or necessity, or to means/ends considerations. Justice is "natural" and "sacred." Natural because it derives from human nature and is inevitably expressed where there is human interaction; sacred, because according to Smith, nature itself is ultimately the expression of divinity operating in the universe. Justice is derived from that "general fellow-feeling which we have with every man." The "sense of what is due to his fellow-creatures . . . is the basis of justice and society." [*MS*, 149]

Justice does not only preserve society, it makes society possible. Human society is the consequence of the moral nature of man. It is through his intrinsic sense of justice and related senses of "remorse and consciousness of merit" [*MS*, 119] that man "who can subsist only in society was fitted by nature to that situation for which he was made." [*MS*, 124] Society, for Smith, means mutual interaction, mutual assistance, and the possibility of mutual injury. Justice controls injury so that mutual interaction and assistance may flower and it thereby also makes possible the development and exercise of the higher virtues. Some measure of justice is the natural 'state' of human nature and society. It is the natural condition for a more comprehensive moral life in which mutual interaction and assistance reflect not only "mere justice" but are tendered "from love, from gratitude, from friendship, and esteem, [and then] society flourishes and is happy." [*MS*, 124]

For Smith, justice is distinguished from all the other virtues by its legitimate public enforceability and therefore by its necessary connection to policy and government. This further helps to explain its position as the organizing concept for the *Wealth of Nations*. According to Smith, the highest virtues are direct expressions of our sympathetic social nature, freely directed and with great sensitivity to the welfare of *others*. These "social and benevolent affections" e.g. beneficence, kindness, gratitude, compassion, friendship, love, are moral virtues and attributes of human relations which, by their very nature, cannot be enforced by legal or political instruments. [*MS*, 112, 114] Their intrinsically voluntary character is an essential part of their genuinely being what they are; the highest expression of human morality and human freedom. Since a necessary connection with 'choice' is a part of their very definition, the practice of the higher virtues cannot be 'enforced' except by advice, persuasion and example.

Justice, on the other hand, is that part of the morally desirable which public force may legitimately be used to attain. Justice refers to that which is *due* to man and *enforceable* by the state and is directed to those conditions of social life, which though they do not guarantee the good life, yet they make it possible. Smith's idea of justice is related to the question, "for what purpose shall force be used in society?"

The close connection between justice and force, resting on the absolute necessity of justice for social order, and the merely conditional character of justice in respect to the exercise of the higher virtues, explains the well known negative character of Smith's notion of justice i.e., "mere justice." If we do not abide by the rules of justice, if we are not just in the Smithian sense, we are rightly exposed to coercion and punishment. On the other hand, if we do so in every way, we are not entitled to any great merit or admiration. "Mere justice is, upon most occasions, but a negative virtue, and only hinders us from . . . violating either the person or the estate, or the reputation, of [our] neighbours." [*MS*, 117] Smith is not denigrating justice, he is distinguishing it from other virtues as that one "of which the observance is not left to the freedom of our own wills, which may be extorted by force, and of which the violation exposes to resentment and consequently to punishment." [*MS*, 114]

The nature of government reflects both the importance of social justice and the necessary connection between justice and force. "The violation of justice is what men will never submit to from one another," [*MS*, 501] says Smith, and government is that peculiar social institution responsible for "protecting, as far as possible, every member of the society from the injustice and oppression of every other member of it." [*Wealth*, 651, 669] Government is justice institutionalized. "The liberty, reason, and happiness of mankind . . . can only flourish where civil government is able to protect them." [*Wealth*, 754]

The justice purpose of government implies that government is an institution inextricably connected with coercion and force. This is not to say that government *is* force. For Smith, the institution is defined by its purpose, justice. Force and coercion are justifiable only in terms of this purpose. But despite the negative character of government due to its intimate relationship with force and its merely conditional nature with respect to the development of the higher virtues, Smith's theory emphasizes the great importance of government in preventing those violations of justice which do "real and positive hurt to some particular persons." [*MS*, 114]

The *Wealth of Nations* is organized by a conception of justice which functions on three different and inter-related levels: 1) "natural justice" or the basic normative principles implied by human nature, which are or ought to be the basis of positive law and entitled to support by public force, 2) the principles and system of general rules which are derived from natural justice, and which are or ought to be the immediate basis of positive law, and 3) the administration of positive law and order, i.e. justice as the impartial carrying out of the law.

Natural justice is Smith's ultimate standard in the *Wealth of Nations*. It illuminates his fundamental purpose and general principles, and is the basis for his critique of the unjust economic ideas and practices of his time. The second level of justice embodies the system of rules and principles he proposed for the ordering of economic life; his own "liberal plan of equality, liberty and justice." The *Inquiry into the Nature and Causes of the Wealth of Nations* is an attempt to express "the rules which the natural sense of justice would dictate" [*MS*, 502] for the economic order so that they may be embodied in positive law and law and government thereby made more just. The third level of justice primarily refers to how the law is administered and upheld. However, the character or quality of administration is itself a moral question and Smith emphasizes "impartial" and "exact" administration as important elements of a just political and economic order and as conducive to economic progress. [Billet, 1975]

The idea of justice and the interplay of the three levels which have been outlined is the essential framework within which all aspects of economic order and progress are discussed in the *Wealth of Nations*. Smith's treatise, however, is clearly aimed at the *second* dimension for it is primarily an explication, elaboration, and defense of the just principles which ought to guide the economic life of every community and which are offered as a contribution to the science of the legislator, "whose deliberations ought to be governed by general principles which are always the same." This distinguishes the true legislator from "that insidious and crafty animal, vulgarly called a statesman or politician, whose councils are directed by the momentary fluctuations of affairs." [*Wealth*, 435] Thus, it can be seen that the three levels of justice in the *Wealth of Nations* are predicated on the distinction between substantive or normative justice and the existent laws and institutions of society. This critical distinction is particularly necessary in the political order because "sometimes the interest of the government; sometimes the interest of particular men who tyrannize the government, warp the positive laws of the country from what natural justice would prescribe." [*MS*, 502]

III. Liberty

It is the proper business of law, not to infringe but to support . . . natural liberty. [*Wealth*, 308] Nothing is more difficult than perfectly to secure liberty. [*Lectures*, 144]

In the discussion so far, I have demonstrated that in the hierarchical model of social science inquiry followed by Adam Smith, political economy is a part of jurisprudence, which is the most important part of moral philosophy, and that justice which is considered the cornerstone of society is also the cornerstone of political economy. I have argued that justice as the enforceable virtue links the *Wealth of Nations* to the *Theory of Moral Sentiments* and that the former work's concern with improving the material condition of the "great body of the people" distinguishes its approach to wealth from that in Smith's work on morality. By elucidating Smith's view of the necessary relationship between justice, force and government and his notion of the "free" nature of higher virtue, I have attempted to lay the foundation for understanding why economic liberty is so central to the just economy of the *Wealth of Nations*. It remains to suggest that for Smith, justice also necessarily implies liberty (religious, political, economic), by virtue of the notion of human nature upon which it rests.[6]

The view of human nature as a complex many sided, if not always many splendored thing, which emerges from a reading of Smith's works may be summarized as follows. Human nature is characterized by social or "fellow-feeling" capacities, which, as I have noted previously, lead man to be concerned with the situation and views of others and which naturally result in morality, justice and society. The "social and benevolent affections" such as generosity, compassion, kindness, pity, mutual friendship make possible a human and virtuous life for the individual, as well as a "happy" society. Yet there are powerful anti-social elements and capacities in the human breast; "envy, malice and resentment," [*Wealth*, 670] "pride . . . which makes him love to domineer," [*Wealth*, 365, 751] "selfishness" [*MS*, 3] and "hatred, resentment, anger, spite . . . which drive men from one another." [*MS*, 48-49] Still, mankind is reasoning and reasonable. Indeed "reason is undoubtedly the source of the general rules of morality, and of all the moral judgments which we form by means of them." [*MS*, 470] But man finds it hard to sustain reason and is easily blinded by his passions, by self-love and superficial glitter. Man is prone to "levity and inconsistency" [*Wealth*, 75] to presumption and excessive self-confidence, [*Wealth*, 107] to comparison and emulation. [*MS*, 70-71] He is attracted to liberty and to authority; an active restless, imaginative, creature; generally responsive more than anything else, to social approval and disapproval, [*MS*, 83; WN, 147] having different talents and differing in the intensity, character and object of his desires. Man, though capable of wisdom [*MS*, 81] is hardly ever distinguished by it or by the pursuit of it. [*MS*, 81, 84-5]

What is the most just guiding notion (enforceable if necessary by public authority) for social life, implied by the nature of such a choosing and sentient being, "so imperfect a creature as man" [*MS*, 28] with differing notions of the good life and of happiness? What is the general rule of social justice appropriate to the nature and society of man? Smith's answer is "liberty" i.e., "self" expression, the possibility of fulfillment; living according to one's ideals and bettering one's own condition in one's own way as far as this is possible. It has already been suggested that part of the meaning of the human condition involves, for Smith, conceptions of choice and the "free" nature of all higher moral virtue. Since a true regard for others cannot be "enforced," Smith believes the exercise of force contradicts the nature of higher virtue and prevents the expression of man's humanity. Liberty and virtue go together. "Man's natural love for society," [*MS*, 127] justice and moral socialization can contain and inhibit the expression of his anti-social characteristics while permitting the social and humane virtues to blossom.

Justice also implies, in particular, economic liberty because for Adam Smith, "labour" or "toil" and "ingenuity" are essential parts of human self-expression and the moral basis of economic order. [*Wealth*, 122]

> The property which every man has is his own labour, as it is the original foundation of all other property, so it is the most sacred and inviolable. The patrimony of a poor man lies in the strength and dexterity of his hands; and to hinder him from employing this strength and dexterity in what manner he thinks proper without injury to his neighbour, is a plain violation of this most sacred property. It is a manifest encroachment upon the just liberty both of the workman, and of those who might be disposed to employ him. [*Wealth*, 122]

Labour was the first and remains the ultimate source of economic wealth, "Labour, it must be remembered, is the ultimate price which is paid for everything." [*Wealth*, 30, 189] Since every man possesses to some degree the ability to toil and imagine (labor), Smith sees the free exercise of labor as the means for achieving both an increase in the production of goods and a more widely diffused and equitable distribution of property and goods in society. The principles of economic liberty are desirable and just because they permit and encourage man's labor to develop in accord with his capacities and purposes and enable him as much as possible to gain the rewards and "produce" of his labor. From this point of view Smith's justification for his system is that it maximizes the opportunities for all men to creatively labor, to express their prudent aims and abilities and to better their own condition most effectively.

Smith's analysis of the character of government provides a second and better known foundation for the system of economic liberty. Government, he believed, is inherently imperfect, subject to corruption, prone to injustice, and hard to control. "The violence and injustice of the rulers of mankind is an ancient evil, for which, I am afraid, the nature of human affairs can scarce admit of a remedy." [*Wealth*, 460] When government administration directs investment and production, allocation or distribution, individuals and groups become much more vulnerable to political and legal injustice and error. It is one thing, difficult enough, to require that government correct, as it must, the injustices which inevitably arise in economic relations. It is quite another and potentially dangerous matter to enormously increase the ability of government to *commit* injustices by giving it significant control over the direction of labor and capital.

> The statesman, who should attempt to direct private people in what manner they ought to employ their capitals, would not only load himself with a most unnecessary attention, but assume an authority which could safely be trusted, not only to no single person, but to no council or senate whatever, and which would nowhere be so dangerous as in the hands of a man who had

folly and presumption enough to fancy himself fit to exercise it. [*Wealth*, 423]

The *Wealth of Nations* is a veritable catalog of injustices committed against groups, individuals and nations consequent to the economic authority of statemen who did have the "folly and presumption to think themselves capable of exercising it." Smith stressed, as examples, the oppression of the laboring poor by wage controls [*Wealth*, 66, 131] and restrictions on their mobility (the "law of settlements"), [*Wealth*, 135ff] anti-union laws; [*Wealth*, 66] the exploitation of rural areas and agriculture by the industry of the towns; [*Wealth*, 124-25] the discrimination against consumers in favor of producers, [*Wealth*, 625-66] and the oppression of colonial people by "mother" countries. [*Wealth*, Book 4, chap. 7] He proposed, in the *Wealth of Nations*, to illuminate the general objections and problems consequent to government being decisively engaged in an endeavor which he argues it cannot succeed in doing with requisite wisdom and justice. A great virtue therefore of the system of economic liberty is that

> the sovereign is completely discharged from a duty, in the attempting to perform which he must always be exposed to innumerable delusions, and for the proper performance of which no human wisdom or knowledge could ever be sufficient, the duty of superintending the industry of private people, and of directing it towards the employment most suitable to the interest of the society. [*Wealth*, 651]

Smith is very much concerned with the fact that those with authority and power can not only commit injustice but can also make mistakes. Injustice is often the unintended consequence of error and lack of wisdom. The *Wealth of Nations* is replete with examples of the often enormous gap between intention and consequence in policy, law and human activity generally. [*Wealth*, 298, 391-92, 424, 495] Smith was extremely sensitive to the problem of unintended consequences in social and economic life, as few other thinkers have been. Marx, for example, ignores the question of injustice as unintentional consequence of error. In *Capital*, such fundamental questions of social life as intention and wisdom are not considered meaningful since they are "historical" and not intrinsic elements of human nature or "species being." Smith, on the contrary, was fascinated by observations in political and economic life of how, on the one hand, a person pursuing his own interest "frequently promotes that of society more effectively than when he really intends to promote it" [*Wealth*, 423] and, on the other hand, how often "it is meant by one law to promote the general interest of the country . . . without perhaps its being well understood how this was to be done." [*Wealth*, 495] The result of the latter kind of ignorance was that the value of a nation's production "instead of being increased according to the intention of the lawgiver" was often diminished. [*Wealth*, 424] Government is often much less well-informed than it is well-meaning and Smith was keenly aware "that governmental action, no matter how well intentioned, frequently made bad worse, rather than better." [Ginzberg, p. 206]

Two sources of economic injustice, therefore, which Smith considered intrinsic (though variable) in government were the danger of abuse of an authority unwisely and unnecessarily given to it, and lack of wisdom to accomplish a task unsuitable to it. Although political authority is always responsible for establishing appropriate principles of economy and for regulating and keeping economic relationships in just order as much as possible [Billet, 1976], restraining and coercing the legitimate economic activities of individuals and groups enlarges the arena for political misjudgment and multiplies the number of injustices flowing from economic miscalculation. The injustices arising from authority backed by law and force are likely to be of greater extent, longer duration and more severe consequence than those of individuals and groups. They are usually more difficult to remedy, for the correction of political abuse and error usually requires action by the very authority responsible for committing them. This authority must be brought to recognize its mistakes, or be replaced; neither is easy or quick.

The rectification of established injustices is extremely difficult not only by virtue of the fact that it must be carried out by government but because it is likely to be opposed by those who benefit from the existing injustices. In addition, although justified in the public interest, reform usually entails genuine hardships or inconvenience for some, and upsets established practices. Every unjust regulation "introduces some degree of real disorder into the constitution of the state, which it will be difficult afterwards to cure without occasioning another disorder." [*Wealth*, 438-29] Where the system of economic liberty prevails, the unjust and unwise actions and reactions of private persons can be offset or counter-balanced by each other more effectively and immediately than can the unjust consequences of policy and law. Smith thoroughly understood what many frustrated citizens feel today. Government *is* hard to control. Therefore its functions and powers need to be restricted as much as possible consistent with the purpose of jutice, so that there will be *less* to control, or, less "out of control".

Smith's theory of economic liberty was based pre-eminently on the view that it is the most just as well as the most productive system of economic order, and the heart of his criticisms of economic despotism and governmentally directed enterprise was the observation that they greatly multiplied injustices. "Adam Smith considered the current commercial policies of Great Britain abhorrent largely because they promoted and sustained grave injustices." [Lindgren, p. 110] The *Wealth of Nations* does not argue, as is often thought, against *all* restraints on the economic liberty of individuals and groups, but against all *unjust* restraints on the freedom of individuals and groups to determine their own economic goals and to use their own labor and time, the power of their mind and imagination and their resources of goods and services, to pursue legitimate economic ends.

Every man, *as long as he does not violate the laws of justice*, is left perfectly free to pursue his own interest his own way and to bring both his industry and capital into competition with those of any other man or order of men [*Wealth*, 651, my emphasis]

Smith argues that such liberty, in the context of a due regard for the rights of others and the requirements of the public interest, does not threaten justice. On the contrary, justice and the public interest are constantly threatened and undermined by individuals and groups who seek unfairly to use the results of differential accomplishment, effort and advantage, against their fellow citizens, [*Wealth*, 363, 392-93] and by governments persuaded or pressured into unjust legislation and economic policy by ignorant or self-interested and powerful individuals and classes [*Wealth*, 250, 434, 438, 460, 845] or by the prejudices of the people. [*Wealth*, 438, 483, 522, 589]

Smith does not maintain that economic development is impossible except under his system or deny that Britain, and to a lesser extent France were making substantial progress, although he thought this was partly a consequence of British liberty and a much looser application of mercantilist principles than, for example, in Spain or Portugal. [*Wealth*, 508] He argues that his own "plan" is far more just and reliable than any alternative method for the social determination of what, when, and how to produce. Furthermore, his treatise solidly established some of the fundamental and familiar standards of equity which have continued to guide criticism of economic institutions and policies. In the political economy of his day, Smith complained, "the interest of the consumer is almost constantly sacrificed to that of the producer." [*Wealth*, 625] Although "the interest of those who live by wages is . . . strictly connected with the interest of the society" [*Wealth*, 249], the worker and the disadvantaged were treated unfairly. [*Wealth*, 134-35, 609] In addition, certain types of business enterprise were given unfair advantages over others, having convinced "the wisdom of the nation, that the safety of the commonwealth depends upon the prosperity of their particular manufacture." [*Wealth*, 233] The interests of agriculture and farming were often subordinated to those of industry and commerce, [*Wealth*, 124ff] restricting markets [*Wealth*, 509], artificially depressing the prices of farm produce relative to that of manufacturing goods. [*Wealth*, 125] The economic development of the American colonies was held back in order "to prevent them from making all they can of every part of their own produce, or from employing their stock and industry in the way they judge most advantageous to themselves." [*Wealth*, 549] Other nations, such as India, were allowed to be exploited by a company of merchants who "were enabled to commit with impunity every sort of injustice in those remote countries." [*Wealth*, 590] In general, economic policy was too often the product of the "passionate confidence of interested falsehood" [*Wealth*, 463] reflecting not the interests of the public but the class interest of the owners and employers of capital "who by their wealth tend to draw to themselves the greatest share of public consideration." [*Wealth*, 250] Thus it seems evident that throughout the *Wealth of Nations* the meaning and application of economic principles and their consequences are tested by the standard of justice to individuals and groups and the public. [*Wealth*, 438-39, 618]

IV. Concluding Remarks

It is frequently maintained that the *Wealth of Nations* is the "product" of a pre-industrial era and therefore that its ideas are irrelevant to contemporary political-economic life and incapable of making a contribution to contemporary understanding. The system of political economy which Smith's treatise condemned and to which he opposed the principles of natural liberty is usually thought of as essentially "historical," ending in the 19th century and superseded by "free trade" or "industrial capitalism." Though Smith's analyses are based on the particular problems, situations and data of his own time, they can however be used to illuminate the general conflict between the principles of what I would call "economic despotism" and economic liberty. The statist and administrative character of the mercantilist economy, its view of wealth primarily in terms of national power, national security and national rivalry, its emphasis on production rather than consumption and its marked class bias are not unfamiliar to the twentieth century.

The unjust employment of the coercive power of the state to directly control, regulate and promote production and commerce primarily for the benefit of the few or for the minority at the expense of the working public has not disappeared. The "clamour and sophistry" of special interests are still capable of persuading the public that "the private interest of a part, and of a subordinate part of the society, in the general interest of the whole." [*Wealth*, 128] Mercantilism, or more properly, "the mercantile system" is the name given by Adam Smith to the particular variety of economic nationalism and despotism with which he was familiar; a glorified system of economic *raison d'etat* based on "national prejudice and animosity." [*Wealth*, 441] By the maxims of the day, Smith asserted, "each nation has been made to look with an invidious eye upon the prosperity of all the nations with which it trades, and to consider their gain its loss." [*Wealth*, 460] The essential ideas and methods of mercantilism, and its zero-sum approach to economic relationships, in a variety of guises, in many societies and cultures and in both extreme and mild forms, seem to be persistent and recurring aspects of modern polity.

In contrast to economic depotism, Smith visualizes his system of economic liberty to be a "participatory" economy in the fullest sense and in a way that no publicly administered economy can possibly be. It roots individual and social wealth in the creativity, efforts and decision making capabilities of each and every person who is engaged in economic endeavor. Smith believed that the wealth of society increases most justly when it results from the desires of persons to improve their lives, utilizing the more comprehensive, acurate and prudent knowledge they have of their own needs and resources. For Adam Smith, the system of economic liberty is the only genuinely "peoples" economy.

In his system, liberty and justice are inextricable. Justice, however, is the more comprehensive notion. It not only implies liberty but also restraints on liberty, i.e. *just* liberty. Thus, justice with liberty for all, is the central theme of the *Wealth of Nations*.

Notes

I am grateful to the Earhart Foundation for the Fellowship Grant which enabled me to do the research for this article.

1.   *MS* refers to Adam Smith's *Theory of Moral Sentiments, Lectures,* to the *Lectures on Justice, Police, Revenue and Arms,* and *Wealth of Nations,* page number following.

2.   A recent noteworthy work in this direction is Lindgren, *The Social Philosophy of Adam Smith.* See also W.F. Campbell.

3.   This view is aptly represented in T.D. Campbell's *Adam Smith's Science of Morals.* "The aspect of justice which features most prominently [in the *Wealth*] is the form and expense of the administration of law." [Campbell, p. 186]

4.   One of the earliest sources of this view is Dugald Stewart's *Account of the Life and Writing of Adam Smith,* published in 1793 which quotes John Millar, a student of Smith's, as saying that the principle of "expediency" was the foundation of his political economy. (*Lectures,* xvii) Buckle's influential 19th century *History of Civilization in England* stated that the central notion of the *Wealth of Nations* was "selfishness." He [Smith] makes man naturally selfish ... he represents them as pursuing wealth for sordid objects." [p. 353]

5.   The view that Smith has an essentially Hobbesian notion of man is imaginatively argued by Joseph Cropsey in *Polity and Economy.* It is however based on an inadequate understanding of Smith's idea of "self-preservation." For a well developed refutation, see Lindgren.

6.   Because Cropsey misconstrues Smith's notion of justice to be merely the virtue of commercial society, he does not appreciate the intrinsically moral relationship between justice and liberty. He therefore concludes that Smith intended economic liberty to be instrumental to preserving political and religious liberty. This may be an important contemporary argument for economic liberty but there is no evidence that Smith himself viewed it in this manner.

References

Billet, L. "Political Order and Economic Development: Reflections on Adam Smith's *Wealth of Nations,*" *Political Studies,* Dec. 1975 23, 430-441.
———. "The role of Government in a Just Economy: The *Wealth of Nations* Reconsidered," (unpublished), Adam Smith Bicentennial Lecture Series, Ohio University, Athens, Ohio, May 26, 1976.
Buckle, H.T. *History of Civilization in England,* New York, 1883, II, pp. 340-360.
Campbell, T.D. *Adam Smith's Science of Morals,* London, 1971.
Campbell, W.F. "Adam Smith's Theory of Justice, Prudence and Beneficience," *American Economic Review,* May 1967, 57, 571-77.
Cooke, C.A. "Adam Smith on Jurisprudence," *Law Q. Review,* April 1935, 51, 326-332.
Cropsey, J. *Polity and Economy,* The Hague, 1957.
Ginzberg, *The House of Adam Smith,* New York, 1934.
Grampp, W.D. "Adam Smith and the Economic Man," *J. Political Economy,* August 1948, 56, 315-336.
Lindgren, J.R. *The Social Philosophy of Adam Smith,* The Hague, 1973.
Macfie, A.L. *The Individual in Society,* London, 1967.
Marx, K. "Critique of the Gotha Program," *The Marx Engels Reader,* ed. R.C. Tucker, New York, 1972.
Morrow, G.R. *The Ethical and Economic Theories of Adam Smith,* Clifton, 1973.
Rosenberg, N. "Some Institutional Aspects of the *Wealth of Nations,*" *J. Political Economy,* Dec. 1968, 68, 557-70.
Small, A.W. *Adam Smith and Modern Sociology,* Chicago, 1907.
Smith, Adam. *An Inquiry into the Nature and Causes of the Wealth of Nations* (1776), New York 1937.
———. *Lectures on Justice, Police, Revenue and Arms* (1896), New York, 1937.
———. *The Theory of Moral Sentiments* (1759), New York, 1966.
West, E.G. "Adam Smith's Philosophy of Riches," *Philosophy,* April 1969, 44, 101-15.

73

Euge! Belle! Dear Mr. Smith: The *Wealth of Nations*, 1776-1976

H.M. Robertson

Source: *South African Journal of Economics*, Vol. 44 (4), December 1976, pp. 378-411.

On 5th June, 1723, a new-born son of a recently widowed mother was baptized in Kirkcaldy, a small town in Scotland. His actual date of birth is not recorded. He grew up, his mother's only child, in a fatherless household. He never married, never made a "great stir in the world", but lived a quiet life as student, independent "free-lance" lecturer, university professor, private tutor and civil servant. He died on 17th July, 1790, in Edinburgh just across the Firth of Forth from his birthplace, and there he was buried. Yet this year economists all over the world are celebrating his bicentenary – the bicentenary of his intellectual and liberary masterpiece, the *Wealth of Nations*, the first edition of which was published on 9th March, 1776.

In the course of all the celebrations and the conferences being held, at which learned papers upon all aspects of Adam Smith's work are being presented, I have no doubt that he will be thoroughly taken apart, dusted, examined in detail and repaired – and then, I fear, too often be put back on the shelf. His "paradigms" will be carefully identified, classified and labelled, and their subsequent vicissitudes – the whole morphology of change out of "old paradigm" into "new paradigm" – will, doubtless, be learnedly explained. Adam Smith himself, one may be sure, was as ignorant of thinking in "paradigms" and of creating "paradigms" for others to think in, as M. Jourdain was ignorant of talking in prose; though his extremely vigorous characterization of the stages through which the ancient Greek philosophy degenerated into the shabby patchwork encountered in the English universities in the 18th century[1] suggests that, had he entered upon this paradigm-identification business, he might have proved a very formidable exponent indeed.[2]

For many reasons, I would have liked to have gone to Chicago and then to Britain, and to have made some contribution to the bicentenary programmes arranged there. But I have learnt that "retirement" does not mean less work but only less income. Moreover, there are, of course, no travel subsidies. I have, therefore, had to accommodate my future views and designs to the real mediocrity of my circumstances.[3] After all, Adam Smith himself, after his Grand Tour[4] and his Great Success, was still content with later years spent actively but stay-at-homedly (and not luxuriously) in Kirkcaldy or Edinburgh.

Yet, I would not like the bicentenary to pass without some tribute to the great master whom all are honouring

> *di cui la fama ancor nel mondo dura*
> *e durerà quanto 'l mondo lontana . . .*

Even did I not lack the skill, I would still lack the inclination to honour him, so to speak, under the scalpel. So, instead of paying a tribute of scholarship, I offer, instead, merely a tribute of friendship.[5]

Bagehot, writing one hundred years after the publication of the *Wealth of Nations*, said of Adam Smith that "the most striking point is that he never seems aware that he is dealing with . . . an abstract science at all. The *Wealth of Nations* does not deal, as do our modern books, with a fictitious human being hypothetically simplified, but with the actual concrete men who live and move. It is concerned with Greeks and Romans, the nations of the middle ages, the Scotch and the English, and never diverges into the abstract world . . ." Yet almost immediately he continued, "Adam Smith approximates to our modern political economist, because his conception of human nature is so limited. It has been justly said that he thought 'there was a Scotchman inside every man'. His *Theory of Moral Sentiments*, indeed, somewhat differs in tone, but all through the *Wealth of Nations*, the desire of man to promote his pecuniary interest is treated as far more universally intense, and his willingness to labour for that interest as far more eager and far more commonly diffused, than experience shows them to be . . . The conception of human nature which underlies the *Wealth of Nations* is near enough to the fictitious man of economic science, to make its reasonings often approximate to, and sometimes co-incide with, those which stoutest of modern economists might use . . ."[6] Such a characterization, indeed, appears to provide the backbone for what is, even now, for both Smithian and post-Smithian economics, the standard article on display upon the academic "paradigm" markets.[7]

Yet, I wonder . . . Smith was well acquainted with Scotsmen and he mentioned them frequently, not as in Bagehot's "ideal-type" but – in greater conformity with Bagehot's earlier statement – as a very miscellaneous collection of real people in a great variety of different circumstances. Among them, for instance, were the 800 clansmen who – surely for no mercenary or self-regarding motive – followed Cameron of Lochiel to join Prince Charles Edward in 1745, when the "Young Pretender" raised the Stuart standard at Glenfinnan; and Lochiel himself (to use the Scots way of referring to a man by his lands not by his surname), who could command their loyalty and obedience – and, without any authority from the Crown, as chief of the clan, exercise jurisdiction over them, which he did very justly – although his rent roll had never exceeded £500 a year.[8] Surely the "half-starved Highland woman" who frequently bore twenty children and ended up not having two alive[9] was no apostle of enlightened self-interest. Were the Shetland hand-knitters of stockings which "are wrought much cheaper than they can anywhere be wrought on the loom"[10] really showing an intense desire to promote their pecuniary interests? Or, departing from the Celtic or Norse fringe, the woman engaged in the spinning of linen yarn? "In most parts of Scotland, she is a good spinner who can earn twenty pence a week." For, in Scotland there were not those obstacles to the migration of labour in order to seek better employment which the Acts of Settlement imposed in England.[11]

In fact, the Scotchman inside every Scot had not yet managed, according to Adam Smith's observations, to save Scotland from any of the problems that typically beset what now seems to be known as an LDC – whether to save ink, or because all the terms employing actual words that have been tried, very soon seem to have become regarded as disparaging. The Scots "labouring poor seldom eat butcher's-meat, except upon holidays, and other extraordinary occasions".[12] With deficient demand for meat, the price of cattle had hardly yet risen high enough to make it generally profitable to grow corn as stock-feed; and live-stock management remained poor and primitive, even though "that stunted breed which was common all over Scotland thirty or forty years ago . . . is now much mended . . ."[13] Through the consequent lack of manure, the infield- and outfield-system still largely prevailed – the manure would be applied only to small areas, "the most fertile, or those, perhaps in the neighbourhood of the farm-yard", and these were subjected to continuous cropping, with sporadic cultivation of parts of the remaining rough pasture, temporarily brought under the plough. A vicious circle was set up: "Without some increase of stock, there can be scarce any improvement of land, but there can be no considerable increase of stock but in consequence of a considerable improvement of land . . ." Thus, "a long course of industry and frugality" would be needed before a better system could be established.[14] For similar reasons, Scots dairying was inferior to English.[15] Enclosed land was scarce in Scotland, even though on this account it yielded high rents.[16] Scots noblemen with the most extensive estates, who, apart from cultivating 200 or 300 acres round the family seat, allowed the rest "to lie waste, almost uninhabited and entirely unimproved, not worth a shilling the hundred acres, without thinking themselves answerable to God, their country and their Posterity for so shameful as well as so foolish a neglect . . .", were yet, for the little that they did, regarded as "improvers".[17] Although Smith made it plain that, in Scotland, considerable economic development was taking place, his Scotchmen were not exerting themselves to bring about as rapid a transformation of a backward agriculture as Bagehot's Scotchman would have done, or even as contemporary Englishmen were actually doing.

Not was it only in agriculture that Scottish energy and initiative fell short. Perhaps the Scots' traditional diet bore some of the responsibility for this. "The common people of Scotland, who are fed with oatmeal, are in general neither so strong nor so handsome as the same rank of people in England, who are fed with wheaten bread. They neither work so well, nor look so well . . ." Since there was no such difference between Scots and English people of fashion, all of whom enjoyed a more varied diet, unsupplemented oatmeal must be nutritionally inferior.[18] But, perhaps added to and a greater hindrance than unsatisfactory diet, were the less favourable expectations afforded in the Scots economy, with its relatively low wage structure. "The wages of labour are the encouragement of industry, which, like every other human quality, improves in proportion to the encouragement it receives. A plentiful subsistence increases the bodily strength of the labourer, and the comfortable hope of bettering his condition, and of ending his days perhaps in ease and plenty, animates him to exert that strength to the utmost. Where wages are high, accordingly, we shall always find the workmen more active, diligent and expeditious, than where they are low; in England, for example, than in Scotland . . ."[19]

The Highlanders, most Scots farmers, most Scots "servants, labourers and workmen of different kinds", who "make up the far greater part of every great political society", must all, it seems, have fallen short of Bagehot's "economic Scotchman". The merchants, indeed, showed up better (or in some cases, with their abuses of bank credit, worse!) and they alone were singled out as Scotsmen of Bagehotian breed. It was in this manner that he explained recent developments – and excesses – in Scots banking. As in the American colonies, so in Scotland, where the use of gold and silver had practically disappeared from domestic commercial transactions, and had been replaced by paper, ". . . it is not the poverty, but the enterprising and projecting spirit of the people, their desire of employing all the stock which they can get as active and productive stock, which has occasioned this redundancy of paper money".[20] Yet, in general it would appear that it was, perhaps, because so many Scots did not correspond with their stereotype, that Scottish economic progress in the 18th century, compared with English, appeared to Adam Smith to be that of a country which "is not only much poorer, but the steps by which it advances to a better condition, for it is evidently advancing, seem to be slower and more tardy".[21]

Such a brief glance at a few of the riches of Smith's storehouse indicates how much is lost by those who do not read the *Wealth of Nations* "as it was written" but through blinkers, whether paradigmatic or other. I suggest, indeed, that when Bagehot described Adam Smith as seeing a Scotchman in every man, he was not describing what Adam Smith saw, but what he himself, on account of his own preconceptions, saw in Smith, after concentrating only on those aspects of the *Wealth of Nations* in which he himself was most interested and after skipping lightly over those in which he was not. Another, later editor of *The Economist*, Francis Hirst, I think achieved a truer focus when he wrote: "The *Wealth of Nations* is a book to be read as it was written. More than half its nutriment and all its fascination is lost if you cut away the theory from its historical setting."[22] I would be inclined to go rather further, and to suggest that the reader himself has to be something of an economic historian fully to appreciate the *Wealth of Nations*, whilst other economists, who are without a true historical bent, somehow truncate it in their own minds, as Bagehot surely did in his oft-quoted passage.[23]

So far I have been concerned only with the real Scotsmen, whom Adam Smith, in order to illustrate a point, from time to time brought into his narrative in the *Wealth of Nations*. I could adduce other, sometimes more direct, denials of the universality of "economic man". "It seldom happens that a great (landed) proprietor is a great improver." In the past it has been shown that such a person "often wanted the inclination and almost always the requisite abilities". "To improve land with profit . . . requires an exact attention to small savings and small gains, of which a man born to a great fortune, even though naturally frugal, is very seldom capable . . ."[24] Indeed landowners were frequently defective in a tolerable knowledge of their own interest. They were too often not only ignorant but incapable of the necessary application of mind, because of the "indolence, which is the natural effect of the ease and security of their situation . . ." But labourers, also, were often incapable of understanding how their interests were bound up with those of society as a whole. The labourer's "condition leaves him no time to receive the necessary information, and his education and habits are commonly such as to render him unfit to judge even though he was fully informed".[25]

Moreover, common observation showed that, in all walks of life, it was a frequent occurrence to be deceived in one's expectations. "The over-weening conceit, which the greater part of men have of their own abilities, is an ancient evil remarked by the philosophers and moralists of all ages. Their absurd presumption in their good fortune, has been less taken notice of. It is, however, if possible, still more universal. There is no man living who, when in tolerable health and spirits, has not some share of it. The chance of gain is by every man more or less over-valued and the chance of loss is by most men under-valued, and by scarce any man, who is in tolerable health and spirits, valued more than it is worth . . . The contempt of risk and presumptuous hope of success, are in no period of life more active than at the age at which young people chuse their professions. How little the fear of misfortune is then capable of balancing the hope of good luck, appears still more evidently in the readiness of the common people to enlist as soldiers, or to go to sea . . . What a common soldier may lose is obvious enough. Without regarding the danger, however, young volunteers never enlist so readily as at the beginning of a new war . . . Their pay is less than that of common labourers, and in actual service their fatigues are much greater . . ."[26] Surely there were big gaps in the enlightment available to give free play to enlightened self-interest.

Yet, in spite of the absence of "economic man" from the *Wealth of Nations*, within the division of labour, and as a necessary cause and consequence of the division of labour, there was a "division of knowledge". And this involved a specialization of awareness about his own particular concerns, upon the part of each individual within the economy, quite beyond the capacity of any Government official, or official of a privileged corporation, exercising powers of compulsion – say of the East India Company, or the Corporation of the Glasgow Hammermen (if it was the Hammermen) which had harassed James Watt.[27] Smith was not the first to have sensed this. Indeed, that most absolutist of political philosophers, Thomas Hobbes, had conceded: "A plain husbandman is more Prudent in affaires of his own house, then a Privy Counceller in the affaires of another man."[28] But, to Hobbes, the husbandman's prudence was only capable of dealing with small affairs. It would be irrelevant to matters within the sphere of the statesman, who must determine a policy on the basis of a prudent emanating from wider experience: so much so that, for example, in the commercial sphere "it belongeth to the Common-wealth (that is, to the Soveraign only), to approve or disapprove both of the places, and the matter of forraign Traffique".[29] The pre-Smithian consensus, it has been said, was that "government should have a detailed economic policy which required active intervention in the affairs of the community in a thousand and one ways, all with the great purpose of achieving exactly the aim that Adam Smith wanted to accomplish: the most rapid possible increase in the country's wealth . . . The

Mercantilists held that if every man tried to do those things which were for his own advantage, grievous national ills would arise unless some statesman, who was looking out for the fortunes of individuals in the interest of the whole commonwealth, should formulate a general plan and by ordered regulations get it executed."[30]

On this sort of regulation – in the following citation specifically on import duties or prohibitions of the import of particular products, in order to foster import-replacing production of these articles at home – Adam Smith made a resounding attack: "What is the species of domestic industry which his capital can employ, and of which the produce is likely to be of the greatest value, every individual, it is evident, can, in his local situation, judge much better than any statesman or lawgiver can do for him. The statesman, who should attempt to direct private people in what manner they ought to employ their capitals, would not only load himself with a most unnecessary attention, but assume an authority which could safely be trusted, not only to no single person, but to no council or senate whatever, and which would nowhere be so dangerous as in the hands of a man who had folly and presumption enough to fancy himself fit to exercise it. To give the monopoly of the home-market to the products of domestic industry in any particular art or manufacture . . . must in all cases be either a pointless or a hurtful regulation . . ." If, in the absence of a tariff or prohibition, domestic production was competitive with foreign imports, its imposition was superfluous; if not, its imposition hampered the division of labour in which all "employ their whole industry in a way in which they have some advantage over their neighbours . . ."[31]

In fact, the major instances where self-interest was harmful – save to the individual who had miscalculated, and not to society – were where it succeeded in creating a monopoly. This, for the most part, though not always, involved a political, rather than a purely economic, activity.

The "intricate . . . and . . . fruitless cares" with which attempts were made to regulate trade under the "mercantile system of political economy", though undertaken and enforced by the State, were concocted by merchants. Their arguments "were addressed by merchants to parliaments, and to the councils of princes, to nobles and to country gentlemen, by those who were supposed to understand trade, to those who were conscious to themselves that they knew nothing about the matter" . . .[32] In so far as they had a capacity for organizing in such ways – or by simple collusion amongst themselves – profitable shared monopolies within the "mercantile system of political oeconomy" which Smith regarded as prevalent in his day, the self-regarding motives of the merchants and manufacturers did not, in his view, lead, as if guided by an "invisible hand", to unintended benefits for the whole society. On the contrary, as they derived a far greater advantage from the monopoly of the home market in their easily transportable wares than the graziers derived from the prohibition of cattle imports or the arable farmers derived from the corn laws, it was the merchants' and manufacturers' interests which were at the bottom of the whole system of prohibitions and highly protective duties in which the consumers' interests were sacrificed. The merchants and manufacturers "seem to have been the original inventors of those restraints upon the importation of foreign goods, which secure to them a monopoly of the home market. It was probably in imitation of them, and to put themselves on a level with those who, they found, were disposed to oppress them that the country gentlemen and farmers of Great Britain so far forgot the generosity that is natural to their station, as to demand the exclusive privilege of supplying their countrymen with corn and butcher's-meat."[33] Moreover, it "is the industry which is carried on for the benefit of the rich and powerful, that is principally encouraged by our mercantile system. That which is carried on for the benefit of the poor and indigent" – like the spinners of linen yarn, poor, scattered and without support or protection – "is too often, either neglected or oppressed".[34]

In their campaigns for a guaranteed market, "merchants and manufacturers complain much of high wages in raising the price, and thereby lessening the sale of their goods both at home and abroad. They say nothing concerning the bad effects of high profits. They are silent with regard to the pernicious effects of their own gains. They complain only of those of other people."[35] Adam Smith, of course, *did* have several things to say about the bad effects of high profits resulting from imperfections of competition, and concluded his remarks on this topic with a general observation quite incompatable with any naïve belief in predestined harmonies: "But besides all the bad effects to the country in general, which have already been mentioned as necessarily resulting from a high rate of profit; there is one more fatal, perhaps, than all these put together, but which, if we may judge by experience, is inseparably connected with it. The high rate of profit seems everywhere to destroy that parismony which in other circumstances is natural to the character of the merchant. When profits are high, that sober virtue seems to be superfluous, and expensive luxury to suit better the affluence of his situation. But the owners of great mercantile capitals are necessarily the leaders and conductors of the whole industry of every nation, and their example has a much greater influence upon the manners of the whole industrious part of it than that of any other order of men. If the employer is attentive and parismonious, the workman is very likely to be so too; but if the master is dissolute and disorderly, the servant who shapes his work according to the pattern which his master prescribes to him, will shape his life too according to the example which he sets him . . . Light come, light go, says the proverb; and the ordinary tone of expense seems every where to be regulated, not so much according to the real ability of spending as to the supposed facility of getting money to spend. It is thus that the single advantage which the monopoly procures to a single order of men, is in many different ways hurtful to the general interest of the country."[36]

Self-interest, then, coincided with community interest only where "the impertinent jealousy . . . the mean rapacity, the monopolising spirit of merchants and manufacturers" were "prevented from disturbing the tranquility of any body but themselves";[37] they co-incided only where the law, which could not prevent, without tyranny, meetings of people of the same trade, even though they "seldom meet together, even for merriment and diversion, but the conversation ends in a conspiracy against the public, or in some contrivance to raise prices", neither facilitated nor promoted such gatherings.[38] Self-interest could be relied upon to operate within the economy in a manner beneficial to society only if it had to operate under those constraints which free competition imposed: "Monopoly . . . is a great enemy to good management, which can never be universally established but in consequence of that free and universal competition which forces everybody to have recourse to it for the sake of self-defence . . ."[39]

In view of all this, it is difficult to understand how, from so many quarters, an inconsistency has been alleged between the basic premisses of the *Wealth of Nations* and those of the *Theory of Moral Sentiments*, even to the extent of its having been labelled by some German students as "Das Adam Smith Problem". This "Problem" was, indeed, solved to the satisfaction of one of them by the explanation that while Smith remained in Britain, under the influence of Hutcheson and Hume, he remained an idealist and wrote the *Moral Sentiments*; but after going to France and coming into close touch with the materialism prevalent there, he returned a materialist, and wrote the *Wealth of Nations*![40] It is quite true that the self-regarding motives – quite rightly for a treatise on economics largely devoted to the elucidation of an exchange economy in which they prove an effective motor force – are drawn to the attention more frequently in the *Wealth of Nations*, and are there, for the most part, treated as having useful functions to perform within such an economy. Yet they are still regarded as having utility for society only within the same limitations as were set out, in the *Moral Sentiments*, as conditions for the self-regarding virtues to obtain approval. Only if the competition was fair could the "impartial spectator" within each of us approve of the actions taken under their impetus. To outstrip, by greater and more effective exertions, all competitors in "the race for wealth, and honour and preferments" is fit and right; but to obstruct or trip up, to "justle or throw down any of them", offends Society's sense of justice.[41] The observance of such rules of justice is essential to the cohesion of human society, which "cannot subsist among those who are at all times ready to hurt and injure one another". Yet, if the rule of not actually hurting any of one's neighbours for one's own advantage is observed, human society may well "subsist among different men, as among different merchants, from a sense of its utility . . . It may still be upheld by a mercenary exchange of good offices according to an agreed valuation." And this possibility is fortunate, since "it is thus that man, who can subsist only in society, was fitted by nature to that situation for which he was made".[42]

What real inconsistency does this show with the exposition in the *Wealth of Nations*, that man, in civilized societies, "stands at all times in need of the co-operation and assistance of great multitudes, while his whole life is scarce sufficient to gain the friendship of a few persons . . . It is in vain to expect it from their benevolence only . . . It is not from the benevolence of the butcher, the brewer, or the baker, that we expect our dinner, but from their regard for their own interest . . ."[43] Indeed, there is much to be said for Francis A. Walker's remark, applied to the Smith of both the *Moral Sentiments* and the *Wealth of Nations*, that "Adam Smith left the love of wealth in human minds, not rebuked but enlightened".[44] Moreover, it is worth noting that the much-mocked (yet instructive) "hidden hand" metaphor was employed in a far more fundamental justification of a laisser-faire economy in the *Moral Sentiments* than in the *Wealth of Nations*. In the latter the example chosen was merely that of the investor who was led to support more productive labour in home industry, and thereby also to accumulate home-based capital more rapidly, and thus provide still more employment of home-domiciled labour, but who only did so because he wished to avoid the greater risks inherent in more distant employments of his capital. It was this more timorous and circumspect investor who, in the *Wealth of Nations*, was led by an invisible hand to promote the public interest without having intended to. But in the *Moral Sentiments*, it was the whole process of the circular flow of wealth. The overestimation of the pleasures of wealth and greatness which "keeps in continual motion the industry of mankind", and which has "turned the rude forests of nature into agreeable and fertile plains, and made the trackless and barren ocean a new fund of subsistence, and the great high road of communication to the different nations of the earth . . .", had functions to perform in the distribution as well as the production of wealth. "It is to no purpose that the proud and unfeeling landlord views his extensive fields, and without a thought for the wants of his brethren, in imagination consumes himself the whole harvest that grows upon them . . . The capacity of his stomach bears no proportion to the intensity of his desires, and will receive no more than that of the meanest peasant . . . The rich only select from the heap what is most precious and agreeable. They consume little more than the poor; and . . . though they mean only their own conveniency, though the sole end which they propose from the labours of all the thousands they employ be the gratification of their own vain and insatiable desires, they divide with the poor the produce of all their improvements. They are led by an invisible hand to make nearly the same distribution of the necessaries of life which would have been made had the earth been divided into equal portions among all its inhabitants; and thus without intending it, without knowing it, advance the interest of the society."[45]

Francis Hirst brought his commonsense to bear on all this. "The truth," he wrote, "as Smith conceived it, is that men are actuated at different times by different motives, benevolent, selfish, or mixed. The moral criterion of an action is: will it help society, will it benefit others, will it be approved by the Impartial Spectator? The economic criterion of an action is: will it benefit me, will it be profitable, will it increase my income? . . . But there is nothing whatever either to excite, surprise or to suggest inconsistency in the circumstance that a philosopher, who . . . distinguished between self-regarding and other-regarding emotions, should have formed the first group into a system of economics and the second group into a system of ethics."[46]

But what sort of distribution did Adam Smith imagine emerged for those who, in view of the circular flow of wealth, enjoyed, by way of the expenditure of proud and unfeeling landlords, almost the same distribution of the necessaries of life as they would have been afforded in a less unequal society, and so found that "when providence divided the earth among a few lordly masters, it neither forgot nor abandoned those who seemed to have been left out in the partition. These last, too, enjoy their share of all that it produces."[47] Lord Robbins – surely a friend – had no comforting view of what their share, in the long run, was likely to be. He has written that "Adam Smith who believed . . . that population tended to multiply until it pressed on the limits of subsistence, gives a most frightening picture of what may be expected if the funds destined for the maintenance of labour should ever cease to increase. He illustrated this by reference to China where he thought such a dreadful state of affairs actually prevailed . . . Only a continuous increase of saving could, he thought, avert such horrors or even worse. It would be difficult to regard such a picture as implying any very sanguine view of the results of the economic process."[48]

It is true that Smith, in the very passage from the *Moral Sentiments* in which he referred to the "invisible hand", did premise his view of the distribution of the surplus, after the proud, unfeeling landlords had taken their delicate but, in total, insignificant pick, upon the assertion that "the produce of the soil maintains at all times nearly that number of inhabitants which it is capable of maintaining". He did not, however, indicate that this represented a fixed maximum of produce, or people. On the contrary, because of the way in which nature imposes expectations – as it would appear, irrationally optimistic expectations – and incentives, "the earth, by these labours of mankind, has been obliged to redouble her natural fertility, and to maintain a greater multitude of inhabitants".[49] It is also true that he wrote that: "Every species of animals naturally multiplies in proportion to the means of their subsistence, and no species can ever multiply beyond it", and that, amongst men, the adjustments of numbers to inadequate means of subsistence was not random, as in the case of other species, but concentrated upon the poor "by destroying a great part of the children which their fruitful marriages produce".[50] It is further true that this occurs in his chapter "Of the wages of labour", and that it leads up to the assertion that: "the demand for men, like that for any other commodity, necessarily regulates the production of men, quickens it when it advances too slowly, and stops it when it advances too fast. It is this demand which regulates and determines the state of propagation in all the different countries of the world, in North America, in Europe, and in China; which renders it rapidly progressive in the first, slow and gradual in the second, and altogether stationary in the last."[51]

Yet Adam Smith nowhere seems to have suggested that economies are destined to pass, in counter-Rostowian manner, through the North American to the European stage and then, inevitably, to the stationary Chinese continuum. It was Gibbon, not Adam Smith, who concerned himself in 1776 with decline and fall. If this had been Adam Smith's message, there would, indeed, have been a glaring inconsistency between this Smith of foreboding, and the Smith who was the apostle of the division of labour, which improves its own "productive powers" and the "skill, dexterity and judgment with which it is . . . directed or applied", so that, in contrast to the "miserably poor" "nations of hunters and fishers", it "occasions, in a well-governed society, that universal opulence which extends itself to the lowest ranks of the people".[52] There would also at least have been a great imbalance in emphasis as compared with the long and magnificent Book III, in which he delineated, with little suggestion that it was coming to an end, the progress of Europe's opulence upwards from the low levels to which it had been reduced in the confusions that followed the fall of the Roman Empire.[53]

Robbins's frightening picture in this book was based upon a fuller treatment on the same lines which he had published many years earlier. In the historical introduction with which, in 1930, he began his article "On a certain ambiguity in the concept of stationary equilibrium", Robbins started off with Adam Smith's theories of wages. He said that Smith commenced his treatment with a "buyer's monopoly theory of subsistence wages". By a tacit combination of employers, the worker's wages "are forced down to subsistence level – a wage, that is to say, which will keep him alive and enable him to bring up a family of just such a size as . . . will keep the population constant". Then, he said, Smith's strong sense of reality forced him at once to abandon this, for one in which workers escaped from the monopsony pressure when funds available in the masters' hand for employing labour increased. But this escape would only be temporary because, as capital accumulates, the rate of profit declines and this discourages further accumulation. So the wage fund becomes stationary and the "wretched labourers multiply, and their share per head of this constant fund is reduced until it reaches that level which is sufficient to maintain the labourer and enable him to support a family of the size necessary to keep population constant".[54]

I do not believe that this is a true expression of Adam Smith's admittedly difficult thought. Robbins, I fancy, was led to form his interpretation under the guidance and rather through the eyes of his own teacher, Edwin Cannan. Now Cannan ought certainly to be enrolled high up in the list of Adam Smith's friends. To him we owe, not only his painstaking and careful editing of the *Wealth of Nations*, for which "to discover a reference has often taken hours of labour: to fail to discover one has often taken days". It was also his pursuit of vague clues which led to the finding of a manuscript copy of a student's notes of a portion of Smith's lectures to his Glasgow classes, which he edited just as meticulously, and revolutionized posterity's knowledge of Smith's intellectual development.[55] But Cannan was a candid friend and, upon occasion, his candour might verge on the pernicketty. One such occasion, I believe, was in treatment of this topic in his *History of the theories of production and distribution*. There Professor Cannan wrote that Adam Smith confined his initial "kind of anticipation of the produce theory", in which the produce of labour "constitutes the natural recompence of wages of labour", to "the original state of things which precedes both the appropriation of land and the accumulation of stock".

Canan then proceeded:

"For the actual state of things, Adam Smith is content, so far as ordinary circumstances are concerned, with the prevailing subsistence theory. Wages are settled by a bargain between master and men, but *'upon all ordinary occasions'* the masters 'have the *advantage in the dispute* and force' the men 'into a compliance with their terms'. They are able to do so because, being fewer in number, and not, like the men, hindered by the law, it is easier for them to combine, and because, though 'in the long run the workmen may be as necessary to his master as his master is to him' 'the necessity is not so immediate' . . . However, the masters cannot force wages down *below a certain point*: 'A man must live by his work, and his wages must at least be sufficient to maintain him. They must even *upon most occasions* be somewhat more; otherwise it would be impossible for him to bring up a family, and the race of such workmen could not last beyond the first generation.'

"This statement of the subsistence theory is far from making it invulnerable. If the combination of masters has the power of depressing wages with which it is credited, why should it leave the labourers enough to support a family?

Doubtless if it did not, then 'the race of such workmen could not last beyond the first generation'; but why should the masters of the present generation concern themselves about that? . . . That Adam Smith himself felt that his doctrine was rather weak on this point we may infer from the prominence which he gives to the irrelevant fact that wages sufficient to support such a family as is required to keep up the population are the lowest 'consistent with common humanity'.

"Observing that, as a matter of fact, wages are often above this rate, Adam Smith decided to restrict his subsistence theory to *'ordinary occasions' or the stationary state*. For the advancing and the declining state he put forward the supply and demand theory . . . This theory of Adam Smith, though in form it supplements his subsistence theory, in reality supersedes it. The power of the masters to depress wages to the subsistence level by combination, and their 'common humanity' which prevents them killing the goose that laid the golden eggs, by depressing them below that level, both disappear. Everything is settled by the demand and supply of labour, and *subsistence appears as nothing more than a condition of the supply being equal to the demand in the stationary state. . .*"[56]

It is, I think, true, that Smith limited the phenomenon of (bare physiological) subsistence wages to the stationary state; but not so true that he regarded the stationary state as an "ordinary occasion" or inevitable; or even in general, as very likely. He had a very shrewd idea that: "The uniform, constant, and uninterrupted effort of every man to better his condition, the principle from which public and national, as well as private opulence is originally derived, is frequently powerful enough to maintain the *natural progress of things towards improvement*, in spite both of the extravagance of government, and of the greatest errors of administration. Like the unknown principle of animal life, it frequently restores health and vigour to the constitution, in spite not only of the disease, but of the absurd prescriptions of the doctor."[57] In the case of the only stationary state which he gave as an example, China, it appeared that some of the doctor's prescriptions had, indeed, been absurd. He doubted whether any country had even yet arrived at the "degree of opulence" which would result in its being "a country fully stocked in proportion to all the business it had to transact". "China", indeed, "seems to have been long stationary, and had probably long ago acquired that full complement of riches which is consistent with the nature of its laws and institutions. But this complement may be much inferior to what, with *other* laws and institutions, the nature of its soil, climate, and situation might admit of. A country which neglects or despises foreign commerce, and which admits the vessels of foreign countries into one or two of its ports only, cannot transact the same quantity of business which it might do with different laws and institutions. In a country, too, where, though the rich or the owners of large capitals enjoy a good deal of security, the poor or the owners of small capitals enjoy scarce any, but are liable, under the pretence of justice, to be pillaged and plundered at any time by inferior mandarines, the quantity of stock employed in all different branches of business transacted within it, can never be equal to what the nature and extent of that business might admit." In illustration of this latter point Smith suggested that, in the current conditions of Chinese society, only if the marginal efficiency of capital exceeded a 12 per cent rate of discount would investment be maintained at a high enough level to prevent the economy slipping backwards into the declining state.[58]

Cannan's gloss, that Adam Smith decided to restrict the efficacy of masters' combinations in depressing wages to subsistence level (yet not below it), to "'ordinary occasions' *or the stationary state*", is, I am sure, unjustified. Adam Smith did not specifically equate ordinary occasions with the stationary state, as Cannan's inverted commas only for 'ordinary occasions' and the fact that his page reference to the *Wealth of Nations* comes after "ocasions", and not after "state", bear witness. This point is perhaps made clearer by comparing the gloss which another of Cannan's pupils, my former colleague and good friend for many years, put upon the same words. Professor Hutt was more concerned with controverting Adam Smith's view that, in the wage bargain, labourers were at a disadvantage *vis-à-vis* employers. Picking on the term "upon all *ordinary* occasions", he asked "Do the *exceptional* occasions help us to understand the theory?"[59] Why isolate the word "ordinary" rather than the word "occasions"? The simplest explanation is, surely, that Adam Smith believed that, at any given time, market rates of wages depended upon the terms of the bargain reached between employers and employed – the "ordinary occasions" being the actual occasions on which a bargain was struck. When the bargaining led to a dispute – and Smith's phrase that "it is not, however, difficult to see which of the two parties must, upon all ordinary occasions, *have the advantage in the dispute*",[60] confirms that Smith tended to slip into considering, in particular, ordinary occasions of disputed bargains – in the institutional circumstances of late 18th century Britain, he believed that the masters were in a stronger bargaining position.[61] Nor did Adam Smith say anything about employers, on such occasions, or in any short-run situation, finding subsistence level a lower limit to their capacity, in a bargaining situation, for forcing wages down.[62] Obviously, any employer could dismiss a man, and in such a case pay no wage at all, which would be considerably below subsistence; and in the case of byemployments, where the continuance of the labour supply could be assured through the existence of other sources of family income, then even the long-run wage, thought Adam Smith, could remain almost indefinitely depressed: "When a person derives his subsistence from one employment which does not occupy the greater part of his time; in the intervals of his leisure he is often willing to work at another for less than would otherwise suit the nature of the employment." Whole industries were, in fact, said to be organized upon this basis.[63]

Though diffuse, Adam Smith's wage theory (or interlocked, rather than competing theories) seems less inconsequent than his critics have alleged. As a result, the threat of the stationary state as a reality of existence, and not merely as a convenient construction of the mind to help in elucidating problems of production and distribution under the three cases or "models" of the progressive, the stationary and the declining state of the economy, loses most of its actuality. Of course, Adam Smith, with his distaste for mere abstractions and his genius for putting forward practical examples, found no difficulty here. North America served as an example of the progressive state, India of the retrogressive state and China of the stationary state. And though in such a classification it may be tempting to think of China, with nothing to disturb the steady maintenance through time of an economy proceeding in a manner that could be represented on a diagram by a horizontal line, as somehow the normal case (and thus "ordinary"); and North America, depicted by one climbing steeply upwards, and India, sliding downwards, as representing temporary deviations from the ordinary, there appears to be no warrant for such an interpretation in the *Wealth of Nations*. If anything, a progressive state – with a curve of European rather than North American slope – would appear to have been regarded in Adam Smith's thought as the norm; North America was looked on as, for the present, exceptionally fortunate; China as stultified by its neglect of opportunities still open; and India as ruined by usury, capital consumption, mismanagement and oppression.[64]

The conclusion, therefore, seems to be that Adam Smith did paint a frightening picture of a stationary state, in which wages would be at a subsistence level and profits also would be at a minimum (leaving no scope for an augmentation of the wage fund) and one in which the population had, therefore, to be kept from outstripping the size for which available resources could furnish subsistence, by such practices as infanticide. But he did not regard this stationary state as, in Cannan's words, ordinary, nor as something about which he was, in Robbins's words, fatalistic.

So much was this the case that, although he found interesting the attempt by Cantillon to set up conditions for determining a poverty datum line at which the labour supply (taking account of life expectancies) might be kept constant, he regarded it as of so little practical importance that he could not be bothered to enter into refinements or recalculations or further discussion of Cantillon's hypotheses.[65] Moreover, it seems appropriate to look at his interesting and questionable arguments concerning corn bounties, in which Smith asserted that: "The nature of things has stamped upon corn a real value which cannot be altered by merely altering its money price. No bounty on exportation, no monopoly of the home market can raise that value. The freest competition cannot lower it." For here he made it quite clear that the subsistence wage (which common humanity ought to prescribe as a minimum) was not the bare physiological subsistence wage to which all labouring humanity must sink if the stationary state became universal, but one based upon current standards and customary expectations, varying as between economies in different stages of growth. "Through the world in general," he had gone on to say, the real price of corn "is equal to the quantity of labour which it can maintain, and in every place is equal to the quantity of labour which it can maintain *in the way, whether liberal, moderate, or scanty, in which labour is commonly maintained in that place*".[66] He designated it as a most exceptional occurrence – for Britain – that: "In 1740, a year of extraordinary scarcity, many people were willing to work for bare subsistence." For this exceptional case he had to go back three and a half decades.[67]

It is rather piquant that, in the issue of the *Economic Journal* immediately preceding that in which Robbins wrote on the stationary state, C.R. Fay contributed an article on "Adam Smith and the dynamic state". And in this he had written: "In wages Adam Smith is a realist. Without being under any illusion about the danger of surplus population, he rejoices in the liberal reward of labour . . . But how did he guard against the objection that people would react to the increase of wealth by breeding up to the limit? His retort is: Look around you. Wages are 'nowhere in this country regulated by the lowest rate which is consistent, with common humanity'. (I. 75) Population will only grow within its customary standards, and in England this standard is accustomed to rise. Not only does he evade thus the Malthusian impasse, but he drives right through the sanctities of the Wage Fund Doctrine . . ." The "workers of industrialism", Fay added, "strive always to broaden the fringe of optional expenditure which lifts existence into civilized life".[68]

When it is realized that Adam Smith's belief (in 1776), in masters generally having the advantage in a wage dispute, is not linked, as Cannan and Hutt wrongly supposed, with a power to drive wages down to subsistence level, but not below it, their inference that, realizing the unreality of the limit, he therefore abandoned his views on labour's disadvantage,[69] becomes untenable. There is no reason to suppose that he abandoned his belief that; in a dispute, labour (in Britain in 1776) stood at a disadvantage, any more than he abandoned his idea that the market price of a commodity was determined by the immediate market forces, when, for "natural prices", he adopted a labour theory of value. However, some more persistent influences than the immediate bargaining situation must determine prices (including the threshold price of a labour supply) in the longer run. In the case of wages, he did not look for the explanation in the labour cost of production of labour power – that he left for some quite distinguished successors – but, with a sensible enough asymmetry, and as Cannan and Robbins in this instance rightly interpreted him, he applied a longer-run supply and demand theory to this aspect. In this, wages depended on an equilibrium of labour supply on the one hand, and the demand for labour on the other hand. The supply was dependent on population which in the long run accommodated itself to labour demands (but not necessarily at bare physiological subsistence); while the demand was mainly dependent upon the state of development of the economy, and the associated *rate* of capital accumulation.[70]

Though net capital accumulation could cease, or even, in the declining state, become negative, these "dull" or "melancholy" states were not regarded as the only eventual prospect to which men could look forward. If the Malthusian trap could be avoided, so could secular stagnation. To begin with, even though profit rates might be pared, capital accumulation and hence the demand for labour might still progress quite rapidly. "A great stock, though with small profits, generally increases faster than a small stock with great profits."[71] Second, in seeking markets, "in countries which are fast advancing to riches, the low rate of profit may, in the price of many commodities, compensate the high wages of labour, and enable those countries to sell as cheap as their less thriving neighbours . . ."[72] Third, where, as a result of low rates of profit, the market rate of interest was so low that it was impracticable to live off interest income unless very rich, "all people of small or middling fortunes would be obliged to superintend themselves the employment of their own stocks. It would be necessary that almost every man should be a man of business, or engage in some sort of trade. The province of Holland seems to be approaching near to this state . . ."[73] Accumulation would not cease, but it would be accumulated out of many small surpluses of active entrepreneurs, not out of the fewer but larger surpluses accruing to rentiers. Growth of real output would be maintained.

Moreover – and it may have been overlooked that Adam Smith, in giving China as an example (as the sole example) of a stationary state, gave China also as an example of a country which voluntarily laid itself open to having to be content with a stationary technology[74] – in discussing "thriving" economies, where the increase of capital used for employing labourers drives up wages, he also held that the same cause tends to increase the productive powers of labour, "and to make a smaller quantity of labour produce a greater quantity of work. The owner of the stock which employs a great number of labourers, necessarily endeavours, for his own advantage, to make such a proper division and distribution of employment, that they may be enabled to produce the greatest quantity of work possible. For the same reason, he endeavours to supply them with the best machinery which either he or they can think of. What takes place among the labourers in a particular workhouse takes place, for the same reason, among those of a great society. The greater their number, the more they naturally divide themselves into different classes and subdivisions of employment. More heads are occupied in inventing the most proper machinery for executing the work of each, and it is, therefore, more likely to be invented . . ."[75] Yet Adam Smith has been said to have been oblivious of the dawn of the Industrial Revolution! "Smith seems not to have been aware of the technology that was emerging in his day."[76]

Magister dilectissime! Dearest Master (as you were juvenis dilectissimus to the never-to-be forgotten Francis Hutcheson, when you went to Glasgow college as a student to sit under him), I know that, when an address grew boring and over-long, you had a habit of nodding a little, overcome by drowsiness. So it is well for me quickly to end my bicentenary tribute of friendship and gratitude for all that you have given me. If confusedly – since I have not your own skill in making a rich and intelligible mosaic design out of scattered pieces of material – I have tried to fit together again, in my own way, some of your interconnected pieces of wisdom, to form what seems to me a truer interpretation of your meaning than sometimes has been afforded by other cleverer but not more assiduous pupils than I. A very early student of yours amongst these cleverer ones, that grand Jean-Baptiste Say, wrote: *"Lorsqu' on lit Smith comme il mérite d'être lu, on s'aperçoit qu'il n'y avait pas avant lui d'économie politique."*[77] If, Master, I have not yet managed to read you as you deserve to be read, may I at least echo what Say wrote of you to another, whom I have learnt, through you, also to number among my friends, Thomas Robert Malthus? *"Je révère Adam Smith: il est mon maître. Lorsque je fis les premiers pas dans l'économie politique . . . je bronchait à chaque pas, il me montra la bonne route. Appuyé sur la* Richesse des Nations, *qui nous découvre en même temps la richesse de son génie, j'appris à marcher seul . . ."*[78]

Notes

My title is taken from the start of David Hume's letter of congratulation (and criticism) of 1st April, 1776, on his first reading of the *Wealth of Nations* (*The letters of David Hume*, ed. J.Y.T. Greig, Oxford, Clarendon Press, 1932, Vol. II, pp. 576-7). I too subscribe to the Bravo! and the Fine! and also to there being points deserving of criticism. But often I believe that Adam Smith is both blamed and praised for assumptions and arguments which were not his. In this tribute, I take up a few – but only a few – such points. Some of the ambiguities of my first draft have been at least partially remedied as a result of close scrutiny by Sean Archer and Peter Wickins.

H.M. Robertson is Emeritus Professor of Economics, University of Cape Town.

1. *Wealth of Nations*, Book V, Ch. I, Pt. III, Article 2nd, especially Vol. II, pp. 290-5. The best edition of the *Wealth of Nations* is that by Edwin Cannan, originally published in London by Methuen in two volumes in 1904. Unfortunately the exact pagination was not retained either in the 2 volumes-in-one Modern Library edition (New York, 1937) or in the reset 2 volume Methuen paperback (and clothbound) version issued from 1961 onwards. On the assumption that most of those copies of the earlier Cannan editions stolen from libraries and from the studies of university teachers are now inactive, and that the current replacements in use are of the more recent, reset edition, page references have been supplied to this latter. But full chapter references have been given as well. Any owner of another edition who finds himself re-reading a few more pages of the *Wealth of Nations* in the course of locating any passage cited, will find that this represents time well spent. Perhaps Smith's latent skill in paradigm construction might also be gauged from his accounts of the "mercantile" and the "agricultural" systems of political economy in Book IV. But these seem to point to the vulnerability of the concept of the "paradigm" in the history of thought. They suited admirably Smith's limited (and largely polemical) purposes in the *Wealth of Nations* but could not pretend to give full and fair synopses of the whole range of mercantilist or physiocratic doctrine.

2. The "paradigm" mode of thought manages to ensure its own apparent justification. When real, living thought has been desiccated (by those who do not actually and still actively partake of it), so that sterile stereotypes have been substituted for lively and fertile actuality; when it has thus been forced into the mould of "old paradigm", the sequence "revolution, new paradigm" becomes inevitable.

3. The reader will observe that this phrase is taken, with only the substitution of the first for the third person, from the concluding sentence of the *Wealth of Nations*, where (not in 1976 but in 1776!) it was offered as advice for the British Empire.

4. I wonder how far the young Buccleuch – who seems at any rate to have retained an affectionate regard for the tutor who supervised him on the Grand Tour, and whose rejection of Adam Smith's offer to forego his pension on his appointment as Commissioner of Customs did as much credit to the Duke as Smith's offer did to him – recognized in later years the full glory of the fact that some part of the excellence of the *Wealth of Nations* was due to Adam Smith's observations in the course of his travels, to his contacts in Paris with the *Économistes*, and, not least, to his perpetual pension, which had formed part of the contract with Buccleuch's step-father, Townshend, and which allowed him more leisure for writing.

I spent a slice of my early childhood in Buccleuch country, in Liddesdale, and never heard of continuing family pride in those days over the connection; but then I do not remember having myself heard of Adam Smith at that age. What I do remember – I imagine from the fringe of grown-up conversation – were grumbles about the Duke's niggardliness over tenancies. I do not know how far they were justified; but I can imagine that some might have resulted from occasional still-operative entails, which might have survived despite legislation designed to stop them. In 1776 Smith estimated that such entails, invented by the Scots lawyers, covered between one-fifth and one-third of the area of Scotland, and obstructed the beneficial extension of long leases (*Wealth of Nations*, Bk. III, Ch. II, Vol. I, pp. 410, 415-6).

I also remember a tale of another five- or six-year-old boy, son of one of the tenantry, who was presented to pay his respects to the Duke in the course of a day's grouse or pheasant shooting. "Are ye a duik (duke)?" asked my contemporary. "Yes." – "Can ye soom (swim)?" – "No." "A' (All) me faither's duiks (ducks) can soom." I never heard that the possessor of this devastating interview technique developed, in later life, into a masterful exponent of the Social Survey. It is more likely that he was unmistakably discouraged by the tawse from developing such a talent as soon as His

Grace was out of hearing. Had Adam Smith had a story like this up his sleeve, I imagine he might have enjoyed telling it in Paris – and certainly to David Hume.

5.   These words might indeed appear presumptuous. But the 115 years between Adam Smith's death and my birth must make it obvious that I am not trying to claim a non-existent connection with the great, in order to exalt my own small importance. Anybody who has been lucky enough to have had, at College, an outstanding tutor, even for the short period for which, in the nature of things, College days can last, will know how, long after distance and even death have parted, the pupil can still feel a warmth of friendship which increases throughout his life. (The pupil must also be fortunate in himself as well as in his tutor, for not all who have had the chance of warming themselves at the same hearth manage to pick up the same vital spark.) I have come to regard Adam Smith as an old tutor and friend; and as binding me in friendship with others – present and past – to whom he has evidently appeared in a similar light.

I feel that I am warranted, in this bicentenary year, in borrowing for Adam Smith two lines from Beatrice's invocation to Virgil (*Inferno*, Canto 2). Smith admired Italian rhymed poetry, which he preferred to English blank verse. The *Divina Commedia*, in an edition of 1757, was in his library. (J. Bonar, *A Catalogue of the Library of Adam Smith*, London, Macmillan, 2 ed. 1932, p. 54); and John Rae mentioned (*Life of Adam Smith*, London, Methuen, 1895, p. 23) that "Smith had read the Italian poets too, and could quote them easily". I surmise that there may be an echo of these very lines in *The Theory of Moral Sentiments* (1759), Part V, Ch. I: "a well-written poem may last as long as the world". (London, Bohn's Standard Library, 1853, p. 283). The passage will hardly bear translation. The version by Charles Singleton (*The Divine Comedy*, Vol. I, Routledge and Kegan Paul, 1971) is spare but elegant: ". . . whose fame still lasts in the world and shall last as long as the world . . ."

6.   Walter Bagehot, Adam Smith and our modern economy (c. 1876), in *Economic Studies*, 3 ed., R.H. Hutton, ed. (London, Longmans, 1895) pp. 125-7.

7.   D.F. Gordon, The role of the history of economic thought in the understanding of modern economic theory, *American Economic Review*, Vol. LV, No. 2, May 1965, pp. 122-5.

8.   *Wealth of Nations*, Bk. III, Ch. IV, Vol. I, p. 436.

9.   *Ibid.*, Bk. I., Ch. VIII, Vol. I., p. 88.

10.   *Ibid.*, Bk. I., Ch. X, Pt. I, Vol. I., p. 131.

11.   *Ibid.*, Bk. I., Ch. X, Pt. I, Vol. I., p. 131; Pt. II, Vol. I, p. 157.

12.   *Ibid.*, Bk. I., Ch. IX, Digression concerning silver . . . Vol. I, p. 209. In an antiquarian collection made in the earlier 19th century by R. Chambers, *The popular rhymes of Scotland, with illustrtions* (Edinburgh, W. Hunter; Chas. Smith, 1826), pp. 140-3, one reads: "It is said that the burgh of Lanark was, till very recent times, so poor, that the single butcher of the town, who also exercised the calling of a weaver, in order to fill up his spare time, would never venture upon the speculation of killing a sheep, till every part of the animal was ordered beforehand. When he felt disposed to engage in such an enterprise, he usually prevailed upon the minister, the provost, and the town-council, to take shares; but when no person came forward to bespeak the fourth quarter, the sheep received a respite . . . The Bellman . . . often used to go through the streets . . . with:

Bell -ell -ell!
There's a fat sheep to kill!
A leg for the provost,
Another for the priest,
The bailies and deacons,
They'll tak the neist;
And if the fourth leg we cannot sell,
The sheep it maun leeve, and gae back to the hill!

. . . Yet (Lanark) is not, or was not, alone in this . . . The ceremony of advertisement is still gone through, at the death of a sheep, in the town of Auchtermuchty . . . and there is scarcely, we believe, a small town in Scotland, where it is not customary to announce, by the bell, the drum, or the *clap*, the joyful intelligence of bovicide. Even in Edinburgh, we remember seeing announced . . . the death (in 1795) of a *cadie*, or market-porter, who was old enough to remember the time when the circumstance of beef being for sale in the market was publicly announced in the streets of the capital!"

13.   *Wealth of Nations*, Bk. I, Ch. XI, Pt. I, Vol. I, p. 166; Bk. I, Ch. XI, Digression concerning

silver, Vol. I, pp. 244-5, 246, 248.

14. *Ibid.*, pp. 245-7.

15. *Ibid.*, pp. 251-2.

16. *Ibid.*, Bk. I, Ch. XI, Pt. I, Vol. I, p. 168.

17. Adam Smith to Lord Shelburne, 4 April, 1759, in W.R. Scott, *Adam Smith as student and professor* (Glasgow, Jackson, 1937, repr. New York, A.M. Kelley, 1965), p. 245.

18. *Wealth of Nations*, Bk. I, Ch. XI, Pt. I, Vol. I, pp. 179-80. Adam Smith had gone on to say that, in contrast, a potato diet appeared to be much more adequate, since "the strongest men and the most beautiful women perhaps in the British dominions" were to be found amongst Irish immigrants to London, reared on potatoes. These remarks show him as an acute observer, although it was not until the 20th century that Sir Frederick Gowland Hopkins, and other biochemists following his lead, were to demonstrate the inferiority of oats, unless supplemented by protective foodstuffs to remedy their deficiencies; and the superior nutritional value of potatoes, with their high vitamin C content. After the Irish potato famine of the 1840s, one is able to appreciate Smith's prescience (or his powers of generalization from observation of contemporary trends) in prognosticating a great increase in population, should potatoes, with a high yield per acre, anywhere become a staple crop; yet in doubting whether they could supplant bread because of the extreme risk which their poor keeping qualities introduced, which should discourage reliance upon them as the sole mainstay of subsistence.

19. *Ibid.*, Bk. I, Ch. VIII, Vol. I, p. 91.

20. *Ibid.*, Bk. II, Ch. II, Vol. I, pp. 314-338; Bk. V, Ch. III, Vol. II, p. 479.

21. *Ibid.*, Bk. I, Ch. IX, Vol. I, p. 101; Bk. I, Ch. XI, Digression concerning silver . . ., Vol. I, p. 211. France, on the other hand, "though no doubt a richer country than Scotland, seems not to be going forward so fast . . ." (p. 102).

22. Francis W. Hirst, *Adam Smith* (English Men of Letters Series, London, Macmillan, 1904), p. 168. Francis Hirst was a sound economist, if somewhat rigid, a staunch free-trader, a distinguished editor, and a prolific and effective public speaker. He had a very practical bent. Whilst taking a breather in my house during a lecture tour of South Africa, he once told me that whenever a member of an audience, at question time, trotted out such phrases as "marginal utility" or "consumers' surplus", he got cold shivers down his spine. The examples he evinced of the "airy-fairy" discourse that troubled him, I suppose helps to date the conversation to relatively unsophisticated days. Nowadays he would have had a different selection of much more esoteric jargon from which to choose. W.H.B. Court, *A concise economic history of Britain* (Cambridge University Press, 1954), p. 118, made the remarkable statement, "Historical understanding is not to be found in the writings of Adam Smith . . ." This remark itself can only be understood, if at all, as an *obiter dictum* on Smith's treatment of the mercantilists in Book IV, which was intended more as a polemic than as history. My own judgement coincides much more closely with C.R. Fay's, that: "every chapter of the *Wealth of Nations* gives evidence of historical insight, and nowhere more than in the price history of Book I (the Digression on Silver) and the historical framework of Book III. Even if Smith and Gibbon had not been personal friends, publishing with the same publishers in the same year, one could not resist a comparison of the two, of Smith the constructive critic of imperial economy, with Gibbon the majestic historian of imperial Rome". C.R. Fay, *Adam Smith and the Scotland of his day*, publications of the Department of Social and Economic Research, University of Glasgow No. 3, Cambridge University Press, 1956, p. 10.

23. I would not even exempt historians of economic analysis, however learned, completely from this criticism. Indeed the very attempt to separate the history of economic analysis, narrowly defined, from a more broadly conceived history of economic thought, predisposes to a selective view of economic writings, particularly noticeable in adjudging and in giving an account of such a far-ranging work as the *Wealth of Nations*. It admits to consideration of only those aspects which appear to lead to rigorous argument (or to fall short of it!) according to some technique of analysis approved by the historian of economic analysis himself. (This might give the appearance that I am implicitly accepting a "paradigm" approach; and am in fact foisting a "paradigm" on the Schumpeterian school, though indicating that I prefer the "paradigms" adopted by economic historians. I do not, however, wish to argue the point here. I am concerned with Adam Smith's thought, not with my own.)

24. *Wealth of Nations*, Bk. III, Ch. II, Vol. I, p. 410.

25. *Ibid.*, Bk. I, Ch. XI, Conclusion of the chapter, Vol. I, pp. 276-7.

26. *Ibid.*, Bk. I, Ch. X, Pt. I, Vol. I, pp. 120-3.

240 *Smith's* Wealth of Nations

27. Cf. F.A. Hayek, Individualism, true and false; Economics and knowledge; The use of knowledge in society, in *Individualism and Economic Order* (London, Routledge, 1949), especially pp. 11-19, 50-51, 77-91.

28. Thomas Hobbes, *The Leviathan*, Ch. 8 (Reprint of 1651 edition, introduction by W.G. Pogson Smith, Oxford, Clarendon Press, 1909), p. 56.

29. *Ibid.*, Ch. 24, p. 192.

30. Wesley C. Mitchell, *Types of Economic Theory*, ed. J. Dorfman (New York, A.M. Kelley, 1967), Vol. I, p. 51. This does not mean that all mercantilists believed everywhere in direct state action. Their thought had increasingly developed in the direction of a more "liberal" recommendation of harnessing the self-interested actions of individuals towards state-determined ends, by dangling the carrot rather than by compelling with the stick. Cf. the suspicion with which a "paradigm" of "mercantilism" is viewed in note 1 above.

31. *Wealth of Nations*, Bk. IV, Ch. II, vol. I, p. 478.

32. *Ibid.*, Bk. IV, Ch. I, Vol. I, pp. 455-6.

33. *Ibid.*, Bk. IV, Ch. II, Vol. I, pp. 480-4. Moreover, in thus acting in imitation of the merchants and manufacturers, "they did not act with that complete comprehension of their own interest which commonly directs the conduct of those two other orders of people". (Bk. IV, Ch. V, Vol. II, p. 22).

34. *Ibid.*, Bk. IV, Ch. VIII, Vol. II, pp. 160-1. It was because merchants and manufacturers had proved so successful in getting their advice accepted, when (even in those cases in which it was given with the greatest candour) it was nevertheless founded on their intimate knowledge of what was best for themselves, that "the proposal of any new law or regulation of commerce which comes from this order, ought always to be listened to with great precaution . . . It comes from an order of men whose interest is never exactly the same with that of the public, who have generally an interest to deceive and even oppress the public, and who accordingly have, upon many occasions, both deceived and oppressed it." (Bk. I, Ch. XI, Conclusion, Vol. I, p. 278.)

35. *Ibid.*, Bk. I, Ch. IX, Vol. I. p. 110.

36. *Ibid.*, Bk. IV, Ch. VII, Pt. III, vol. II, pp. 127-9.

37. *Ibid.*, Bk. IV, Ch. III, Pt. II, Vol. I. p. 519.

38. *Ibid.*, Bk. I, Ch. X. Pt. II, Vol. I, p. 144.

39. *Ibid.*, Bk. I, Ch. XI, Pt. I, Vol. I, p. 165.

40. Quoted from Skarzynski, *Adam Smith als Moralphilosoph*, 1878, in W.R. Scott, "Adam Smith", *Proceedings of the British Academy*, Vol. X (1921-23), pp. 442-3; Francis W. Hirst, *op cit*, pp. 181-2.

41. *Theory of Moral Sentiments*, Pt. II, Sect. II, Ch. II, pp. 119-20 in edition cited.

42. *Ibid.*, Pt. II, Sect. II, Ch. III, pp. 124-5. Indeed, in Pt. VII, Sect. II, Ch. III, pp. 445-6, Smith criticized his own revered teacher, Francis Hutcheson, for unwillingness to recognize that "Regard for our own private happiness and interest, too, appear upon many occasions very laudable principles of action. The habits of economy, industry, discretion and application of thought, are generally supposed to be cultivated from self-interested motives, and at the same time are apprehended to be very praiseworthy qualities, which deserve the esteem and approbation of everybody . . ." However, the lack of such praiseworthy qualities was unlikely to be much noticed. "We are not ready to suspect any person of being defective in selfishness. This is by no means the weak side of human nature . . ."

43. *Wealth of Nations*, Bk. I, Ch. II, Vol. I, p. 18. For some further remarks on this issue, cf. H.M. Robertson, *The Adam Smith Tradition: Inaugural Lecture* (Cape Town, Oxford University Press, 1950), pp. 12-14, 17-18.

44. Francis A. Walker, *Political Economy*, (New York, Holt; London, Macmillan, 3 ed. 1892) pp. 2-3. He enlarged this by saying that "So far from ministering to greed . . . the study of Political Economy has tended . . . to banish a ravening, ferocious greed which seeks to snatch its objects of desire . . . at whatever cost of misery to others, to replace this by an enlightened sense of self-interest, which seeks its objects through exchanges mutually beneficial, and which supports social order and international peace as the conditions of general well-being. Political Economy does not plant the love of wealth in human minds. It finds it there, a strong native passion, which, but for enlightened views, is likely to break out into private rapine and public war . . ." In *The Wages Question* (London, Macmillan, n.d. (1879)) Walker several times (e.g. pp. 58-60, 164, 386) pointed to both avarice and unawareness as being antagonistic to true self-interest. I remember, when much younger, going through both these once well-known books, dismissing one passage as

obvious, another as rather inept, yet another as fallacious . . . and the general tone as too obtrusively sermonizing. Nowadays, when I re-read them, I appreciate how Marshall came to stress their importance; and, indeed, with undue modesty, to suggest that his own chapters on the earnings of labour, in the *Principles*, consisted merely in following the leads which Walker had given.

45.   *Wealth of Nations*, Bk. IV, Ch. II, Vol. I, pp. 475-8; *Theory of Moral Sentiments*, Pt. IV, Ch. I, pp. 263-5. Much of the argument of this passage of the *Theory of Moral Sentiments* finds expression, in somewhat different form, in the *Wealth of Nations*, Bk. I. Ch. XI, Pt. II, Vol. I, pp. 182-3.

46.   F.W. Hirst, *op. cit.*, p. 182.

47.   *Theory of Moral Sentiments*, Pt. IV, Ch. I, p. 265.

48.   Lionel Robbins, *The Theory of Economic Policy in English Classical Political Economy* (London, Macmillan, 1952), pp. 26-28. Cf. *ibid.*, pp. 73-5.

49.   *Theory of Moral Sentiments*, Pt. IV, Ch. I, pp. 263-4.

50.   *Wealth of Nations*, Bk. I, Ch. VIII, Vol. I, p. 89. Edwin Cannan, *A History of the Theories of Production and Distribution, 1776-1848* (London, P.S. King, 1893, 3 ed., reprinted, 1924), p. 127, sardonically noted regarding this passage that "Adam Smith, who as an observer of the facts of everyday life was seldom at fault, believed the chief 'check' to be infant mortality caused by poverty".

51.   *Ibid.*,Bk. I, Ch. VIII, Vol. I. pp. 89-90.

52.   *Ibid.*, Introduction and plan of the work and Book I, Ch. I. Phrases quoted are in Vol. I. pp. 2, 7, 15.

53.   I would almost have written "no suggestion" rather than "little suggestion" but for the cryptic remark to which C.R. Fay drew attention (Adam Smith and the dynamic state, *Economic Journal*, Vol. XL, No. 157, March, 1930, p. 26): "It is now more than two hundred years since the beginning of the reign of Elizabeth, a period as long as the course of human prosperity usually endures." (Bk. III, Ch. IV, Vol. I, p. 443). But the context of this remark makes it clear that he viewed Englands's economic development as far from any danger of running down.

54.   *Economic Journal*, Vol. XL, No. 158, June, 1930, pp. 196-9. Economists' Greek had not yet substituted "monopsony" for "buyer's monopoly". In a review of Robbins's *Theory of Economic Policy*, (*S. Afr. J. Econ.*, Vol. 21, No. 3, September, 1953, pp. 263-4), I criticized this and one or two other aspects. I received a demurrer in which Robbins's position was clearly and succinctly put: "For the rest, I feel that there is substance in what you say about my treatment of the relation between the *Wealth of Nations* and the *Theory of Moral Sentiments*, which is a problem that, in spite of Smith and Dugald Stewart, I have always found very perplexing. My withers are not quite so wrung about the reference to Smith's passage on China. Perhaps fatalistic is a wrong word to use about the Smithian theory. But, surely, the main contrast with the Ricardians is correct; namely that whereas Smith thought that, while wages might be kept over subsistence level for a very long time while capital was increasing, in the end they must come down to something like physiological subsistence level, the Ricardians, following the second edition of Malthus, thought that the equilibrium level of wages in the stationary state could be very much above that level if only the rate of multiplication were sufficiently controlled. Or have you found some passage in Adam Smith which suggests that he had perceived more cheerful possibilities for the eventual stationary state?" (Private letter, 2 December, 1953). My brief answer would be that I doubt whether Adam Smith envisaged the inevitable coming of a stationary state at all. Much of the immediately preceding paragraphs and most of those following here are based upon my own reply to Robbins. (Private letter, 7 January, 1954).

55.   *Wealth of Nations*, editor's preface, Vol. I, p. vii; *Lectures of Adam Smith*, reported by a student in 1763 and edited with an introduction and notes by Edwin Cannan (Oxford, Clarendon Press, 1896). One might also adduce, *inter alia*, such fine appreciations as Cannan's lectures in honour of the 200th anniversary of Smith's birthday in 1923 and the 150th anniversary of the *Wealth of Nations* in 1926, reprinted in E. Cannan, *An Economist's Protest* (London, P.S. King, 1927), pp. 335-340, 417-430.

56.   E. Cannan, *History of the Theories of Production and Distribution*, pp. 234-237. To assist in the argument certain words, not italicized by Cannan, have been italicized here.

57.   *Wealth of Nations*, Bk. II, Ch. III, Vol. I, p. 364 (italics added).

58.   *Ibid.*, Bk. I. Ch. IX, Vol. I, pp. 106-7 (italics added).

59.   W.H. Hutt, *Theory of Collective Bargaining*, (London, P.S. King, 1930) 1st edition, pp.

22-4. (The italics are Professor Hutt's).

60.   *Wealth of Nations*, Bk. I, Ch. VIII, Vol. I, p. 74 (italics added).

61.   This is a question of fact, not of economic theory. Hutt doubts whether combinations of employers to agree on maximum wages were common, or, where they occurred, efficacious. Adam Smith, however, (Bk. I, Ch. X, Pt. II, Vol. I, p. 159) wrote explicitly and circumstantially: "When masters combine together in order to reduce the wages of their workmen, they commonly enter into a private bond or agreement, not to give more than a certain wage under a certain penalty. Were the workmen to enter into a contrary combination of the same kind, not to accept a certain wage under a certain penalty, the law would punish them very severely . . ." In Book I, Ch. VIII, Vol. I, p. 75, he wrote: "We rarely hear, it has been said, of the combinations of masters, though frequently of those of workmen. But whoever imagines, upon this account, that masters rarely combine, is as ignorant of the world as of the subject . . . These are always conducted with the utmost silence and secrecy, till the moment of execution, and when the workmen yield, as they sometimes do, without resistance, though severely felt by them, they are never heard of by other people." If Smith was right about all this, a lack of evidence extant today may be inadequate to prove that such combinations did not quite commonly exist in Adam Smith's days, as Smith evidently believed.

If, then, such agreements on the part of employers were "commonly entered into", yet severely punished in the case of workmen, *when it came to a dispute*, the masters would upon *ordinary occasions* have had a bargaining advantage. But in cases which did not lead to a dispute, there would have been little clear-cut evidence whether the absence of dispute was due to a scarcity of hands, which could "sometimes give the labourers an advantage" (*Wealth of Nations*, I, p. 77), or an overwhelming advantage on the part of the confederated employers.

62.   Hutt, *op. cit.*, p. 23: "First, there existed particular combinations of masters who agreed to force down wages *to subsistence level* . . . The emptiness of the theory becomes clear when we consider the limits he assigned to the employers' power in this respect." But in this connection, Smith did not set a lower limit. What he did say was "to sink the wages of labour even below this rate", i.e. below the "actual rate" or existing market rate reached by competitive bargaining. However, he reckoned that the workmen, possessing smaller reserves and therefore anxious to come to terms quickly, were already likely to be weak bargainers (Bk. I, Ch. VIII, Vol. I, pp. 74-75). Smith drew an explicit distinction between the *market* rate which might be set by a disputed wage bargain, and the subsistence level as a minimum possible *long-run* wage rate, viz.: "But though *in disputes with their workmen* masters generally have the advantage, there is, however, a certain rate below which it seems impossible to reduce, *for any considerable time*, the ordinary wages even of the lowest species of labour. A man must always live by his work'. . ." (Vol. I, p. 76). Cannan summarized this merely as: "However, the masters cannot force wages down below a certain point: 'A man must always live by his work'. . ." (*op. cit.*, p. 235). This does not seem an adequate paraphrase (italics added).

63.   *Wealth of Nations*, Bk. I, Ch. X, Pt. I, Vol. I, pp. 130-1.

64.   *Ibid.*, Bk. I, Ch. VIII, Ch. IX, Vol. I, pp. 78-82, 101-107.

65.   *Ibid.*, Bk. I, Ch. VIII, Vol. i, pp. 76-7. As regards "what is precisely necessary . . .", wrote Adam Smith, "I shall not take it upon me to determine."

66.   *Ibid.*, Bk. IV, Ch. V, Vol. II, p. 21 (italics added).

67.   *Ibid.*, Bk. I, Ch. VIII, Vol. I, p. 96.

68.   *Economic Journal*, Vol. XL, No. 157, March, 1930, pp. 30-31. In the 1961 and later re-issues of the *Wealth of Nations* Fay's reference would be to Bk. I, p. 83.

69.   W.H. Hutt, *op. cit.*, p. 24-5, put it that "Adam Smith himself seems to have unconsciously given up the idea". In a more recent publication, *The strike-threat system* (New Rochelle, N.Y., Arlington House, 1973), pp. 61-2, Hutt wrote that "Since I treated the subject in 1930, my interpretation of Adam Smith's famous passage about 'labor's disadvantage' has changed slightly." He seems to indicate that his interpretation has now come closer to mine. I have not yet managed to confirm how much closer. A second edition of his *Collective Bargaining* has just been published in London by the Institute of Economic Affairs, but unfortunately I have not yet managed to procure a copy. (I can subsequently report that the new edition, entitled *The theory of collective bargaining 1930-1975*, (Hobart Paperback No. 8), London, Institute of economic Affairs, 1975, reprints the first edition verbatim, but adds a long new section "45 years after: who exploits whom?", which does not bear on the matter. Pages 22-24 of the first edition, which are considered here, form pp. 17-18 of the second enlarged edition.)

Cannan's scoffing about the "irrelevant fact" that wages equal to minimum subsistence needs are the lowest "consistent with common humanity" (p. 235) also loses force because, if the wage bargain was not equal but favoured the masters, the impartial spectator in the employers' breasts, making them ashamed of offering wages which implied only starvation (rather than considerations of long-run policy in not letting the race of such workmen die out), might have helped to set a lower limit to the harshness of their bargain. In dealing with individuals they might indeed have preferred not to offer a job at all rather than offer one at starvation wages – and no wages at all is indeed below subsistence. However, though this might have made the situation still worse for the unfortunates who were laid off, it would not have appeared to be the employer's responsibility in the same way. It is not irrelevant to the determination of the lowest levels of wages paid in South Africa at present, that independent calculations of the effective minimum family subsistence income are regularly re-calculated at intervals for the main centres of employment, and are circulated amongst their members by employers' associations. Nor is it irrelevant that separate calculations are made for Coloured and African families, and that these do not coincide for all, at exactly the same level of basic needs.

70. At a level of analysis beyond the rule-of-thumb which allows for asymmetries if they are sensible enough, even a "longer-run" supply and demand theory (the term "long-run" is deliberately avoided) might appear a contradiction in terms or, at the least, circular. When one takes account, however, of Smith's dynamic view of the demand for labour and of the associated changes in labour supply, in which it is not the "size" of the wage-fund or of the population at any given time, but the rate and the direction of change of capital accummulation in relation to the rate and direction of change in the labour force (i.e. of those who live by wages) that determines the real remuneration of labour, it seems legitimate to regard this as a longer-run view. The adjustment of real wages which Smith appears to have been considering, in one sense was strictly operative only over a period of historical time and in another sense it was timeless – though never coming to finality save in the chance of equilibrium of a far from inevitable stationary state.

71. *Wealth of Nations*, Bk. I, Ch. IX, Vol. I, p. 104.

72. *Ibid.*, p. 109.

73. *Ibid.*, p. 108.

74. *Ibid.*, Book IV, Ch. IX, Vol. II, pp. 201-2: "The Chinese have little respect for foreign trade . . . A more extensive foreign trade, however . . . could scarce fail to increase very much the manufacturers of China, and to improve very much the productive powers of its manufacturing industry. By a more extensive navigation, the Chinese would naturally learn the art of using and constructing themselves all the different machines made use of in other countries, as well as other improvements of art and industry which are practised in all the different parts of the world. Upon their present plan they have little opportunity of improving themselves by the example of any other nation; except that of the Japanese."

75. *Ibid.*, Bk. I, Ch. VIII, Vol. I, pp. 96-7.

76. W.D. Grampp, On the history of economic thought and policy, *American Economic Review*, Vol. 55, Pt. 2, May 1965, p. 130.

77. J.-B. Say, *Traité d'économie politique* (1803) (6 ed., ed. Horace Say, Paris, Guillaumin, 1841), p. 29. ("When one reads Smith as he deserves to be read, one perceives that before him there was no political economy.")

78. J.-B. Say, Correspondence avec M. Malthus (1820), in *Oeuvres diverses de J.-B. Say*, ed. C. Comte, E. Daire and Horace Say, (Paris, Guillaumin, 1848), p. 455. ("I revere Adam Smith: he is my master. When I took my first steps in political economy . . . I stumbled at every step; he showed me the right way. Supported by the *Wealth of Nations*, which at the same time makes us aware of the richness of his genius, I learned to walk on my own . . ."). On his visit to Britain in 1815, after the end of the Napoleonic wars, Say, while in Adam Smith's chair in the University. John Rae's account in his *Life of Adam Smith*, p. 61, of the reverence with which he took advantage of the invitation, confirms what he wrote in the letters to Malthus. Say afterwards described the episode "not without emotion" to the students of the *Conservatoire des Arts et Métiers*, where he was appointed Professor of Industrial Economy in 1820. (*Oeuvres diverses*, p. xi).

74

The Wealth of Nations – The Vision and the Conceptualization

K.R. Ranadive

Source: *Indian Economic Journal*, Vol. 24 (3), January-March, 1977, pp. 295-332.

> The failure of the social sciences to think through and to integrate their several responsibilities for the common problem of relating the analysis of parts to the analysis of the whole constitutes one of the major lags crippling their utility as human tools of knowledge.
>
> — R.S. Lynd, *Knowledge for What?*, 1939, p. 15.

Adam Smith's place in the intellectual heritage of the present-day economists is unquestionable. Smith's 'invisible hand', mentioned only once and almost in passing in the *Wealth of Nations*, has held successive generations of economists in firm grip. His picture of the apparent chaos of competition transmuted into an orderly system of economic cooperation by means of which the community's needs are met and its wealth increased has provided the 'basic' model for the later economists to *analyse*.[1] The bicentennial of the *Wealth of Nations* should be an occasion not only to pay homage to its author but to be introspective. Such introspection is particularly necessary because by sheer accident the bicentennial has happened to fall during a period when economic theory has entered into the phase of a 'second crisis'.[2] The 'state of the art' is being questioned in the highest quarters of our profession. Yet the current state of our discipline cannot be understood without linking it with the genesis and the evolution of our subject. By examining afresh Smith's own approach to the problem he posed for the later economists to *analyse*, we may understand better the current malaise. The present paper is an attempt in that direction.

Current Disquiet about the 'State of the Art'

The present happens to be a period when many leading members in the profession have expressed serious disquiet about the state of the subject.[3] Doubts on the part of economists about their own activities have, of course, persisted in arising from the earliest period. Economists' self-assessment of their role as scientists varies depending on whether the economy seems to be performing 'well' or is experiencing rough weather. Yet the fact that the phases

244

of optimism and pessimism have shown a distinct trend, with the latter phase becoming more frequent, persistent and pronounced, would seem to suggest that the 'crisis' in economic theory is deepening.

Implicit in the current disquiet about the state of our discipline is the acceptance of economics as a 'policy science'. Economic thought has been influenced by the economic issues of the day, and in the development of economics as a *positive* discipline, need for policy has played a significant role. In the writings of the classical economists, description and analysis of facts were not sharply distinguished from policy prescription; the latter-day economists have been more wary. Yet the latter are as much concerned with the real world, whether or not all of them 'prescribe for the real world'. Most economists would claim that their purpose in seeking to understand economic phenomena is to contribute, if not directly, to solutions of practical problems. Those who do not claim this and are satisfied with their self-chosen field of 'theory' are also not found emulating G.H. Hardy who once attempted to justify pure mathematics by explicitly proclaiming its 'uselessness'.

The concern of the economists who have expressed themselves on the current state of the subject, except for Kaldor, is with 'the evident bankruptcy of economic theory which has nothing to say on the questions that to everyone, except economists, appear to be most in need of an answer.'[4] The problems referred to are: co-existence of unemployment and inflation, poverty in affluent countries, problems of poor countries, environmental problems, quality of life etc.[5] The dissatisfaction is all the greater because of the gap between 'the increasing power of economists to elaborate trains of subtle and rigorous reasoning and build complex models' and 'the slow advance of their power to *diagnose and prescribe* for the problems of the day'.[6]

Kaldor, on the other hand, is not concerned with success or otherwise of economics in 'prescribing' for the problems of the day. He sets for economics as a *science* a more 'modest' task in keeping with the concept of economics as a positive science. Using the term 'science' in the sense of 'a body of theorems based on assumptions that are *empirically* (emphasis in the original) derived (from observations), and which embody hypotheses that are capable of verification both in regard to the *assumptions* and the *predictions*' (emphasis added), Kaldor argues that 'equilibrium economics' is 'barren and irrelevant'. It cannot explain how economic forces operate – except in a purely logical sense – and therefore cannot serve as a basis for 'predicting' the likely consequences of economic changes, whether induced by exogenous factors or policy variables.

Yet, unlike natural scientists, economists are not induced by 'crisis' or recurring disquiet to go back to the 'sources of knowledge' in their field. The current phase of pessimism is no exception. The reason suggested for the imbalance between 'formidable progress in techniques' and 'the performance of economics' is 'the weak and all too slowly growing *empirical* foundation which cannot support the proliferating superstructure of *pure* or. . .*speculative* economic theory.'[7] Differences, of course, are there but the main thrust of the argument is on the need 'to widen the *empirical* foundations of economic analysis' (emphasis added).

Joan Robinson attributes the 'bankruptcy of economic theory' to tackle the questions which 'appear to be most in need of an answer' to the dominance of the notions of equilibrium and of the rationality of a market economy. Her disquiet is all the greater because the lessons of the Keynesian revolution on the plane of theory have been forgotten. The traditional dichotomy between 'real' and 'monetary' theory, which Keynes sought to break down, has reappeared in the form of micro and macro theory. Keynes' success in '[breaking] out of the cocoon of equilibrium' and in considering 'the nature of life lived in time' has proved short-lived and equilibrium is once again back in the saddle.

Kaldor questions 'equilibrium economics' *even as a conceptual framework* for 'explaining' the behaviour of decentralized economic system because some of its assumptions are unverifiable (e.g. 'maximizing' postulate), others are contrafactual (e.g. perfect competition, linear and homogeneous production function, perfect foresight) and some of the concepts are not *operationally* defined (e.g. commodities, processes of production). He attributes the present none-too-happy state of economics to the concentration on the *allocative* functions of market to the exclusion of their *creative* functions – to the fact that the theory of value holds the centre of the stage.

Both Joan Robinson and Kaldor would seem to be seeking to substitute equilibrium by 'history' but there is a difference. Joan Robinson sees the 'crisis' in the difficulty of reconciling Walras with Keynes – the failure to integrate micro with macro theory which even those who espouse 'equilibrium economics' regard as 'one of the major scandals of current price theory'.[8] Kaldor, integrating Smith-Young doctrine of increasing returns with the Keynesian doctrine of effective demand, finds that the distinction between resource allocation and resource creation has no validity except for short-run problems.

Those who regard the achievements of equilibrium economics as 'both impressive and in many ways beautiful' would seem to be schizophrenic.[9] For instance, Hahn admits that 'it cannot be denied that there is something scandalous in the spectacle of so many people refining the analyses of economic states which they give no reason to suppose will ever, or have ever, come about.' Yet he maintains that equilibrium is so 'singularly well suited to study' and its study has produced '*technically* best work'.[10] While rightly emphasizing that 'equilibrium economics' is 'not engaged in description [of a real world economy] at all', he maintains that '[it] is of great practical significance simply because it is of the greatest relevance to *action* in the present state of economic debate,' and can serve as 'a starting point from which it is possible to advance towards a descriptive theory.'[11]

Neo-Classical Economics and Adam Smith

The price-theoretical theorems of equilibrium economics constitute one of the important components of the 'formidable progress in techniques' referred to earlier. 'The prestigious status of the purest of pure economic theory' is in no small degree due to these theorems. Logical theory of rational choice from which these theorems have been derived would seem to have fulfilled Jevons' ambition to reform economics on the lines of natural science.[12] Yet equilibrium economists do not claim Jevons as their souce of inspiration but Adam Smith! They claim to be 'making precise an economic tradition which is two hundred years old and deeply ingrained in the thinking of many'.[13] Adam Smith's hypothesis of 'invisible hand' is *interpreted* as implying that 'a decentralized economy motivated by self-interest' leads to coherence and not chaos, coherence being taken to imply 'disposition of economic resources that could be regarded, in a well-defined sense, as superior to a large class of possible alternative dispositions.'[14] The purpose is not so much to *verify* the hypothesis as to make it precise.[15] The equilibrium economics, therefore, seeks to work out the 'basic assumptions' necessary for the existence of equilibrium set of prices that is unique, stable and meets the conditions of Pareto optimality – a situation where it is not possible to make any one better off without making someone else worse off through any reallocation.

This interpretation put on Adam Smith's hypothesis of 'invisible hand' would seem to make him a precursor of Walras on positive side and Pareto on normative. Smith, in fact, is hailed as a 'creator of general equilibrium theory'.[16] It is undeniable that in the *Wealth of Nations* Smith provided a pioneering description of the mechanism by which a society of 'perfect liberty' maintains internal cohesion and stability. Yet neither the concept of equilibrium,[17] nor the concept of autonomous 'maximizing' individuals with given resources, tastes and technology implicit in the General Equilibrium system including Pareto-optimum, is to be found in Adam Smith's work. It is the purpose of the following sections to argue that the interpretation put on Adam Smith's work by the latter-day economists in terms of their own epistemological preconceptions has failed to capture both his Vision and his conceptualization of economic problems.

'Ideological' Element in Scientific Knowledge

Empirical facts constitute the basis of all scientific knowledge and theories are mental constructs imposed on these empirical facts. Yet the choice of a particular field of investigation, the choice of a given range of concepts for investigating that field, the way in which observations are organized depend on the scientists' 'presuppositions' and are subjective in that sense. The *subjective* factor in this sense enters even in the study of natural sciences and is related to the socio-historically conditioned environment in which man operates.

This socio-historical interpretation of ideological element in the development of scientific knowledge must be distinguished from Schumpeter's concept of Vision. According to Schumpeter

> 'every comprehensive "theory" of an economic state of society consists of two complementary but *essentially* distinct elements . . . the theorist's view about the basic features of that state of society, about what is and what is not important in order to understand its life at a given time [which is his vision] and the theorist's technique, an apparatus by which he conceptualizes his vision'.[18]

Schumpeter's concept of 'Vision' which 'enters on the very ground floor, into the *pre-analytic* cognitive act', is 'ideological almost by definition [since] it embodies the picture of things as we see them' and according to Schumpeter 'the way in which we see things can hardly be distinguished from the way in which we wish to see them'.[19] Schumpeter would thus seem to be stressing the hopes and aspirations of the observer rather than his socio-historically conditioned perspective. This also leads him to draw what would seem to be a spurious distinction between 'Political Economy' and 'Economic Thought' as ideologically conditioned and 'economic analysis' proper as independent and objective.[20]

In the development of a new field, social needs and values play a major role in determining the problems on which the early practitioners concentrate. The concepts and methods they use in solving problems are, on the one hand, influenced by the specific features of the period and, on the other – and to a large extent –, conditioned by the prevailing philosophical tradition and also by the most prestigious contemporary science. The choice of a particular field of investigation, conceptualization of the problem and the technique of analysis are therefore *inter-related*. They reflect the scientists' 'Vision' interpreted not in the Schumpeterian sense but in the sense of the 'world view' which is socio-historically conditioned.

The recognition of the 'ideological' element in economic thought should make it easy to understand the reason why the interpretation of the doctrines of the earlier writers has been beset with pitfalls. There are certainly areas like policy-making in which using other man's framework can prove dangerous. Unless, however, the doctrines of the earlier writers are judged in the context of their own framework and in the light of the questions they were interested in, there is a risk of misinterpreting them. In the case of Adam Smith, the risk is all the more. The *Wealth of Nations* marked the '*dawn* of a science' in economics. That 'much of what [Smith] presented [should seem] imperfect' and more it 'loosely articulated' is hardly surprising, because 'a body of principles grows like a living body'. A present-day economist is bound to feel impatient with what Smith offered as 'laws' which were often 'unverified' theories. 'Limpid style, picturesque details. . . emotional warmth' cannot also make up for logical inconsistencies, even though there is a lot to be learnt even from the errors of an able thinker. In fact the passages which would receive a high rating by the literary standards of the eighteenth century are not likely to find favour with the present-day reader more at home with writings replete with axioms, theorems and lemmas. Besides Smith was more than an economist. That the *Wealth of Nations* contains diverse topics – aspects of medieval life and civilization, economic development of Europe since the fall of the Roman Empire, evolution of temporal power of the church – reflects more than Smith's own penchant for facts and historical perspective. The *Wealth of Nations* belongs to an age when intellectual division of labour was limited.

Historical Context of the Wealth of Nations

The central theme that inspires the *Wealth of Nations* is the accumulation of capital. Smith's reliance on free competition to ensure 'optimum' allocation of resources *within* and *between* industries was prompted by his belief that such a system would ensure extension of division of labour by widening the scope of the market. He attached great importance to division of labour because of its *dynamic* effect in promoting accumulation of capital. It is not so much that he was 'the spokesman of manufacturing interest' – in the ordinary sense of the word 'spokesman' – as the 'prophet of industrial revolution'. To counter this by citing either his harsh denunciation of the manufacturing interests – 'the mean rapacity, the monopolizing spirit of merchants and manufacturers who neither are, nor ought to be the rulers of mankind' – or his failure even to mention the inventions which were revolutionizing textile and coal industry[21] is to fail to realize that the historical concept of the *Wealth of Nations* was far too complex to be implied by a particular phrase or by the mention of a particular fact.

The *Wealth of Nations* belongs to the period of transition. With the sharpening of the conflict of interests as the upcoming bourgeoisie sought freedom form the feudal institutions and 'mercantilist' policies which were constraining the growth of productive forces, the old order was breaking up. The new order based on fully developed capitalist relations was yet to take shape. Capital accumulation and technical progress were still confined predominantly to agriculture. Even here wages, profit and rent were still not clear-cut categories of income because functional differentiation was still imperfect. In the field of industry, capitalists who were benefiting from the gradual concentration of the means of production were not industrialists but merchants for whom industry was only a form of trade. 'Manufacture', as Marx called the early forms of industrial organisation, was still an exception. The basic social pattern of landlords, labourers and capitalists which figures in the *Wealth of Nations* was developing in some of the commercial and industrial centres like Glasgow, but for the country as a whole, it was certainly not typical.[22] Smith, of course, was not the only economist to become aware of '*profit on capital* as a general category of class income which accrued to all who used "stock" in the employment of wage-labour, and which was qualitatively distinct both from the rent of land, and from the wages of labour.'[23] He deserves, however, credit for having appreciated its enormous significance much more than any of his contemporaries and discerned the *potential* for the release of productive forces held in the new socio-economic relations which were then developing.

Role of the Markets in the Wealth of Nations

In characterising Adam Smith as a 'creator of general equilibrium system', reference is made to his discussion of the equalization of rates of return as enforced by the tendency of resources to move from less to more remunerative uses. This is taken to imply that the markets play a role in Smith's analysis analogous to that in equilibrium economics. This contrasts rather sharply with Allyn Young's emphasis on the *creative* function of markets in Smith's analysis implied by the central role of the principle of division of labour in his work.[24]

It is not that markets do not play *allocative* function but this function of the market is complementary to and dominated by their basic *creative* function and the nature of the 'allocative' problem is also *different*. The role of competitive markets is not that of improving the allocative efficiency to satisfy *given* wants within a *given* productive framework but that of increasing the physical productivity of labour and the total volume of economic activity. The physical output approach of the labour theory made the *proportion* in which labour is used in 'productive' purposes crucial, the allocation between the two being supposed to be determined by the requirements of increasing the volume of physical output of commodities with '*value-in-use*'. The *creative* function of the markets, on the other hand, is to be seen in the fact that the impulse to change is transmitted through interdependence between markets. The fact that the very process of allocation provides impetus to economic change makes change endogenous to the system. The fact that change is 'progressive and propagates itself in a cumulative way' also makes the notion of 'equilibrium of costs and advantages' irrelevant, as Allyn Young's elaboration of Adam Smith's proposition about division of labour in terms of increasing returns clearly brings out. The recognition of the interdependence between resource allocation and resource creation does not, however, require that the theory of value should be displaced from the centre of the stage, as Kaldor's criticism of equilibrium economics would seem to suggest. The interdependence between markets explains only the mechanism through which the change propagates. The role of prices in relation to the interdependence between resource allocation and resource creation can be seen in proper perspective only by looking at Smith's characterization of the 'changeless'.

Vision and Conceptualization

While Adam Smith grasped the prospects of complex relations of trade and industry of a developed economy, the 'early and rude state of society', which he took as the starting point of his analysis, was suggested by a primitive community of self-employed peasants, largely self-sufficient and requiring only a rudimentary system of exchange. The importance which Smith attached to the size of the annual produce of labour is to be attributed to his concentration on the essential nature of economic life – *physical* process in which commodities are annually produced and consumed. Not only was production treated as consisting of transformation of natural resources into *physical* products but satisfaction was also thought of primarily in terms of physical properties of commodities or their 'value-in-use'.

The central role which capital accumulation plays in Smith's analysis is to be attributed to its implications for the two major determinants of the size of the annual produce which Smith emphasized *viz.*, (i) 'the skill, dexterity, and *judgement* with which . . . labour is generally applied' and (ii) 'the proportion between the number of those who are employed in *useful* labour, and that of those who are not so employed.'[25] While the former was linked to the possibilities of increasing productivity through division of labour, the latter was linked to the possibility of increasing the supply of labour by increasing the 'productive' use of labour. 'Productive' use of labour basically meant use of labour for investment in circulating capital or 'advances to labour'. Thus the crucial factor is the proportion of labour used for the production of basic necessities, because it increases both the total volume of economic activity and also the physical productivity of labour. The very process of production increases the production potential, the larger the proportion of labour used for 'productive' purposes. While analysing the mechanism of exchange Smith recognises that in additiopn to increase in physical productivity, exchange makes possible a further gain:

'It gives a value of their superfluities, by exchanging them for something else, which may satisfy a part of their wants, and increase their enjoyments.'[26]

Yet this argument is neither fully developed nor integrated into the main analysis. In fact by emphasizing conditions of production, Smith definitely shifted the focus away from exchange relations which had held the centre of the stage under the 'mercantilist' influence.

It is possible to explain the physical output approach in terms of economic conditions prevailing at the time when Smith wrote. On the one hand, wage goods consisted of a few basic necessities which could be lumped together into a single commodity 'corn' and distinguished from 'luxuries', on the other, a large part of the luxury consumption took the form of direct personal services. With land assumed to be fixed and limited role of fixed capital in economic life, social output could be treated as consiting of a single commodity and as a function of quantity of labour. Yet Adam Smith's expository device of a society *as if* it were one giant firm employing mainly one variable factor labour and producing a single 'commodity' was more than a method of abstraction. It implied his specific views about 'individual in society' as a component of his Vision.

In the case of Adam Smith it is necessary to consider explicitly his Vision because for Smith himself his work was not primarily economic but social. Even in the *Wealth of Nations* Smith was not merely an economist. As common with the other writers of the Englightenment, he did not draw a sharp distinction between philosophy and science. In conformity with the Scottish tradition in economic thought, Smith would have regarded economics as only one component of the study of individuals living in societies involving psychology, ethics, law, politics and social philosophy.[27]

The fundamental doctrines of the *Wealth of Nations*, particularly in regard to the economic motive and natural liberty, have served as the basis for characterizing Smith as 'apostle of individualism' or even 'self-interest'. These cannot, however, be understood independently of Smith's *Theory of Moral Sentiments* which, on the one hand, reflects the common ethical background of the eighteenth century and, on the other, Smith's own individual contributions within that common framework. Relationship between the two books has been a matter of controversy. For instance, Viner sees 'irreconcilable conflict' *between* the two on the ground that 'a beatific state which [Smith] dreamed about in the *Theory of Moral Sentiments*' (on the basis of the natural harmony of private interests as safeguarded by a benevolent and all-wise Deity) is quite different from 'the economic order under the system of natural liberty' in the *Wealth of Nations*.[28] Cropsey, on the other hand, argues that the two books are not inconsistent, both being based on the same deterministic psychological explanation of human conduct accepted in the eighteenth century, according to which the controlling force behind human motivation is 'passions' or 'instincts'.[29] The fact that there are conflicts and inconsistencies *within* both books and that too the same major ones would seem to be more relevant for our purpose.[30] The eighteenth century thinkers, following synthetic as against analytic approach, neither regarded consistency as a necessary virtue nor found it feasible to practise it in dealing with facts of experience in *totality*.[31]

Concept of Man

Adam Smith traces Division of Labour to the basic human 'propensity to truck, barter and exchange' by making a simple observation:

> 'Nobody ever saw a dog make a *fair* and *deliberate* exchange of one bone for another with another dog.'[32]

For him the ultimate economic propensity is not, however, 'trucking dispositions', as it is assumed because of the central role which division of labour plays in the *Wealth of Nations*, but self-love which is the source of exchange activity.[33] Smith remarks that man who has 'almost constant occasion for the help of his breathern' would in vain expect it 'from their benevolence only'. He is more likely to succeed by appealing to 'their self love in his favour' and talking to them not of [his] own necessities but of their advantages.[34] Reading in Smith's analysis 'maximizing postulate' has involved interpretation of self-interest in the present-day too exclusively subjective sense and of 'economic man' (a phrase which Adam Smith never used) in terms of 'instrumental rationality'. Yet the *Wealth of Nations* reflects the philosophy implicit in the *Theory of Moral Sentiments* and it is more appropriate to regard self-interest of 'economic man' as the economic counterpart of self-love of prudent man of the *Theory of Moral Sentiments*.

Adam Smith's concept of man involved his eclectic views of both human nature and of the purpose of human existence.[35] The starting point is his view (like that of Aristotle and Hume) that man is by nature *social* and like Hume he regarded the dominant human end as the interests or 'welfare' of society. His emphasis on natural liberty of the individual (reflecting the influence of the concept of life according to Nature of the Stoics) acquires a different significance when seen in the context of his view that man is *socially* motivated, though he need not be conscious of it. That he recognized the importance of self-love, of urge to 'better our conditions' is obvious from his criticism of both Mandeville and Hutchison, of the former for a merely selfish interpretation of self-love, of the latter for not giving due weight to the importance of self-love in human affairs in his benevolent system. He himself did not regard self-love as necessarily anti-social and tried to show how self-love could develop into socially valuable prudence in a *free society made up of critical but social individuals*. He did not play down human inadequacies . . . 'the coarse clay of which the bulk of mankind is formed' – nor did he rely on altruism. He recognised that man's self-love needed outlet. His theory of graduated individual values begins with vanity, the common human motive in its lowest form and moves from vanity to pride and from pride to magnanimity. Education is supposed to direct vanity into proper channels. He made out a case for inducing active self-love, if necessary by 'illusions', because he *believed* man could be expected to act for social benefit, being by nature social.

One of the 'illusions' is 'the pleasure of wealth and greatness' which is dubbed as 'self-deception' but is recognised as force 'which rouses and keeps in continual motion the industry of mankind.' The other is to be found in the concept of 'the impartial and well-informed spectator.' The link between the concept of the prudent man with his self-love and of the society as the prudent man's ultimate end is provided through sympathy and reason. For Smith it is 'a sense of propriety quite distinct from the sense of utility' which is the basis of 'virtue', 'approbation' or judgement of the good. Utility is no more than a means. Smith's positive doctrine of the nature of 'virtue' has two basic components: (i) individual's regard for the 'order' of society, for the 'beauty' of the 'well-contrived machine' and (ii) 'virtue' lying 'not in any one affection, but in the proper degree of all affections' with the 'natural' and original measure of this proper degree lying in *sympathy* and not *utility*. For Smith it is sympathy and not utility which is the bond for society[36] and he put justice as prior to utility.[37] Between justice and benevolence also he accorded priority to justice because benevolence cannot be forced whereas utility depends on justice being enforced.

'Society may subsist, though not in the most comfortable state, without beneficence but the prevalence of injustice must utterly destroy it.'[38]

He accepted Hume's view of sympathy as the moralizing factor but put rational content into it by interpreting it as the sympathy of the 'impartial and well-informed spectator'. The subjective side of the moral activity implied in the sympathetic feelings of the 'impartial and well-informed spectator' is the conscience, 'the man in the breast' who can 'imagine' himself in another man's position. The 'man in the breast' has a double function: he provides individuals with criteria for judgements of the conduct of others and also with standards for their own actions. Smith rejected Hutchison's intuitive 'view of 'moral sense'. He traced it to experience of social life and social rules which man observes because he has innate desire for social approbation and fear of social disapprobation. The objective side of moral activity is rationalized social rules – the reflection of sympathy in informed public opinion and in a code of social behaviour. The obvious 'illusion' involved in [putting] ourselves in their situation' implies that *rational* sympathy and *proper* self-regard (or enlightened self interest) are the basis for *gradual* building up of a system of moral rules, customs, conventions and institutions which provide the bond for society and also the basis of progress of society.

That Adam Smith created the 'economic' man as an abstraction which typifies *social* behaviour in the market place cannot be denied. But he is a very different 'creature' than the one later invented by the economists. Even in the *Wealth of Nations*, where he is transformed into a down-to-earth man of the world from the 'disembodied creature with hypersensitized sympathies' (of the *Theory of Moral Sentiments*), he reveals four different levels of conduct: (i) seeking to gratify physical needs; (ii) pursuing his self-interest in the context of which he is proud, vain, wilful, indolent, acquisitive; (iii) using his 'resources' (fortune and talent) in a more calculating manner to acquire the highest returns in terms of a *wide* range of objectives; (iv) *thinking about the proper ends to pursue.* The last is regarded as the highest level of conduct because through it the environment in which the 'economic' man operates is consciously changed. Thus the kind of choices he makes involves selecting from among different modes of conduct the particular one which conforms best with his nature as a social individual, although his behaviour is not necessarily rational.

The *Wealth of Nations* need not be regarded as simply a special case – the economic case – of the philosophy implicit in the *Theory of Moral Sentiments,*[39] but it is the *Wealth of Nations* which makes more clear the nature and the limitations of the Vision. The two 'illusions' which provide the link between social and individual interest in the *Theory of Moral Sentiments* are weaker because the gap between the two is particularly obvious in economic affairs. The more explicit counterpart of economic motives for 'place' and the 'trinkets' is 'the uniform, constant, and uninterrupted effort of every man to better his condition.' The clashes of self-interest are sharper and more frequent when we come down to the market place. The impartial spectator is replaced by the impersonal market. The subjective side of moral activity implied in the 'sympathetic feelings of the impartial and well-informed spectator' is weaker, if not absent; the objective side of the 'sympathy-spectator' mechanism implied by public opinion, fair play, justice is replaced by business ethics, conventions, and legal redress which is a slow process. Smith, as a result relies on the stabilizing operation of a *theoretical* perfect machine – natural liberty and *free markets* – to reconcile the conflict of individual interests. The exceptions that he himself lists to the harmonizing influence of this economic stabilizer are so numerous and substantial[40] as to make 'optimality' – in the Smithian sense – of 'perfect' competition a hypothesis to be verified by facts.

Yet *ultimate* natural harmony is an important component of Smith's vision and it is essential to be clear about its source. The invisible hand would seem to play in Adam Smith's work a role comparable in importance to the mechanism of dialectics in Marx. The natural theism is not, however, basic in Smith's *inductive* moral theory based on sympathy-spectator mechanism, interpreted in the context of *gradually* evolving societies. In fact the theistic invisible hand type of argument plays hardly any role in the *Wealth of Nations.* The actual phrase 'an invisible hand' is used only once where its purpose is to show how the individual is led by 'nature' to benefit society by a deception:

> 'Every individual is continually exerting himself to find out the most advantageous employment for whatever capital he can command . . . he intends only his own gain, and he in this, as in many other cases, led by an invisible hand to promote an end which was no part of his intention.'[41]

The invisible hand is used as a metaphor for the beneficent outcome of the process of competition, the emphasis being on the mutual advantage of free exchange.

It would seem that the source of the ultimate natural harmony would have to be sought *not* in resolution of conflicts but in the concept of society as a 'well-contrived machine'. Smith constantly talks of the 'beauty', of 'fitness', of the 'well contrived machine' which provides 'a thousand agreeable effects', while a rusty jarring one 'would displease' and be 'necessarily offensive'. The aesthetic delight in the perfect system or machine derived (along with rationalism) from Platonism is reflected in Smith's statement:

> 'Human society, when we contemplate it in a certain abstract and philo-sophical light, appears like a great, an immense machine, whose regular and *harmonious* movements produce a thousand agreeable effects.' (emphasis added).

The source of the concept of natural harmony would again seem to be *theological* because the source of society as a 'great machine' is said to be God, described as 'All-wise architect and conductor'. In this Smith reflected the prevailing attitude of his period, influenced by the development of Newton's 'System of the World' which showed the universe as a great machine.

Yet Smith more often uses the analogy of the judge (who is not infallible) and the law than the watch-maker and the watch or the engineer and the machine. This can be interpreted as implying that he wanted to stress also that society as a 'great machine' may not be perfect. It would seem more appropriate to seek the philosophical basis (without denying its theistic roots) for the theory of natural liberty (with its corollary of free and fair competition) in the concept of *Order* in society or *Social Balance*. That 'the society persists' does not, however, provide and adequate basis for inferring about the *nature* of Order or the *process* by which it is ensured without an adequate theory of society. As the most general interpretation that can be put on the concept of equilibrium is Order, in respect of which the present day economists can claim two hundred years old tradition, the adequacy of Adam Smith's theory of society becomes a crucial issue.

Theory of Society

A word about Smith's *method* of investigation would be necessary for this purpose. Some of the inconsistencies *within* his two major works can be traced to the combination of deductive and inductive *method*. Smith did not explicitly discuss his method of investigation. His description of the inductive method in the *Theory of Moral Sentiments* would seem to suggest that he regarded it as scientific:

> 'We observe in a great variety of particular cases what pleases or displeases our moral faculties . . . and by *induction* from this experience, we establish the general rules.'

On the basis of some of Smith's posthumously published essays, Bittermann has argued that Smith denied the possibility of *a priori* knowledge.[42] He did not deny the possibility of discovering laws but these were to be induction from sense data implying that for him experience alone provided the basis for casual connections.

Smith was influenced by many thinkers among whom Hume was one of the most important. It would seem reasonable to presume that Hume, whom he called 'by far the most illustrious philosopher and historian of the present age' and from whom, according to him, he differed 'a little',[43] might have influenced him in his *empirical* method. The fact the Newton's *System of the World* was Smith's ideal also acquires a new dimension as a result. It represented not only the religion of the Enlightenment but also the possibility of developing a 'system' or a 'theory' in the form of empirical generalizations. Smith's emphasis on the importance of induction did not involve careful distinction between the functions of deductive and inductive *reasoning* but by 'induction' he probably meant the Newtonian method which Jevons called 'inverse deduction'. Newton's 'experimentalism' combined both methods – inductive and deductive – but its merit was supposed to be its inference of causes from effects as opposed to the purely 'rationalistic' procedure which derived 'conjectural inferences from uncertain premises.'

Without denying frequent normative overtones in Smith's *Theory of Moral Sentiments*, the *inductive* moral theory contained in it can be interpreted as being designed to '*explain*' the causes of moral decisions, treated as data.[44] Smith's theory was more descriptive and 'explanatory' than normative. Inductive nature of the *Wealth of Nations* would suggest that his static equilibrium should be interpreted as *a posteriori* construct of actual economic order at any point of time taken as *datum*. The purpose is not to evaluate but to 'explain' the result of economic activity. The concept of static equilibrium, if interpreted otherwise, would be out of place in the study of societies regarded as '*natural* growths in their own unique environment', which requires an historical approach. Yet in economic theory of the *Wealth of Nations*, the prescriptive elements are embedded in descriptive-predictive 'system'. Order in Society has both a positive and a normative connotation about it so that the adequacy of Smith's theory of society becomes important.

Society is the 'natural' and the ultimate unit for Smith as for the other Scottish thinkers of his period. Theory of society requires, however, a precise concept of society. Appropriateness of the concept depends on the purpose for which it is to be used. If the interest is in the mechanism that permits a society to exist, functional concept of society as a social system may be adopted. On the other hand, if the interest is in different types of social order and in the way in which they change over *historical* time, the concept of society as a *process* – an evolving entity – is more relevant. Social disorder instead of being taken as prior to and different from social order needs to be interpreted as the result of the same elements, although occuring in different combinations. Dynamics of social order focuses on the mechanism by which social order is transformed using the framework of the same conditions which determine its continuity. In either case the problem of the relation between individuals and society has to be faced. Society is neither an aggregate of individuals nor an entity *sui generis*. At the same time society as a living organism does not represent a unity of the *integrated whole* unless it is merely used as a frame of reference. It is a working mechanism. Various conditions are essential to the continuance of society and the functioning of the social mechanism underlying such continuance. As such the study of the interdependence of the component parts of the system is indissolubly linked with how the component parts work in relation to one another and in relation to the whole.

Adam Smith's concept of society is of growing – or more appropriately an evolving – society, embodying 'virtues of system and balance.' Smith, the empiricist, took the 'civil society' – the concept of society as an entity distinct from and prior to state, which was the product of the Age of Reason – as *given*. Unlike some of the thinkers of the Enlightenment, Smith did not use the 'philosophic fiction' of the state of nature and the social contract for discussing the nature of human relations in the absence of government.[45] Such a 'philosophic fiction' can be interpreted in two ways. It reflected the fact that the Enlightenment thought was founded on the concept of reason and the method of reason is analytical. Whole has to be reduced to fundamental parts so that it can be built by a process of deduction from 'laws' governing parts. Secondly, it was an attempt to derive social coherence and order from the basic human faculty of reason. State could be as a result shown to be a dependent sector of a larger social order. This involved resolution of the problem of conflicting ends by postulating metaphysical concepts like natural rights, natural identity of interests or spirit of sociability. As such the ultimate premise continued to be 'war of all against all' – social disorder which Hobbes used as a starting point for analysis of the possibility of social order.

Smith's frequent use of the terminology of natural law has resulted in his being bracketed with those thinkers of his period who used such a 'philosophic fiction'. Yet he rejected the notion of both the state of nature and the social contract. In the *Glasgow Lectures* of 1763, he wrote:

> 'It in reality serves no purpose to treat of the laws which would take place in a state of nature, or by what means succession to property was carried on, as there is no such state existing.'

He also rejected Rousseau's notion of an original contract – more on this later – and its corollary of an implied contract existing in modern states. His rejection is partly to be attributed to his empirical method of investigation. There is also another, and perhaps more important, reason. Order did not imply for Adam Smith absence of conflict between the interests of individuals or groups. In the *Theory of Moral Sentiments* the absence of conflict is ascribed only to benevolent actions. The qualifications to the theory of natural liberty in the *Wealth of Nations* are all related to conflict of interests.

Yet it would be difficult to include Smith's concept of society in the category of 'conflict theory', which regards society as a product of 'antagonistic cooperation' of competing organisms. The basic element in 'conflict theory' is that men as organisms must compete for access to the resources of life and the theory therefore has ecological perspective. The theory seeks to explain not only how conflict is stabilized, or regulated but also how the 'rate' and direction of change of society is related to the nature and substance of conflict. While Adam Smith's man-against-nature view of economic problem is consistent with the concept of society as 'a device for regulating the struggle for existence and for relating man to his environment', his concept of man being by nature social is not.

Smith's concept of 'individual in society' ruled out Mandeville's notion of the fall from man's 'primitive innocence' as the cause of his becoming 'that sociable creature he is now'. Societies were not created to protect individuals from dangers posed by the vices of individuals. The factors binding individuals in society are *emotional and moral* and not merely *biological*.

> 'Man, it has been said, has a natural love of society. . . . The orderly and flourishing state of society is agreeable to him, and he takes delight in contemplating it.'

The 'fellow-feeling' or sympathy is even more important in the sociality of man, because it is the essential condition to the development of morality. Smith rejected the abstraction of a Robinson Crusoe 'from his birth' because *moral* issues could not arise for him. He would neither have interests beyond his own nor standards for comparison. Adam Smith's letter to the *Edinburgh Review* of 1755, with its apparently strange juxtaposition of Rousseau and Mandeville, was designed to stress man's essentially social nature and at the same to deny that man is *a priori* a 'social' being and a 'moral' person.[46]

Yet in another sense Rousseau and Mandeville do stand in juxtaposition *vis-a-vis* Smith. Both Rousseau and Mandeville emphasized the basic contradiction of 'civil society' which lies in the fact that social relationships in 'civil society' are not based on mutual solidarity but on competition. Of course, for Mandeville 'private vices' are 'public benefits' and the pursuit of his own selfish interest by each man forms the basis of national prosperity. The contradictions of 'civil society' which provide the basis of Rousseau's critique of it are in fact exalted by Mandeville. Also for Mandeville 'man is an *animal* in permanent conflict with his kind', while for Rousseau it is the advent of private property which drives a wedge between interests of different individuals. Thus Mandeville's concept of man is ahistorical while Rousseau's is not.[47] On the other hand, Smith's concept of 'individual in society' makes his concept of man as well as of society ahistorical. The fact that for Smith the starting point of investigation is individual, although society is the ultimate unit, is not surprising, because individual is regarded as *socially motivated*. It is in social life and in the creation of good social customs, conventions and institutions that individual finds his 'propriety' and happiness, whether he intends it or not. With the concept of a socially-motivated individual, learning from social experience and guided by internalized social conscience, the difficulties faced by the Benthamites in passing from individual to social utility do not arise for Smith. Smith's concept of society is better classified as 'one in many and many in one' – philosophical rather than sociological and therefore ahistorical.

The inadequacy of Adam Smith's theory of society lies precisely in its underlying concept of society. Smith shared with the other members of the Scottish Historical School his interest in the study of the 'natural history' of society.[48] In the *Glasgow Lectures* Smith treats history as a sequence of epochs identifying four main stages through which various societies had passed: hunting, pasturage, agriculture and commerce. Each is defined in terms of 'mode of subsistence', with 'inequality of fortune' owing to the institutions of private property and government to defend it developing in the second stage.

'Till there be property', Smith remarks, 'there can be no Government, the very end of which is to secure wealth, and to defend the rich from the poor'. The causal connection between 'mode of subsistence' and property relationships on the one hand, and the juridical and political system, on the other, is pointed out. The transition from one stage to another is also traced to changing economic conditions. Yet this 'materialist conception of history' does not lead to more explicit analysis of the nature of conflict. Smith recognises ubiquity of conflict but antagonistic cooperation is supposed to be regulated by sympathetic reason. Emphasis is on *gradual* evolution of moral rules, customs and institutions *which regulate conflicts of interest without ever resolving them completely*. Smith's reply to Mandeville's sharp satire may be 'rather flat and feeble,'[49] but while Mandeville *rejoices* in the selfish interest, which he calls a *vice*, Smith pins his faith in the possibility of the same, which he calls '*virtue*', *developing into enlightened self-interest*. If his solution of Mandeville's paradox is only *apparent*, all the more so because he puts the problem in a much sharper focus, it is better explained by linking it directly to the inadequacy of his theory of society rather than to his 'theory of harmony' as Coletti does.[50] The 'vulgar economics' has read in Smith's doctrine of harmony resolution of Mandeville's paradox but Myrdal's contention that in the doctrine of 'harmony', 'the possibility of conflicts of interest is simply ignored',[51] is not valid for Smith. As pointed out earlier, not only is conflict of interest recognized, but resolution of conflicts is also not implied in Smith's concept of harmony.

That Smith should have neglected the role of conflict in determining the direction and 'rate' of change of society should not be a matter of surprise. Even Adam Ferguson, the Scottish sociologist who stressed the importance of social conflict, drawing particular attention to the possibility of revolutionary change, shared the belief common to the thinkers of the Scottish Historical School that 'society . . . developed blindly'. Changes were regarded as 'the result of human action but not the execution of any human design.'[52] Even John Millar, who in his *Origin of the Distinction of Ranks* more explicitly used 'materialist' approach to the study of society, stressed that it is 'by . . . gradual advances in rendering their situation more comfortable that the most important alterations are produced in the state and condition of a people'. He stressed 'a *natural* progress from ignorance to knowledge, and from rude to civilized manners in human society'.[53]

Smith himself emphasized the gradual and continuous character of social development[54] relating 'individual's morals to the stage in moral stature society has reached.' There was a hope or belief in *future* growth and social improvement through 'the slow influence and unfolding of reason' over *historical* time. It would be more appropriate to say that Smith had a philosophy of history rather than a theory of society. While Smith adopted an historical approach to the study of men's relations to one another, history would seem to have stopped for him with the advent of 'civil society'. What remained was sure, even if slow, march to progress not as a result of 'conscious deliberate planning' but 'as a by-product of the development of society.'[55] In the 'optimistic quietism' of Smith's is 'the desire for better men',[56] rather than for economic growth in the present-day sense of the term.

Distribution not a 'puzzle' in Smith's Analysis

With society as the ultimate unit, it is not surprising that Smith regarded the *level of average* output, together with its *growth*, as the aim of social policy. It would be more appropriate to characterize the prime objective of Smith's social policy as 'maximization' of the *level* of average output. There is, of course, no basic conflict between the *level* of average output and the rate of *growth* of average output in Smith's physical output approach. Yet 'maximization' of rate of growth of average output would seem to be regarded as more crucial. Smith mentions that the wage earner was better off in a progressive state in which capital was growing faster than population, its complement. In a stationary state, by contrast, the wage earner's lot was hard and dull.[57] A developing society is also more consistent with his method of relating individual's morals to the moral stature which society has attained.

Adam Smith's treatment of the division of labour has been much discussed by the later writers. Adam Smith has been credited with two views on the division of labour on the basis of the apparent contradiction between the analysis of the gains from division of labour in Book I and the reference to the deleterious effects of the division of labour on the work force in Book V. More important fact to note is that the division of labour is looked upon 'as a process which had not only an historical but necessarily also an important *social dimension.*'[58] Given the fact that division of labour is the dynamic force in Smith's analysis, it is interesting to note that it is judged in terms of its implication for society. The very process which increases the 'collective intelligence of society' causes the 'inferior ranks of people' to become 'stupid and ignorant.' The brunt of the deleterious effect falls on the industrial labour force. The scope for division of labour is limited in agricultural sector and the upper ranks of a society are insulated because they do not derive their incomes from menial activities. The *modal* level of understanding is low, the dispersion of understanding is greater but the *collective* level of intelligence is greater. Smith attached greater importance to the potential for growth through improved creativity of the society.

With society treated as the ultimate unit, production – the level and growth of output – was Smith's main concern. *Distribution is not a 'puzzle' in Smith's analysis.* Smith took differences in rank, inequality in the distribution of wealth and income, differences in the consumption pattern and the consequent differences in the consumption pattern and the consequent differences in the composition of output, as *given.* Smith's limited analysis of sociological implications of division of labour as related to dynamics of capitalist production can be easily understood. While he tried to reconstruct the evolutionary process in the development of human artifacts on the basis of 'conjectural history', he could not have been expected to foresee fully its future course. In any case, at least in the early stages of development, division of labour could be expected to increase the worker's dexterity and alertness, if not intelligence or understanding. The picture in regard to distribution is, however, different even in the early stages of capitalist development.

The 'uniform, constant and uninterrupted effort of every man to better his condition' is regarded as the driving force of individual action. The reason why man pursued riches, avoided poverty and put forth every effort after his elementary wants have been satisfied is traced to man's 'regard to the sentiments of mankind'. Vanity, emulation, desire for favourable notice, aspirations to advancement in rank are emphasized as psychological determinants of human behaviour. Both the hierarchy of wants[59] and the insatiability of wants other than the basic ones are clearly recognized.[60] The desire for these 'non-basics' is regarded as being governed by socio-economic conditions external to the individual and not fixed by his elementary needs. Yet there is no analysis of the *composition* of output in terms of the *pattern* of demand as determined by the distribution of income. Consumption is, of course, mentioned as 'the sole end and purpose of all production'. That is however in the aggregate sense and that too in the context of making out a case for the more numerous as against the less numerous groups.[61] Monopoly is both injurious to the consumers and also wasteful because it harms the interests of capitalists seeking advantageous outlets.[62] From the view point of *increasing* output, consumption is regarded as what is necessary for production.

Difficulties in having *'fair'* and free exchange are recognized.

> 'People of the same trade seldom meet together, even for meriment and diversion, but the conversation ends in a conspiracy against the public, or in some contrivance to raise prices.'[63]

The weaker position of the workers vis-a-vis employers is recognized. Though the employers cannot reduce wages below a certain level, they have a decided advantage.

> 'Masters are always and everywhere in a sort of tacit, but constant and uniform combination, not to raise the wages of labour above their actual rate. . . . Masters too sometimes enter into particular combinations to sink the wages of labour even below this rate.'[64]

The interests of the workers are linked with the interests of society. Yet

> 'in the public deliberations, . . . his voice is little heard and less regarded, except upon some particular occasions, when his clamour is animated, set on, and supported by his employers, not for his, but their own particular purpose.'[65]

Yet economic problem is conceptualized as a problem of production rather than distribution. The reason is not far to seek. Man's universal desire of bettering 'his own condition' is to Smith, a 'powerful . . . principle capable of carrying on the *society* to wealth and prosperity.'

As we noted earlier Adam Smith had criticized Rousseau (along with Mandeville) in a letter to the *Edinburgh Review* of 1755, stressing man's essentially social nature. Yet Rousseau's original contract was not designed to derive social order from 'war of all against all'. Rousseau's purpose was to distinguish between inequality of men (which he called natural because men are not exactly alike even at birth) and inequality *among* men which depended on a kind of convention – *agreement among 'free' individuals who have no power over each other*. Underlying Rousseau's original contract was the concept of 'democratic individualism' – of a society of free and equal individuals, free because equal. His broad conclusion was that the advent of property and inequality in wealth marked the beginning of a new psychology of man. Smith's criticism of Rousseau cannot be attributed merely to the fact that the 'philosophical fiction' of state of nature was anathema to his empirical approach. Smith regarded inequality as functionally necessary if society is to grow. Given the importance of capital accumulation for increasing employment and average output, conditions favourable to accumulation of capital (including its optimum use) assume a crucial significance. To Smith even the landlord's prodigality would seem to be a worthwhile price to pay if it can induce him to play an effective role in the process of capital accumulation. His consumption of 'nonbasics' cuts into the surplus over and above the necessary consumption but it is not on par with the support of idle retainers and 'unproductive' labourers. The maximum output potential of a society would also seem to be regarded as determined by the stage of its development, – by the forces of production – and as *independent of its institutional structure.*[66]

In the *Theory of Moral Sentiments* Smith always adds the rules of 'fair play' and the system of justice to his advocacy of natural liberty. In the Stoic tradition 'fair play' has reference to the game of life. Playing fairly implied that an individual 'may run as hard as he can, and strain every nerve . . . to outstrip all his competitors [but not] justle, or throw down any of them.' In the *Wealth of Nations* 'the second duty of the sovereign' is that of 'protecting, as far as possible, every member of the society from the injustice or oppression of every other member of it, or the duty of establishing an exact administration of justice.'[67] Smith is not explicit whether he meant the justice implied by the law of property, contract or some ideal ethical justice. In view of the discussion above, it would seem that the laws of justice are the legal requirements. They may be criticized in terms of social ideals and policy but are to be treated as binding so long as they prevailed. It is in the course of social progress that they would be revised to embody the higher moral stature to which progress would carry the society.

In the same way that Adam Smith underestimated the psychological costs of division of labour and their sociological implications, he underestimated the potential for wealth to breed and to perpetuate inequality and privileges. It would seem that he had even less reason to do so. Yet he shared the belief common in his century that innate ability was fairly equally spread and consequently opportunities were more or less equally distributed.[68] Rousseau's inequality of men was not important and inequality *among* men was not only socially useful but could be accepted in so far as there was equality of opportunity. There was a belief that a 'general plenty diffuses itself through all the different ranks of society' and that there was enough social mobility so that the problem of ranks did not need to be investigated.

A thinker has to be understood in the context of his times. Bertrand Russel's advice that 'in studying a philosopher, the right attitude is neither reverence nor contempt, but first a kind of hypothetical sympathy, until it is possible to know what it feels like to believe in his theories', is no less true in regard to a scientist.

Adam Smith's *theoretical* advocacy of freedom for the individual can be understood better when seen as a reaction to the kind of society he lived in. It was mainly rigid, stratified on both economic and religious basis, controlled by out-of-date practices and institutions. The development of productive forces was hampered by powerful vested interests, in particular by the feudal aristocracy acting directly or through the government and aided by entrenched commercial monopolies. On the other hand, the classical ethical background of the eighteenth century – Platonic-Aristotelian-Stoic – provided the *vision* of a *rational* and *free* society made up of critical but social individuals. Economic individualism and political democracy were two inseparably connected aspects of the same vision of *free* society. Smith, like other classical economists, was fighting not only for something but also – and perhaps more – against something. He, like other thinkers of the period, refused to accept the values of the society he lived in, though he could not transcend the historical limitations of his own time. One need not subscribe fully to Goethe's generous saying that 'a man's defects are the faults of his time, while his virtues are his own';[59] but even the most prophetic minds have not been able to transcend the limitations of their own time. Kepler mingled 'mysticism' with his science'.[70] Rousseau's critique of 'civil society' was far ahead of his time but his 'equalitarianism' did not encompass inequality of men. He emphasized the need for social recognition of the individual's 'merits' and not of 'needs' as Marx later did.[71]

It would be wrong to seek in Smith's concern with order in society the spectre of Hobbes which haunted the eighteenth century, although statements supporting such an interpretation can be found in the *Theory of Moral Sentiments*.[72] It would be equally wrong to read a Ricardian finale to the growth process in Smith's reference to the countries that have acquired their 'full complement of riches' or to attribute to him a notion of alienation, which Marx later formulated, on the basis of his reference to the deleterious effects of division of labour on the work force. Smith was a 'progressist', to use Pareto's terms, but without 'progress' implying the present-day narrow concept of economic growth. Not only did he forsee the potential for development of productive forces in the emerging bourgeois order, recognize the need to throw off the crippling fetters of the feudal society if the potential was to be realized but he also expected that the internalized social conscience' would create a *free* society. Yet Smith had no illusion that the 'optimum' would be ever attained. To him to expect it 'is as absurd as to expect that . . . Utopia should ever be established. . . .' He recognized that even if the entrenched prejudices of the public against free competition could be overcome, the more formidable resistance of *vested interests* would prevent the possibility of establishing harmonious social order.[73]

What is Wrong with Economics?

In the Kuhnian sense the mainstream economics has never had a major revolution.[74] It has been dominated throughout its history by a single paradigm in characterizing which both the implications of the concept – 'way of viewing the world' and 'puzzles' – need to be kept in mind. In fact the two are closely interlinked in a science like economics which is a policy science and in which 'experimental' work in the sense in which it has in physical sciences is not possible. The 'puzzles' present themselves, as a result, sometimes in the form of 'stylized facts', (like historical constancy of the share of wages in national income) which then serve as assumptions, and sometimes in the form of concrete issues. As such what may be called the 'basic' puzzle and the 'world-view' implicit in it become all the more important. Keeping in mind this inter-relation, the single paradigm which has dominated mainstream economics can be characterized in terms of the two components: the 'basic model' implies commitment to liberal philosophy and the basic puzzle is production rather than distribution.

Economic theory has concentrated on 'improving' the articulation of the paradigm implicit in Adam Smith's philosophy of history. It is doubtful whether the 'conscious efforts to improve' has been 'progression from error to truth' as is often alleged.[75] Adam Smith's sociological approach has given way to analysis of economic process as 'isolated system'. His empirical method in the sense of 'inverse deduction' and historical approach have given way to equilibrium analysis. In place of *rational society* is substituted the concept of *rational market* resulting in the problem of economic life being approached from the viewpoint of market process, abstracted to a varying extent from the underlying social relations. Economics as a general science of rational activity, the principles of which apply even to Robinson Crusoe, can incorporate social relationships, if at all, in the process of exchange. As such it has lost its point of contact with political economy as a science dealing with laws of economic development, i.e., the processes of production and distribution in the course of which relationships among men are generated through material objects.

Adam Smith's concept of socially-motivated individual, transmitting (through 'internalized social conscience') the accumulated social experience to the next generation, has been replaced by that of atomistic individual standing in isolation from his predecessors, contemporaries and successors. His concept of society as an evolving entity embodying 'virtues of system and balance' has been replaced by society as an aggregate of atomistic individuals. Reading in Smith's analysis 'maximizing postulate has involved interpretation of self-interest in the present-day too exclusively subjective sense and of 'economic man' in terms of 'instrumental rationality'. The postulate of 'economic man' with the implicit concept of means-ends relationship not only endows man with rationality, although he is often irrational and rationalizing, but also assumes away the more difficult problem of choice of ends by assuming them as 'given'. The highest level of conduct of Adam Smith's social individual *viz., thinking about the proper ends to pursue*, has no place in the decision-making of 'economic' man. This is as much true of 'satisficing' interpretation of rationality as of 'maximizing'. While the former does recognize that the alternatives are not given but must be sought, the reference is to the inadequate information about his environment on the part of 'economic' man. While the emphasis has rightly shifted from equilibrium to the processes and mechanisms through which the adaption takes place, the environment itself remains outside the pale of analysis. The trend towards value-free analysis in the interest of 'objectivity' has resulted in the existing scale of values being taken as given.

It would be tempting to read in the concept of atomistic man, choosing from 'given' ends, the alienated man of the capitalist society.[76] Such interpretation would be unwarranted for two reasons. On the one hand it would conceal the deeper process of alienation involved in the fragmented mode of scientific activity as determined by the institutionalized framework of the capitalist mode of production. On the other, it would imply failure to recognize that unlike Adam Smith's concept of socially-motivated man which was based partly upon the behavioural properties he imputed to man and partly upon the behavioural tendencies he inferred from the activities of man, the concept of atomistic man is a pure abstraction. The recognition that man is not *socially motivated* but *socially conditioned* should have logically led to questioning the basic postulate underlying liberal philosophy.

Economics has in fact ceased to be 'an empirical science'. The liberal case for capitalism in terms of individual initiative is a nostalgic yearning in the context of the bureaucratic structure of managerial capitalism. Emphasis on 'consumer sovereignty' in the midst of 'Hidden persuaders', on the devolution of power implicit in decentralized decision-making in the midst of central-ization and concentration of capital, on the state as 'an impartial arbitrator' in the midst of symbiotic relationship between corporations and the state, are suggestive of economic theory having lost its link with contemporary reality.

The concept of atomistic man has to be understood as a component of analytical method. It is not just an accident of history that the *method* of static equilibrium in Book I of the *Wealth of Nations* provided the basis for the later more mechanistic interpretations. It suited the analytical approach and the deductive method which triumphed in the century that followed the *Wealth of Nations*. The Enlightenment thought was founded on the concept of reason and the *method* of reason is analytical. Treatment of economics as 'isolated system' reflects not only the growing intellectual division of labour but the fact that analytical method requires analytical boundary even though 'reality is seamless'. Consequently economics becomes a technical exercise which ignores the relations of production and the role of conflict, power and coercion in economic process, while political theory ignores the basic economic forces. Deductive method also requires that the whole should be reduced to funda-mental parts so that it can be built by process of deduction from 'laws' governing parts. In the course of 'improving' the articulation of the paradigm implicit in Adam Smith's philosophy of history, emphasis has come to be placed on *technique of analysis*.

The participants in the current debate on the 'state of the art' have also focused essentially on two issues: (i) empirical foundations of economic theory and (ii) technique of analysis. The interdependence between resource allo-cation and resource creation involves the question of *mechanism* through which change is transmitted and productive forces grow. The difficulty of reconciling Walras with Keynes is also partly a matter of technique of analysis. The theorems derived from conventional assumptions of independence among individual units cannot be applied when there is interdependence in aggre-gation. Equilibrium and history as *techniques of analysis* cannot also coalesce. The former seeks to carve a path of rigorous deduction from the part to the whole without 'causality'; the latter either infers cause from effect by using the method of 'inverse deduction' or concentrates on the *mechanism* by which the whole operates by postulating direction of causal relationship in terms of the behavioural properties of the whole (e.g., in the Keynesian theory economic activity tends towards a level where savings and investment are equal and investment *determines* savings).

Interestingly enough neither the boundary of economic process (the scope of economics, to use the old-fashioned phrase) nor the underlying Vision has been questioned.[77] Lynd's critical diagnosis, more than thirty five years ago, of the crippling state of social sciences because of their operating as 'isolated systems', hardly seems to have had any impact on the economists. In fact compartmentalization of social sciences is breaking down precisely in that dimension which is making all of them 'barren and irrelevant'. With the extension of the neo-classical theoretical framework to the analysis of political behaviour, public choice and decision-making in general, all social analysis is getting reduced to a common denominator in terms of *technique of analysis*. Yet this expanding 'academic imperialism' of economics has also implied more rigidly-drawn boundaries for all of them. Compartmentalization of social sciences in the more basic sense of splitting up of investigation which prevents the underlying determinants of the social formation from coming into view has strengthened.

Compartmentalization is in fact defended. In contrast to Wicksteed who emphasized that 'economic laws must not be sought and cannot be found on the properly economic field' and that 'economics must be the handmaid of sociology',[78] the latter-day economists have insisted on autonomy and specialization of economic analysis. Duesenberry defends the neglect of psychology on the ground that 'it allows one to avoid getting on a psychological limb which may collapse at any moment.'[79] Stigler rejects the case for interdisciplinary work on the ground that 'specialism' is necessary for *efficiency* in intellectual as in economic life.[80] The exclusive concern with *technique of analysis* reflects the deeper process of alienation involved in the fragmented mode of scientific activity. The present-day social scientist seeks 'know-how but ... not ... the know-why, nor the know-what-for.'[81]

Efficiency in intellectual life, as in economic life, cannot, however, be conceived independently of ends and the ends are to be sought in the kind of questions which appear to be most in need of an answer. The problems of poverty and affluence, unemployment and unutilized capacity, stagnation and inflation, environmental disruption and international disorganization, represent not only the growing contradictions of the capitalist system, as it has evolved since the time of Adam Smith, but the crisis of liberal philosophy. The problems reflect the conflict between 'socialized' production and 'individual appropriation' in the context of which the basic postulate of the liberal philosophy – the postulate of social harmony (in the sense of, if not identity of interests, at least absence of irreconcilable conflict of interest) – stands exposed.

If economic activity is viewed as an extension of man's biological evolution, the dual nature of man's evolution – physical and ideational – would require economic process to be treated as an *open* system in continuous interaction with social and physical environment. Economic problem would also need to be conceptualized as the problem of distribution. The interdependence between resource allocation and resource creation has implications not only for the mechanism through which productive forces grow but also for distribution of product among individuals. Production and distribution are, of course, two different aspects of the same process but it is distribution which determines *what* is produced and by *whom* it is determined. The fact that the needs and, therefore commodities, can be arranged in a hierarchical order with near-identity for all individuals upto a level is significant from the viewpoint of distribution. In 'natural' economy it would determine the composition of output and also the dynamics of the structure of relative 'prices'. If 'corn' can be used to produce 'bread' which meets primary need and 'cake' which satisfies less essential need, output-mix will shift in favour of cake only after the primary need has been met. The shift in the pattern of corn-use would be brought about by the rise in the 'price' of cake relative to that of bread. The 'natural' mechanism does not in fact operate because of unequal distribution of 'corn' and its implications for the *pattern* of demand, the *composition* of output and the structure of relative prices. Concentration on the relations among commodities without any reference to 'relations of production' would be inadequate in the context of the problem of distribution.

Economists may not set out to lay bare the law of motion of society but they cannot analyse problems of distribution without relating economic process to social environment. Without a sociological perspective and dialectics of social change based on explicit recognition of conflict of interest and of power as a ubiquitous social process, the questions which are surfacing to social awareness to-day cannot be answered. To analyse the interdependencies and cumulative causation, the treatment of economic process as a self-contained and self-sustaining system has to be discarded and so also the equilibrium technique of analysis. The most important, however, is the need to discard the basic postulate of social harmony which the bourgeois economists have adhered to for two hundred years in spite of mounting evidence to the contrary. Yet 'socialized production' and 'individual appropriation' must present a *rationally* insoluble problem until it is decided to solve it practically. The 'crisis' of economic theory is the crisis of capitalist system itself. If, following Marx, we accept that theory is itself practice or life in the sense of being both one of its *parts* and also its form[82] (in the sense that it reflects it), the resolution of the two crises is interrelated. Adam Smith's historically-conditioned Vision belongs to the period of transition. The hope-for 'better' men in a society which is basically characterized by *antagonistic contradictions* is out of tune with contemporary reality. The best homage we can pay to Adam Smith is to respond effectively to the challenges of our period as he did to those of his.

Notes

1. Economists' box of tools consists of two components: the 'basic' models relating to an unspecified social space and 'augmented' versions of the basic models provided *after* the phenomena sought to be explained has occurred – 'ingenious devices which take the form of general, flexible *ex post facto* explanatory schemata'. See Papandreou, A.G., *Economics as a Science*, U.S.A., Lippincott, 1958, p. 139.

2. See Robinson, J., 'The second crisis of Economic Theory' *American Economic Review*, 62, May 1972, pp. 1-10.

3. See (i) Leontief, W., 'Theoretical Assumptions and Nonobservable Facts', *American Economic Review*, 61, March 1971, pp. 1-7; (ii) Phelps Brown, E.H., 'The Underdevelopment of

Economics', *Economic Journal*, 82, March 1972, pp. 1-10. (iii) Worswick, G.D.N., 'Is Progress in Economic Science Possible?', *Economic Journal*, 82, March 1972, pp. 73-86; (iv) Kaldor, N. (a) 'The Irrelevance of Equilibrium Economics', *Economic Journal*, 82, December 1972, pp. 1237-55; (b) 'What is Wrong with Economic Theory?' *Quarterly Journal of Economics*, 89, August 1975, pp. 347-57; (v) Robinson, *op. cit.*

4.   Robinson, *op. cit.*, p. 10.
5.   *Ibid.*, pp. 6-8. See also Leontief *op. cit.*, p. 1 and Phelps Brown, *op. cit.*, p. 1.
6.   Phelps Brown *op. cit.*, pp. 6-7, emphasis added. See also Worswick.
7.   Leontief, *op. cit.*, p. 1; emphasis added; see also Phelps Brown.
8.   See Arrow, K.J., 'Samuelson Collected', *Journal of Political Economy*, 75, October, 1967, pp. 730-7.
9.   See Hahn, F.H., 'Some Adjustment Problems' *Econometrica*, 38, January 1970, pp. 1-17.
10.   *Ibid.*, p. 1; emphasis added.
11.   See Hahn, F.H., 'The Winter of Our Discontent' *Economica*, 40, August 1973, pp. 322-30; emphasis added.
12.   Jevons had written to his sister: '. . . does it not strike you that just as in physical science there are general and profound principles deducible from a great number of apparent phenomena, so in treating Man or Society there must also be general principles and laws . . .?' *vide* Jevons, W.S., *Papers and Correspondence of William Stanley Jevons*, Black, R.D.C., (ed.), London, Kelley, 1973, Vol. II., p. 361.
13.   Hahn (1973) *op. cit.*, p. 324.
14.   Arrow, K.J. and Hahn, F.H., *General Competitive Analysis*, San Francisco. Holden Day and Edinburgh, Oliver and Boyd, 1971, pp. vi-vii.
15.   "It is important to know not only whether it is true but also whether it *could be* true', *Ibid.*, p. vii.
16.   Arrow and Hahn, *op. cit.*, p. 2.
17.   The definition of equilibrium is: 'prices and input-output combinations are said to be equilibrium prices and input-output combinations if, when they rule, no economic agent has any inducement to change his method of production and no input or outputs is in excess demand'. See Hahn, F.H. *The Share of Wages in the National Income*, London, Weidenfeld and Nicholson, 1972, p. 3.
18.   Schumpeter, J.A., *Ten Great Economists*, London, Allen and Unwin, 1952, p. 268; emphasis added.
19.   Schumpeter, J.A., *History of Economic Analysis*, New York, Oxford University Press, 1954, pp. 41-2; emphasis added.
20.   *Ibid.*, p. 38.
21.   See Blaug, M., *Economic Theory in Retrospect*, London, Heinemann (1962) 1970, p. 39.
22.   See Meek, R.L., *Economics and Ideology and Other Essays*, London, Chapman and Hall, 1967, pp. 23-8.
23.   *Ibid.*, p. 18.
24.   See Young, A., 'Increasing Returns and Economic Progress', *Economic Journal* 38, December 1928, pp. 527-42.
25.   See Smith, A., *The Wealth of Nations* (1776) (ed. Cannan), London, Methuen, 1930, Vol. I, p. 1, emphasis added.
26.   *Ibid.*, p. 413.
27.   See Macfie, A.L., *The Individual in Society*, London, Allen and Unwin, 1957, pp. 19-41.
28.   Viner, J., 'Adam Smith and Laissez-Faire' in *Adam Smith 1776-1926*, New York, Kelley, (1928), 1966, p. 149.
29.   Cropsey, *Polity and Economy*, Hague, Martinus Nijhoff, London, Batsford, 1957.
30.   See Macfie, *op. cit.* There were six editions of the *Theory of Moral Sentiments* between 1759 and 1770. Only the last edition involved extensive revision of the text without however any basic change in arguments. In the last edition Smith explained in the preface that the *Wealth of Nations* (published in 1776) was to be regarded as *partial fulfilment* of the promise to publish a work on justice. This would seem to suggest that Smith himself regarded his two works as complementary.
31.   See Macfie, *op. cit.*, pp. 22, 107-8, 126-9.

32. Smith, Vol. I., *op. cit.*, p. 15; emphasis added.
33. Trucking propensity is described as being possibly *cultural* instead of originally-natural.
34. Smith, Vol. I., *op. cit.*, p. 16.
35. The references to the *Theory of Moral Sentiments* are carefully compiled by Macfie from all editions. The quotations without citations in this and the next section are from the *Theory of Moral Sentiments* as taken from Macfie. See Macfie, *op. cit.*, pp. 42-125.
36. 'Society may subsist among different men . . . from a sense of its utility, without any mutual love or affection [but it cannot] subsist among those who are at all times ready to hurt and injure one another.' Thus Smith was not a utilitarian even in the sense of Hume who regarded utility to society as 'a foundation of the chief part of morals, which has reference to mankind and our fellow creatures.'
37. 'Justice . . . is the main pillar that holds the whole edifice.'
38. Justice carried implication of 'fair play' interpreted most broadly to refer to the game of life in the Stoic tradition. The Stoics considered 'human life . . . as a game of great skill . . . In such games, the stake is commonly a trifle and the whole pleasure of the game arises from playing well, from playing fairly, and playing skilfully'. The second duty of the sovereign (next to defence) is mentioned as 'protecting, as far as possible, every member of the society from the injustice or oppression of every other member of it, or the duty of establishing an exact administration of justice', *vide*, Smith, Vol. II, p. 202.
39. See Macfie, *op. cit.*, p. 75.
40. See Viner, *op. cit.*
41. Smith, Vol. I, *op. cit.*, pp. 419-21.
42. Bittermann, H.J., 'Smith's Empiricism and the Law of Nature', *Journal of Political Economy*, 48, August and October, 1940, pp. 487-520, 703-34.
44. It is interesting to note that Smith explicitly states: '. . . the present inquiry is not concerning a matter of right, . . . but concerning a matter of fact. We are not examining upon what principles a perfect being would approve of the punishment of bad action; but upon what principles so weak and imperfect a creature as man actually and in fact approves of it'.
45. Smith's 'early and rude state of society' resembles the state of nature of Locke and Pufendrof in its economic organisations. It corresponds however to what was known of primitive cultures, even allowing for some element of 'conjectual history'. In any case its analytic function was different.
46. *Edinburgh Review*, July 1755 to January 1756, Second edition, 1818, 'A Letter to the Authors', pp. 121-35.
47. See Colletti, L., 'Mandeville, Rousseau and Smith', in *From Rousseau to Lenin*, London, NLB (1969) 1972, pp. 195-216.
48. See Meek, *op. cit.*, pp. 36-46.
49. Robinson, J., *Economic Philosophy*, London, Watts, (1962) 1966, p. 18.
50. Colletti, *op. cit.*, pp. 208-14.
51. Myrdal, G., *The Political Element in the Development of Economic Theory*, London, Routledge and Kegan Paul, 1953, p. 44.
52. See Meek, *op. cit.*, p. 38.
53. *Ibid.*, p. 41.
54. Smith, Vol. I., *op. cit.*, pp. 389-90.
55. Hutchison, T.W., *,"Positive" Economics and Policy Objectives*, Cambridge, Harvard University Press, 1964, p. 130.
56. Stigler, G.J., *Five Lectures on Economic Problems*, 1950, p. 4.
57. Smith, Vol. I., *op. cit.*, pp. 71-5.
58. See Rosenberg, N., 'Adam Smith on the Division of Labour: Two Views or One', *Economica*, 32, May 1965, pp. 127-39; emphasis added.
59. Smith, Vol. I., *op. cit.*, pp. 162-5.
60. 'The desire of food is limited in every man by the narrow capacity of the human stomach; but the desire of the conveniences and ornaments of buildings, dress, equipage and household furniture, seems to have no limit or certain boundary', *ibid.*, p. 165.
61. Smith, Vol. II., *op. cit.*, p. 159; Smith regards it as *self evident* that the interest of the consumer should have primacy over that of the producer. He emphasizes it because 'in the mercantile system the interest of the consumer is almost constantly sacrificed to that of the producer.'

62.   Smith, Vol. I., p. 63, and Vol. II., *op. cit.*, p. 245.

63.   Smith, Vol. I., *op. cit.*, p. 130.

64.   *Ibid.*, pp. 68-9.

65.   *Ibid.*, pp. 248-9.

66.   'The distribution of the necessities of life [is the same as it would have been] had the earth been divided into equal portion among all its inhabitants' *vide* the *Theory of Moral Sentiments*, 1st ed., pp. 349-50.

67.   Smith, Vol. II., *op. cit.*, p. 202.

68.   'The difference between the most dissimilar characters; between a philosopher and a common street porter, for example, seems to arise not so much from nature, as from habit, custom, and – education' *vide* Smith, Vol. I., *op. cit.*, p. 17.

69.   Quoted in Durant, W. and Durant, A., *The Age of Reason Begins*, New York, 1961, p. 599.

70.   *Ibid.*

71.   See Colletti, *op. cit.*, 'Rousseau as Critique of Civil Society', pp. 127-8.

72.   For instance, Smith writes: 'the peace and order of society is of more importance than even the relief of the miserable'.

73.   Smith, Vol. I., *op. cit.*, p. 435.

74.   See Kuhn, T.S., *The Structure of Scientific Revolution*, Chicago University Press (1962), 1970. Crucial to Kuhn's 'catastrophist' conception of scientific progress are two concepts: dominant paradigm which provides the framework for extending the knowledge of 'relevant' facts and improving the articulation of the paradigm itself *and* revolution through paradigm change.

75.   See Knight, F.H., 'The Ricardian Theory of Production and Distribution' in *On the History and Method of Economics*, Chicago University Press, 1956.

76.   See Fromme, E., *The Sane Society*, London, Routledge and Kegan Paul (1956), 1959, pp. 78-208.

77.   Even Joan Robinson's questioning of the rationality of a market economy does not go to the heart of the problem beyond saying that 'all economic answers are only political questions'.

78.   Wicksteed, P.H., 'The Scope and Method of Political Economy in the light of the "Marginal" Theory of Value and of Distribution', *Economic Journal*, 24, March, 1914, pp. 11-12.

79.   Duesenberry, J.S., *Income, Saving and the Theory of Consumer Behaviour*, Harvard University Press, 1949, p. 15.

80.   Stigler, G.J., 'Specialism: A Dissenting Opinion', in *The Intellectual and the Market Place and Other Essays*, New York, The Free Press of Glencoe, 1963, p. 11.

81.   Fromme, E., *op. cit.*, pp. 169-172.

82.   See Marx, K., *A Contribution to the Critique of Political Economy*, Moscow, Progress Publishers, 1970, pp. 20-1, and also, Colletti, *op. cit.*, 'Marxism as a sociology', pp. 10-12.

75

A Centenarian on a Bicentenarian: Léon Walras's *Eléments* on Adam Smith's *Wealth of Nations*

W.A. Jaffé

Source: *Canadian Journal of Economics*, Vol. 10 (1), February 1977, pp. 19-33,

A centenarian on a bicentenarian: Léon Walras's Eléments *on Adam Smith's* Wealth of Nations. Walras's *Eléments* mentions the *Wealth of Nations* only twice: to criticize Smith's alleged definition of economic science and to denounce as a sophism Smith's labour theory of value. Walras's failure to appreciate Smith is all the more surprising because Smith had, in fact, adumbrated a theory of general equilibrium similar to Walras's though far less rigorous and comprehensive; because Smith's analysis, like that of Walras, was inspired by Cartesian methodology; because both authors looked to Newtonian celestial mechanics as a model for their vision of social science; and because both had been imbued in their youth with the same natural law philosophy of Grotius and Pufendorf. Walras's blindness to all he had in common with Adam Smith is traceable, in part at least, to his oft-expressed anglophobia.

This year (1976), with the celebration of centenaries all the rage, the two hundredth anniversary of the *Wealth of Nations* is being grandly commemorated, as it deserves to be, all over the world. Occasionally it is remembered, here and there, that this year may also be considered the centenary of another outstanding event in the history of economics, the appearance of the first edition of Léon Walras's *Eléments d'économie politique pure* in 1874-77, just about one hundred years ago. If the *Wealth of Nations* seems to be taking precedence of the *Eléments* in the frequency and in the pomp and circumstance of their respective centenary observances, it is indicative of one of two things. Either we have here an instance of falsification of Newton's famous inverse square law of diminishing attraction with distance, since the greater distance from us of the *Wealth of Nations* apparently lends greater attraction to our view of the work; or the Scots know better than the French how to honour their intellectual forebears.

We may think of Walras's *Eléments* as a sprightly centenarian, still hobbling about and insinuating itself into all sorts of current economic literature where it persists in playing a living role, much to the dismay of the Marshallians and still more to the dismay of the classical neo-Marxists of Cambridge, England. The

Wealth of Nations, on the other hand, has meanwhile been relegated to the role of a venerated dead ancestor, whose memory is saluted on successive centenaries out of respect, but whose words no longer enter as an active ingredient in present-day theoretical discourse. For historians of economics, however, the *Wealth of Nations* continues to be an object of sympathetic critical appreciation which has been nowhere better expressed than by Vincent Bladen in his recent book, *From Adam Smith to Maynard Keynes: the heritage of political economy*. It has remained, above all, an inexhaustible source of material for exegetic commentary, which has been nowhere better conducted than by Samuel Hollander in his recent book, *The Economics of Adam Smith*.

It is precisely in Professor Hollander's masterly treatise that we see most clearly the link between the Walrasian and the Smithian theoretical systems. To reveal this link was indeed Professor Hollander's purpose, for he tells us explicity:

> we adopt the position that the use of modern analytical tools, concepts, and procedures may be of considerable aid in an analysis of the work of an early writer, *provided that he was operating within the general frame of reference for which these devices are appropriate*. In particular, we believe that there is justification for the utilization of the current state of knowledge regarding the general equilibrium process in a study of the economics of Adam Smith insofar as he adopted the position that the price mechanism can be relied upon to clear product and factor markets. (Hollander, 1973, 13)

And Professor Hollander quotes with approval Lord Robbins' earlier remark that 'from the point of view of theoretical Economics, the central achievement of [Adam Smith's *Wealth of Nations*] was his demonstration of the mode in which the division of labour tended to be kept in equilibrium by the mechanism of relative prices – a demonstration which . . . is in harmony with the most refined apparatus of the modern School of Lausanne.'[1]

For our present purpose, it does not matter whether we adopt the Robbins-Hollander view of the *Wealth of Nations* as an adumbration of modern general equilibrium theory, or whether we see in it a growth-cum-welfare model to which the allocation principle is subsidiary, or whether we regard the *Wealth of Nations* as an elaborate analytical plea for freedom from mercantilist-inspired state intervention, or whether we see in Adam Smith's great work the harbinger of a theory of capitalistic exploitation because of the emphasis he placed on 'the relations of production' (to use a Marxist phrase) in his analysis of market relations – the important thing is that from whatever prespective we may be inclined to view the *Wealth of Nations* we are bound to confront Adam Smith's pioneer analysis of the mechanism which holds the market system in general equilibrium. If this seems obvious to all historians of economics nowadays, whatever their school, surely one would think it must have been evident to Léon Walras, the celebrated founder of the modern fully-fledged version of general equilibrium economics. Strange to relate, it was not so. In what follows, I propose to offer an explanation for the failure on the part of Walras to recognize in the *Wealth of Nations* the presence of rudiments of his own great theory.

Let us first see what Walras's *Eléments*, now centenarian, had to say about Adam Smith's *Wealth of Nations*, now bicentenarian. The *Eléments* began, promisingly enough, with a tribute to Adam Smith, whom Walras credited with having achieved 'remarkable success' in establishing political economy as an autonomous branch of social science in 1776.[2] Having said this, Walras proceeded immediately to undo the praise by taking issue with what he thought was Adam Smith's too narrow conception of the scope of this autonomous branch of study.[3] To prove his point Walras quoted a passage from the Introduction to Book IV of the *Wealth of Nations*, where Adam Smith announced the topic of that particular Book as follows: 'Political œconomy, considered as a branch of the science of a statesman or legislator, proposes two distinct objects: first, to provide a plentiful revenue or subsistence for the people, or more properly to enable them to provide such a revenue or subsistence for themselves; and secondly, to supply the state or commonwealth with a revenue sufficient for the public services. It proposes to enrich both the people and the sovereign.'[4]

In total disregard of Adam Smith's qualifying phrase, 'considered as a branch of the science of a statesman or legislator,' Walras took this passage to represent a definition of economics in general instead of a characterization of *political* economy in the narrow sense which Adam Smith clearly intended. This characterization was all the more appropriate at the opening of Book IV because Adam Smith was just then embarking upon a particular discussion of various types of government policies in relation to trade and industry. Walras did not see that elsewhere Adam Smith ascribed a wider scope to economics in general – toward the end of Book IV where he defined appositionally 'what is *properly* called Political Economy' as a study of *'the nature and causes of the wealth of nations,'* and nothing else (Smith, 1776/1937, 643, italics mine).

Adam Smith meant by political economy in the large,[5] in contradistinction to 'political œconomy as a branch of the science of a statesman or legislator,' precisely what Léon Walras meant by it. Adam Smith's inquiry into 'the nature and causes of the wealth of nations' is no different, in essence, from Walras's 'théorie de la richesse sociale,' which is the subtitle of his *Eléments d'économie politique pure*. Yet Walras, who looked no further than the introduction to Book IV of the *Wealth of Nations*, and who did not even look into that properly, condemned Adam Smith's 'definition' as excessively narrow, because it confined the scope of the subject to its applied component and ignored all the rest.

For Walras, economics, considered as a whole, is made up of three components: the pure science component, the applied science component and the normative component. Had Walras penetrated more deeply into the *Wealth of Nations*, he could hardly have avoided perceiving that Adam Smith's *Inquiry* encompassed within its rich texture the other aspects of economics which together with the applied science aspect constituted the whole science of economics as Walras saw it. If there were no core of pure theory to the *Wealth of Nations*, the latter-day commentators quoted above could not have discerned foreshadowings, however imperfect, of general equilibrium models of the Lausanne School type in Adam Smith's analysis of the emergence of equilibrium from the spontaneous operations of free markets.

If there were no normative content, in Walras's sense, to the *Wealth of Nations*, Adam Smith could not have denounced 'violations of natural liberty' as 'unjust,' as, in fact, he did (Smith, 1776/1937, 141, 497). Of course, the particular aspect of applied economics, which Walras mistakenly thought made up the totality of Adam Smith's conception of the scope of economics, is the special subject matter of Book IV of the *Wealth of Nations*. There Adam Smith developed the very same theme that Walras did in his *Etudes d'économie politique appliquée*, to which, significantly, he gave the subtitle, *Théorie de la production de la richesse sociale*. The central problem of both Adam Smith's Book IV and Léon Walras's 'economie politique appliquée' was to determine what government policies best promote to production of wealth.

How little Walras understood, or even tried to understand, the *Wealth of Nations* is next seen in his treatment of Adam Smith's theory of value in Lesson 27 of the first edition of the *Eléments*, which later became Lesson 16 of the definitive edition.[6] In all the editions, this Lesson is entitled 'Exposition and refutation of Adam Smith's and J.B. Say's doctrines of the origin of value in exchange'; and in all editions the subhead of this Lesson summarizing Walras's argument reads, so far as Adam Smith is concerned, 'Adam Smith's *labour theory:* this doctrine merely declares that labour alone has value, but since it does not explain why labour has value, it leaves unexplained whence things in general derive their value.' The text that follows starts with the quotation of Adam Smith's well-known second paragraph from chapter V of Book I, which begins, 'The real price of everything, what every thing really costs to the man who wants to acquire it, is the toil and trouble of acquiring it,' and contains also the sentence 'Labour was the first price, the original purchase-money that was paid for all things' (Smith, 1776/1937, 30-1). Walras understood this passage to say that 'all things which have value and are exchangeable are labour in one form or another, so that labour alone constitutes the whole of social wealth.' Then, after brushing aside, as 'peu philosophique' (insufficiently philosophical), the subsidiary objection that there are things not produced by labour which also have value in exchange, Walras mounted the main attack. The argument which he thought clinching ran:

> Whether labour is all or part of social wealth is beside the point. In either case why is labour worth anything? Why is it exchangeable? That is the question before us. Adam Smith neither asked nor answered it. Surely, if labour has value and is exchangeable, it is because it is both useful and limited in quantity, that is to say because it is scarce. Value therefore comes from scarcity. If there are things other than labour which are scarce, they, like labour, will also have value and be exchangeable. So the theory which traces the origin of value to labour is a theory that is completely devoid of meaning rather than too narrow, entirely gratuitous rather than merely deficient.[7]

Thus at one fell syllogistic stroke, Walras imagined he had demolished Adam Smith's theory of value forever, leaving nothing more to be said. It turns out, however, that Walras's argument, which he presumably meant to be truly 'philosophique,' was flagrantly sophistical. What Walras destroyed so effectively was not Adam Smith's theory of value at all, but a caricature of that theory. Where did Adam Smith declare, as Walras alleged, that labour alone has value? Neither I nor anyone else I know of has ever found such an assertion in the *Wealth of Nations* or in any other writing of Adam Smith for that matter. Germain Garnier's French translation of the *Wealth of Nations* from which Walras took his quotation did not contain any such misconstruction of the original.[8] Labour may well have been for Adam Smith the source of value, the substance of value, or the measure of value, but was never represented as the only thing which has value in exchange.

This is not to say that Walras's criticism was devoid of any semblance of validity. Insofar as Adam Smith used his labour theory (be it a labour-cost or labour-command theory) to define an ultimate source of value, whatever that may mean, Walras's argument against it was logically impeccable, even if he was wrong in attributing to Adam Smith the notion that 'labour alone has value.' Though a phrase here and a phrase there in the *Wealth of Nations* may betray a fleeting interest in the ultimate source of value, that was clearly not Adam Smith's major concern. In his chapter V of Book I, devoted to the distinction between 'real and nominal price,' he was primarily interested in value not from the standpoint of evaluation but from two other standpoints, in fact the same two standpoints that Karl Marx subsequently adopted. The two functions that the labour theory of value performed for Adam Smith were, in essence, the same as those Michio Morishima tells us it performed for Marx, '(1) to explain the equilibrium prices (or the exchange values) of commodities, around which actual prices fluctuate over time, and (2) to provide aggregators, or weights of aggregation, in terms of which a large number of industries . . . are aggregated' (Morishima, 1973, 10). Though the principle of aggregation was the same, Karl Marx and Adam Smith nevertheless differed in the uses to which they put their respective aggregates: Karl Marx used his to analyse the relations in the economy between the 'department' producing capital goods taken in the aggregate and the 'department producing consumers' goods, again taken in the aggregate; Adam Smith on the other hand wanted to measure, or at least to estimate, the progress of 'opulence,' i.e. the movement in the aggregate output of the nation over time and under various systems of government policy (cf. Robertson and Taylor, 1957, 195-7).

If Léon Walras had taken the pains to unravel Adam Smith's theory of value in the light of the purpose or purposes it was designed to serve, I don't see how he could have concluded that the theory was irredeemably specious. Instead of saying that the theory was entirely gratuitous rather than merely deficient, he might have put it the other way around, and said that the theory was merely deficient rather than wholly gratuitous. The latter is certainly the judgment of several of our contemporary scholars who have examined the theory. Professor Bladen, who places Adam Smith's theory of value in the context of the problem of measuring *changes* in real price over time, calls the theory 'debatable,' but not one that it is legitimate to regard as nonsense (Bladen, 1974, 24; cf. Bladen, 1975). Joseph Schumpeter, whom no one would accuse of being excessively partial to Adam Smith and who found no better place for Adam Smith than in a chapter on 'Consultant administrators and pamphleteers,' nevertheless opposed no 'logical objection' to Adam Smith's choice of labour as *numéraire* for making intertemporal and interlocal comparisons of value in exchange (1954, 188). Yet Léon Walras thought the labour theory deserved nothing better than cavalier dismissal.

This is not an appropriate occasion, nor am I qualified, to puzzle out what Adam Smith really meant by his bewildering variety of pronouncements on value. As Jacob Viner once observed: 'Smith can be quoted in support of all of the following propositions: that labour is the sole regulator of exchange value; that labour has, among the elements entering into production, a peculiar and perhaps even an exclusive value-creating power; that the relative values of different commodities are, or should be, proportional to their labour-time costs; that all incomes are extracted from the product of labour' (1968, 327). No wonder, then, that the *Wealth of Nations* is so often read, as Marcel Proust tells us novels are read, allowing the reader to find his own innermost preoccupations mirrored in the book. Nor is it any wonder that the *Wealth of Nations* is susceptible of as many interpretations as there are commentators, whose preoccupations range from those of Ronald Meek or Maurice Dobb at one end of the ideological spectrum to those of Friedrich Hayek at the other end (Hayek, 1976).

What can we say was Léon Walras's preoccupation that led him to condemn Adam Smith's theory of value out of hand as a logical absurdity? It turns out that the cavilling interpretation of the theory we find in the *Eléments* was not Léon Walras's, but that of his father, Auguste Walras. Léon Walras did little more than repeat in summary what his father had written before him in chapter XII of *De la nature de la richesse et de l'origine de la valeur*, published in 1831.[9] The little more that Léon Walras added was unfortunate, for Auguste Walras had made a better job of it.

Auguste Walras perceived more clearly than his son that Adam Smith had been principally concerned with the measure of value and had considered only peripherally and inferentially its origin. To illustrate the weakness of Adam Smith's implicit understanding of the origin of value he cited the very same passage from the *Wealth of Nations* that Léon Walras used as the basis for his argument. Auguste Walras, on his side, reproached Adam Smith not only for implying in this passage that all exchangeable goods are produced in one way or another by labour, but also and more importantly for failing even to inquire why labour has value. The question of the ultimate source of value in some absolute, rather than relative, sense loomed large in Auguste Walras's mind because of his point of departure when he turned from philosophy and law to economics (Walras, 1908, 171-2). His interest in economics was first aroused when he attempted to clarify the concept of property in order to meet the challenge of the socialists of his day who were denouncing the institution of property with more vehemence than understanding. Seeking guidance from economics and not finding it there, he came to the conclusion that both property and value in exchange have a common origin in the limitation in quantity of certain objects of desire. If all desirable things were not scarce, there would be no property, nor would there be value in exchange. The source of value, irrespective of its measure, was then for Auguste Walras, not Adam Smith's labour, but scarcity.

There is no need to retell here the well-known tale how Léon Walras metamorphosed his father's nebulous notion of scarcity into an analytical precision tool which he still called 'rareté,'[10] but which we usually call marginal utility;[11] nor need we repeat how Léon Walras used the tool as a unifying and organizing principle to endow his general equilibrium model with over-all consistency. It suffices to note that, though it was altogether irrelevant to the construction of his general equilibrium model, he attributed to his new 'rareté' the same capacity to generate absolute value his father had attributed to the old 'rareté.'[12] This he did in deference to his father's central proposition that 'la rareté est la cause de la valeur,' a proposition which, to say the least, had nothing to do with Léon Walras's multi-equational system of general equilibrium. Nevertheless, he seized upon it as the ultimate standard of a correct theory of value, thus permitting him to reject Adam Smith's theory as he did all other theories that did not conform to the standard.

It is a great pity that Léon Walras foreclosed in this way all true communication with his great predecessor. In fact, outside of Walras's misbegotten criticism of Smith's alleged 'definition' of economics and his peremptory attack on Smith's theory of value, there is no mention of Adam Smith's name in the *Eléments*. Indeed, it is doubtful that Walras ever read the *Wealth of Nations* attentively, even in the Garnier translation. Not only in the *Eléments*, but on the rare occasions that he cited Adam Smith elsewhere, the quotations appear to be, if not second-hand, at least drawn from references already made by others.[13] In this and other ways, Léon Walras's occasional excursions into the history of economics show him up as an execrable historian. His only interest was either to bolster his own theoretical contributions by involving the posthumous support of respected forerunners, or else to berate as fatal flaws anything he found in the writings of others that did not accord with his own ideas.[14]

Had Léon Walras been a better historian, had he read the entire *Wealth of Nations* with care, and, above all, had he contemplated the *Wealth of Nations* in the light of Adam Smith's other writings which were available to him, he might have found that he had much more in common with the reputed founder of his science than he suspected. Other writings of Adam Smith were, in fact, available to him, as is clear from the existence in his day of French translations not only of *The Theory of Moral Sentiments*, but also of *The Essays on Philosophical Subjects*, the latter of which contained Adam Smith's all-important 'Principles which Lead and Direct Philosophical Inquiries, Illustrated by the History of Astronomy.'[15]

If Walras had read the 'History of Astronomy' in the original English (which he was perfectly capable of doing) or in translation, he could hardly have failed to inquire into its relation to the *Wealth of Nations*, which he might then have found was methodologically as much inspired by Newtonian celestial mechanics as his own *Eléments d'économie politique pure*. The *Wealth of Nations* alone could have told Walras as much, for in Article 2nd of chapter I in Book V, Adam Smith distinctly drew an analogy between the sciences which account for 'the great phenomena of nature, the revolutions of the heavenly bodies, eclipses, comets; thunder, lightning and other extraordinary meteors' on the one hand, and moral philosophy, which we would to-day classify as social or behavioural science, on the other. According to Adam Smith, after natural philosophy had set the example of 'a systematical arrangement of different observations connected by a few common principles,' then 'something of the same kind was attempted in morals' (Smith, 1776/1937, 723-4).

Certainly the attempt was made in Adam Smith's *Theory of Moral Sentiments*, where 'sympathy' in the etymological sense served as the common principle regulating the conduct of individuals in such a manner as to create a harmonious human society. And in the *Wealth of Nations* it was the joint principle of an alleged primordial 'propensity to truck, barter and exchange' and a universal 'desire of bettering our condition,' which, working in tandem, bound together the operations of innumerable markets in such a way as to promote the orderly progress of 'opulence.' In each of these systems the connecting principles played the same role as Newton's principle of universal gravitation; and, as may be surmised from Adam Smith's 'History of Astronomy,' they were probably intended to do so in much the same mechanical fashion.

Walras, having also been guided by the precedent of Newtonian celestial mechancis, used his 'rareté' as the connecting common principle in the construction of his general equilibrium model. One of Léon Walras's last publications, 'Economique et mécanique' (1909), published the year before he died, was a reaffirmation of his reliance on the pattern of Newtonian mechanics to inform his conception of catallactic mechanics. From the age of nineteen on, when Walras first read Louis Poinsot's *Eléments de statique*, he had sought to create a theory of economics with the same formal properties that characterized celestial mechanics.[16] A hundred years or so before Walras, when Adam Smith was still at the threshold of his intellectual career, he too had imprinted upon him for life the Newtonian ideal of science founded on chains of reasoning deducible from mechanistic laws. It appears from Adam Smith's 'Letter to the Authors of the *Edinburgh Review*,' dated July 1755, that in his case it was d'Alembert who pointed the way by his articles in Diderot's *Encyclopédie* on the rise, progress, and affinities of the various sciences (Lindgren, 1967, 18; cf. Scott, 1937, 53). We now have Herbert F. Thomson's article (1965) on 'Adam Smith's philosophy of science' to demonstrate how Adam Smith pursued the Newtonian ideal of science both in the *Theory of Moral Sentiments* and in the *Wealth of Nations*.

In their analytical mode of thinking, Adam Smith and Walras were, at bottom, Cartesians. One being a child and the other the grandchild of the Enlightenment, they both employed in their economic reasoning the method that Descartes was the first to define and that served the physical sciences so spectacularly during the Enlightenment. How far Adam Smith was Cartesian has been very well shown in a recent book on *Philosophy and Economics* by Piero V. Mini, a book which, though uneven in other respects, is excellent for its discussion of the Cartesian inspiration of the *Wealth of Nations* (Mini, 1974, chap. 4). It should be noted that Adam Smith's repudiation of the *substance* of Descartes' theories of vortices, and so on, did not prevent him from holding the *form* of Descartes' analysis in the highest regard. In his *Lectures on Rhetoric and Belles Lettres* Adam Smith declared that Descartes was in reality the first 'in Natural Philosophy, or any science of that sort' to attempt a method of laying down 'certain principles, primary or proved, in the beginning, from whence we account for the several phenomena, connecting all together by the same chain.' Though Adam Smith took Descartes' application of the method to be, to say the least, 'dubious,' he thought the method itself 'most philosophical' since it was the very same method that Newton employed (quoted by Thomson, 1965, 214-15).

Léon Walras proved to be more wholeheartedly Cartesian. We know from his 'Notice autobiographique' and from his letters that he studied Descartes, Newton, and Lagrange at an early age.[17] Toward the end of his life, he was delighted to read in an article, 'Les mathématiques dans les sciences sociales,' by Vito Volterra, that the new mathematical economics, which Walras, among others, was instrumental in creating, belonged methodologically to the same class of scientific achievements as those of Descartes in geometry, of Lagrange in mechanics, of Maxwell in physics, and of Helmholtz in physiology.[18]

This is not all that Walras might have discovered he had in common with Adam Smith. Though more than a century apart in the years of their birth, though they were brought up in quite different lands and different social and cultural settings, nevertheless, in their early, most impressionable years they had imbibed the same philosophy of natural law. While the particular streams from which each of them drew this philosophy were wide apart, the separate streams had their source in the writings of Grotius and Pufendorf. It is well known that between the ages of fourteen and seventeen, Adam Smith studied these two great exponents of natural law in Francis Hutcheson's class at Glasgow College, where an edition of Pufendorf's *De officio hominis et civis* annotated by Francis Hutcheson's teacher, Gershom Carmichael, was used as a text (Taylor, 1965, 25-8). Walras, on his side, absorbed this same philosophy from his father, Auguste Walras, who had studied a textbook presentation of Pufendorf in the *Eléments du droit naturel* by a Swiss publicist, Jean Jacques Burlamaqui. Besides, Burlamaqui was cited by both Auguste Walras and Léon Walras as an anticipator of the scarcity theory of value.[19]

Moreover, had Walras been so inclined, he might have learned from the *Theory of Moral Sentiments* that he and Adam Smith were kindred souls in their philosophical contempt for those advances in modern technology which corrupt and contaminate our private lives. In one of those striking figures of speech which adorn Adam Smith's writings, he conjured up the vision of 'enormous and operose machines contrived to produce a few trifling conveniences to the body, consisting of springs the most nice and delicate, which must be kept in order with the most anxious attention, and which in spite of all our care are ready every moment to burst into pieces, and to crush in their ruins their unfortunate possessor'[20] – a perfect premonition, if there ever was one, of the modern automobile. Had Walras known this passage, it would have warmed his heart. In 1909 when the rector of the University of Lausanne, who knew Walras's eccentricities well, offered to take Walras to his Jubilee ceremony in an automobile, he added, 'if you are not afraid of this sort of conveyance.'[21] Before that, writing to his friend Georges Renard in 1896, Walras described with horror the new electric tramway in Lausanne, with its ugly overhead trolley wires and screeching wheels, and then exclaimed: 'We have too much chemical and mechanical progress and not enough political and economic progress. We are going to the devil by electric tramway!'[22] Walras longed for the peace and quiet he knew in his childhood in Evreux, Normandy, in the pre-railway days. In 1892 he wrote to another friend, Gustave Maugin, 'For my part, I prefer the simpler life that France led around 1847, before the advent of railways.'[23]

Actually, Walras and Adam Smith were very much of the same temper in their attitude to life and the world. Léon Walras was born in the apartment of the principal of the Collège d'Evreux, where his father, besides being principal, taught rhetoric and philosophy. Adam Smith came from a family of higher civil servants with connections in the professions and in the Aberdeen universities (Scott, 1937, 395-408). Both Adam Smith and Léon Walras were university professors for whom, whatever their particular occupation was at any moment of their careers, intellectual life was all. I venture to say that this circumstance is reflected in their respective economic theories, each in its own way. Adam Smith belonged to an ancient line, now nearly, if not wholly, extinct, of philosophers who turned their attention to economics – primarily, so it seems to me, to discover a way to make the world safe for philosophy. If Aristotle concerned himself with justice in exchange, it was because without such justice, intellectual and social merit, which he measured not in physical or market valued productivity but in virtue, would not receive the material support it deserved.

Adam Smith, who perceived more clearly than Aristotle the dependence of the cultivation of philosophy on the material conditions of society, urged the suppression of all impediments to the natural growth of the wealth of nations. Though he was keenly aware of the existence of flagrant injustices in the distribution of wealth and income in 'civilized societies,' though he attributed the glaring disparities not only to 'violence,' as Boisguilbert and Cantillon had done before him, but also to what he called, in an unforgettable phrase, 'the more orderly oppression of law' (Scott, 1937, 327) he nevertheless refrained from suggesting any remedy for these acknowledged injustices. Why is that so? I should say that it was because, in his eyes, the inequitable distribution of wealth and income possessed the saving grace of creating and preserving the 'distinction of ranks,' without which there would be no class possessing sufficiently 'liberal fortunes' to permit its members to pursue 'study for its own sake, as an original pleasure or good in itself, without regarding its tendency to procure the means of other pleasures' (Lindgren, 1967, 47-50). As Adam Smith meant his philosophers' paradise for this side of eternity, he had to take into account the world here below. His economics, then, consisted of a systematic analysis of the workings of human society, such as he knew it and such as he conceived it to have evolved in the course of history. It was an analysis directed primarily to an understanding of the growth of the opulence within a society humanely organized for the cultivation of philosophy.

Walras, without being anything like the complete philosopher we find in Adam Smith, was none the less a devotee of natural law philosophy and designed his general equilibrium model as an analytical expression of ethical ideals derived from that philosophy. Though the *Eléments* appears on the surface as a completely *wert-frei* synoptic view of the interdependent operations of an economic system under a hypothetical regime of perfect competition, it can be shown that the model is through and through informed and animated by Walras's moral convictions.[24] His latent purpose in contriving his general equilibrium model was not to describe or analyse the workings of the economic system as it existed, nor was it primarily to portray the purely economic relations within a network of markets under the assumption of a theoretically perfect regime of free competition. It was rather to demonstrate the possibility of formulating axiomatically a rationally consistent economic system that would satisfy the demands of social justice without overstepping the bounds imposed by the natural exigencies of the real world.

Why did Léon Walras stubbornly refuse to open his eyes to so many resemblances between himself and Adam Smith? The only explanation I can offer lies in his fanatical anglophobia, an anglophobia which in the nineteenth century made no distinction between the Scots and the English. This is not surprising when we remember that Léon Walras's father was a lad in Montpellier during the Napoleonic Wars and that thenceforth for the whole Walras family everything across the Channel betokened 'perfidious Albion.'

Lest it be imagined that I am inventing this explanation out of whole cloth or exaggerating, let me cite in the original two typical expressions of Léon Walras's deep-seated feelings against the English. In 1881 he wrote to a Dutch correspondent, d'Aulnis de Bourouill, 'Quant à vous, ami des Anglais, je vous souhaite bien du plaisir avec eux, mais mon expérience ne leur est pas favorable. Leur philosophie est nulle; leur science étroite et bornée; et [leur] point de vue égoïste et mesquin.'[25] Ten years later, writing to the Russian economist Bortkiewicz, he declared, 'les Anglais sont d'autant plus gracieux qu'on est plus ferme avec eux. On peut, jusqu'à un certain point, leur appliquer notre ancien proverbe français: "Oignez vilain, il vous poindra, Poignez vilain, il vous oindra."'[26]

If there is a lesson to be learned from this sad story of Walras's failure to appreciate Adam Smith, it is that science and scholarship suffer grievously when national, sectarian, and ideological animosities are allowed to invade their realm.

Notes

This is a slightly revised version of the paper I presented at the Tenth Annual Meeting of the Canadian Economic Association, Laval University, Quebec City, 1 June 1976. In the revision I have taken no account of the excellent comments of Professor Dusan Pokorny, the discussant of the paper at the meeting, in order to leave intact the full force of his criticism and supplementation, with which I am largely, if not wholly, in agreement. I am indebted for editorial guidance to two constant friends, Professor Samuel Hollander of the University of Toronto and Professor John Buttrick of York University, who, in all fairness, must be absolved from blame for the contents of the paper. The research was supported by a Killam Senior Research Scholarship of the Canada Council, for which I am most thankful.

1. Hollander (1973, 19-20), quoted from Robbins (1932, 68-9). Before Lord Robbins, Jacob Viner had observed in 1927 in his justly famous lecture, 'Adam Smith and laissez faire': 'There is much weight of authority and of evidence . . . that Smith's major claim to originality, in English thought at least, was his detailed and elaborate application to the wilderness of economic phenomena of the unifying concept of a co-ordinated and mutually interdependent system of cause and effect relationships which philosophers and theologians had already applied to the world in general' (reprinted in Viner, 1958, 213).

2. Walras (1874-77/ . . .), § 3 in all eds of the *Eléments*.
3. Ibid., § § 4-5 in all eds.
4. Smith (1776/1937, 397). Here as elsewhere the pages referred to in the *Wealth of Nations* are those of the Modern Library edition.
5. We must not allow ourselves to be misled by the ambiguity of Adam Smith's use of the term 'political economy.' The short and simple term 'economics' to designate our subject in the large was not brought into current use until 1879 when Alfred and Mary Paley Marshall introduced it in their *Economics of Industry* (2).
6. Walras (1874-77/ . . .), § § 157-158 of definitive ed.).
7. Walras, (1874-77/ . . .). § 158 of the definitive ed.).
8. The French translation of the *Wealth of Nations (Recherches sur la nature et les causes de la richesse des nations)* which was considered standard in the nineteenth century was that of Germain Garnier. The first edition of this translation, which appeared in 1805, was followed through the century by a series of revised editions, annotated and amplified by a succession of editors. The best known was the Guillaumin edition, published in 2 vols in 1843-4.
9. Auguste Walras (1831 [167-72]/1938 [188-91]).
10. Jaffé (1972 [387-9]/1973 [121-3]).
11. Walras (1874-77/ . . .) English transl., 506-7, Translator's Note 9 to Lesson 8.
12. Ibid., § 98 (§ 101 of definitive ed.). Cf. English transl., 512-13, Translator's Note 3 to Lesson 10.
13. This is the case, for example, with one of the quotations from Adam Smith in Walras (1880 [1898/1936, 370]). The passage quoted from Book II, chapt. II of the *Wealth of Nations* (304-5) had appeared (in a different French translation) in Say (1819) 1, 446-7.
14. E.g. Lessons 16 and 37-39 of the definitive edition of Walras (1874-77/ . . .).
15. Adam Smith's *théories des sentiments moraux* 2d ed. (Paris: Barrois, 1830) translated by the Marquise de Condorcet in 1798 is generally considered the best of the early French translations of *The Theory of Moral Sentiments*. Adam Smith's posthumously published *Essays on Philosophical Subjects*, ed. Joseph Black and James Hutton (London: Cadell and Davies; Edinburgh: Creech, 1795), was translated as *Essais philosophiques* by P. Prevost (Paris: Agasse, 1797). The 'History of Astronomy,' first published in the *Essays on Philosophical Subjects*, has recently been reprinted in Lindgren (1967, 30-109).
16. Jaffé (1965, III, 148-50, Letter 1483, esp. n. 7).
17. Jaffé (1965, I, 2; III, 149, Letter 1483, and 252-3, Letter 1576).
18. Ibid. (III, 296, Letter 1618, n. 2). Vito Volterra's article appeared in *La revue du mois*, 10 Jan. 1906, 1, 1-21.
19. Burlamaqui (1821). See also Auguste Walras (1831/1938, chap. 15) and Léon Walras (1874-77/ . . ., § 159) (§ 161 of definitive ed.).
20. Smith (1759/1797), I, 462 [8th ed.]).
21. Jaffé (1965, III, 416, Letter 1750).
22. Ibid. (II, 690-1, Letter 1256).
23. Ibid. (II, 493, Letter 1057).
24. From his very first book on economics, *L'économie politique et la justice* (1860), to his last public utterance on the occasion of his Jubilee in 1909, Walras's predominant occupation was with the problem of social justice, (see my article, Jaffé (forthcoming) and cf. Jaffé, 1965, *I*, 208-12, Letter 148).
25. Jaffé (1965, I, 704, Letter 513).
26. Jaffé (1965, II, 428, Letter 996).

References

Bladen, V. (1974) *From Adam Smith to Maynard Keynes: the heritage of political economy* (Toronto: University of Toronto Press).
Bladen, V. (1975) 'Command over labour: a study in misinterpretation.' This JOURNAL 8, 504-19.
Burlamaqui, J.J. (1821) *Elémens du droit naturel*. Nouvelle édn (Paris: Delestre-Boulage).
Hayek, F.A. (1976) 'Adam Smith's foresight: open society and disorder.' *Globe and Mail* (Toronto, March 23).

Hollander, S. (1973) *The Economics of Adam Smith* (Toronto: University of Toronto Press).
Jaffé, W., ed. (1965) *Correspondence of Léon Walras and Related Papers* 3 vols (Amsterdam: North Holland, for the Royal Netherlands Academy of Sciences and Letters).
Jaffé, W. (1972) 'Léon Walras's role in the marginal revolution of the 1870s. '*History of Political Economy* 4, 379-405; Republished in Black et al., eds, *The Marginal Revolution in Economics* (Durham, North Carolina: Duke University Press).
Jaffé, W. (forthcoming) 'The normative bias of the Walrasian mode: Walras vs Gossen.' *Quarterly Journal of Economics*.
Lindgren, J.R., ed. (1967) *The Early Writings of Adam Smith* (NY: A.M. Kelley).
Marshall, A. and M.P. Marshall (1879) *The Economics of Industry* (London: Macmillan).
Mini, P.V. (1974) *Philosophy and Economics* (Gainesville: University of Florida Press).
Morishima, M. (1973) *Marx's Economics, A dual theory of value and growth* (Cambridge: University Press).
Robbins, L. (1932) *An Essay on the Nature and Significance of Economic Science* (London: Macmillan).
Robertson, H.M. and W.L. Taylor (1957) 'Adam Smith's approach to the theory of value.' *Economic Journal* 67, 181-98.
Say, J.B. (1819) *Traité d'économie politique* 4th ed., 2 vols (Paris: Deterville).
Schumpeter, J.A. (1954) *History of Economic Analysis* (New York: Oxford University Press).
Scott, W.R. (1937) *Adam Smith as Student and Professor* (Glasgow: Jackson, Son and Co).
Smith, A. (1759/1797) *The Theory of Moral Sentiments* (London: Millar; 8th ed., 2 vols; London: Cadell and Davies).
Smith, A. (1776/1937) *An Inquiry into the Nature and Causes of the Wealth of Nations* (London: Strahan and Cadell; Modern Library edn, Edwin Cannan, ed, New York: Random House).
Taylor, W.L. (1965) *Francis Hutcheson and David Hume as Predecessors of Adam Smith* (Durham, North Carolina: Duke University Press).
Thomson, H.F. (1965) 'Adam Smith's philosophy of science.' *Quarterly Journal of Economics* 79, 212-33.
Viner, J. (1958) *The Long View and the Short* (Glencoe, Illinois: Free Press).
Viner, J. (1968) 'Smith, Adam.' In David L. Sills, ed., *International Encyclopedia of the Social Sciences* 14, 322-8.
Walras, Auguste (1831/1938) *De la nature de la richesse et de l'origine de la valeur* (Paris: Johanneau; 2d edn, ed. Gaston Leduc, Paris: Alcan).
Walras, L. (1860) *L'économie politique et la justice* (Paris: Guillaumin).
Walras, L. (1874-77/ . . .) *Eléments d'économie Politique pure ou Théorie de la richesse sociale* (1st ed. [in two instalments], Lausanne: Corbaz, 1874-77; 2d ed., Lausanne: Rouge, 1889; 3rd ed., Lausanne: Rouge, 1896; 4th ed., Lausanne: Rouge, 1900; definitive ed. (published posthumously), 1926. Reprinted Paris: Pichon and Durand-Auzias, 1952. English translation by William Jaffé, *Elements of Pure Economics*, London: Allen and Unwin, 1954 [Reprints of Economic Classics, New York: Augustus Kelley, 1969]).
Walras, L. (1880) 'Théorie mathématique du billet de banque.' *Bulletin de la société vaudoise des sciences naturelles* 2d Series, 16 (80), 553-92. Republished in Walras (1898/1936, 339-75).
Walras, L. (1898/1936) *Etudes d'économie politique appliquée (Théorie de la production de la richesse sociale)* Lausanne: Rouge. 2d edn, ed. G. Leduc, Paris: Pichon and Durand-Auzias).
Walras, L. (1908) 'Un initiateur en économie politique: A.A. Walras.' *Revue du Mois* 6 (2), 170-83.
Walras, L. (1909) 'Economique et mécanique.' *Bulletin de la société vaudoise des sciences naturelles* 5th Series, 45 (166), 313-27.

76

The Wealth of Nations

R.H. Coase

Source: *Economic Inquiry*, Vol. 15, July 1977, pp. 309-25.

We meet today, on the ninth of March, to commemorate the 200th anniversary of the publication of the *Wealth of Nations*. We do this, I believe, not simply because of its historical importance as a landmark in the development of economics, but because it is a book that still lives and from which we continue to learn. Commentaries such as mine are only of value as a preliminary to reading the *Wealth of Nations* itself or, if this has already been done, to rereading it.

The *Wealth of Nations* is a masterpiece. With its interrelated themes, its careful observations on economic life, and its powerful ideas – clearly expressed and beautifully illustrated – it cannot fail to work its magic. But the very richness of the book means that each of us will see it in a somewhat different way. It is not like a multiplication table, or a modern textbook with a few simple messages which, once absorbed, makes a rereading unnecessary. The *Wealth of Nations* has many ideas from which to choose and many problems to ponder. Though the time may come when we will have nothing more to learn from the *Wealth of Nations* or, more accurately, when what we would learn would be irrelevant to our problems, that time has not yet been reached, nor will it, in my view, for a long time to come.

Adam Smith was born in 1723. He went to the University of Glasgow when he was fourteen years old, according to Scott somewhat older than was usual at the time. In 1740, when he was seventeen years old, he graduated with an MA. He was then elected to what we would call a post-graduate fellowship at Oxford. There, neglected by his teachers who, as he observes in the *Wealth of Nations*, received their pay whether they taught or not, he studied on his own for six years. He then returned to Scotland and, in the period between 1748 and 1751, gave public lectures in Edinburgh on literature, rhetoric, and jurisprudence. It seems clear that the lectures on jurisprudence included an early version of some of the leading ideas which were to appear later in the *Wealth of Nations*. In 1751, he was appointed professor at the University of Glasgow, at first of logic, but shortly afterwards of moral philosophy.

In 1759 he published, in *The Theory of Moral Sentiments*, the substance of a major part of his lectures. But Adam Smith also gave lectures on jurisprudence and, in them, he presented his views on economics under the heading, "Police."

As Cannan points out, this may appear strange to us, but this is only because Adam Smith believed that the economic system should be controlled through the operations of the market, a view which, largely because of his work, many of us share. Had Adam Smith been, in Cannan's words, "an old-fashioned believer in state control of trade and industry," as were many of his contemporaries and most of his predecessors, this would, of course, have seemed the most natural heading in the world under which to discuss the determination of prices.[1] The surprise felt by those listening to his lectures at Glasgow would not have been at the heading, but at his conclusion.

Adam Smith resigned his professorship in 1764 to become tutor to the young Duke of Buccleuch and passed the next two and a half years with him, mainly in France. This position brought with it a pension of £300 a year for life and, after his return to Britain in 1766, Adam Smith spent most of his time in Kirkcaldy, his birthplace, where he devoted himself to study and the writing of the *Wealth of Nations*.

From this account of Adam Smith's life it is possible to discern the special circumstances which, his genius apart, made the *Wealth of Nations* so extraordinarily influential. First, many of his main ideas were conceived very early in his life, very probably in his days at Oxford. He thought about these ideas and enriched his analysis by reading and observation for about thirty years. His life included long periods, in Oxford and later in Kirkcaldy, in which he worked out his position completely alone, with little or no contact with others interested in economic questions. Adam Smith called himself a "solitary philosopher," and though he also seems to have been a "clubable" man, there can be no doubt that he enjoyed his own company and could work well on his own without requiring any stimulus from others. In a letter to his friend David Hume, written from Kirkcaldy, he says: "My business here is study . . . My amusements are long solitary walks by the seaside. You may judge how I spend my time. I feel myself, however, extremely happy, comfortable, and contented. I never was perhaps more so in all my life."[2]

Adam Smith's independence of mind and his liking for solitude which gave his independence free reign, must have helped greatly in writing a book which was to launch a new subject. It is perhaps no accident that Adam Smith and Isaac Newton were both posthumous children. Historians of economic thought tell us, I am sure correctly, of the works of others, such as Hutcheson and Mandeville, that influenced Smith. But he absorbed their ideas and made them serve purposes of his own.

The popular success of the *Wealth of Nations*, however, depended on another factor: its readability. Adam Smith, as is clear from the subjects dealt with in the Edinburgh lectures and later at Glasgow, was interested in the art of writing – and James Boswell was one of his pupils. Schumpeter acknowledges Adam Smith's skill in rather grudging terms: ". . . he disliked whatever went beyond plain common sense. He never moved above the heads of even the dullest readers. He led them on gently, encouraging them by trivialities and homely observations, making them feel comfortable all along."[3] What Schumpeter means is that the *Wealth of Nations* can be read with pleasure. It is clear, amusing, and persuasive. Adam Smith's style is, of course, very different from that of most modern economists who are either incapable of writing simple

English or have decided that they have more to gain by concealment.

That Adam Smith worked alone and wrote the *Wealth of Nations* over half a lifetime was in part responsible for the qualities which made it so influential. But it also brought with it some disadvantages. It has often been remarked that the *Wealth of Nations* is not particularly well constructed, with sections awkwardly placed. Indeed, Adam Smith himself labels some very long sections, "Digressions." The explanation normally given is that as he wrote the *Wealth of Nations* over a very long period, completing sections one at a time, he found it too onerous a task to make the substantial revisions in earlier sections which a finer construction would have called for. I accept this explanation. It seems clear that Adam Smith found writing extremely painful. This seems to have been true even for the physical act of writing and he usually composed by dictating to an amanuensis.

The *Wealth of Nations* also contains some obscurities and inconsistencies which might have been removed had Adam Smith not been so solitary but had consulted more with others, although it has to be confessed that not many of his contemporaries were capable of a close analysis of his work. There is, however, another reason why Adam Smith did not give that added attention which might have removed some of the inconsistencies: he did not know that he was Adam Smith. Had he known that we would be discussing his work 200 years after it was published, he would undoubtedly have been even more careful about his writing. But I think we may be glad that he could not have foreseen this great interest in his work, for the most probable result would have been an unwillingness to publish the *Wealth of Nations* at all. When Adam Smith was dying he asked that his surviving manuscripts be burnt which, to the despair of all lovers of Adam Smith's work, was in fact done. A man so anxious that work not properly finished should be withheld from the public, would have been greatly concerned about the kind of scrutiny which the *Wealth of Nations* has come to receive. Another remark he made as he awaited death was to regret that he had done so little: ". . . I meant to have done more."[4] All of which suggests that he never knew what he had achieved – that his concentrated study had produced the most important book on economics ever written, a work of genius.

What Adam Smith did was to give economics its shape. The subjects he dealt with, the approach that he used, even the order in which the various topics are treated can be found repeated in economics courses as they are given today. From one point of view, the last 200 years of economics have been little more than a vast mopping up operation in which economists have filled in the gaps, corrected the errors, and refined the analysis of the *Wealth of Nations*.

Adam Smith succeeded in creating a system of analysis – our system – by a series of masterstrokes. Some are very familiar to us. Others, it seems to me, are not, even yet, fully appreciated. Adam Smith's starting point is well-known. He abandoned the idea, held by many mercantilists, that wealth consists of gold or money. To Adam Smith, the wealth of a nation was what people get for their money, that is, what is produced, either directly, or indirectly by exchange with other nations. This is the viewpoint he expresses in the opening words of the *Wealth of Nations*:

The annual labour of every nation is the fund which originally supplies it with all the necessaries and conveniencies of life which it annually consumes, and which consist always either in the immediate produce of that labour, or in what is purchased with that produce from other nations. According therefore, as this produce, or what is purchased with it, bears a greater or smaller proportion to the number of those who are to consume it, the nation will be better or worse supplied with all the necessaries and conveniencies for which it has occasion.[5]

We can see immediately that what Adam Smith is concerned with is the flow of real goods and services over a period of time and its relation to the numbers of those who are to consume. The emphasis is on real income, not money income: "The labourer is rich or poor, is well or ill rewarded, in proportion to the real, not to the nominal price of his labour."[6]

This is Adam Smith's starting point. The welfare of a nation depends on its production. But the amount that is produced depends on the division of labour: "The greatest improvement in the productive powers of labour, and the greater part of the skill, dexterity, and judgment with which it is anywhere directed or applied, seem to have been the effect of the division of labour."[7] To produce even the most ordinary commodities requires the cooperation of a vast number of people:

Observe the accommodation of the most common artificer or day-labourer in a civilized and thriving country, and you will perceive that the number of people of whose industry a part, though but a small part, has been employed in procuring him this accommodation, exceeds all computation. The woollen coat, for example, which covers the day-labourer, as coarse and rough as it may appear, is the produce of the joint labour of a great multitude of workmen. The shepherd, the sorter of the wool, the wool-comber or carder, the dyer, the scribbler, the spinner, the weaver, the fuller, the dresser, and many others, must all join their different arts . . .[8]

And so Adam Smith continues, adding more and more detail, until at the end he is able to conclude: ". . . if we examine, I say, all these things, and consider what a variety of labour is employed about each of them, we shall be sensible that without the assistance and co-operation of many thousands, the very meanest person in a civilized country could not be provided, even according to, what we very falsely imagine, the easy and simple manner in which he is commonly accommodated."[9]

Schumpeter remarks that "nobody either before or after A[dam] Smith, ever thought of putting such a burden upon division of labour."[10] But Adam Smith was right to insist on the importance of division of labour and we do wrong to slight it, for it turns economics into a study of man in society and poses an extremely difficult question: How is the cooperation of these vast numbers of people in countries all over the world, which is necessary for even a modest standard of living, to be brought about? Adam Smith's answer is that it is done by means of trade or exchange, the use of the market fueled by self-interest:

. . . man has almost constant occasion for the help of his brethren, and it is in vain for him to expect it from their benevolence only. He will be more likely to prevail if he can interest their self-love in his favour, and shew them that it is for their own advantage to do for him what he requires of them. Whoever offers to another a bargain of any kind, proposes to do this. Give me that which I want, and you shall have this which you want, is the meaning of every such offer; and it is in this manner that we obtain from one another the far greater part of those good offices which we stand in need of. It is not from the benevolence of the butcher, the brewer, or the baker, that we expect our dinner, but from their regard to their own interest. We address ourselves, not to their humanity but to their self-love, and never talk to them of our own necessities but of their advantages.[11]

This is a familiar quotation which you and I have read on innumerable occasions in one textbook or another. It seems to assert that man is wholly dominated by self-interest and not at all by feelings of benevolence. Furthermore, it seems to imply that benevolence, or love, could not form the basis on which an economic organization could function. Neither of these inferences would be correct. Man's behavior, as the author of *The Theory of Moral Sentiments* knew, is influenced by feelings of benevolence – and the division of labour within a family, even an extended family, may be sustained by love and affection. Adam Smith is, I believe, making a more subtle and more important point than we normally assume. Benevolence or love is personal; it is strongest within a family, but it may also exist between associates and friends. However, the more remote the connection the less strongly, in general, are we influenced by feelings of love or benevolence. This is indeed what Adam Smith says in *The Theory of Moral Sentiments*.

It is very strange but I do not recall anyone who, when giving this famous quotation – and it has been repeated on innumerable occasions – also includes what Adam Smith says in just the sentence but one before. "In civilized society [man] stands at all times in need of the co-operation and assistance of great multitudes, while his whole life is scarce sufficient to gain the friendship of a few persons."[12] This, as I see it, completely alters one's perception of Adam Smith's argument. To rely on benevolence to bring about an adequate division of labour is an impossibility. We need the cooperation of multitudes, many of whom we do not even know and for whom we can therefore feel no benevolence, nor can they for us. Indeed, if we did know them, their lives and circumstances would often be so different from our own that it would be hard for us to sympathize with them at all. Reliance on self-interest is not simply one way in which the required division of labour is achieved; for the division of labour needed for a civilized life, it is the only way.

We just do not have the time to learn who the people are who gain from our labors or to learn of their circumstances, and so we cannot feel benevolence towards them even if benevolence would be justified were we to be fully informed. The fact that when discussing Adam Smith's treatment of the division of labour economists have usually quoted his famous pinmaking example – where everyone is situated within a single factory – rather than the long passage from which I quoted earlier – where the participants in the division of labour are scattered all over the world – has also helped to divert attention from the extremely limited role benevolence could play in bringing about the division of labour in a modern economy.

I have remarked that the earlier sentence about one's whole life being "scarce sufficient to gain the friendship of a few persons" is never quoted. Neither, curiously, are the sentences which follow and which make the same point: "Nobody but a beggar chuses to depend chiefly upon the benevolence of his fellow-citizens. Even a beggar does not depend upon it entirely . . . The greater part of his occasional wants are supplied in the same manner as those of other people, by treaty, by barter, and by purchase. With the money which one man gives him he purchases food. The old cloaths which another bestows upon him he exchanges for other old cloaths which suit him better, or for lodging, or for food, or for money, with which he can buy either food, cloaths, or lodging, as he has occasion."[13]

Adam Smith's main point, as I see it, is not that benevolence or love is not the basis of economic life in a modern society, but that it cannot be. We have to rely on the market, with its motive force, self-interest. If man were so constituted that he only responded to feelings of benevolence, we would still be living in caves with lives "nasty, bruteish and short."

The efficient working of the market thus becomes the key to the maintenance of a comfortable standard of living and to its increase. What Adam Smith does first, is to show that an efficient market system is one in which, because of the inconveniences of barter, we use money, in terms of which all prices are expressed. He then shows that the pricing system is a self-adjusting mechanism which leads to resources being used in a way that maximizes the value of their contribution to production: "Every individual is continually exerting himself to find out the most advantageous employment for whatever capital he can command. It is his own advantage, indeed, and not that of the society, which he has in view. But the study of his own advantage naturally, or rather necessarily, leads him to prefer that employment which is most advantageous to the society."[14] He is "led by an invisible hand to promote an end which was no part of his intention. Nor is it always the worse for the society that it was no part of it. By pursuing his own interest he frequently promotes that of the society more effectually than when he really intends to promote it."[15]

Adam Smith's analytical system may seem primitive to us but in fact he reaches results we accept as correct today. He uses the concept of the natural price, what we would call the long-run supply price. The effectual demand is the amount demanded at that price. This is how Adam Smith describes the position of equilibrium:

> When the quantity brought to market is just sufficient to supply the effectual demand and no more, the market price naturally comes to be either exactly, or as nearly as can be judged of, the same with the natural price. The whole quantity upon hand can be disposed of for this price, and cannot be disposed of for more. The competition of the different dealers obliges them all to accept of this price, but does not oblige them to accept less.[16]

He also goes through the operation familiar to those taking introductory courses in economics of supposing that the amount supplied is less than the amount demanded at the equilibrium price:

> When the quantity of any commodity which is brought to market falls short of the effectual demand, all those who are willing to pay for whole value of the rent, wages, and profit, which must be paid in order to bring it thither, cannot be supplied with the quantity which they want. Rather than want it altogether some of them will be willing to give more. A competition will immediately begin among them, and the market price will rise more or less above the natural price . . .[17]

And, of course, he also examines what happens when the amount supplied is more than the amount demanded at the equilibrium price:

> When the quantity brought to market exceeds the effectual demand, it cannot be all sold to those who are willing to pay the whole value of the rent, wages, and profit, which must be paid in order to bring it thither. Some part must be sold to those who are willing to pay less, and the low price which they give for it must reduce the price of the whole. The market price will sink more or less below the natural price, according as the greatness of the excess increases more or less the competition of the sellers, or according as it happens to be more or less important to them to get immediately rid of the commodity. The same excess in the importation of perishable, will occasion a much greater competition than in that of durable commodities; in the importation of oranges, for example, than in that of old iron.[18]

As an example of the way in which Adam Smith examined an actual situation, consider his discussion of the effect of a public mourning which increases the demand for black cloth: "A public mourning raises the price of black cloth (with which the market is almost always understocked upon such occasions), and augments the profits of the merchants who possess any considerable quantity of it. It has no effect upon the wages of the weavers. The market is under-stocked with commodities, not with labour; with work done, not with work to be done. It raises the wages of journeymen taylors. The market is here under-stocked with labour. There is an effectual demand for more labour, for more work to be done than can be had. It sinks the price of coloured silks and cloths, and thereby reduces the profits of the merchants who have any considerable quantity of them upon hand. It sinks too the wages of the workmen employed in preparing such commodities, for which all demand is stopped for six months, perhaps for a twelvemonth. The market is here over-stocked both with commodities and with labour."[19]

There is a surefootedness about this analysis which demonstrates Adam Smith's ability to get at the heart of the matter. His tools may be primitive, but his skill in handling them is superb. He may not work with schedules, but implicit in his analysis is the view that if one did construct a demand schedule, more would be demanded at a lower price. Consider, again, Adam Smith's discussion of the effects of price regulation:

> When the government, in order to remedy the inconveniencies of dearth,

orders all the dealers to sell their corn at what it supposes a reasonable price, it either hinders them from bringing it to market which may sometimes produce a famine even in the beginning of the season; or if they bring it thither, it enables the people, and thereby encourages them to consume it so fast, as must necessarily produce a famine before the end of the season. The unlimited, unrestrained freedom of the corn trade, as it is the only effectual preventative of the miseries of a famine, so it is the best palliative of the inconveniences of a dearth; for the inconveniencies of a real scarcity cannot be remedied; they can only be palliated.[20]

Could we do much better today if we were discussing government control of the price of oil and natural gas?

Adam Smith's handling of economic analysis has not, however, occasioned universal praise. The clumsiness of his treatment and its lack of finish have been strongly criticized by some economists, so strongly, indeed, as to suggest that if only these writers had been around in 1776 Adam Smith would not have been necessary. Many economists have criticized the way in which Adam Smith discusses the distinction between "value in use" and "value in exchange": "The things which have the greatest value in use have frequently little or no value in exchange; and on the contrary, those which have the greatest value in exchange have frequently little or no value in use. Nothing is more useful than water: but it will purchase scarce any thing . . . A diamond, on the contrary, has scarce any value in use; but a very great quantity of other goods may frequently be had in exchange for it."[21] This passage is, it is true, neither original nor particularly helpful. But Adam Smith's economics in no way suffers because he did not also give us the theory of diminishing marginal utility. Utility theory has always been an ornament rather than a working part of economic analysis.

Another passage which has offended economists is Adam Smith's statement about monopoly price: "The price of monopoly is upon every occasion the highest which can be got. The natural price, or the price of free competition, on the contrary, is the lowest which can be taken, not upon every occasion indeed, but for any considerable time together. The one is upon every occasion the highest which can be squeezed out of the buyers, or which, it is supposed, they will consent to give: The other is the lowest which the sellers can commonly afford to take, and at the same time continue their business."[22] What is found objectionable is that Adam Smith, by speaking of the "highest possible price" rather than the "price which maximizes profits," seems not to take into consideration that at a higher price less would be demanded, or alternatively assumes that the decrease in the amount demanded takes place in a discontinuous fashion. But it is apparent from the quotations I gave earlier, and is quite explicit elsewhere in the *Wealth of Nations*, that Adam Smith knew that the demand schedule was downward sloping. What does seem clear is that he was not able to formulate the determination of monopoly price in the rigorous manner of Cournot. However, Adam Smith's view of competition was quite robust. He thought of competition, as the quotations given earlier illustrate, as rivalry, as a process, rather than as a condition defined by a high elasticity of demand, as would be true for most modern economists. I need not conceal from you my belief that ultimately the Smithian view of competition will prevail.

Adam Smith also discusses the relation between the number of competitors and the price that will emerge. He says that if the trade "is divided between two different grocers, their competition will tend to make both of them sell cheaper than if it were in the hands of one only; and if it were divided among twenty, their competition would be just so much the greater, and the chance of their combining together, in order to raise the price, just so much the less."[23] What Adam Smith believed was that a greater number of competitors leads to lower prices, both directly through the competitive process and also indirectly by making collusion less likely. It is not a very thorough treatment but I am not sure that modern economists can do much better. We should not object because Adam Smith left us some problems to solve, although it may be a legitimate complaint that in the 200 years since the *Wealth of Nations* we have made such little progress in solving them.

Adam Smith showed how the operations of the market would regulate an economy so as to maximize the value of production. to accomplish this required little assistance from government: "Every man, as long as he does not violate the laws of justice [should be] left perfectly free to pursue his own interest his own way, and to bring both his industry and capital into competition with those of any other man . . . The sovereign is completely discharged from a duty, in the attempting to perform which he must always be exposed to innumerable delusions, and for the proper performance of which no human wisdom or knowledge could ever be sufficient; the duty of superintending the industry of private people, and of directing it towards the employments most suitable to the interest of society."[24] Note that Adam Smith, as his reference to the "laws of justice" shows, saw the necessity for the government establishing what we would call a "property-rights system." But he did not favor government action that went much beyond this.

Adam Smith's opposition to more extensive government action did not arise simply because he thought it was unnecessary, but because government action would usually make matters worse. Governments lacked both the knowledge and the motivation to do a satisfactory job in regulating an economic system. He says: "Great nations are never impoverished by private, though they sometimes are by public prodigality and misconduct."[25] Again: "It is the highest impertinence and presumption . . . in kings and ministers, to pretend to watch over the economy of private people, and to restrain their expence. . . . They are themselves always, and without any exception, the greatest spendthrifts in the society. Let them look well after their own expence, and they may safely trust private people with theirs. If their own extravagance does not ruin the state, that of their subjects never will."[26]

Adam Smith explains that government regulations will normally be much influenced by those who stand to benefit from them, with the result that they are not necessarily advantageous to society:

The interest of the dealers . . . in any particular branch of trade or manufactures, is always in some respects different from, and even opposite to, that of the public. To widen the market and to narrow the competition, is always the interest of the dealers. To widen the market may frequently be aggreeable enough to the interest of the public; but to narrow the competition must always be against it, and can serve only to enable the dealers, by raising their profits above what they naturally would be, to levy, for their own benefit, an absurd tax upon the rest of their fellow-citizens. The proposal of any new law or regulation of commerce which comes from this order, ought always to be listened to with great precaution, and ought never to be adopted till after having been long and carefully examined, not only with the most scrupulous, but with the most suspicious attention. It comes from an order of men, whose interest is never exactly the same with that of the public, who have generally an interest to deceive and even to oppress the public, and who accordingly have, upon many occasions, both deceived and oppressed it.[27]

According to Adam Smith, the government has only three duties. The first is to protect society from "the violence and invasion of other independent societies."[28] As he says, "defence . . . is much more important than opulence."[29] The second duty is to establish a system of justice, by which he means a legal system which defines everyone's rights. Economists are prone to think of Adam Smith as simply advocating the use of a pricing system, but throughout the *Wealth of Nations* one finds Adam Smith discussing the appropriate institutional framework for the working of a pricing system. Whether one agrees or disagrees with his views on apprenticeship laws, land tenure, joint-stock companies, the administration of justice, or the educational system, what distinguishes Adam Smith's approach from much of what has come since is that he obviously thinks this a proper and important part of the work of an economist. It is, I believe, only recently that economists in any number have come to realize that the choice of an institutional framework is a subject which deserves to be studied systematically.

The final duty Adam Smith gives to the government is the establishment of certain public works and public institutions. What he mainly has in mind are roads, bridges, canals, and suchlike. It seems to me that the list of public works that Adam Smith thought should be undertaken by government, although quite limited, was as extensive as it was because he did not foresee the potentialities of the modern corporation and a modern capital market, a position understandable in the light of the history up to his day of joint-stock companies, of which he had a very unfavourable opinion. But there is nothing ordinary even about his treatment of a subject such as this. In his discussion of how these public works should be financed and administered, Adam Smith argued that they should be financed by payments from consumers rather than by grants from the public revenue: "It does not seem necessary that the expence of those public works should be defrayed from the public revenue . . . The greater part of such public works may easily be so managed, as to afford a particular revenue sufficient for defraying their own expence, without bringing any burden upon the general revenue of the society."[30]

"A highway, a bridge, a navigable canal, for example, may in most cases be both made and maintained by a small toll upon the carriages which make use of them: a harbour, by a moderate port-duty upon the tunnage of the shipping which load or unload in it." If this were done, such works would only be provided where they were needed: "When high roads, bridges, canals, &c. are in this manner made and supported by the commerce which is carried on by means of them, they can be made only where that commerce requires them and consequently where it is proper to make them . . . A magnificent high road cannot be made through a desart country where there is little or no commerce, or merely because it happens to lead to the country villa of the intendant of the province, or to that of some great lord to whom the intendant finds it convenient to make his court. A great bridge cannot be thrown over a river at a place where nobody passes, or merely to embellish the view from the windows of a neighbouring palace: things which sometimes happen, in countries where works of this kind are carried on by any other revenue than that which they themselves are capable of affording."[31] It is clear that Adam Smith, had he been presented with a proposal for marginal cost pricing, would not have neglected the effect such a policy would have on what would be supplied.

In making this survey of the *Wealth of Nations* I have concentrated on what I see as Adam Smith's main contributions to economics: the division of labour, the working of the market, and the role of government in the economic system. I am acutely aware that this does less than justice to Adam Smith's great work. It would require, however, many lectures and many lecturers to do that. In the *Wealth of Nations* a number of subjects are dealt with doubtless as important as some of those I have mentioned. It is enough to note his discussion of economic development, of public finance, of education, of religious establishments, and, above all, his discussion of colonies – and particularly the American colonies. On all these subjects, and still others, Adam Smith has much to say that is profound, and his ideas appear striking and even, paradoxically, novel to someone reading him today.

I will illustrate this by considering the one subject which, on such an occasion as this, I can hardly avoid: Adam Smith's view of the American Revolution. In the *Wealth of Nations* America becomes, in effect, the minor theme accompanying the major theme, the working of a pricing system. As Fay says: "America was never far from Adam Smith's thought. Indeed, in the end it was almost an obsession."[32] On America, Adam Smith's views were liberal. He saw the future greatness of America: it was likely to become "one of the greatest and most formidable [empires] that ever was in the world."[33] He had little faith in the conduct of British policy. In a letter written from Kirkcaldy in June 1776, a month before the Declaration of Independence was adopted, he wrote that "the American campaign has begun awkwardly. I hope, I cannot say that I expect, it will end better. England tho' in the present times it breeds men of great professional abilities in all different ways, great Lawyers, great watchmakers, and great clockmakers etc. etc., seems to breed neither Statesmen nor Generals."[34]

Adam Smith did not underestimate the fighting quality of the American military forces. In discussing defense expenditures, he argued that although normally a militia would be inferior to a standing army, yet after a few years in the field it would become its equal. He added: "Should the war in America drag out through another campaign, the American militia may become in every respect a match for that [British] standing army, of which the valour appeared. . . not inferior to the hardiest veterans of France and Spain."[35] It was no doubt in part with this in mind that Adam Smith said elsewhere in the *Wealth of Nations*: "They are very weak who flatter themselves that . . . our colonies will be easily conquered by force alone."[36] In a memorandum written in 1778, Adam Smith gave as the probable outcome of the American conflict, out of four possibilities, that one which actually materialized.[37] And towards the end of the war, he wrote a letter of introduction to Lord Shelburne, who was to become Prime Minister, on behalf of Richard Oswald, who became the chief British peace negotiator with the Americans. Oswald signed the preliminary articles of peace in 1782 on Britain's behalf. He then lost his job, being attacked as one who supported "the Cause of America" rather than that of Britain, a view which may not have been too far from the truth. For example, Oswald not only forwarded Franklin's proposal that Britain cede Canada to the United States, but seems to have favoured it.[38]

However, while all this is no doubt indicative of Adam Smith's attitude, he was by no means a cheering supporter of the American cause. In the *Wealth of Nations* he describes the motives of the leaders of the American Revolution in the following terms: "Men desire to have some share in the management of public affairs chiefly on account of the importance which it gives them . . . The leading men of America, like those of all other countries, desire to preserve their own importance. They feel, or imagine, that if their assemblies, which they are fond of calling parliaments, and of considering as equal in authority to the parliament of Great Britain, should be so far degraded as to become the humble ministers and executive officers of that parliament, the greater part of their importance would be at an end. They have rejected, therefore, the proposal of being taxed by parliamentary requisition, and like other ambitious and high-spirited men, have rather chosen to draw the sword in defence of their own importance."[39]

To Adam Smith, what the American leaders wanted was, not liberty nor democracy, but position. He therefore devised a plan which would give it to them. He proposed to give the colonies representation in the British parliament in proportion to their contributions to the public revenues. If this were done, "a new method of acquiring importance, a new and more dazzling object of ambition would be presented to the leading men of each colony. Instead of piddling for the little prizes which are to be found in what may be called the paltry raffle of colony faction; they might then hope, from the presumption which men naturally have in their own ability and good fortune, to draw some of the great prizes which sometimes come from the wheel of the great state lottery of British politics."[40] That is to say, an ambitious American could hope to become Prime Minister and, in effect, the ruler of the British Empire, Adam Smith also argued that Americans could ultimately expect that the capital of the British Empire would cross the ocean. "Such has hitherto been the rapid progress of that of [America] in wealth, population and improvement, that in the course of little more than a century, perhaps, the produce of America might exceed that of British taxation. The seat of the empire would then naturally remove itself to that part of the empire which contributed most to the general defence and support of the whole."[41]

Professor Stigler quotes Adam Smith's account of the motives of the American leaders with approval as a discussion of "political behavior in perfectly cold-blooded rational terms," and considers Adam Smith's plan to be shrewd. He contrasts this discussion with other passages in the *Wealth of*

Nations in which men are apparently "hot-blooded" or even "irrational" in their political behavior, passages which are inconsistent with the view that political behavior is "cold-blooded" and "rational" and are therefore wrong.[42] But the behavior of Americans in the Revolution demonstrates to me that men can be both "cold-blooded" and "hot-blooded." I do not myself find it difficult to understand why George Washington and Thomas Jefferson supported the American Revolution – Adam Smith adequately explains a large part of their motives. But why did they secure the support of the masses who suffered and died? Self-interest successfully pursued seems an inadequate explanation of their actions. Revolution is a risky business for all who take part in it, with the prizes going to the successful revolutionary leaders if the revolutionaries win.

Adam Smith does give an explanation of why the American leaders had followers, but this is to be found, not in the *Wealth of Nations*, but in *The Theory of Moral Sentiments*, in his discussion of the distinction of ranks. "The great mob of mankind are the admirers and worshippers, and, what may seem more extraordinary, most frequently the disinterested admirers and worshippers, of wealth and greatness."[43] This defence to the powerful, on which the distinction of ranks is based, is, Adam Smith explains, a human propensity necessary for the maintenance of order. But we can see that it is also, on occasion, capable of producing disorder.

Was it better for the ordinary American to have secured independence from British rule? It certainly got rid of those absurd restrictions on trade imposed for the benefit of British merchants and manufacturers which Adam Smith denounced. But the American government, through its tariff policy, was to reintroduce similar absurdities for the benefit of American merchants and manufacturers. And were taxes lower with independence than they would have been without it? As the main expenditure in America by Britain was for defense, to Adam Smith the taxation question became simply, who was the low-cost supplier of defense and, if it was the British government, would the colonies pay for it? If they would not, there was no reason for Britain to retain its control. "If any of the provinces of the British empire cannot be made to contribute towards the support of the whole empire, it is surely time that Britain should free herself from the expence of defending those provinces in time of war, and of supporting any part of their civil or military establishments in time of peace, and endeavour to accommodate her future views and designs to the real mediocrity of her circumstances."[44] These are the last words of the *Wealth of Nations*.

There is indeed some reason to suppose that Adam Smith may have had a hand in Charles Townshend's taxation schemes which helped to precipitate the American Revolution.[45] Adam Smith regarded the taxes as a method of paying for the services which the mother country provided the colonies. The colonists, or rather their leaders, turned an economic problem into a political one. But had Adam Smith's whole plan been agreed to, there would have been no American Revolution. A child's essay on 1776 which I heard read on the radio in Chicago contained the following sentence: "If it had not been for 1776, England would now rule America." But had Adam Smith's plan been followed, there would have been no 1776, America would now be ruling England, and we would today be celebrating Adam Smith not simply as the author of the *Wealth of Nations*, but hailing him as a founding father.

The *Wealth of Nations* is a work that one contemplates with awe. In keenness of analysis and in its range it surpasses any other book on economics. Its preeminence is, however, disturbing. What have we been doing in the last 200 years? Our analysis has certainly become more sophisticated, but we display no greater insight into the working of the economic system and, in some ways, our approach is inferior to that of Adam Smith. And when we come to views on public policy, we find propositions ignored which Adam Smith demonstrates with such force as almost to make them "self-evident." I really do not know why this is so, but perhaps part of the answer is that we do not read the *Wealth of Nations*.

Notes

The author is at the University of Chicago Law School. This paper was delivered originally as a public lecture at UCLA under the auspices of the Department of Economics, UCLA, and The Foundation for Research in Economics and Education. It was first published for private circulation by The Foundation for Research in Economics and Education which has graciously given The Editor permission to reprint the address for readers of *Economic Inquiry*.

1.   Adam Smith, *An Inquiry Into the Nature and Causes of the Wealth of Nations*, editor's introduction, pp. xxix-xxx (Modern Library edition: 1937).
2.   E.G. West, *Adam Smith, the Man and his Works*, p. 153 (1969).
3.   Joseph A. Schumpeter, *History of Economic Analysis*, p. 185 (1954).
4.   John Raw, *Life of Adam Smith*, p. 434 (1895).
5.   Smith, *Wealth of Nations*, p. 1vii.
6.   Ibid., p. 33.
7.   Ibid., p. 3.
8.   Ibid., p. 11.
9.   Ibid., p. 12.
10.   Schumpeter, *Economic Analysis*, p. 187.
11.   Smith, *Wealth of Nations*, p. 14.
12.   Ibid.
13.   Ibid.
14.   Ibid., p. 421.
15.   Ibid., p. 423.
16.   Ibid., p. 57.
17.   Ibid., p. 56.
18.   Ibid., p. 57.
19.   Ibid., p. 59.
20.   Ibid., p. 493.
21.   Ibid., p. 28.
22.   Ibid., p. 61.
23.   Ibid., p. 324.
24.   Ibid., p. 651.
25.   Ibid., p. 325.
26.   Ibid., p. 329.
27.   Ibid., p. 280.
28.   Ibid., p. 653.
29.   Ibid., p. 431.
30.   Ibid., p. 682.
31.   Ibid., pp. 682-683.
32.   C.R. Fay, *Adam Smith and the Scotland of His Day*, p. 98 (1956).
33.   Smith, *Wealth of Nations*, p. 588.
34.   Quoted in W.R. Scott, *Adam Smith, An Oration*, p. 23 (1938).
35.   Smith, *Wealth of Nations*, pp. 662-663.

36. Ibid., p. 587.
37. Reproduced in Fay, *Adam Smith*, pp. 110-114.
38. See Richard Oswald's *Memorandum on the Folly of Invading Virginia*, pp. 38-43. (edited, with an essay on Richard Oswald by W. Stilt Robinson, Jr., 1953).
39. Smith, *Wealth of Nations*, pp. 586-587.
40. Ibid., p. 587.
41. Ibid., p. 590.
42. George J. Stigler, "Smith's Travels on the Ship of State," pp. 265, 270-272 in vol. 3, *History of Political Economy* (Fall 1971).
43. Adam Smith, *The Theory of Moral Sentiments*, p. 85 (E.G. West, ed.: 1969).
44. Smith, *Wealth of Nations*, p. 900.
45. Fay, *Adam Smith and Scotland*, pp. 115-116.